Lecture Notes in Computer Science　　　8769

Commenced Publication in 1973
Founding and Former Series Editors:
Gerhard Goos, Juris Hartmanis, and Jan van Leeuwen

Lecture Notes in Computer Science 8169

Commenced Publication in 1973
Founding and Former Series Editors:
Gerhard Goos, Juris Hartmanis, and Jan van Leeuwen

Editorial Board

David Hutchison
Lancaster University, UK
Takeo Kanade
Carnegie Mellon University, Pittsburgh, PA, USA
Josef Kittler
University of Surrey, Guildford, UK
Jon M. Kleinberg
Cornell University, Ithaca, NY, USA
Alfred Kobsa
University of California, Irvine, CA, USA
Friedemann Mattern
ETH Zurich, Switzerland
John C. Mitchell
Stanford University, CA, USA
Moni Naor
Weizmann Institute of Science, Rehovot, Israel
Oscar Nierstrasz
University of Bern, Switzerland
C. Pandu Rangan
Indian Institute of Technology, Madras, India
Bernhard Steffen
TU Dortmund University, Germany
Madhu Sudan
Microsoft Research, Cambridge, MA, USA
Demetri Terzopoulos
University of California, Los Angeles, CA, USA
Doug Tygar
University of California, Berkeley, CA, USA
Gerhard Weikum
Max Planck Institute for Informatics, Saarbruecken, Germany

Daniel Amyot   Pau Fonseca i Casas
Gunter Mussbacher (Eds.)

System Analysis and Modeling: Models and Reusability

8th International Conference, SAM 2014
Valencia, Spain, September 29-30, 2014
Proceedings

 Springer

Volume Editors

Daniel Amyot
University of Ottawa
School of Electrical Engineering and Computer Sience
800 King Edward St., Ottawa, ON K1N 6N5, Canada
E-mail: damyot@eecs.uottawa.ca

Pau Fonseca i Casas
Universitat Politècnica de Catalunya - Barcelona Tech
Department of Statistics and Operations Research
North Campus - C5218 Room, 08034 Barcelona, Spain
E-mail: pau@fib.upc.edu

Gunter Mussbacher
McGill University
Department of Electrical and Computer Engineering
3480 University Street, Montreal, QC H3A 0E9, Canada
E-mail: gunter.mussbacher@mcgill.ca

ISSN 0302-9743   e-ISSN 1611-3349
ISBN 978-3-319-11742-3   e-ISBN 978-3-319-11743-0
DOI 10.1007/978-3-319-11743-0
Springer Cham Heidelberg New York Dordrecht London

Library of Congress Control Number: 2014949191

LNCS Sublibrary: SL 2 – Programming and Software Engineering

Typesetting: Camera-ready by author, data conversion by Scientific Publishing Services, Chennai, India

Printed on acid-free paper

Springer is part of Springer Science+Business Media (www.springer.com)

Preface

The System Analysis and Modeling (SAM) conference provides an open arena for participants from academia and industry to present and discuss the most recent innovations, trends, experiences, and concerns in modeling, specification, and analysis of distributed, communication, and real-time systems using the Specification and Description Language (SDL-2010) and Message Sequence Chart (MSC) notations from the International Telecommunication Union (ITU-T), as well as related system design languages such as UML, ASN.1, TTCN-3, SysML, and the User Requirements Notation (URN).

While the first seven instances of SAM (Berlin 1998, Grenoble 2000, Aberystwyth 2002, Ottawa 2004, Kaiserslautern 2006, Oslo 2010, and Innsbruck 2012) were workshops, in 2014, SAM has become a conference to better reflect its structure, audience, and overall quality.

This 8th SAM conference (http://sdl-forum.org/Events/SAM2014/) was co-located with the ACM/IEEE 17th International Conference on Model Driven Engineering Languages and Systems (MODELS 2014) in Valencia, Spain, during September 29-30, 2014.

Theme for 2014: Models and Reusability

Model reuse is a powerful concept defined as the process of creating new models using existing model artefacts. To make model reuse applicable, reusing an artefact should be easier than constructing it from scratch. This entails that the reusable artefacts are easy to understand, find, and apply. Commonly reusable artefacts include classes, components, patterns, frameworks, and, services, and emerging ones include product lines, aspects, and concerns.

SAM 2014 invited contributions related but not limited to the reuse of model artefacts and the design of reusable artefacts for ITU-T languages and other related system design languages. In addition to models and reusability, researchers and practitioners were invited to provide contributions on language development, model-driven development, and applications.

Review Process

SAM 2014 utilized a multi-tier review process. First, all papers were reviewed by at least three Program Committee members. The papers and reviews were then made available to Program Committee members who did not have a conflict of interest with the authors. The papers were discussed during a three-day, online meeting before the final decisions were made.

Out of 63 long papers and 8 short papers received (for a total of 71 submissions), 18 long papers (acceptance rate: 29%) and 3 short papers (acceptance rate: 37%) were selected.

SAM 2014 is truly an international conference. We received submissions from 27 different countries covering all continents. Among the accepted papers, we have authors from 13 countries in Europe, North-America, South-America, Asia, and Africa.

Proceedings Overview

This volume contains the 21 papers selected for presentation at SAM 2014 as well as the abstracts of two keynote presentations. The volume structure reflects the six sessions of the conference.

The first day was closely aligned with the conference theme with a session on Reuse followed by a keynote presentation from Prof. Jean-Marc Jézéquel (Université de Rennes and IRISA, France) on *Safely Reusing Model Transformations through Family Polymorphism*, a second session on Availability, Safety, and Optimization, and a third session on Sequences and Interactions.

The volume contents for the second day are a session on Testing followed by a second keynote presentation, this time from Prof. Lionel Briand (FNR PEARL chair in software engineering and Vice-Director at the Centre for ICT Security, Reliability, and Trust (SnT), University of Luxembourg) about *Making Model-Driven Verification Practical and Scalable: Experiences and Lessons Learned*. The last two sessions target Metrics, Constraints, and Repositories, and finally SDL and Validation & Verification.

Acknowledgments

The 8th edition of SAM was made possible by the dedicated work and contributions of many people and organizations. We thank the authors of submitted papers, the 46 members of the Program Committee, the 18 additional reviewers, and the board members of the SDL Forum Society. We thank the MODELS 2014 local Organization Committee at the Universitat Politècnica de València for their logistic support. The submission and review process was run with the EasyChair conference system (`http://www.easychair.org/`), and we therefore thank the people behind this great tool. We finally thank the sponsors of SAM 2014: SDL Forum Society, ITU-T, ACM, IEEE, Springer, the University of Ottawa, McGill University, and the Universitat Politècnica de Catalunya.

September 2014

Daniel Amyot
Pau Fonseca i Casas
Gunter Mussbacher

SDL Forum Society

The SDL Forum Society is a not-for-profit organization that, in addition to running the System Analysis and Modeling (SAM) conference series of events (once every two years), also:

- Runs the System Design Languages Forum (SDL Forum) conference series every two years between SAM conference years;
- Is a body recognized by ITU-T as co-developing System Design Languages in the Z.100 series (Specification and Description Language), Z.120 series (Message Sequence Chart), Z.150 series (User Requirements Notation), and other language standards;
- Promotes the ITU-T System Design Languages.

For more information on the SDL Forum Society, see
http://www.sdl-forum.org.

Organization

Organizing Committee

Chairs

Daniel Amyot	University of Ottawa, Canada
Pau Fonseca i Casas	Universitat Politècnica de Catalunya, Spain
Gunter Mussbacher	McGill University, Canada

SDL Forum Society

Reinhard Gotzhein	Chairman (TU Kaiserslautern, Germany)
Ferhat Khendek	Secretary (Concordia University, Canada)
Martin von Löwis	Treasurer (Beuth-Hochschule für Technik Berlin, Germany)
Rick Reed	Non-voting board member (TSE, UK)

Local Facilities Chair

Javier González Huerta	Universitat Politècnica de València, Spain

Program Committee

Program Chairs

Daniel Amyot	University of Ottawa, Canada
Pau Fonseca i Casas	Universitat Politècnica de Catalunya, Spain
Gunter Mussbacher	McGill University, Canada

Members

Shaukat Ali	Simula Research Laboratory, Norway
Rolv Bræk	NTNU Trondheim, Norway
Reinhard Brocks	HTW Saarland, Germany
Jean-Michel Bruel	University of Toulouse, France
Laurent Doldi	TransMeth, France
Anders Ek	IBM Rational, Sweden
Stein Erik Ellevseth	ABB Corporate Research, Norway
Joachim Fischer	Humboldt University of Berlin, Germany
Emmanuel Gaudin	PragmaDev, France
Birgit Geppert	Avaya, USA
Abdelouahed Gherbi	École de technologie supérieure, Canada

Reinhard Gotzhein	TU Kaiserslautern, Germany
Jens Grabowski	University of Göttingen, Germany
Øystein Haugen	SINTEF, Norway
Loïc Hélouët	Inria Rennes, France
Peter Herrmann	NTNU Trondheim, Norway
Dieter Hogrefe	University of Göttingen, Germany
Ferhat Khendek	Concordia University, Canada
Tae-Hyong Kim	Kumoh National Institute of Technology, Korea
Jacques Klein	University of Luxembourg, Luxembourg
Finn Kristoffersen	Cinderella, Denmark
Anna Medve	University of Pannonia, Hungary
Pedro Merino Gómez	University of Malaga, Spain
Birger Møller-Pedersen	University of Oslo, Norway
Patricio Moreno Montero	ACCIONA, Spain
Ileana Ober	University of Toulouse, France
Iulian Ober	University of Toulouse, France
Fei Peng	Siemens CT, China
Dorina Petriu	Carleton University, Canada
Andreas Prinz	Agder University College, Norway
Rick Reed	TSE, UK
Laurent Rioux	Thales R&T, France
José Luis Risco-Martín	Universidad Complutense de Madrid, Spain
Manuel Rodriguez-Cayetano	Valladolid University, Spain
Richard Sanders	SINTEF, Norway
Amardeo Sarma	NEC Laboratories Europe, Germany
Ina Schieferdecker	Freie Universität Berlin, Germany
Edel Sherratt	University of Wales Aberystwyth, UK
Eugene Syriani	University of Alabama, USA
Maria Toeroe	Ericsson, Canada
Peter Tröger	Potsdam University, Germany
Hans Vangheluwe	University of Antwerp, Belgium and McGill University, Canada
Martin von Löwis	Beuth-Hochschule für Technik Berlin, Germany
Thomas Weigert	Missouri University of Science and Technology and UniqueSoft, USA
Manuel Wimmer	Technische Universität Wien, Austria
Steffen Zschaler	King's College London, UK

Additional Reviewers

Sabas Arsène	Franck Chauvel	Christopher Henard
Bruno Barroca	Amine El Kouhen	Steffen Herbold
Robert Bill	Fabian Glaser	Tanja Mayerhofer
Tegawende Bissyande	Patrick Harms	Assaad Moawad

Phu Nguyen   Margarete Sackmann   Daniel Varro
Frank Roessler   Markus Scheidgen   Anatoly Vasilevskiy

Sponsoring Organizations and Institutions

Keynotes

Safely Reusing Model Transformations through Family Polymorphism

Jean-Marc Jézéquel

IRISA, University of Rennes, France
jean-marc.jezequel@irisa.fr

First Keynote Speaker – Abstract. The engineering of systems involves many different stakeholders, each with their own domain of expertise. Hence more and more organizations are adopting Domain Specific Languages (DSLs) to allow domain experts to express solutions directly in terms of relevant domain concepts. This new trend raises new challenges about designing DSLs, evolving a set of DSLs and coordinating the use of multiple DSLs. In this talk we explore various dimensions of these challenges, and outline a possible research roadmap for addressing them. We detail one of these challenges, which is the safe reuse of model transformations.

Indeed both DSL definition and tooling (e.g., checkers, document or code generators, and model transformations) require significant development efforts, for a limited audience (by definition), because the current state of the art of Model Driven Engineering still makes it hard to reuse and evolve these definitions and tooling across several DSLs, even when these DSLs are conceptually very close to one other. We outline a new extension to the Kermeta language that leverages Family Polymorphism to allow model polymorphism, inheritance among DSLs, as well as evolution and interoperability of DSLs.

Making Model-Driven Verification Practical and Scalable: Experiences and Lessons Learned

Lionel C. Briand

SnT Centre for Security, Reliability and Trust, University of Luxembourg
lionel.briand@uni.lu

Second Keynote Speaker – Abstract. Verification challenges in the software industry, including testing, come in many different forms, due to significant differences across domains and contexts. But one common challenge is scalability, the capacity to test and verify increasingly large, complex systems. Another concern relates to practicality. Can the inputs required by a given technique be realistically provided by engineers? Though, to a large extent, Model-Driven Engineering (MDE) is a significant component of many verification techniques, a complete solution is necessarily multidisciplinary and involves, for example, machine learning or evolutionary computing components.

This talk reports on 10 years of research tackling verification and testing problems, in most cases in actual industrial contexts, relying on MDE but also metaheuristic search, optimization, and machine learning. The focus of the talk will be on how to scale to large system input spaces and achieve practicality by decreasing the level of detail and precision required in models and abstractions. I will draw from past and recent experiences to provide practical guidelines and outline possible avenues of research.

Concrete examples of problems we have addressed, and that I will cover in my talk, include schedulability analysis, stress/load testing, CPU usage analysis, robustness testing, testing closed-loop dynamic controllers, and SQL Injection testing. Most of these projects have been performed in industrial contexts and solutions were validated on industrial software.

Further information is available in the following selected references.

References

1. Ali, S., Iqbal, M.Z., Arcuri, A., Briand, L.C.: Generating test data from OCL constraints with search techniques. IEEE Transactions on Software Engineering 39(10), 1376–1402 (2013)
2. Briand, L., Labiche, Y., Shousha, M.: Using genetic algorithms for early schedulability analysis and stress testing in real-time systems. Genetic Programming and Evolvable Machines 7(2), 145–170 (2006)
3. Iqbal, M.Z., Arcuri, A., Briand, L.: Empirical investigation of search algorithms for environment model-based testing of real-time embedded software. In: Proc. ISSTA 2012, pp. 199–209. ACM, New York (2012)
4. Matinnejad, R., Nejati, S., Briand, L., Bruckmann, T., Poull, C.: Search-based automated testing of continuous controllers: Framework, tool support, and case studies. Information and Software Technology (to appear, 2014)

5. Nejati, S., Briand, L.C.: Identifying optimal trade-offs between CPU time usage and temporal constraints using search. In: Proc. ISSTA 2014, pp. 351–361. ACM, New York (2014)
6. Nejati, S., Di Alesio, S., Sabetzadeh, M., Briand, L.: Modeling and analysis of cpu usage in safety-critical embedded systems to support stress testing. In: France, R.B., Kazmeier, J., Breu, R., Atkinson, C. (eds.) MODELS 2012. LNCS, vol. 7590, pp. 759–775. Springer, Heidelberg (2012)

Table of Contents

Metrics, Constraints and Repositories

SDL and V&V

BVR – Better Variability Results

Øystein Haugen[1] and Ommund Øgård[2]

[1] SINTEF, P.O. Box 124 Blindern, NO-0314 Oslo, Norway
oystein.haugen@sintef.no
[2] Autronica Fire & Security, P.O. Box 5620, NO-7483 Trondheim, Norway
Ommund.Ogaard@autronicafire.no

Abstract. We present BVR (Base Variability Resolution models), a language developed to fulfill the industrial needs in the safety domain for variability modeling. We show how the industrial needs are in fact quite general and that general mechanisms can be used to satisfy them. BVR is built on the OMG Revised Submission of CVL (Common Variability Language), but is simplified and enhanced relative to that language.

Keywords: Variability modeling, Typing, BVR, CVL.

1   Introduction

BVR (Base Variability Resolution models) is a language built on the Common Variability Language (CVL) [1-3] technology, but enhanced due to needs of the industrial partners of the VARIES project[1], in particular Autronica. BVR is built on CVL, but CVL is not a subset of BVR. In BVR, we have removed some of the mechanisms of CVL that we are not using in our industrial demo cases that apply BVR. We have also made improvements to what CVL had originally.

Our motivation has mainly been the Fire Detection demo case at Autronica, but we have also been inspired by the needs of the other industrial partners of VARIES through their expressed requirements to a variability language.

This paper contains a quick presentation of the Common Variability Language in Chapter 2. In Chapter 3, we relate our work to its motivation in the Autronica fire alarm systems, but argue that we need a more compact and pedagogical example and our car case is presented in Chapter 4. Then we walk through our new BVR concepts in Chapter 5, discuss the suggested improvements in Chapter 6, and conclude in Chapter 7.

2   CVL – The Common Variability Language

The Common Variability Language is the language that is now a Revised Submission in the Object Management Group (OMG) [3] defining variability modeling and the

---

[1] http://www.varies.eu

D. Amyot et al. (Eds.): SAM 2014, LNCS 8769, pp. 1–15, 2014.
© Springer International Publishing Switzerland 2014

means to generate product models. CVL is in the tradition of modeling variability as an orthogonal, separate model such as Orthogonal Variability Model (OVM) [4] and the MoSiS CVL [1], which formed one of the starting points of the OMG CVL. The principles of separate variability model and how to generate product models are depicted in Fig. 1.

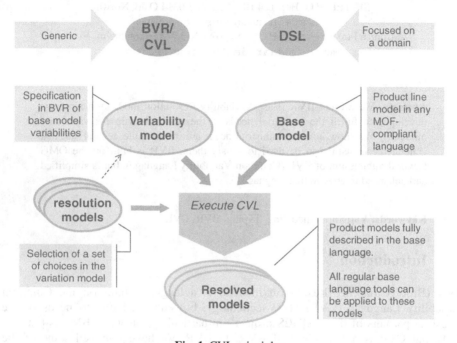

Fig. 1. CVL principles

The CVL architecture is described in Fig. 2. It consists of different inter-related models. The variability abstraction consists of a VSpec model supplemented with constraints, and a corresponding resolution model defining the product selections.

The variability realization contains the variation points representing the mapping between the variability abstraction and the base model such that the selected products can be automatically generated. The configurable units define a layer intended for module structuring and exchange. In this paper we have not gone into that layer.

The VSpec model is an evolution of the Feature-Oriented Domain Analysis (FODA) [5] feature models, but the main purpose of CVL has been to provide a complete definition such that product models can be generated automatically from the VSpec model, the resolution model and the realization model.

BVR (named from Base, Variability, Resolution models) is an evolution from CVL where some constructs have been removed for improved simplicity and some new constructs have been added for better and more suited expressiveness. The new constructs are those presented in this paper.

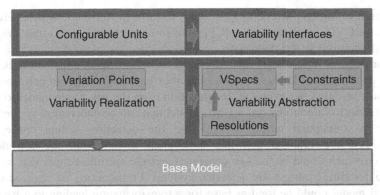

Fig. 2. CVL architecture

3   The Autronica Fire Detection Case

The main motivator has been the Autronica Fire Detection Case. Autronica Fire & Security[2] is a company based in Trondheim that delivers fire security systems to a wide range of high-end locations such as oil rigs and cruise ships. Their turnover is around 100 MEUR a year.

The Autronica demo case is described schematically in Fig. 3.

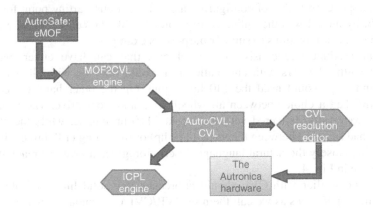

Fig. 3. The Autronica demo case

The purpose of the demo case was to explore the ways in which the Autronica specific model "AutroSafe" could be applied for two different purposes. Firstly, after transforming the MOF metamodel into CVL the CVL tools could be used to define AutroSafe configurations. Secondly, and possibly more interestingly, from the CVL

---

[2] http://www.autronicafire.com

description it would be possible to apply analysis tools to AutroSafe which were made generally for CVL. In particular the ICPL tool [6-8] could be used to find an optimal set of configurations to test AutroSafe.

For our purpose in this paper, the Autronica use-case provided the real background for understanding what kinds of product line they have to manage. In performing our use case at Autronica, we explored the transition from the AutroSafe model to a CVL model. The AutroSafe model was a UML model that can be understood as a reference model or a conceptual model of how the fire detection system concepts are associated [9]. We realized that this conceptual model could be considered a metamodel, which could be used to generate language specific editors that would be limited to describing correct fire detection systems. Furthermore, we realized that the conceptual model could be used as base for a transformation leading to a variability model. We explored this route by manually transforming the AutroSafe metamodel through transformation patterns that we invented through the work. At the same time Autronica explored defining variability models for parts of the domain directly, also for the purpose of using the variability model to generate useful test configurations.

4   The Example Case – The Car Configurator

Since the Autronica case is rather large and requires special domain knowledge we will illustrate our points with an example case in a domain that most people can relate to, namely to configure the features of a car.

Our example case is that of configuring a car. In fact our starting point for making the variability model was the online configurator for Skoda Yeti in Norway[3], but we have made some adaptations to suit our purpose as example.

Our car product line consists of diesel cars that can have either manual or automatic shift. The cars with automatic shift would only be with all wheel drive (AWD) and they would need the 140 hp engine. On the other hand the cars with manual shift had a choice between all wheel drive and front drive. The front wheel drive cars were only delivered with the weaker 110 hp engine, while the all wheel drive cars had a choice between the weak (110 hp) or the strong (140 hp) engine.

Following closely the natural language description given above, we reach the CVL model shown in Fig. 4.

Readers unfamiliar with CVL should appreciate that solid lines indicate that the child feature (or VSpecs as we call them in BVR/CVL) is mandatory when the parent is present in a resolution. Dashed lines on the other hand indicate optionality. A small triangle with associated numbers depicts group multiplicity giving the range of how many child VSpecs must and can be chosen. Thus when *AWD* has children *hp140* and *hp110* associated with a group multiplicity of 1..1, this means that if *AWD* is chosen, at least 1 and at most 1 out of *hp140* and *hp110* must be selected.

---

[3] http://cc-cloud.skoda-auto.com/nor/nor/nb-no/

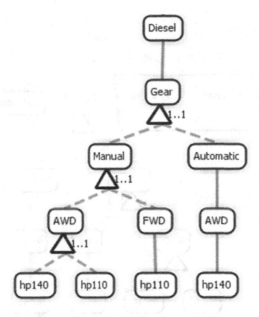

Fig. 4. The example diesel car in CVL

5 The BVR Enhancements

In this chapter, we will walk through the enhancements that we have made to accommodate for general needs inspired by and motivated by industrial cases.

5.1 Targets – The Power of the Variability Model Tree Structure

Our CVL diagram in Fig. 4 is not difficult to understand even without the natural language explanation preceding it given some very rudimentary introduction to CVL diagrams (or feature models for that matter). We see that the restrictions are transparently described through the tree structure and our decisions are most easily done by traversing the tree from the top.

It is also very obvious that the diesel car has only one engine, and that it has only one gear shift and one kind of transmission. Therefore everybody understands that even though there are two elements named "hp140" they refer to the same target, namely the (potential) strong engine. In the same way "AWD" appears twice in the diagram, but again they both refer to the same target. It turns out that CVL and other similar notations do not clearly define this. In fact CVL defines that the two choices named "hp140" are two distinct choices with no obvious relationship at all.

When does this become significant? Does it matter whether the two choices refer to the same target? It turns out that it does both for conceptual reasons and technical ones.

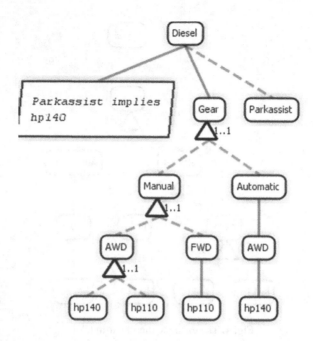

Fig. 5. Adding a Parking assistant

In Fig. 5, we have added an optional parking assistant to the car. However, to be allowed a parking assistant, you need to buy the strong engine. This is intuitive and easily understood, but formally this means that any of the occurrences of "hp140" should satisfy the constraint. Thus, constraints talk about the targets and not the choices.

5.2   Beyond One Tree

We see that the tree structure of variability models convey in a very transparent way the restrictions of the decisions to be made. However, trees are sometimes not enough. In our Autronica experiment, we wanted to reflect in the CVL model the structure of variability in a way that would abstract the actual configurations of fire detection systems in airports and cruise ships. In this way our variability model became close to the structures of the base model. Our car example model has the opposite focus as it highlights the restrictions of interrelated decisions.

In variability models that are close to the base model, one can expect that tree structures are insufficient to describe the necessary relationships and in the Autronica case the physical layout of detectors and alarms was overlaid by an equally important structure of logical relationships and groups. To represent the alternative, overlaid structures, we need ways to refer between variability elements and our obvious suggestion is to introduce references (or pointers as they are also called).

References can also serve as traces and indicate significant places in other parts of the model.

In our Autronica experiment we had to encode references since references were not available as a concept in CVL. To encode references, we used integers to indicate identifiers and corresponding pointers. This required a lot of manual bookkeeping that turned out to be virtually impossible to perform and even more impossible to read.

In BVR, we want to reflect the physical structure that is represented in the conceptual model as composition through the main hierarchical VSpec tree. The logical structure that is modeled by associations in the conceptual UML model would be represented by variability references in BVR.

5.3   From Proper Trees to Properties

Judging from the tool requirements elicited from the VARIES partners, they wanted a lot of different information stored in the variability (and resolution) models. Some of the information would be intended for their own proprietary analysis tools, and sometimes they wanted to associate temporary data in the model.

When working with the Autronica case and experiencing the difficulties with encoding the needed references we ourselves found that we wished that we had a way to explain the coding in a natural language sentence. Thus we felt the very common need for having comments.

5.4   Reuse and Type – The First Needs for Abstraction

Fire alarming is not trivial. Autronica delivers systems with thousands of detectors and multiple zones with or without redundancy to cruise ships and oil rigs where running away from the fire location altogether is not the obvious best option since the fire location is not easily vacated. In such complicated systems it was not a big surprise that recurring patterns would be found.

Without going into domain-specific details, an AutroSafe system will contain IO modules. Such IO modules come in many different forms and they represent a whole product line in its own right; this actually applies for most of the parts a fire alarm system is composed of, e.g., smoke detectors, gas detectors, panels, etc. Some IO modules may be external units and such external units may appear in several different contexts. As can be guessed, external units have a very substantial variability model and it grows as new detectors come on the market.

In our experiment, we encoded these recurring patterns also by integers as we did with references with the same plethora of integers and need for bookkeeping as a result. It was clear that concepts for recurring patterns would be useful in the language. We investigate introducing a type concept combined with occurrences referring the types.

Our example car product line has no complicated subproduct line, but we have already pointed out that *AWD* recurs twice in the original model. We express *AWD* as a type and apply two occurrences of it.

The observant reader will have seen that replacing the two occurrences of *AWD* in Fig. 6 with replications of the type will not yield exactly the tree shown in Fig. 5 since for Automatic shift only the strong engine can be chosen. Such specialization should be expressed by a constraint associated with the occurrence.

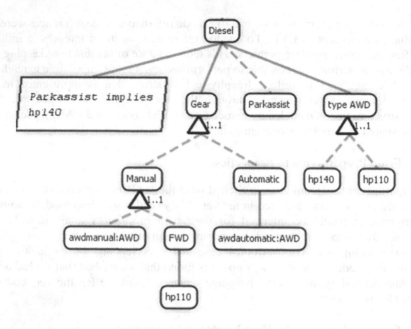

Fig. 6. The AWD variability type

We note that the type itself is defined on a level in the tree which encloses all of the occurrences. It is indeed not obvious where and how the type should be defined and we have shown here what was sufficient to cover the Autronica case.

In Fig. 6 *awdautomatic:AWD* is a ChoiceOccurrence, which represents an occurrence or instantiation of the *AWD* VType. A question is whether a ChoiceOccurrence can itself contain a tree structure below it since it is indeed a VNode? If there was a subtree with a ChoiceOccurrence as root, what would be the semantics of that tree acknowledging that the referred VType defines a tree, too? It is quite obvious that there must be some consistency between the occurrence tree and the corresponding VType tree. Intuitively, the occurrence tree should define a narrowing of the VType tree. There are, however, some serious challenges with this. Firstly, to specify the narrowing rules syntactically is not trivial. Secondly, to assert that the narrowing rules are satisfied may not be tractable by the language tool. Thirdly, the narrowing structures may not be intuitive to the user. Therefore, we have decided that only constraints will be allowed to be used to further specify a choice occurrence. In our example case, the diagram in Fig. 6 would add a constraint below *awdautomatic:AWD* with exactly one target reference to *hp140* and thus the semantics would be the same as in Fig. 5.

Our example model has only Choices as VSpecs, but the Autronica system has multiple examples of elements that are sets rather than singular choices. Such decision sets that represent repeated decisions on the same position in the VSpec tree are described by VClassifiers. Similar to ChoiceOccurrences that are typed Choices, we have VClassOccurrences that are typed VClassifiers. We appreciate that VClassifiers are not VTypes even though they represent reuse in some sense, but sets are not types. A type may have no occurrences or several occurrences in different places in the VSpec tree.

5.5   Resolution Literals – Describing Subproducts

Once we have the VType with corresponding occurrences in the variability model, we may expect that there may be consequences of these changes in the associated resolution models and realization models.

What would be the VType counterpart in the resolution model?

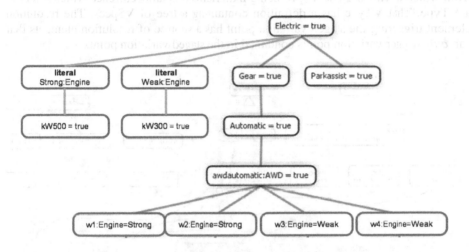

Fig. 7. Resolution literals

In Fig. 7, we show a resolution model of an imaginary electric car that has one engine for each wheel. We have defined two literals of the *Engine* type, one named *Strong* and one named *Weak*. The literals represent sub-products that have been fully resolved and named. In reality, it is often the case that there are named sub-products that already exist and have product names. Thus such literals make the resolution models easier to read for the domain experts.

5.6   Staged Variation Points – Realizing Occurrences

Having seen that the VType has consequences for the resolution model, the next question is what consequences can be found in the realization model that describes the mapping between the variability model and the base model?

We have already reuse related to the realization layer since with fragment substitutions we can reuse replacement fragment types. Replacements represent general base model fragments that are cloned and inserted other places in the base model base.

Replacement fragment types do not correspond to VType directly and we find that with fragment substitutions as our main realization primitive we would need a hierarchical structure in the realization model to correspond to the hierarchy implied by occurrences of VTypes in the variability model. The "staged variation points" correspond closely with subtrees of the resolution model. They are not type symbols, but rather correspond to the expansion of occurrences (of VTypes and resolution literals).

In BVR (and CVL) variation points refer to a VSpec each. Materialization of a product is driven by the resolutions. They refer to VSpecs and trigger those variation points that refer to that same VSpec. A staged variation point refers to an occurrence of a VType.

The semantics of a staged variation point is to limit the universe of variation points from which to choose. The VSpec being materialized is an occurrence which refers to a VType. That VType has a definition containing a tree of VSpecs. The resolution element triggering the staged variation point has a subtree of resolution elements that can *only* trigger variation points contained in the staged variation point.

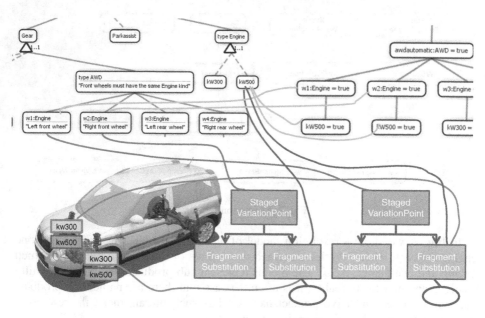

Fig. 8. Staged Variation Points example

In Fig. 8, we illustrate how staged variation points work. In the upper right, we have the resolution model and we will concentrate on resolutions of *w1* and *w2*. *w1* is resolved to true and the rightmost staged variation point refers the *w1:Engine* choice on the very left in the VSpec model indicated by the (green) line. Now since the *w1:Engine* has been chosen, we need to look into the *Engine* VType for what comes next, and the choice of the power of the engine comes next. For *w1* the resolution model indicates that *kw500* is chosen and this is also indicated by a (yellow) line from the resolution element to that of the VSpec model. The actual transformation of the base model is given by the variation points in the realization model, and we are now limited to the variation points enclosed by the staged variation point already found (the rightmost one). The rightmost fragment substitution of said staged variation point refers to the chosen *kw500* VSpec inside the *Engine* VType and thus this is the one that will be executed. The figure indicates that what it does is to remove the *kw300* option and leaving only the *kw500* engine option on the right wheel of the car.

In the very same way, we may follow the resolution of *w2* and we find that due to the staged variation point for *w2* is the leftmost one, a different fragment substitution referring the *kw500* of the *Engine* VType will be executed for *w2*, which is exactly what we need.

6   Discussion and Relations to Existing Work

Here we discuss the new mechanisms and why they have not appeared just like this before.

6.1   The Target

Introducing targets was motivated by how the VSpec tree structure can be used to visualize and define restrictions to decisions. The more the tree structure is used to define the restrictions, the more likely it is that there is a need to refer to the same target from different places in the tree.

Our example car in Fig. 4 can be described in another style as shown in Fig. 9 where the restrictions are given explicitly in constraints and the tree is very shallow. The two different styles, tree-oriented and constraint-oriented, can be used interchangeably and it may be personal preference as well as the actual variability that affects what style to choose. It is not in general the case that one style is easier or more comprehensible but constraints seem to need more familiarity with feature modeling [10].

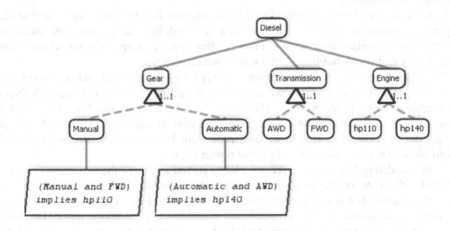

Fig. 9. The example car with explicit constraints

Given that a tree-oriented style is applied and there are duplications of target, why is this a novelty? It is a novelty because CVL does not have this concept and it is unclear whether other similar feature modeling notations support the distinction that we have named targets as distinguished from VSpecs (or features). Batory [11] and Czarnecki [12, 13] seem to solve duplication by renaming to uniqueness. The Atego OVM tool[4] implicitly forces the user into the style of using explicit constraints and thus circumvents the problem. OVM [4] does not contain the general feature models of FODA [5].

VSpecs are distinct decision points and every VSpec is in fact unique due to the tree path to the root. Targets are also unique, but for a different reason. Targets are unique since they represent some substance that is singular. This substance needs not be base-model specific, but it is often closely related to the base model. What makes this distinction essential is that explicit constraints talk about targets and not VSpecs. In Fig. 5 we have a variability model which is properly satisfied by (*Parkassist, Manual, AWD, hp140*) and by (*Parkassist, Automatic, AWD, hp140*) showing that *hp140* may refer to any of two distinct VSpecs.

6.2   The Type and Its Consequences

Introducing a type concept to BVR should come as no surprise. As pointed out in [14] concepts for reuse and structuring normally come very early in the evolution of a language. Since the feature models have a fairly long history [5], it may be somewhat surprising that type concepts for subtrees have not been introduced before. A type concept was introduced in the MoSiS CVL [1], and this was fairly similar to the one we introduce to BVR. The CVL Revised Submission [3] has a set of concepts related to "configurable units" that are related to our suggested VType concept, but those concepts were intended mainly for sub-product lines of larger size. The concept was also much related to how variabilities are visible from the outside and the inside of a product line definition.

Other notations have not introduced type concepts and this may indicate that the suggested notations were not really seen as modeling languages, but more as illustrations. Another explanation may be that type concepts do introduce some complexity that imply having to deal with some challenges.

One challenge is related to notation. The type must be defined and then used in a different place. In the singular world definition and usage were the same. VTypes must appear somewhere. We have chosen to place them within the VSpec tree, but it would also be attractive to be able to define VTypes in separate diagrams. A VType in fact defines a product line in its own right. Our Engine VType implied in Fig. 7 could contain much more than only horse power choice.

In the modeling language Clafer, which has served as one of the inspiration sources of BVR, the type declarations must be on the topmost level [15], which in our example would have made no difference. Locally owned types, however, have been common in languages in the Simula/Algol tradition [16] for many years. The local ownership gives tighter encapsulation while the top ownership is semantically easier.

---

[4] http://www.atego.com

The usage occurrences refer to the type. How should this be depicted? We have chosen to use textual notation for this indicating the type following a colon. The colon is significant for showing that the element is indeed an occurrence of a VType.

Another challenge is related to how the VType and its occurrences are placed in the model at large. This has to do with what is often called scope or name space. We have defined that VTypes or VPackages (collections of VTypes) can be name spaces and thus occurrences of a VType *X* can only appear within the VType enclosing the definition of *X*, but VTypes may be nested. Similar to the discussion on targets, again names are significant because they designate something unique within a well-defined context.

Are targets and types related? Could we say that targets appearing in multiple VSpecs are in fact occurrences of a VType (named by the target name)? At first glance this may look promising, but they are conceptually different. The target is something invariant that the decisions mentioning it are talking about. A VType is a pattern for reuse, a tree structure of decisions representing a subproduct line. There are cases where the two concepts will coincide, but they should be kept distinct. While VTypes are defined explicitly and separately, we have chosen to let targets be defined implicitly through the names of VSpecs.

CVL already recognized types as it had VariableType, which was quite elaborate and which also covered ReplacementFragmentType and ObjectType. Could VType be a specialized VariableType and the occurrences specialized variables? This may also be tempting, but variables are given values from the base model by the resolutions, while occurrences refer to patterns (VTypes) of the variability model.

6.3   The Note

The Note is about a significant element that has no direct significance in the language. Adding a note concept is an acknowledgement of the fact that there may very well be information that the user wants to associate closely with elements of the BVR model, but which is of no consequence to the BVR language or general BVR tooling.

Such additional information may be used for tracing, for expressing extra-functional properties or it may be pure comments. The text may be processed by proprietary tooling or by humans. Having no such mechanism made it necessary to accompany a CVL diagram with a textual description if it should be used by more than one person or more than one community.

Since variability modeling is oblivious to what varies, the Note can be more important than it might seem. The Note is where you can associate safety critical information with the variants and the possibilities. The Note is where you can contain traces to other models. The Note is where you can put requirements that are not connected to the variability model itself.

The Note will be significant for the tools doing analysis.

We foresee that once we have experimented with using notes in BVR, there will be recurring patterns of usage which may deserve special BVR constructs in the future, but at this point in time we find such constructs speculative.

6.4   The Reference

References in the BVR model are similar to what can be found in commercial tools like pure::variants[5]. A reference in the variability model is defined as a variable and as such it enhances the notion that variables hold base model values only. A *Vref* variable is resolved by a *VRefValueSpecification* where the pointers of the resolution model and the pointers of the variability model correspond in a commutative pattern.

Why are references necessary? They represent structure beyond the tree and this can represent dependencies that are hard to express transparently in explicit constraints.

In our motivation from the Autronica case our need for references came from describing an alternative product structure that overlaid the hierarchical physical structure of the configured system. We may say that our Autronica variability model is a very product-oriented (or base-oriented) variability model meaning that structures of the product was on purpose reflected in the variability model. The opposite would have been a property-oriented variability model where VSpecs would have represented more abstract choices such as "Focus on cost" vs. "Focus on response time".

7   Conclusions and Further Development

We have been motivated by needs of the use cases and found that the needs could be satisfied by introducing some fairly general new mechanisms. At the same time we have made the BVR language more compact than the original CVL language such that it serves a more focused purpose.

Our next step is to modify our CVL Tool Bundle to become a true BVR Tool Bundle to verify that the demo cases can more easily be expressed and maintained through the new language.

The future will probably see improvements along two development paths. One line of improvements will be related closely with needs arising from variability analysis techniques for safety critical systems. We suspect that the generic Note construct could be diversified into several specific language mechanisms associated with analysis techniques. This would migrate the insight from the analysis tools to the BVR language.

The second line of improvements will follow from general language needs. The VType concept should potentially form the basis for compact concepts of interface and derived decisions serving some of the same goals as the elaborated mechanisms around "configurable units" in CVL. We think this line of development will also include partial binding and default resolutions without introducing additional conceptual complexity.

Acknowledgements. This work has been done in the context of the ARTEMIS project VARIES with Grant agreement no: 295397.

---

[5] http://www.pure-systems.de

References

1. Haugen, O., Møller-Pedersen, B., Oldevik, J., Olsen, G.K., Svendsen, A.: Adding Standardized Variability to Domain Specific Languages. In: Geppert, B., Pohl, K. (eds.) SPLC 2008, vol. 1, pp. 139–148. IEEE Computer Society, Limerick (2008)
2. Haugen, O., Wasowski, A., Czarnecki, K.: CVL: common variability language. In: Proceedings of the 17th International Software Product Line Conference, pp. 277–277. ACM, Tokyo (2013)
3. Object Management Group: Common Variability Language (CVL). Revised Submission, OMG (2012)
4. Pohl, K., Böckle, G., van der Linden, F.J.: Software Product Line Engineering. Springer (2005)
5. Kang, K., Cohen, S., Hess, J., Novak, W., Peterson, A.: Feature-Oriented Domain Analysis (FODA) Feasibility Study. Software Engineering Institute, Carnegie Mellon University (1990)
6. Johansen, M.F., Haugen, Ø., Fleurey, F.: An algorithm for generating t-wise covering arrays from large feature models. In: SPLC 2012 Proceedings of the 16th International Software Product Line Conference, vol. 1, pp. 46–55. Association for Computing Machinery (ACM) (2012)
7. Johansen, M.F., Haugen, Ø., Fleurey, F., Eldegard, A.G., Syversen, T.: Generating Better Partial Covering Arrays by Modeling Weights on Sub-product Lines. In: France, R.B., Kazmeier, J., Breu, R., Atkinson, C. (eds.) MODELS 2012. LNCS, vol. 7590, pp. 269–284. Springer, Heidelberg (2012)
8. Johansen, M.F.: Testing Product Lines of Industrial Size: Advancements in Combinatorial Interaction Testing. Ph.D. thesis, Department of Informatics, University of Oslo, Oslo (2013)
9. Berger, T., Stanciulescu, S., Ogaard, O., Haugen, O., Larsen, B., Wasowski, A.: To Connect or Not to Connect: Experiences from Modeling Topological Variability. In: SPLC 2014. ACM (to appear, 2014)
10. Reinhartz-Berger, I., Figl, K., Haugen, Ø.: Comprehending Feature Models Expressed in CVL. In: Dingel, J., van de Stadt, R. (eds.) MODELS 2014. LNCS, vol. 8767, pp. 501–517. Springer, Heidelberg (2014)
11. Batory, D.: Feature Models, Grammars, and Propositional Formulas. In: Obbink, H., Pohl, K. (eds.) SPLC 2005. LNCS, vol. 3714, pp. 7–20. Springer, Heidelberg (2005)
12. Czarnecki, K., Helsen, S., Eisenecker, U.: Staged Configuration Using Feature Models. Software Process Improvement and Practice 10(2), 143–169 (2005)
13. Czarnecki, K., Helsen, S., Eisenecker, U.: Formalizing cardinality-based feature models and their specifications. Software Process Improvement and Practice 10(1), 7–29 (2005)
14. Haugen, O.: Domain-specific Languages and Standardization: Friends or Foes? In: Reinhartz-Berger, I., Sturm, A., Clark, T., Cohen, S., Bettin, J. (eds.) Domain Engineering, pp. 159–186. Springer, Heidelberg (2013)
15. Bąk, K., Czarnecki, K., Wąsowski, A.: Feature and Meta-Models in Clafer: Mixed, Specialized, and Coupled. In: Malloy, B., Staab, S., van den Brand, M. (eds.) SLE 2010. LNCS, vol. 6563, pp. 102–122. Springer, Heidelberg (2011)
16. Birtwistle, G.M., Dahl, O.-J., Myhrhaug, B., Nygaard, K.: SIMULA BEGIN. Petrocelli/Charter, New York (1975)

MID: A MetaCASE Tool
for a Better Reuse of Visual Notations

Amine El Kouhen[1], Abdelouahed Gherbi[1], Cédric Dumoulin[2], Pierre Boulet[2],
and Sébastien Gérard[3]

[1] Software Engineering Dept., École de technologie supérieure, Montréal, Canada
{amine.el-kouhen.1,abdelouahed.gherbi}@etsmtl.ca
[2] University of Lille, LIFL CNRS UMR 8022,
Cité scientifique - Bâtiment M3, Villeneuve d'Ascq, France
{cedric.dumoulin,pierre.boulet}@lifl.fr
[3] CEA LIST, Gif-sur-Yvette, France
sebastien.gerard@cea.fr

Abstract. Modeling tools facilitate the development process from modeling to coding. Such tools can be designed using a Model-Driven approach in metamodeling environments called *MetaCASE tools*. However, current MetaCASE tools still require, in most cases, manual programming to build full tool support for the modeling language. In this paper, we want to specify, using models, diagram editors with a high graphical expressiveness without any need for manual intervention. The second axis is dedicated to the reuse of this specification in other contexts. The redundancy in a diagram editor specification raises the problem of inconsistency during the evolution or the update of this specification. We propose then *MID*, a tool based on a set of metamodels supporting the easy specification of modeling editors with reusable components.

Keywords: Graphical user interface design, Visual languages, Model reuse, Concrete syntax, Design tools.

1 Introduction

After the object-oriented paradigm in the 80's and a brief stint in aspect-oriented approaches, software engineering is moving today towards model-driven engineering (MDE), in which the studied system is not seen as a sequence of lines of code but as a set of more abstract models describing each concern or point of view of this system.

The evolution of a paradigm requires the evolution of the tools and languages that support it. We can see then the rise of UML (Unified Modeling Language)[20], which has emerged as the most used modeling language in industrial and academic environments.

While models are very widespread, an explicit definition of a modeling language and an explicit manipulation of its models are closely connected to some specific tools, called Computer-Aided Software Engineering tools, or simply

D. Amyot et al. (Eds.): SAM 2014, LNCS 8769, pp. 16–31, 2014.

"CASE tools". These tools have been very successful in software engineering: they manipulate models to generate code and vice versa (reverse engineering).

The design and generation of such tools can be done either using program-based environments or by applying model-based approaches supported by Meta-CASE tools. The intent of MetaCASE tools is to capture the specification of the required CASE tool and then generate it automatically.

However, many modeling environments still require a considerable amount of manual programming to build diagram editors. Existing MetaCASE tools allow one to specify diagram editors but in a very superficial way. The ergonomics of a generated editor is often not up to expectations. Additional programming effort is required to specify complex forms, manage interactions, edit labels, providing property views, etc. This becomes a problem for developers, who must invest a significant amount of time and other resources to complete tasks considered as secondary to their main purpose: the development and integration of language modeling and code generation.

In addition to manual intervention to specify that kind of tools, several gaps did appear [6,11,16], mainly in terms of their low visual expressiveness and of the limited reuse of their specifications.

To explain these issues, we evaluated the technologies currently used to specify diagram editors [11]. The design of a graphical tool such as Papyrus [7] for example, brings up an important need in terms of diagram definition reuse. The main reason for these gaps is the lack of reusability in this kind of technologies. UML diagrams for example have several common elements, yet these elements are manually duplicated in the specification, thus increasing risks of errors, problems of consistency, redundancy in the specification, and maintenance effort.

At a high level of abstraction, the study of editor specification tools allows us to identify some needs and criteria in terms of reusability, graphical completeness, model consistency and maintainability of diagram specifications. Compliance with these criteria led us ultimately to produce an alternative meta-tool based on a set of metamodels called Metamodels for user Interfaces and Diagrams (*MID*), to easily design, prototype and evolve graphical editors for a wide range of visual languages. We base MID's design on two overarching requirements: graphical expressiveness and simplicity of diagram editor (de)composition for a better reusability. The main goal of this work is the specification of modeling tools from reusable, pre-configured components. For that purpose, we take advantage from MDE benefits, component-based modeling, separation of concerns and an inheritance mechanism to increase the reuse of editors' components. In this paper, we present a more comprehensive version of *MID* metamodels that offers a high visual expressiveness and advanced reuse capabilities.

2   Foundations

The concrete syntaxes (CS) of a language provide users one or more formalisms, graphical and/or textual, to manipulate abstract syntax concepts and thus create instances (i.e., models). Thus, models obtained are conforming to the structure defined by the abstract syntax (i.e, metamodel). Our proposal is at the level of graphical concrete syntax definition. A key concept of this syntax is the *Diagram*.

In the literature, numerous definitions can be found for the concept of diagram. The widely accepted ones include Kosslyn's [10] and Larkin's [13]: *Diagrams are an effective medium of human thinking and problem solving. Diagrams are thus bi-dimensional, geometric, symbolic and human-oriented representations of information; they are created by humans for humans. They have little or no value for communicating with computers, whose visual processing capabilities are primitive at best* [18].

According to Moody [17], elementary components of a visual representation are called visual notations (visual language, diagramming notations or graphical notations) and consist of a set of graphical symbols (**visual vocabulary**), a set of compositional / structural rules (**visual grammar**) and definitions of the meaning of each symbol (**semantics**). The visual vocabulary and visual grammar form together the **concrete** (or **visual**) **syntax**.

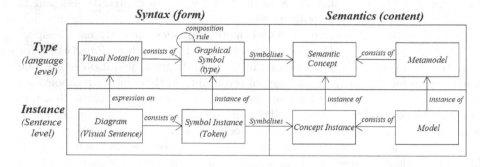

Fig. 1. The nature of a visual notation [17]

Graphical symbols are used to symbolize (perceptually represent) semantic constructs, typically defined by a metamodel. The meanings of graphical symbols are defined by mapping them to the constructs they represent. A valid expression in a visual notation is called a **visual sentence** or **diagram**. Diagrams are composed of symbol instances (tokens), arranged according to the rules of the visual grammar [17]. Such distinction between the content (semantics) and the form (syntax: vocabulary and grammar) allows us to separate the different concerns of our proposition. These definitions are illustrated in Fig. 1.

The seminal work in the graphical communication field is Jacques Bertin's *Semiology of Graphics* [1]. Bertin identified eight elementary visual variables, which can be used to graphically encode information. These are categorized into planar variables (the two spatial dimensions x,y) and retinal variables (Shape, Color, Size, Brightness, Orientation, Texture). The set of visual variables define a *vocabulary* for graphical communication: a set of atomic building blocks that can be used to construct any graphical representation. Different visual variables are suitable for encoding different types of information. The choice of visual variables has a major impact on cognitive effectiveness [3,14,23].

3 Metamodels for User Interfaces and Diagrams (MID)

The aim of our work is to design diagram editors and to allow reusing parts of such design. For that, we propose to use a model-driven approach, to ensure the independence from technology, the ease of maintenance and to enable better sustainability.

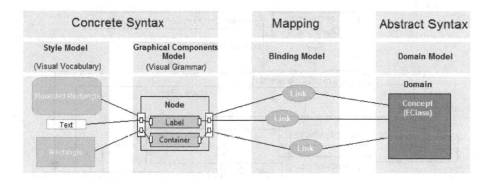

Fig. 2. MID: involved artifacts

Figure 2 shows the linkage of the metamodels involved in our proposal. First, we separate the domain content (**abstract syntax**) and the form (visual syntax or **concrete syntax**) of a diagram at a high level of abstraction (language level). The semantics is out of scope of our paper; it is widely treated in tools and technologies like EMF/Ecore. The form is separated into two parts: the **visual vocabulary** (different variables of shape, color, size, etc.) and the **visual grammar** that describes composition rules of visual representations. The link between the syntax and the semantics is also specified in a separate "binding" model. Thus, our proposal is made of several metamodels, each one used to describe one concern: a visual grammar metamodel, a visual vocabulary metamodel and a mapping metamodel. This work has resulted in our metamodels called *MID*: Metamodels for user **I**nterfaces and **D**iagrams[1].

3.1 Visual Grammar: Graphical Elements Composition

To improve reusability, we propose a component-based approach. This approach aims to take advantage of encapsulation (ease of maintenance and composition) and the benefits of interfacing (interfaces naming mechanism). In addition, our

---

[1] MID artifacts are available on: http://www.lifl.fr/~elkouhen/MID-Updates

approach allows the reuse through inheritance: a component can inherit from another one and it can also override some of its characteristics (style, structure, behaviors, etc.).

The component concept is the main concept of our set of metamodels. It represents the composition of a visual notation. A component could have three kinds of interfaces: *domain interface, style interface* and *event interface*. Interfaces are used as an attachment point between (sub)components and the corresponding concern of each interface (semantics, rendering and interactions). Thus, it helps to improve the maintainability of components by externalizing their descriptions in a unique place.

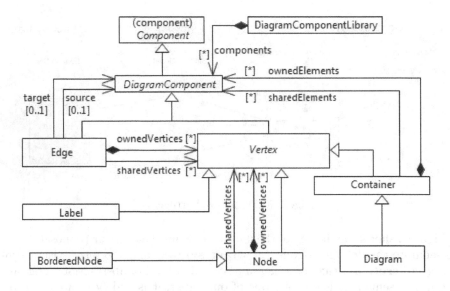

Fig. 3. Diagram grammar

The visual grammar is used to describe the structure of diagrams' elements. This description is hierarchical: a root element can contain other elements. We propose two main types of elements: *vertices* to represent diagrams complex elements and *edges* to represent links between complex elements.

A Vertex is node abstraction that consists of main nodes (top nodes), subnodes (contained vertices in Fig. 3) and attached nodes (nodes that can be affixed to other nodes). A Label is a vertex that allows access to nodes textual elements via their accessors (getters and setters). This will synchronize the data model with the text value represented. A Bordered node is a node that can be affixed to other nodes. Containers (Compartments) are specific nodes that contain diagram elements. A Diagram is itself a Container. An Edge is a connection between two diagram elements; this relationship could be specified semantically (in the domain metamodel) or graphically and could be more complex than a simple line (e.g., buses in Fig. 4).

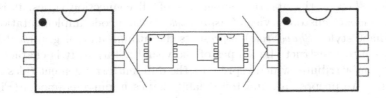

Fig. 4. Bus between two elements

Conceptually, we have added several concepts for a complete description of hybrid visual languages (i.e., languages that combine the characteristics of spacially defined languages, Connection-based or Entity/Relation languages and Containment languages). We can thus describe complex diagrams such as UML sequence and timing diagrams.

3.2   Visual Vocabulary: Visual Variables

The visual vocabulary allows describing the graphical symbols (visual representation) of diagrams' elements. This description is composed of Bertin's [1] visual variables; we regroup all of them in the *Style* concept (Fig. 5) representing the shape, color, size, layout, etc.

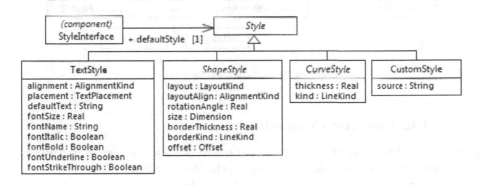

Fig. 5. Visual vocabulary description

All diagram components are associated via their *style interfaces* to visual vocabularies represented in the metamodel by the **Style** concept. As other characteristics of diagrams elements, this relationship can be reused and overloaded through the proposed mechanism of inheritance.

The style is divided into four main categories. The text style (*TextStyle*) is a graphical representation that renders a sequence of characters in a box (label). Text styles specify the alignment of the displayed data, positions and information about the size, color and font. The curve style is the graphical definition of a connection. This is the abstract superclass of all connection styles. It is also possible to create custom styles (*CustomStyle*) with a code implementation.

The shape style (*ShapeStyle*) represents the atomic unit of graphical information used to construct the shapes of the visual notation. It is characterized by the layout attribute, which represents the different arrangement rules in the host figure. We propose around ten default shapes in our metamodel (Fig. 6), and we let users create their own shapes with polygons, images or more complex shapes (*ComposedStyle*).

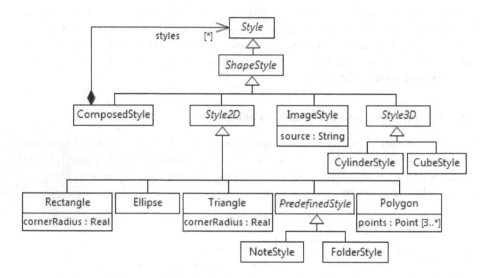

Fig. 6. Shape styles

3.3   CASE Tools (De)Composition

In the current version, the description of bindings with abstract syntax is used as an entry point to the full description of the Diagram editor (Fig. 7).

This is represented by the element *DiagramEditor* containing all bindings. This concept is associated with a diagram and contains tools such as palette, which allows to create graphical elements into diagrams, menus and properties view, which allows to view/edit the properties of the selected item in the diagram.

3.4   Representation Formalism

For simplicity, we propose a graphical formalism to present our concepts. This formalism allows to see graphically the diagrams specification instead of a textual or tree-based form. Diagram components are represented as rectangles with interfaces on their borders. Style interfaces are red and domain ones are blue.

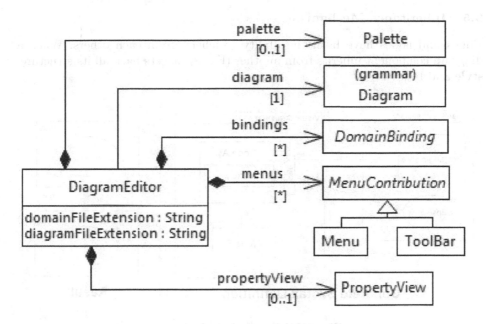

Fig. 7. Diagram editor assembling

We have defined our concrete syntax with *MID* (auto-description), allowing us to propose a modeling tool for our metamodels. Figure 8 shows an example of a component specification with the graphical view (left side) and its result.

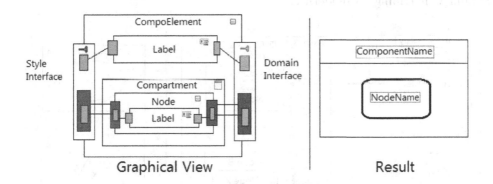

Fig. 8. MID graphical formalism

3.5   Inheritance Mechanism

Edges and nodes have both the ability to inherit from each others. When a diagram component inherits from another (Fig. 9), it gets back all its structure, style and behavior.

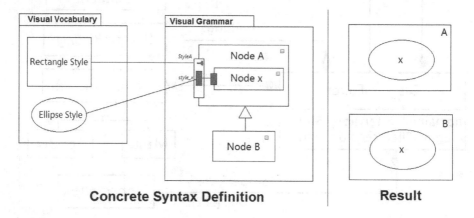

Fig. 9. MID: graphical inheritance

If the inheriting component contains an element with the same name as the inherited component (Fig. 10), this is interpreted by an overload and then we can override the structure, style and behavior. This feature maximizes components reuse and allows creating other derivatives components. Visual grammar elements only represent the structure and should be associated to a visual vocabulary describing its rendering.

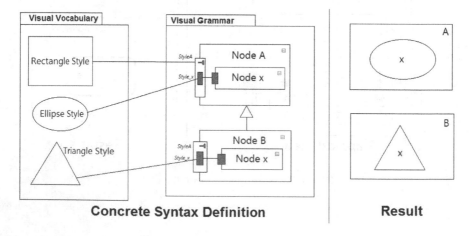

Fig. 10. Example of graphical overriding

Figure 10 shows the overriding of inherited elements. The component "**Node B**" inherits from the component "**Node A**". Both have sub-components named "Node x", in this case the element *"Node x" of B* overrides the description of *"Node x" of A* (initially represented by an ellipse).

4   Validation

The specification method chosen for our approach is based on models. This approach allows us to benefit from the undeniable advantages of MDE in the editors' development cycle. These benefits are reflected in multiple aspects, such as ease of specification and technology independence, which allow greater collaboration and flexibility in the metamodeling cycle of editors.

To validate our metamodels, we have developed several chains of transformations allowing the full generation of designed editors code. Note that MID metamodels are completely independents from technological targets. In the actual implementation, we choose *Spray* [8] and GMF as technological targets.

4.1   Graphical Expressiveness

A circuit diagram (also known as electrical diagram) is a simplified conventional graphical representation of an electrical circuit [22]. A circuit diagram shows the components of the circuit as simplified standard symbols (left side of Fig. 11).

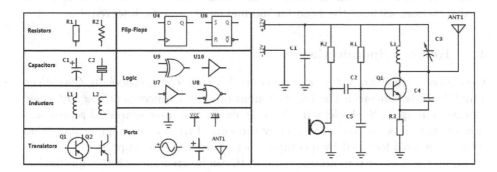

Fig. 11. Electrical symbols (left side) and an example of a circuit diagram (right side)

Our goal is to specify editors able to draw and manipulate electrical components concepts and construct diagrams such as shown in the right part of Fig. 11. Despite its graphical complexity, we could describe this visual language with *MID*. The result of this specification is shown in Fig. 12.

The graphical completeness is defined by the capability to use fully the shape variable (the use of any kind of shapes: complex, composites, 2D/3D, etc.). Unlike tools we have evaluated in [11], our metamodels have a great capacity to use the full range of these variables; we were inspired by tools based on graph

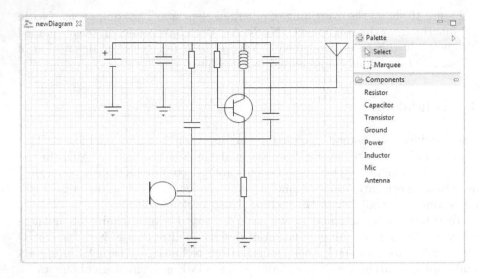

Fig. 12. Electrical diagram editor generated with *MID*

grammar and their approaches to define those variables. We have proposed also other representation mechanismes like SVG representations, and other predefined figures. We solve some problems identified in existing tools and methods found in the industry and in the literature [6]. For example, we have succeeded to specify diagram editors as complex as circuit diagram editors, at a high level of abstraction, without the need for manual programmatic intervention.

4.2 Reuse of Specification

We choose as case study, the reuse between UML concepts, especially *Classifiers*. The Classifier concept is the basic element of several concepts (*Class, Interface, Component*, etc.). Such elements have generally the same graphical representation except for a few variations. They are formed from a rectangular node that contains a label followed by a compartment that contains properties.

Thus, the graphical redundancy in UML can be treated with this mechanism of inheritance. The advantage in terms of the spent time on specification and maintenance is substantially reduced by using reusable graphical elements.

To specify a *Component*, we have to inherit from *Classifier* and add to its structure, a border node representing the ports (attached on components borders).

To Specify the graphical elements *Class* and *Interface*, we have to inherit from *Classifier* and add to its structure two other compartments, the first for operations and the other one for nested classifiers (Fig. 13). In this example, and for simplification, the Interface inherits from the graphical definition of the Class to show the graphical similarity between the two concepts. Fig. 14 shows the generated result.

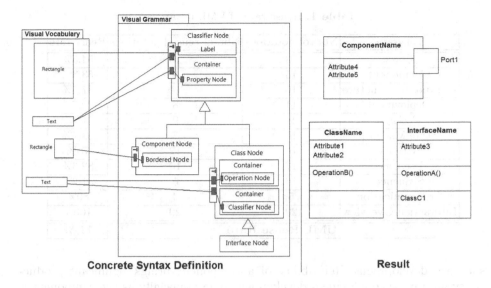

Fig. 13. Reuse of UML graphical elements

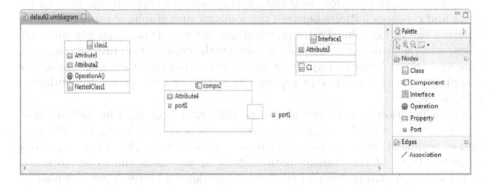

Fig. 14. Generated editor for UML

The specification of UML concrete syntax, allows us to evaluate the reuse rate of UML visual notations with *MID*. Table 1 shows the diagrams specified with *MID*, the number of visual notations in each diagram and the reuse rate of these notations in each diagram. The rate of reuse is calculated as follows:

$$\text{UML Reuse Rate} = \frac{\text{number of reused notations}}{\text{global number of UML notations}} \times 100$$

Reusability was, since the beginning of our research work, the most important and desirable criterion. This criterion motivated us to seek methods that allow more reuse of specification models. For this reason, we chose to introduce the concept of component-based metamodeling to specify graphical editors. A component-based approach ensures better readability and better maintenance of models. It is particularly useful for teamwork and allows industrializing

Table 1. Reuse rate of UML notations

Diagram	Nbr. of notations	Nbr. of reused notations	Reuse rate
Class	33	18	54,5%
Component	15	8	53,3%
Composite Structure	16	14	87,5%
Deployment	11	8	72,7%
Package	9	9	100%
State Machine	16	7	43,7%
Activity	16	12	75%
Use Case	17	14	82,3%
Sequence	16	5	31,2%
Communication	5	4	80%
Interaction Overview	20	20	100%
UML Reuse Rate			**71 %**

software development. Reusability of a component brings significant productivity gain because it reduces development time, especially as the component is reused often.

Unlike existing tools for diagrams specification, we separate the editor's aspects and concerns initially between the semantic and graphical aspects, then we separate the two graphical aspects, which are the visual vocabulary (visual variables) and the visual grammar that represents the composition rules of diagrams. Subsequently, it becomes important to create another part that would make the mapping between the different aspects, in particular between the semantic and graphic aspects.

The separation of concerns is also carried out in the transformation chain, by introducing several intermediate level models and by delaying the introduction of technical details in the latest models of the chain. This allows for better maintainability of the transformation chain in case of a change/evolution in metamodels. A strong separation of concerns allows a better reuse and maintenance of models, it decreases development costs in terms of maintenance time in case of changes in these models and it should allow designing new applications by assembling existing models. It also allows to reuse a complete diagram description in another domain model.

Through the examples presented in this sub-section, we validated our approach in terms of reusability. This approach allowed us to **reuse more than 70%** of components created in our UML specification, which is not negligible. This approach allowed us to define easily the editors' specificities with a model-driven approach and without any need to redefine or manually program changes, which increases the level of maintainability of editors generated with our solution.

Furthermore, we evaluated the reuse rate for other existing approaches: we found that our proposal offers a reuse rate much higher than the other ones. Table 2 shows the UML reuse rate with the other approaches.

Table 2. UML reuse rates for the other tools

Tool	UML Reuse Rate
MetaEdit+	46,9 %
GMF	52,3 %
Obeo Designer	34,8 %
Spray/Graphiti	64 %
MID	**71 %**

Practically, when we developed the Papyrus UML modeler [7], we tried all existing frameworks including GMF, Graphiti, Sirius and other approaches such as those of Bottoni and Costagliola [2]. All of them are limited to design Entity/Relation-like languages and no more. These tools have been widely discussed and compared with our approach in [6,11,16].

Tools based on graph grammars (e.g., $AToM^3$ [12] and DiaGen [15]) provide visual separation between visual vocabulary and visual grammar. However, to define a visual language, developers must invest significant effort to analyze and identify all rules [5].

In [4], the authors propose a tool called VLDesK, which is based on components for specifying visual languages. However, this approach is suffering from several limitations. Using a textual description to define components, this approach rises an additional cost to learn and write the implementation of each component. Users are soon confronted to the difficulty of components maintenance. In addition, users of this tool require specific skills: a good understanding of the Extended Positional Grammars [5] and of YACC [9].

Most diagrams specification methods mix concerns. The common form of mixing is between the visual vocabulary and visual grammar definitions. Most of the tools offering the separation of the graphical part from the semantic one, like *GMF* tooling, TopCased-Meta and even standards like Diagram Definition [19], fail to separate the two graphical syntax concerns, which are visual vocabulary (shapes, colors, styles, etc.) and visual grammar (composition rules of the visual notation).

5   Conclusion

In this article, we present an approach based on MDE and components modeling, allowing the easy specification of diagram graphical editors at a high level of abstraction, in order to model, reuse, compose and generate code. In our proposal, we focus on the component concept, to describe and then assemble concepts emerging from visual languages. We first solved some major problems identified in existing tools and methods found in industry and in the literature, such as the specification at a high level of abstraction without the need for manual programmatic intervention, the separation of concerns, the graphical effectiveness and finally the reusability of editors. To validate our approach, we have developed transformation chains targeting technologies like GMF and Spray, which enable the generation of functional editor's code. This allows us to successfully design diagrams by reusing existing components, and to generate their implementation. We validated our approach on several diagrams.

Our approach presents many advantages. Firstly, through the reuse of models: the models are theoretically easier to understand and to manipulate by business users; which corresponds to a goal of MDE. Secondly, this reuse brings considerable gains of productivity through ease of maintenance of components. It also allows better teamwork and helps for the industrialization of software development; it becomes possible to build libraries of components, and then build the diagram by assembling these components.

Briefly, we can say that our approach opens a new way that shows promises for a wider use of modeling tools and automatic generation of applications. Compared to the current development technologies, the promises of this approach are high due to the ability to create complex applications by assembling existing simple model/components fragments, and especially the possibility for non-computer specialists, experts in their business domain, to create their own applications from a high-level description using an adapted formalism, easy to understand and manipulate for them.

In the current state of our research, many studies are still required to reach a full generation of modeling tools. Firstly, we need to be able to describe and generate ergonomic aspects and interactions with our approach. We can thus use task models [21] to specify user interactions regardless of the modality or implementation technologies. Finally, we need to define other metamodels that would allow describing the other parts of such tools (tree editors, tables/matrices, etc.) following the same approach of component reuse and inheritance.

Acknowledgements. This work was supported by the LIST laboratory of the French Atomic Commission (CEA). This work has also been supported by the Natural Sciences and Engineering Research Council of Canada (NSERC) and the Fond de l'internationalisation de la recherche (FIR) - Bureau de coordination internationale (BCI) of the École de technologie supérieure (ÉTS).

References

1. Bertin, J.: Semiology of graphics: diagrams, networks, maps. University of Wisconsin Press, Madison (1983)
2. Bottoni, P., Costagliola, G.: On the definition of visual languages and their editors. In: Hegarty, M., Meyer, B., Hari Narayanan, N. (eds.) Diagrams 2002. LNCS (LNAI), vol. 2317, pp. 305–319. Springer, Heidelberg (2002)
3. Cleveland, W.S., McGill, R.: Graphical perception: Theory, experimentation, and application to the development of graphical methods. Journal of the American Statistical Association 79(387), 531–554 (1984)
4. Costagliola, G., Francese, R., Risi, M., Scanniello, G., De Lucia, A.: A component-based visual environment development process. In: SEKE 2002, pp. 327–334. ACM, New York (2002)

5. Costagliola, G., Deufemia, V., Polese, G.: A framework for modeling and implementing visual notations with applications to software engineering. ACM Trans. Softw. Eng. Methodol. 13(4), 431–487 (2004)
6. El Kouhen, A.: Spécification d'un métamodèle pour l'adaptation des outils UML. Ph.D. thesis, Université de Lille 1, France (2013)
7. Gérard, S., Dumoulin, C., Tessier, P., Selic, B.: Papyrus: A UML2 tool for domain-specific language modeling. In: Giese, H., Karsai, G., Lee, E., Rumpe, B., Schätz, B. (eds.) Model-Based Engineering of Embedded Real-Time Systems. LNCS, vol. 6100, pp. 361–368. Springer, Heidelberg (2010)
8. Itemis: A quick way of creating graphiti (2012), http://code.google.com/a/eclipselabs.org/p/spray
9. Johnson, S.C.: Yacc: Yet another compiler-compiler. Tech. rep., AT&T Corporation (1970)
10. Kosslyn, S.M.: Image and Mind. Harvard University Press (1980)
11. Kouhen, A.E., Dumoulin, C., Gérard, S., Boulet, P.: Evaluation of modeling tools adaptation. Tech. rep., CNRS (2011), http://hal.archives-ouvertes.fr/hal-00706701
12. de Lara, J., Vangheluwe, H.: Atom3: A tool for multi-formalism and meta-modelling. In: Kutsche, R.D., Weber, H. (eds.) FASE 2002. LNCS, vol. 2306, pp. 174–188. Springer, Heidelberg (2002)
13. Larkin, J.H., Simon, H.A.: Why a diagram is (sometimes) worth ten thousand words. Cognitive Science 11(1), 65–100 (1987)
14. Lohse, G.L.: A cognitive model for understanding graphical perception. Hum.-Comput. Interact. 8(4), 353–388 (1993)
15. Minas, M., Viehstaedt, G.: Diagen: A generator for diagram editors providing direct manipulation and execution of diagrams. In: 11th Int. IEEE Symp. on Visual Languages, pp. 203–210. IEEE CS, USA (1995)
16. Mohagheghi, P., Haugen, Ø.: Evaluating domain-specific modelling solutions. In: Trujillo, J., et al. (eds.) ER 2010. LNCS, vol. 6413, pp. 212–221. Springer, Heidelberg (2010)
17. Moody, D.: The "physics" of notations: Toward a scientific basis for constructing visual notations in software engineering. IEEE Trans. Softw. Eng. 35(6), 756–779 (2009)
18. Moody, D., van Hillegersberg, J.: Evaluating the visual syntax of UML: An analysis of the cognitive effectiveness of the UML family of diagrams. In: Gašević, D., Lämmel, R., Van Wyk, E. (eds.) SLE 2008. LNCS, vol. 5452, pp. 16–34. Springer, Heidelberg (2009)
19. Object Management Group: Diagram Definition. Version 1.0. OMG Document Number: formal/2012-07-01 (2012), http://www.omg.org/spec/DD/1.0/
20. Object Management Group: OMG Unified Modeling Language (OMG UML), Infrastructure. Version 2.5 - Beta 2. OMG Document Number: ptc/2013-09-05 (2013), http://www.omg.org/spec/UML/2.5/Beta2/
21. Rich, C.: Building task-based user interfaces with ansi/cea-2018. Computer 42(8), 20–27 (2009)
22. Wikipedia: Circuit diagram (2013), http://bit.ly/1mVvwMI
23. Winn, W.: Learning from maps and diagrams. Educational Psychology Review 3, 211–247 (1991)

An Empirical Study on the Anticipation of the Result of Copying and Pasting among UML Editors

Daniel Liabeuf, Xavier Le Pallec, and José Rouillard

Université de Lille 1, Laboratoire d'Informatique Fondamentale de Lille,
59655 Villeneuve d'Ascq Cédex, France
{daniel.liabeuf,xavier.le-pallec,jose.rouillard}@univ-lille1.fr

Abstract. Copy and paste is a function that is very popular in software programming. In software modeling, when a person performs a copy and paste, she/he expects that the copy will be similar to the original. The similarity refers to a selection of what properties and references from the original element have to be copied. This problem seems difficult because this feature is not addressed in scientific literature, is rarely available in — de-facto standard — editors of UML class diagram or functions differently from one editor to another. In this article, we will show that a significant part of the solution depends on the metrics used. We propose three families of metrics that produce various copy and paste behaviors. We adopted an empirical approach to assess their ergonomic qualities. We asked 67 people to predict results of a series of copy-pasting experiments. We observed two populations, one influenced by the visual representation and the other by semantics.

Keywords: Copy and paste, Diagram editor, Empirical study.

1 Introduction

Model Driven Engineering (MDE) is claimed to be a convincing way to deal with the increasing complexity of information systems [20]. First, meta-modeling allows the stakeholders of a project to specify requirements, structure and behavior of the future system through different focused models that are easy to visualize. Second, model weaving/transformation techniques allow to merge those submodels and make them productive [6]. However, modeling remains a software development activity and inherits from the same demands. Reusing is part of them and generally receives great attention from the software engineering community. Nevertheless, one of the easiest reuse technique, which is widespread in programming [9,11], did not receive much attention in the MDE community: the Copy and Paste (CnP).

During the practical courses on UML that we oversaw, we observed that most students were not satisfied with the CnP provided by UML editors (Papyrus, Magic Draw, RSA, and Enterprise Architect) and generally did not use it. If

D. Amyot et al. (Eds.): SAM 2014, LNCS 8769, pp. 32–47, 2014.

we look closer at current UML tools, we see that there is no consensus among them for this functionality. Our recent discussions with developers of Papyrus and OpenFlexo have convinced us that implementing CnP in graphical modeling tools is not trivial and have motivated us to deeply investigate this issue. We first analyzed the dimensions that must be considered when CnP-ing graphical model elements. Then we asked UML users to forecast the behavior of CnP (on a series of examples) to see what seemed to be the most intuitive one for them. The results allowed us to determine to what extent previous dimensions intervened within users' anticipation and to detect the type of situations where there would be a *problem* (i.e., no consensus). We concluded by giving directions to solve such problems.

The remainder of the paper is organized as follows. Section 2 reminds us why CnP is strategic in Software Development and why it is more complex when dealing with graphical model elements than the usual CnP or Copy and Paste Special of classic application suites. Here, we also explain why we focus on UML class diagrams. Section 2.4 demonstrates that there is no consensus among UML editors for CnP on class diagrams. Section 3 aims to explain the complexity of the CnP issue by noting the difficulty in finding answers from the three underlying dimensions (syntax, semantics and visual notation) of graphical model elements. Section 4 describes the methodology we adopted to study the anticipations of UML users. In the last section, we discuss the results.

2   Copy and Paste in Software Engineering and in Software Modeling

In this section, we first discuss why CnP is useful in Software Development. After discussing how CnP is implemented in usual application suites, we will identify the reasons why this classic behavior is not suited to the context of Software Modeling.

2.1   A Valuable Tool in Software Development

It is commonly accepted that duplications due to CnP slow down the spread of fixes and improvements. This is one of the main causes of degrading software quality. Despite these shortcomings, the scientific community does not propose replacing CnP and prefers to find solutions for the problems it causes [10,12]. CnP is popular and therefore, it is difficult to imagine alternatives.

This functionality is particularly popular among programmers. In his study on the psychology of programming, Burkhardt [4] shows that CnP is a major player in the understanding of code fragments. Programmers use it to understand a snippet via a trial and error strategy. Thus CnP, combined with the ability to quickly run proto-programs and efficient debugging tools, helps to quickly understand a candidate artifact to reuse. This ability to quickly test artifacts is also present within model-oriented environments thanks to model transformation and code generation mechanisms. CnP remains relevant in Software Modeling.

2.2 Copy and Paste in Editing Tools

In the beginning (Xerox PARC, in the 70s), the CnP technique was limited to text duplication. Today, most editing softwares (for images, text, spreadsheets, diagrams, etc.) propose it. From an interactive perspective, copying and pasting occurs most commonly in an ordered sequence of commands: the selection of what will be copied, the invocation of the copy function, the destination selection, and the invocation of the paste function. We also find a more *advanced* forms of copy and paste called *special*. Paste special is distinguished by an additional step where the operator can reduce their original selection. For example, when one copies rich text with editors like LibreOffice Writer or Microsoft Word, *paste special* will prompt a choice between the full selection (rich text) or a reduced version of it (plain text). This interactional difference between the regular and special CnP incites us to consider copying and pasting from a functional point of view: it is a reproduction technique of editing objects that requires the selection of what should be reproduced and where it should be reproduced. From this point of view, Copy and Paste Special is a regular CnP but offers an *internal refinement* of what should be copied.

2.3 Copy and Paste in Software Modeling

There is little attention from the scientific community given to CnP in Software Modelling. *Domain-Specific Modeling: Enabling Full Code Generation* [7] is probably the most advanced work in this area. In their book that guides the creation of graphical model editors, Kelly & Tolvanen distinguish copy by value versus copy by reference. The first method is similar to the usual CnP: the selected element is duplicated and becomes independent from the original. The originality of the second method comes from the model-diagram duality: it consists in replicating only the graphical element representing its model element. This method creates a new graphic element without creating a new model element or changing the model. But in both cases, the operator must select the graphical representation of the element to be copied. This problem is often solved in UML editors by providing a *paste special* that allows the operator to specify if the selection refers to the model element or to its representation.

Still in their book, Kelly & Tolvanen specify that *copy by value thus always includes the idea that the copy is to a certain depth*. Indeed, the model element is defined by its properties and its relationship with other model elements. When copying by value, it is expected that the copy retains some characteristics to consider it in keeping with the original. When copying to an external model, a copied element will be accompanied by extra elements to the initial selection. Otherwise, the copied element boils down to being a new instance of the same type as the original but with a loss of meaning that will be more or less important according to the context. However, Kelly & Tolvanen did not define how to measure *depth* and the *critical value* beyond which elements cease to be added. These inaccuracies allow a wide range of interpretations and thus, many ways to perform CnP by value.

2.4   CnP in UML Editors: The Case of Class Diagrams

CnP does not seem to be trivial when dealing with graphical model elements. Do all authors of modeling tools agree on how CnP has to behave? Rather than analyzing all current software modeling editors, we limit ourselves to UML editors with a focus on class diagrams. First, UML is widespread, so we can benefit from a large panel of editors. Second, as class diagrams are the most supported type of diagrams in UML editors, we can compare many of them on the same basis. Finally, a class diagram (CD) is a type of very basic diagram with no logic or temporal operators that may alter the way CnP is implemented: structural considerations of CD can be found in many meta-models.

Table 1. Support of copy-paste among editors of UML class diagrams

Product	Release date	Destination model	
		source	foreign
Astah	2014-01-16	Yes	Yes
Modelio	2013-12-20		
Software Ideas Modeler	2013-03-23	Yes	Yes
Visual Paradigm	2013-03-07	Yes	
Papyrus	2013-02-13	Yes	
Enterprise Architect	2013-01-15	Yes	
Innovator	2012-12-13	Yes	Yes
MagicDraw	2012-12-06	Yes	
Together	2012-11-07	Yes	
Metamill	2012-10-30	Yes	
Umodel	2012-10-19	Yes	
Visual Studio	2012-09-12	Yes	Yes
Rational Rhapsody Modeler	2012-09-11	Yes	Yes
eUML2 Modeler	2012-08-30		
AmaterasUML	2012-07-16	Yes	Yes
Rational Software Architect	2012-06-27		
Artisan Studio	2012-05-23		
Open ModelSphere	2012-04-13	Yes	Yes
ArgoUML	2011-12-15		
BOUML	2010-07-14		
EclipseUML	2010-05-09		
Poseïdon for UML	2009-12-01	Yes	
Apollo	2007-12-18		

We performed some CnP on a set of 23 UML editors (listed in Table 1) to determine what relations or properties an editor keeps when CnP-ing a class (attributes, references, associated classes, components, container, etc.). The CnP has been done within two configurations: **internal CnP**, meaning the source and target (models) are the same, and **external CnP**, where the source and target are different. Table 1 shows the status of CnP among the set of tested UML editors in their most recent version. A majority of editors (15 out of 23) support internal CnP (by value) whereas only 7 out of 23 support external CnP.

Table 2 shows the different classes of UML editors that we observed when we performed our series of tests. The classification is related to the UML editors that keep or add an element to/from the initial selection during an external CnP. If the latter is not supported, tests are performed with internal CnP in order to compare the maximum number of editors. The largest family (*Cutters*) includes seven editors, where four support external CnP. When one copies and pastes a class from an editor of this family, it duplicates the name and attributes of the class and the name and cardinality of the attributes. However, the types of attributes are not duplicated but referenced. In the context of external CnP (when the editor supports it), this reference is inconsistent (!) and sometimes causes bugs[1]. This problem of inconsistent relationships is particularly common because it affects five of the seven editors concerned. Associations and generalization links are not duplicated/referenced. It is the same for the concerned properties (that reference associations or superclasses). The *Brokers* family works in almost the same way but duplicates the property related to generalization and references corresponding superclasses in the case of internal CnP (otherwise it stays inconsistent). *Astah* is similar to the *Cutters* family but duplicates types involved in attributes of copied class. *Innovator* adds the duplication of the superclasses (and their referencing). Both editors from the *Preservatives* family, where only internal CnP is available, duplicate types of attributes and associations, but they only reference superclasses.

Table 2. Classification of UML Editors about CnP / class diagrams

Class			Cutters	Brokers	Astah	Innovator	Preservatives
name	**String**						
ownedAttribute ◇—	**Property**						
	name	**String**					
	type ——▶	**Type**					
	aggregation	**AggregationKind**					
	/lower	**Integer**					
	/upper	**Integer**					
	association ——	**Association**					
		ownedEnd ◇—**Property**					
generalization ◇—	**Generalization**						
	general ——▶	**Classifier**					

Key	
	Copied
	Referenced*
	Nonexistent

* references are inconsistent when the destination is a foreign model.

Cutters : AmaterasUML, Software Ideas Modeler, Visual Studio, Open ModelSphere, Visual Paradigm, Metamill & Poseïdon

Brokers : Papyrus, Umodel, Rational Rhapsody Modeler, Enterprise Architect & MagicDraw

Preservatives : Together & Modelio

As we can see, all elements at a distance/depth of 1 (attribute and generalization property) are not considered in the same way by all editors. It is the same with those at distance/depth of 2 (attribute types, superclass reference, association) or 3 (the other end of an association). A way to better understand why there is no consensus is to see if there are as many differences between a set of UML users and to examine those differences with an analytical framework that goes further than the simple syntactic distance.

---

[1] We may mention the model import mechanisms that allow extra-model references and could solve some inconsistent issues. However, this dependence is in conflict with established practice whereby clones are indistinguishable from their originals.

3   Dimensions to Measure the Depth

We just saw that CnP by value implies a decision problem. This problem is choosing what model elements will be added to the explicit selection. These decisions are based on the *critical depth* and the *distance* between the explicitly selected model element and the additional candidates. However, no work has been done that mentions the correct critical depth and how to measure said depth. In this section, we focus on how to measure the depth.

We have established that measuring depth is, in fact, measuring a distance between two model elements. However, it is possible to have different results depending on the selected viewpoint. For example, we may decide that the distance between two model elements correspond to the Levenshtein distance[2] between their names. This proposal does not make much sense but it shows that we need a *dimension* to create a metric. Modeling languages are typically defined by three viewpoints [8]: abstract syntax, concrete syntax and semantics. We propose to use them as dimensions and we will see that the produced distances are different. These differences are illustrated in Fig. 1.

3.1   Abstract Syntax

An abstract syntax defines symbols and construction rules that are allowed in a modeling language. According to its abstract syntax, a model element may be linked to other elements. In practice, a model element is not linked to any other model and should rather be viewed as a directed graph. From this point of view, a model element may have an *indirect* relationship with a known amount of intermediates. We propose to use this property to create a metric: the **syntactic path** is the shortest directed path between two model elements and the **syntactic distance** is the number of arcs in the corresponding syntactic path. For example, the syntactic path between a subclass and its superclass is `Class::generalizations::general` and its syntactic distance is two.

3.2   Concrete Syntax

Although not essential, models are most commonly displayed through *diagrams*. Such types of diagrams have to respect the visual vocabulary and grammar that are associated to the applied abstract syntax. This visual mapping is called the concrete syntax. For example, UML specifications recommend that a class be graphically represented by a rectangle with one, two or three horizontal compartments [14] (respectively containing *class name*, *properties* and *operations* representations). It is highly probable that one considers all these graphic symbols as constituting a single form because they are visually *inside the class shape*. This natural phenomenon can be used to decide which items should be kept during a CnP.

---

[2] The Levenshtein distance is the minimum number of single-character edits (*i.e.,* insertions, deletions or substitutions) required to change one word into the other.

The Gestalt perceptual grouping principles describe the factors that influence the groupings made by our visual perception [22]. Table 3 summarizes the principles to consider when dealing with software diagrams. Gestalt's theory explains how our perception combines visual forms. However, it fails to quantify a visual distance between visual forms only for very simple cases [21]. To the best of our knowledge, measuring visual distances in diagrams cannot be done in a formal way. We set (but not quantify) visual distances according to the theory of Gestalt and get five types of grouping whose influence on visual distance can be ordered.

Table 3. Principles of perceptual grouping most frequently encountered in UML class diagrams

Principles	Effects
Proximity	Spatially close forms tend to be grouped together.
Similarity	The most similar elements (in color, size, and orientation for these examples) tend to be grouped together.
Good Gestal	Forms arranged to create a regular and simple pattern (aligned, curved, hierarchical, radial etc) tend to be grouped together.
Common region	Forms placed inside a closed shape tend to be viewed as components of the enclosing form [16].
Connectedness	Forms connected by a link are more likely to be perceived as components of a larger form [15].
Common fate & synchrony	Forms with correlated behaviors (*e.g.,* moving in the same direction) tend to be grouped together[1,22].

In the case of class diagrams, we consider that the visual encapsulation (which is based on the principle of *common region*) generates the smallest perceptual distances. Thus, the class's name, properties and operations (or package's classes and sub-packages) are visually very close. Even without being visually connected, classes may be perceptually grouped when they are *similar* (*e.g.,* size and color), spatially close or arranged remarkably (*e.g.,* hierarchically). Although not as powerful as encapsulation, connectedness (observed particularly when the association or the generalization are used) decreases significantly the perceptual distance. Finally, the largest visual distance is between elements that benefit only from grouping by proximity. This relates in particular to the association between classes when the property is located outside of the class, close to the associated class.

Risks of inconsistencies are observed if the visual distance is used to solve the problem of decision. These risks vary depending on the critical depth used. In the first step of visual distance (embedded elements), classes are copied with their name, properties and operations. In turn, the properties and operations are copied with their name, cardinality and a *reference* to their type but not necessarily the concerned type itself. In this scenario, the properties and operations are of a type that is not present in the target model, which will make it inconsistent. In the second step (linked elements), the associated classes are grouped perceptually but not in their indissociable properties.

3.3 Semantics

If the abstract syntax defines the building blocks (concepts and their associations) that are to be used to create models, the designer should refer to the semantics of the modeling language to understand their meaning. Semantics has a major impact on how a designer perceives a modeling language and has to be included in the calculation of the distance between two elements. Semantic definition of the modeling language and its interpretation are the two key elements to consider for this goal. The interpretation consists in assigning meaning to a syntactic structure and extracting relevant information. In our case, relevant information is the *contribution of a model element in the definition* of elements that are selected to be CnP-ed. For example, what is the contribution of Properties in the definition of a Class? This objective differs from those encountered in the literature. Indeed, the work that operates semantic metrics is designed to determine the similarity between two elements [2,17,18,19].

The second key to achieve a distance based on semantics is the semantic definition of the language. This definition is the material from which useful material to interpret can be extracted. We have identified several sources/sites that an interpreter could use: the semantic domain, the meta-model and the visual notation.

According to Harel et al., a *[semantic domain] specifies the very concepts that exist in the universe of discourse* [5]. The semantic domain defines what is the concept, its effects and the constraints associated with it. For example, one of the effects of specialization (inheritance) in UML is that "each instance of the specific classifier is also an instance of the general classifier" [14]. One can interpret this definition by a very short semantic distance from a specialized class to its superclass (although not necessarily in the other direction). The UML editor *Innovator* behaves according to this example.

Meta-models define the major part of the abstract syntax, especially "the legal connections between language elements" [7]. These connections are ruled and corresponding rules can be interpreted. The UML meta-model is written with MOF, which allows two kinds of connections: composition or association. The difference between them is important: an object can be associated with several other objects, but on the other hand, an object can be the component of only one. This exclusive relationship created by composition can be interpreted as a shorter semantic distance between composed classes than between associated classes. The editors of the family *Brokers* (*cf.* Table 2) have such a behavior.

When reading a diagram, a human reader is likely to give meaning to visual elements through their positions relative to each other, their sizes, their connections, the direction of arrows, etc. This *intuitive* interpretation is studied about the quality of visual notations that Moody named *semantic transparency*. "Semantic transparency is defined as the extent to which the meaning of a symbol can be inferred from its appearance" [13]. According to Moody, the semantic transparency of a representation can be immediate, opaque or perverse. When transparency is *immediate*, the semantic is fully deductible from the representation – even a novice can understand its meaning. When it is opaque, the semantic is not deductible from the representation. When it is perverse, the semantic deduced from the representation is false. Since UML class diagrams can be qualified as *opaque*, it is difficult to distinguish the influence of visual perception from the influence of semantic transparency. However the influence of semantic transparency decreases with experience of the reader. As a consequence, we will be able to make this distinction if the knowledge level of the reader allows it.

Perceptual	Syntactic	Meta-model's semantic	Semantic domain	Key

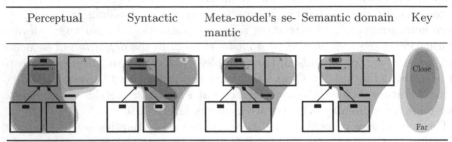

The measurement origin is the upper-left class

Fig. 1. Distances produced through presented metrics

4   Methodology and Experience

We now propose to empirically assess the relevance of the three previous dimensions and their ergonomic qualities for the CnP. To do this, we asked 73 people to predict the behavior of CnP performed by UML editors. We used the series illustrated in section 3 for this purpose. This series has been designed to assess the impact of each of the previous dimensions. In this section, we will describe the details of the methodology we applied.

4.1   Participants

Our target population is compose of people capable to read and draw UML class diagrams. Our sample is composed of 73 people who are mainly students. There are two factors that may have an impact on our survey: the level of knowledge of UML and the CnP experience.

Knowledge of UML. As the level of UML knowledge varies among software practitioners, we have selected participants to reflect these different levels of knowledge thus, attaining a representative sample of UML users. This also allows to evaluate its impact. Our set of participants is composed of 10 students in a

Master of Biology and 61 students in Computer Science, where 19 are in license 2nd year, 16 in license 3rd year and 26 in Master 1st year. The sample also includes one software practitioner and a psychologist. Students in biology will be the main group used to test the impact of semantics in their responses. More than half of the participants claimed to know class diagrams quite well.

Copy and Paste Experience. An operator anticipates the behavior of a tool when she/he invokes one of its functionalities. The quality of this anticipation may vary according to her/his knowledge of the tool and thus can be improved through learning. When one seeks to improve the ergonomics, that means that one wants to reduce the learning curve. So, if we are looking for an ergonomic CnP of model elements, that means that we are aiming to specify it in a way that produces results that conform to anticipations of operators who have no previous experience. Only two participants used a tool that allows CnP by value. They mentioned that their use of CnP was limited. Because of the small number of experienced participants and their low-level of experience, we chose to include them in our sample. Six participants provided incomplete or non-readable responses; therefore, our sample has been ultimately reduced to 67 participants.

4.2 Task

We requested the participants to *predict* the outcome of a CnP that should produce a UML editor. To ensure that experience is relevant, it was necessary that the subject had a minimum of experience in the assigned task. This is the reason why we deliberately chose participants with little experience in UML and associated editors.

To perform the requested task, it was necessary to specify the class to be copied. The class was designated by a marker introduced by a mouse click. In this way, one limits the uploading visual disturbances and makes the task more *realistic*. If we had chosen to designate the class, such as the surrounding, this would have resulted in a significant decrease in visual distance between all elements inside the selection shape and therefore introduce a bias. Still to limit the insertion of bias, the responses are requested free design and without time limit. Finally, we specified that the pasting destination be a blank environment that would not tolerate links with the source environment.

There were eight questions concerning four types of *connections*: composition represented by an attribute [3], composition represented by an association link, inheritance and packages. These types were tested twice, by selecting each end of the connection.

4.3 Variables

Studied Variable. A strong assumption of our approach is that a subject decides to keep an extra element when its distance is below a critical threshold. A second assumption of our approach is that this distance is assessed through *the presented metrics*. Consequently, metrics and critical depth used by a subject are independent and invoked variables (they are inherent to the individual and we can not have an effect on them). Our experiment aims to evaluate to what extent dimensions occur in their decision.

Distance. We assume that distances between graphical model elements are parameters of forecast production. So, we consider them as independent variables. Except for syntactic and meta-model based semantic distances, it is impossible to accurately measure a distance. Nevertheless, it is sometimes possible to decide if a distance is superior to another (ordinal data). For example, two classes connected by a line are closer perceptually than without.

Knowledge of the Subject. We asked people to forecast the result of a copy-paste in a diagram editor. It is possible that subjects have already done this task before. In these circumstances, a subject is likely to answer the observed result rather than the result of its assessment of distances. This variable was supervised during sampling and task development; making it an invoked, independent and secondary variable.

Answers. The answer of a subject is composed of the explicitly selected item and additional items to this selection. According to our theoretical model, the set of additional items depends on the metric used by the subject. Therefore, answers are the dependent variable of the target variable (used metric).

5   Experiment Results

First, we check some hypotheses from simple situations. These hypotheses are specific and it is difficult to draw general conclusions. Still, they can provide credit on the influence of presented metrics. Second, we propose a more descriptive method that is able to take into account more observations simultaneously.

5.1   Influence of Visual Representation

We assume that *a decrease in the visual distance between two classes increases the probability that the class connected to the copied class is part of prognostic.* To verify this hypothesis, we must compare situations where only visual distance changes. These situations are produced using the dual notation of the composition in UML [3]. In the first group, we represent the composition by a class attribute. In the second, the composition is represented using an association. This attribute is visually within the composite class. In the second, the composition is represented using an association. This time, the property is visually outside the composite class. Furthermore, composite and component classes are visually connected. With the connectedness property, this connection reduces the visual distance between classes.

Table 4 shows that participants add a class most often when it is visually connected to the copied class. A Fisher exact test shows a probability less than 1‰ (p-value) that connecting the classes did not influence the response, which means that our hypothesis is correct with less than 1‰ risk of being wrong. The

Table 4. Effect of reducing the visual distance between two classes

		Opposite added?		Total
		No	Yes	
Linked	No	121	13	134
	Yes	88	46	134
Total		209	59	268

visual representation appears to play an important role in prognostics because the visually connected class is added 4.9 as much as the unconnected class. This odd ratio is an average ; there is a 95% chance that the real value is in [2.5; 9.5] (the 95% confidence level). However, we must be careful to not jump to conclusions. Indeed, metric based on semantic transparency is strongly associated with visual distances. Therefore, these observations can be explained because the participants use a perceptual or a semantic transparency-based metric.

5.2 Influence of Semantic Transparency

The previous observation can be explained by the influence of semantic transparency. To demonstrate its influence, we proposed determining whether *the perceived distance between two visually associated classes is the same from one class to the other*. Indeed, the visual metric is symmetric, that is to say that the distance is substantially the same in both directions. However, the semantic transparency based metric is asymmetric: the distances can vary, for example, the direction of an arrow. As the composition association uses a diamond or an arrow at each end, the situation can be analyzed. Discriminatory behavior means that transparency semantic influences the prognosis. On the contrary, homogeneous behavior means that semantic transparency has no influence on the prognosis.

Table 5. Asymmetry in the perception of inter-class distances visually composed

		Opposite added?		Total
		No	Yes	
Selected	Component	52	15	67
class	Composite	36	31	67
Total		46	88	134

Table 5 provides more detail concerning the numbers on the second line of Table 4. This table shows whether their prognostic adds or not the opposite class according to the selected class. A Fisher exact test rejects the independence of answers with a p-value less than 1%. The effect is important because it is 3.0 times more likely that a component class will be added than the composite (95% confidence level = [1.4; 6.3]). It is concluded that semantic transparency significantly and strongly influences the prognosis of participants. Yet it is not enough to completely exclude the use of this visual metric.

5.3 Influence of the Semantic Domain

We have seen that semantic transparency affects the prognosis of participants. According to Moody, semantic transparency has a role in the semantic interpretation of a diagram. However, the importance of this role decreases with increasing knowledge of the interpreter. As our sample is largely composed of students, the level of UML knowledge of our sample is certainly lower than the level of the target population. Therefore, it is essential to ensure that semantic transparency gives way to semantic domain when the level of knowledge increases.

Therefore, we want to verify that *the knowledge improvement affects the prognosis of CnP* and, in turn, that *the semantic domain affects the prognosis of CnP*. To improve the level of knowledge, questions about visual composition are reproduced and then names are changed[3]. Previously anonymous (Unnamed-{two random letters}), the names are switched to be meaningful. In this way, names provide information about the nature of the model elements and their relationships. Thus, the composite and the component classes are respectively named *Car* and *Wheel*.

Table 6. Influence of class names on the prognosis

		Output varies?		Total
		No	Yes	
Semantic	No	62	5	67
distance varies?	Yes	44	22	66
Total		106	27	133

To demonstrate the influence of knowledge (and therefore the distance semantics), we check prognostic changes when no manipulations are done and when meaningful names are used. Table 6 counts prognostic changes between these two situations. A Fisher exact test shows a significant difference with a p-value less than 1 ‰. It is concluded that improving UML knowledge of a subject (with low initial knowledge) leads to a significant change in his prognosis. The odds ratio indicates that a subject changes 6.2 times more often on average (95% confidence level = [2.2; 17.6]) his prognostic when names become meaningful.

5.4 Overall View and Discussion

To demonstrate the influence of a metric, we created situations in which one distance varies. This method showed significant and powerful effects of visual representation, semantic transparency and semantic domain but has some limitations. First, we can neither confirm nor deny the influence of the syntax or meta-model semantic. We were not able to vary these distances independently of others. The second limitation relates to the problem of the internal validity of

---

[3] These questions are at the end of the questionnaire. They were asked for an answer in order and without changing previous answers.

the study. Indeed, there is one specific hypothesis to support each of the three metrics tested. Therefore, it is difficult to expand the scope of our observations. Finally, our demonstrations seem confused because they supported contradictory hypotheses and did not clearly indicate to editor designers what metrics they should focus on.

To address these limitations, we propose a *compatibility score* for each subject-metric tuple[4]. Our score is the ratio between the amount of *non-contradictory* observations and the total of observations done for a tuple. The first issue is resolved by searching the contradictions between the responses of a subject's responses to a theoretical model characterized by a couple metric-critical distances[5]. The second is partially solved because the score is the synthesis of several observations. Consequently, it is easier to compare these scores and draw a conclusion.

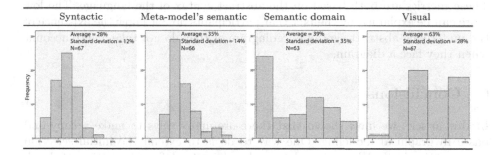

Fig. 2. Compatibility scores of some metric

Figure 2 shows the distribution of compatibility scores for metrics based on syntax, meta-model, semantic domain and visual perception. Added to cluster analysis, these scores reveal two groups. One group performs the prognostic according to the use of a metric based on visual distances with encapsulation as the best critical distance. That is to say, these people are forecasting a copy that retains all graphic shapes located within the copied container and only those shapes. The second group brings together subjects who tend to maintain relationships and elements that play a strong role in the definition of the copied element. For example, three out of four members of this group retain the entire composition if the composite class is copied (not the reverse) or the superclass if the subclass is copied (and not the reverse).

Pearson's correlation coefficient between visual and semantic metric is very significant (p-value less than 1‰) and strong (−0.71). This means that membership in a group causes the exclusion from the other group. This duality is

---

[4] The influence of semantic transparency has only one observation. It is therefore not included.

[5] When the critical distance is an important parameter, we retain the critical distance with the best score, that is to say one that generates the least contradictions and therefore has the highest score.

even more important that the two group's behavior are in contradiction with each other. This large difference in behavior mean that these metrics are in fact *additional*. Therefore, we recommend offering both behaviors rather than one or the other. Editors may propose either one through a *paste special*. Therefore, the prognostic based on semantic transparency can be seen as a transition period. Indeed, we have shown that the domain knowledge affects prognosis.

We note that it is possible to *hide* visual elements, such as attributes, among many UML editors. Considering the strong influence of representation, we recommend paying attention to these hidden elements. Indeed, it is likely that copying them is not the behavior expected by the person that predicted in accordance with a visual perception-based metric. For the same reason, it is recommended to avoid adding *copy of* in the name of the copied element (only one subject showed this behavior).

Syntactic and semantic meta-model-based metrics produce the lowest scores. These metrics are both based on the abstract syntax of the language. The low score can be explained by the fact that participants do not know the existence of the underlying abstract syntax of a diagram or they do not take it into account when they face a diagram.

6   Conclusions

In this article, we have shown that there are many ways to make a copy and paste in graphical modeling. One way to do is to extend the initial selection to a certain *depth*. We proposed several metrics to define the notion of depth in graphical modeling and then we experimentally evaluated their ergonomic qualities. To do this, we asked 67 participants to forecast the result of some copy-paste instances. Their answers allowed us to demonstrate the influence of visual perception and semantics on their prognosis. With these demonstrations, we concluded that copy and paste are made according to these observations. These recommendations are contradictory to most implementations of current UML class diagram editors.

References

1. Alais, D., Blake, R., Lee, S.H.: Visual features that vary together over time group together over space. Nature Neuroscience 1(2), 160–164 (1998)
2. Blok, M.C., Cybulski, J.L.: Reusing UML specifications in a constrained application domain. In: Proceedings of 1998 Asia Pacific Software Engineering Conference, pp. 196–202 (December 1998)
3. Booch, G., Rumbaugh, J., Jacobson, I.: The Unified Modeling Language User Guide. Addison Wesley Professional (2005)
4. Burkhardt, J.M., Détienne, F., Wiedenbeck, S.: Object-oriented program comprehension: Effect of expertise, task and phase. Empirical Software Engineering 7(2), 115–156 (2002), http://dx.doi.org/10.1023/A%3A1015297914742
5. Harel, D., Rumpe, B.: Meaningful modeling: what's the semantics of "semantics"? Computer 37(10), 64–72 (2004)

6. Jézéquel, J.M.: Model driven design and aspect weaving. Software & Systems Modeling 7(2), 209–218 (2008)
7. Kelly, S., Tolvanen, J.P.: Domain-Specific Modeling: Enabling Full Code Generation. John Wiley & Sons, Inc., Hoboken (2007)
8. Caskurlu, B.: Model driven engineering. In: Butler, M., Petre, L., Sere, K. (eds.) IFM 2002. LNCS, vol. 2335, pp. 286–298. Springer, Heidelberg (2002)
9. Kim, M., Bergman, L., Lau, T., Notkin, D.: An ethnographic study of copy and paste programming practices in oopl. In: Proceedings of 2004 International Symposium on Empirical Software Engineering, ISESE 2004, pp. 83–92 (August 2004)
10. Koschke, R.: Identifying and removing software clones. In: Software Evolution, pp. 15–36. Springer, Heidelberg (2008)
11. Li, Z., Lu, S., Myagmar, S., Zhou, Y.: Cp-miner: finding copy-paste and related bugs in large-scale software code. IEEE Transactions on Software Engineering 32(3), 176–192 (2006)
12. Mann, Z.: Three public enemies: cut, copy, and paste. Computer 39(7), 31–35 (2006)
13. Moody, D.: The "physics" of notations: Toward a scientific basis for constructing visual notations in software engineering. IEEE Transactions on Software Engineering 35(6), 756–779 (2009)
14. Object Management Group: OMG Unified Modeling Language (OMG UML), Infrastructure. Version 2.4.1. OMG Document Number: formal/2011-08-05 (August 2011), http://www.omg.org/spec/UML/2.4.1/Infrastructure/PDF/
15. Palmer, S., Rock, I.: Rethinking perceptual organization: The role of uniform connectedness. Psychonomic Bulletin & Review 1(1), 29–55 (1994)
16. Palmer, S.E.: Common region: A new principle of perceptual grouping. Cognitive Psychology 24(3), 436–447 (1992)
17. Robles, K., Fraga, A., Morato, J., Llorens, J.: Towards an ontology-based retrieval of UML class diagrams. Information and Software Technology 54(1), 72–86 (2012)
18. Roddick, J.F., Hornsby, K., de Vries, D.: A unifying semantic distance model for determining the similarity of attribute values. In: Proceedings of the 26th Australasian Computer Science Conference, ACSC 2003, pp. 111–118. Australian Computer Society, Inc., Darlinghurst (2003)
19. Rufai, R.A.: New Structural Similarity Metrics for UML Models. Ph.D. thesis, King Fahd University of Petroleum & Minerals, Saudi Arabia (2003)
20. Schmidt, D.: Guest editor's introduction: Model-driven engineering. Computer 39(2), 25–31 (2006)
21. Wagemans, J., Elder, J.H., Kubovy, M., Palmer, S.E., Peterson, M.A., Singh, M., von der Heydt, R.: A century of Gestalt psychology in visual perception: I. Perceptual grouping and figure-ground organization. Psychological Bulletin 138(6), 1172–1217 (2012)
22. Wertheimer, M.: Untersuchungen zur lehre von der gestalt. ii. Psychologische Forschung 4(1), 301–350 (1923)

Toward a UCM-Based Approach for Recovering System Availability Requirements from Execution Traces

Jameleddine Hassine[1] and Abdelwahab Hamou-Lhadj[2]

[1] Department of Information and Computer Science,
King Fahd University of Petroleum and Minerals, Dhahran, Saudi Arabia
jhassine@kfupm.edu.sa
[2] Electrical and Computer Engineering Department,
Concordia University, Montréal, Canada
abdelw@ece.concordia.ca

Abstract. Software maintenance accounts for a significant proportion of the cost of the software life cycle. Software engineers must spend a considerable amount of time understanding the software system functional attributes and non-functional (e.g., availability, security, etc.) aspects prior to performing a maintenance task. In this paper, we propose a dynamic analysis approach to recover availability requirements from system execution traces. Availability requirements are described and visualized using the Use Case Maps (UCM) language of the ITU-T User Requirements Notation (URN) standard, extended with availability annotations. Our UCM-based approach allows for capturing availability requirements at higher levels of abstraction from low-level execution traces. The resulting availability UCM models can then be analyzed to reveal system availability shortcomings. In order to illustrate and demonstrate the feasibility of the proposed approach, we apply it to a case study of a network implementing the HSRP (Hot Standby Router Protocol) redundancy protocol.

1 Introduction

Software comprehension is an essential part of software maintenance. Gaining a sufficient level of understanding of a software system to perform a maintenance task is time consuming and requires studying various software artifacts (e.g., source code, documentation, etc.) [5]. However, in practice, most existing systems have poor and outdated documentation, if it exists at all. One common approach for understanding what a system does and why it does in a certain way is to analyze its run-time behavior, also known as *dynamic analysis* [6]. Dynamic analysis typically comprises the analysis of system behavioral aspects based on data gathered from a running software (e.g., through instrumentation). Dynamic analysis, however, suffers from the size explosion problem [23]; typical execution traces can be millions of line long. In fact, executing even a small system may generate a considerably large set of events. Hence, there is a need to find ways

D. Amyot et al. (Eds.): SAM 2014, LNCS 8769, pp. 48–63, 2014.
© Springer International Publishing Switzerland 2014

to create higher abstractions from low-level traces that can later be mapped to system requirements. To tackle this issue, many abstraction-based techniques have been proposed [19,16,21], allowing for the grouping of execution points that share certain properties, which results in a more abstract representation of software.

The widespread interest in dynamic analysis techniques provides the major motivation of this research. We, in particular, focus on recovering non-functional requirements, such as availability requirements, from system execution traces. This is particularly important for critical systems to verify that the running implementation supports availability requirements, especially after the system has undergone several ad-hoc maintenance tasks. Avizienis et al. [1] have defined the availability of a system as being the readiness for a correct service. Jalote [15] deemed system availability is built upon the concept of system reliability by adding the notion of recovery, which may be accomplished by fault masking, repair, or component redundancy.

In this paper, we propose the use of Use Case Maps [14] language, part of the ITU-T User Requirements Notation (URN) standard, as a visual means to facilitate the capturing of system availability features from execution traces. Previous work [11,12,10,8,9] has considered availability tactics, introduced by Bass et al. [2], as a basis for extending the UCM [14] language with availability annotations. Bass et al. [2] have introduced the notion of tactics as *architectural building blocks* of architectural patterns. These tactics address fault detection, recovery, and prevention.

This paper serves the following purposes:

- It provides an approach based on the high-level visual requirements description language Use Case Maps to recover system availability features from execution logs. Using our approach, an analyst can select a particular feature of interest, exercise the system with this feature and analyze the resulting execution trace to determine whether or not availability is taken into account. Although, other visualization techniques can be employed, we have selected the UCM language as our visualization method because it allows for an abstract description of scenarios, that can be allocated to a set of components. Furthermore, through the UCM stub/plugin concept, different levels of abstractions can be considered. The resulting UCM can be later analyzed using the UCM-based availability evaluation technique introduced in [9].
- It extends the set of UCM-based availability features introduced in [10,8,9] by introducing UCM-based distributed redundancy modeling. The proposed extensions are implemented using metadata within the jUCMNav [20] tool.
- It demonstrates the feasibility of our proposed approach using a case study of a network implementing the Cisco Hot Standby Router Protocol (HSRP) [4].

The remainder of this paper is organized as follows. The next section introduces briefly the availability description features in Use Case Maps. Our proposed approach for the recovery of availability requirements from execution traces is presented in Section 3. Section 4 demonstrates the applicability of the proposed approach to the Cisco proprietary Hot Standby Router Protocol (HSRP). A discussion of the benefits of our approach and a presentation of the threats to validity is provided in Section 5. Finally, conclusions and future work are presented in Section 6.

2   Describing Availability Requirements in Use Case Maps

In this section, we recall the UCM-based availability requirements descriptions that are relevant to this research. We mainly focus on (1) the implementation of the *exception* tactic, part of the UCM fault detection modeling category, and on (2) the redundancy modeling, part of the UCM fault recovery modeling category. For a detailed description of UCM-based availability features, interested readers are referred to [9], where the UCM-based availability extensions are described using a metamodel.

2.1   Exception Modeling

Exceptions are modeled and handled at the scenario path level. Exceptions may be associated with any responsibility along the UCM scenario execution path. A separate failure scenario path, starting with a failure start point, is used to handle exceptions. The failure path guard condition (e.g., *R1-FD-Cond* in Fig. 1(a)) can be initialized as part of a scenario definition (i.e., scenario triggering condition) or can be modified as part of a responsibility expression. The handling of the exception, embedded within a static stub (e.g., *R1-ExceptionHandling* in Fig. 1(a)), is generally subject to the implementation of fault recovery tactic through some redundancy means (see Section 2.2). Figure 1(c) shows the metadata attributes of a responsibility (within the R1-ExceptionHandling stub) implementing the *StateResynchronization* tactic. After handling the *R1* exception, the path continues explicitly with responsibility *R2*.

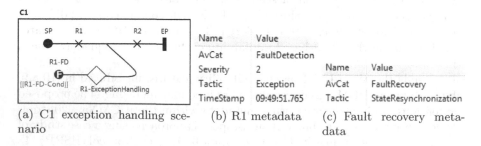

(a) C1 exception handling scenario   (b) R1 metadata   (c) Fault recovery metadata

Fig. 1. UCM exception handling tactic

In addition to the three metadata attributes associated with responsibility *R1* (*AvCat* (specifies the availability category, e.g., *FaultDetection*), *Tactic* (specifies the deployed tactic, e.g., *Exception*), and *Severity* (fault severity, e.g., 1 being the most severe) that have been introduced in previous research [9,10], we add a *timestamp* attribute to be able to capture the occurrence time of the responsibility (extracted from the log files). Other time-based attributes such as *delay* and *duration*, introduced as part of the Timed Use Case Maps language [13], are not necessary in our context.

2.2 Redundancy Modeling

Fault recovery tactic focuses mainly on redundancy modeling in order to keep the system available in case of the occurrence of a failure. To model redundancy, UCM components are annotated with the following attributes: (1) *GroupID* (identify the group to which a component belongs in a specific redundancy model), (2) *Role* (*active* or *standby* role), (3) *RedundancyType* (specifies the redundancy type, e.g., *hot, warm,* or *cold,* (4) *ProtectionType* (denotes the redundancy configuration, e.g., 1+1, 1:N, etc.), and (5) *Voting* (specifies whether a component plays a voting role in a redundancy configuration).

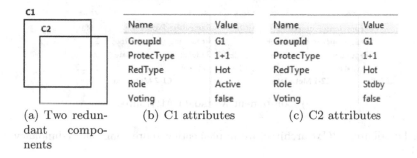

(a) Two redundant components

Name	Value
GroupId	G1
ProtecType	1+1
RedType	Hot
Role	Active
Voting	false

(b) C1 attributes

Name	Value
GroupId	G1
ProtecType	1+1
RedType	Hot
Role	Stdby
Voting	false

(c) C2 attributes

Fig. 2. UCM node protection

Figure 2 illustrates an example of a system with two components *C1* (*active*) and *C2* (*standby*) participating in a 1+1 hot redundancy configuration. It is worth noting that the above redundancy annotations refer to the initial system configuration state. The operational implications, in case of failure for instance, can be described using the UCM scenario path, e.g., as part of an exception handling path (see Section 2.1).

2.3 UCM Distributed Redundancy Modeling

The generic UCM-based annotations describing redundancy [9,10], presented in the previous section, can be refined to cover redundancy of components that are not physically collocated. Two or more components can be part of a redundancy configuration without being physically on the same device. Such a redundancy can be achieved through a redundancy protocol such as HSRP (Hot Standby Router Protocol) [17] and VRRP (Virtual Router Redundancy Protocol) [18] in IP-based networks.

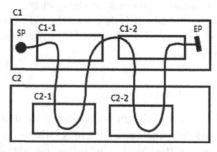

(a) Distributed UCM Architecture

Name	Value	Name	Value
RedundancyProtocol	HSRP	RedundancyProtocol	HSRP
RedundancyProtocolGroup	1	RedundancyProtocolGroup	2
RedundancyProtocolState	active	RedundancyProtocolState	active
VirtualIP	1.1.1.1	VirtualIP	2.2.2.2
C1-1 Metadata		**C2-2 Metadata**	

Name	Value	Name	Value
RedundancyProtocol	HSRP	RedundancyProtocol	HSRP
RedundancyProtocolGroup	1	RedundancyProtocolGroup	2
RedundancyProtocolState	standby	RedundancyProtocolState	standby
VirtualIP	1.1.1.1	VirtualIP	2.2.2.2
C2-1 Metadata		**C1-2 Metadata**	

(b) Component Metadata Attributes

Fig. 3. Distributed UCM architecture implementing more than one redundancy configuration

In order to describe redundancy protocols in UCM, additional metadata attributes need to be incorporated:

- *RedundancyProtocol*: denotes the protocol name, e.g., HSRP, VRRP, etc.
- *RedundancyProtocolGroup*: denotes the redundancy group associated with the redundancy protocol).
- *VirtualIP*: denotes the virtual IP address shared by one or more distributed components.
- *RedundancyProtocolState*: denotes the redundancy protocol state, e.g., active, standby, init, etc.).

Depending on the targeted abstraction level, other relevant metadata attributes may be added like *MacAddress*. Figure 3(a) illustrates a generic UCM architecture with 2 main components C1 and C2. Two HSRP redundancy configurations are described, one for group 1 that involves subcomponents C1-1 (*active* state) and C2-1 (*standby* state), and the other for group 2 that involves subcomponents C1-2 (*standby* state) and C2-2 (*active* state). More details about HSRP can be found in Section 4.

3   Recovery of Availability Requirements from Execution Traces

Figure 4 illustrates our proposed approach. The first step consists of collecting system logs (from a single or multiple systems). Typically, a log file is composed of individual log entries ordered in chronological order. Each entry is described as a single line in plain text format and may contain one or more of the following attributes: a timestamp, the process ID generating the event/error, operation/event prefix, severity of the error, and a brief description of the event/error. Some systems (e.g., Apache and IIS) generate separate log files for *access* and *error*.

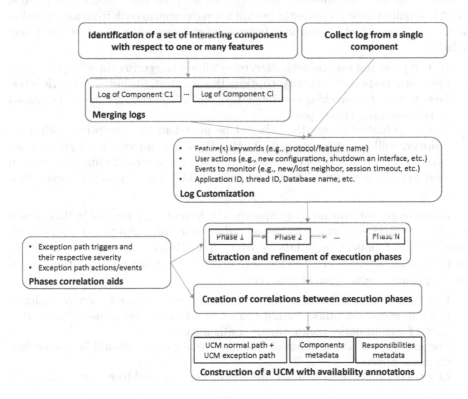

Fig. 4. Recovery of availability requirements from execution traces approach

In case we are targeting systems with more than one component, a prior knowledge of the possible interactions between the involved components (e.g., protocols used to coordinate the interacting components) is required. After identifying the interacting components, their respective log files are merged and sorted based on timestamps. In order to have a focused analysis of the resulting log, we may reduce its size by applying analyst-defined customization criteria. An analyst may reduce or extend a log window, include or exclude log entries based on features/protocols names, administrator operator actions (e.g., add/remove configuration, shut/unshut network interfaces, etc.), events to monitor (e.g., session timeout, network interfaces state changes, neighbors up/down, etc.). To make an insightful decision, these criteria are applied to the merged log rather than individual logs.

The next step deals with the extraction of the system execution phases. An execution phase is a grouping of a set of log entries (into clusters) based on a predefined set of criteria, such as functionality, component ID, system events, user actions, etc. Our ultimate goal is to be able to map log traces into UCMs (the final step of our approach) using the availability annotations presented in Section 2. Given the sequential nature of log file structures, additional analyst input is required in order to distinguish a normal scenario path from an exception path, and to construct correlations between execution phases. Analyst input may include:

– List of potential events/actions/errors/failures triggering the exception path and their respective severity (optional), e.g., shut/unshut a network interface, protocol state changes (down/up), etc. These triggers should be placed in the normal scenario path.
– List of potential events that should be placed in the exception path, e.g., failover, rollback, process restart, HSRP state changes, etc. Typically, an exception path describes the system reaction to an error/failure (i.e., system recovery). Hence, administrator actions should not be placed in the exception path.

Furthermore, an analyst may specify the format and keywords that would help the extraction of components metadata attributes. Section 4 provides an example of component metadata recovery from HSRP log traces. In addition, the following guidelines are developed in order to construct the execution phases and to promote separation of concerns:

– Log entries from different components should be placed into separate phases (i.e., an execution phase cannot span more than one component unless it is part of a component containment configuration).
– Log entries describing different features' events/errors should be placed into separate phases.
– Log entries relative to user actions should be separated from system response log.

It is worth noting that the segmentation of a log into execution phases should not break the causality between different log entries. Finally, the last step consists of mapping the execution phases into UCM models and generating the

UCM component related attributes. The following recommendations guide the mapping process:

- Each log entry is mapped to one responsibility.
- An execution phase with more than one responsibility is described using a plugin enclosed within a static stub (named with the name of the execution phase).
- A phase, part of the exception path, having a single responsibility should be enclosed within a static stub.
- Depending on the targeted level of abstraction, sequential stubs bound to the same component and belonging to one path (regular or exception), may be refactored into a static stub.
- Component related information such as the redundancy protocol, the redundancy group, etc., are mapped to component metadata attributes.
- In case two log entries have the same timestamp, their corresponding responsibilities should be enclosed within an AND-Fork and an AND-Join.

4   Case Study: Hot Standby Router Protocol (HSRP)

In what follows, we apply our proposed approach to the HSRP [4] redundancy protocol.

4.1   Hot Standby Router Protocol (HSRP)

Hot Standby Router Protocol (HSRP) is a Cisco proprietary protocol that provides network redundancy for IP networks [4]. By sharing an IP address and a MAC (Layer 2) address, two or more routers can act as a single "virtual" router, known as an HSRP group or a standby group. A single router (i.e., Active router) elected from the group is responsible for forwarding the packets that hosts send to the virtual router. If the Active router fails, the Standby router takes over as the Active router. If the Standby router fails or becomes the Active router, then another router is elected as the Standby router. HSRP has the ability to trigger a fail-over if one or more interfaces on the router go down. For detailed information about HSRP, the reader is referred to RFC 2281 [17].

4.2   Experimental Setup

Figure 5 illustrates our testbed topology, used to implement and collect router logs relative to the HSRP feature. The testbed has been built using the Graphical Network Simulator 3 (GNS3) simulation software [7]. GNS3 allows researchers to emulate complex networks, since it can combine actual devices and virtual devices together. GNS3 supports the Cisco IOS by using Dynamips, a software that emulates Cisco IOS on a PC. In our setup, we have used 4 Cisco c7200 routers (R1, R2, Site1, and Site2) and two Ethernet switches (SW1 and SW2). Two networks are configured (10.10.10.0/24 on the left hand side of the topology, and 10.10.20.0/24 on the right hand side of the topology). Two HSRP groups are configured: Group1 (virtual IP address: 10.10.10.10) on interfaces f0/0 of R1 and R2, and Group2 (virtual IP address: 10.10.20.20) on interfaces f0/1 on R1 and R2. R1 is the active router for Group 1, while R2 is the active router for Group 2.

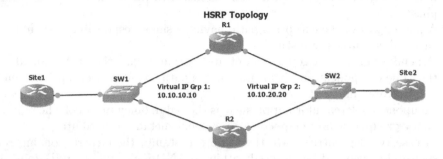

Fig. 5. HSRP experimental setup

4.3 Cisco IOS Logging System

Logs can be collected from Cisco IOS routers through console logging (default mode), terminal logging (displays the log messages on VTY lines), buffered logging (use the router's RAM to store logs), syslog server logging (use of external syslog servers for log storage), and SNMP trap logging (send log messages to an external SNMP server).

Any collected log may have one or more components from the following three types:

1. System log messages: They can contain up to 80 characters and a percent sign (%), which follows the optional sequence number or/and timestamp information, if configured [3]. Messages are displayed in this format:

   seq no:timestamp: %facility-severity-MNEMONIC:description

   The *seq no* provides sequential identifiers for log messages (it can be enabled using the command *"service sequence-numbers"* in configuration mode). The *timestamp* is configured using the command *service timestamps log datetime msec* in configuration mode. In this case study, we enable timestamp only. *facility* refers to the system on the device for which we want to set logging (e.g., Kern (Kernel), SNMP, etc.). *Severity* is a single-digit code from 0 to 7 specifying the severity of the message (e.g., 0:emergencies, 1:alerts, 2:critical, 3:errors, 4:warnings, 5:notifications, 6:informational, 7:debugging). *MNEMONIC* is a text string that uniquely describes the message. *description* is a text string containing detailed information about the event being reported.

2. User actions: Cisco IOS stores configuration commands entered by users (e.g., configuring an interface or a protocol) using the config logger. For example, the following log shows that the user has shut down the FastEthernet0/0 interface:

   *May 27 09:04:37.227: %PARSER-5-CFGLOG_LOGGEDCMD: User:console logged command:interface FastEthernet0/0
   *May 27 09:04:38.475: %PARSER-5-CFGLOG_LOGGEDCMD: User:console logged command:shutdown

3. Debug messages: They should only be used to troubleshoot specific problems because debugging output is assigned high priority in the CPU process. Hence, it can render the system unusable. The following debug output is produced after enabling debugging for the HSRP feature (using the command *"debug standby events"*). It illustrates a state change from Speak to Standby on interface Fa0/0 for Group 1:

   *May 24 11:15:41.255: HSRP: Fa0/0 Grp 1 Redundancy "hsrp-Fa0/0-1" state Speak -> Standby

4.4 Log Collection and Segmentation

Figure 6 illustrates the collected log from router R1 (without enabling the sequence number and debugging options). Following the guidelines introduced in Section 3, the log has been decomposed into 10 execution phases, where each phase targets a single component and describes one and only one type of actions/events. We distinguish two sub-components R1-F0/0 and R1-F0/1, denoting the FastEthernet interfaces within router R1. Phase numbering follows sequential order and are provided for each component separately. For instance, the first phase, named R1-F0/0, in Fig. 6 illustrates system log messages describing the state of the interface FastEthernet0/0, while the second phase of R1-F0/0 component describes an HSRP state change (i.e., %HSRP-5-STATECHANGE) from Standby to Active. Phase 3 of R1-F0/0 shows that the user has entered the config mode and shut down the interface F0/0.

Next, correlations between the extracted execution phases are identified. In our context, exception path triggering events/actions/errors include interface state changes (e.g., up or down) and the administrator shutting/unshutting down interfaces. Events involving HSRP state changes are considered to be part of exception paths since they are supposed to implement fault recovery mechanism. For example, shutting down the interface F0/0 in phase 3 of R1-F0/0 have triggered an HSRP state change moving the protocol state from *Active* to *Init*. Finally, the correlations between the execution phases are mapped to the UCM notation as shown in Fig. 7(a). Figures 7(b), 7(c), 7(d), 7(e), and 7(f) illustrate examples of UCM plugins corresponding to some execution phases stubs. Figure 7(g) illustrates metadata attributes relative to the responsibility *HSRP-STATECHANGE-F0/0-Grp1-Listen-Active*, while Fig. 7(h) illustrates the metadata attributes relative to the subcomponent F0/0.

To demonstrate the applicability of our approach in the presence of more than one system log, we have captured the log from router R2. Figure 8 illustrates the

Fig. 6. Log from router R1

merged log for routers R1 and R2. Sixteen phases, involving 4 subcomponents, have been identified. The resulting UCM is depicted in Fig. 9.

It is worth noting that our choice to consider the entire log without neither customization nor chopping some parts is two-fold. First, we would like to demonstrate the UCM visualization of more than one subcomponent. Second, although the scenario focuses on the HSRP group 1, it is important to show that actions/events related to this group do not impact group 2 (i.e., absence of feature interactions).

5   Discussion and Threats to Validity

One important objective of this research is to capture non-functional requirements from system execution traces. Our approach uses the high-level requirement description language Use Case Maps to describe visually and using metadata availability requirements. UCMs offer a flexible way to represent such requirements at different levels of abstractions using the stub/plugin concept. However, our proposed approach and the experimental case study are subject to several limitations and threats to validity, categorized here according to three important types of threats identified by Wright et al. [22].

Regarding *internal validity*, it might not be sufficient to establish accurate correlations between execution phases without additional semantic information about the running system. For example, in our case study, the log entries corresponding to stubs R1-F0/0-Ph2 and R1-F0/1-Ph2 take place after both interfaces F0/0 and F0/1 came up (Fig. 7(a)). Although, these two events represent the triggers for the R1-F0/0-Ph2 (HSRP group 1) and R1-F0/1-Ph2 (HSRP group 2) phases, we cannot refine such correlation with the available information at hand (i.e., triggers and exception path events). Actually, R1-F0/0-Ph2 and R1-F0/1-Ph2 should be triggered by R1-F0/0-Ph1 and R1-F0/1-Ph1, respectively. Additional, semantic rules are needed in order to achieve accurate

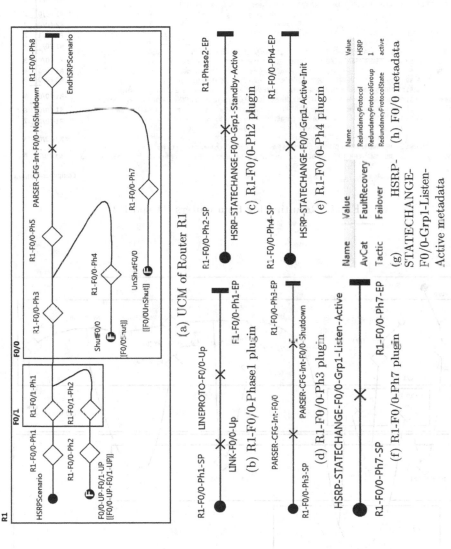

Fig. 7. R1 UCM and its related plugins and metadata attributes

Fig. 8. Resulting log from routers R1 and R2

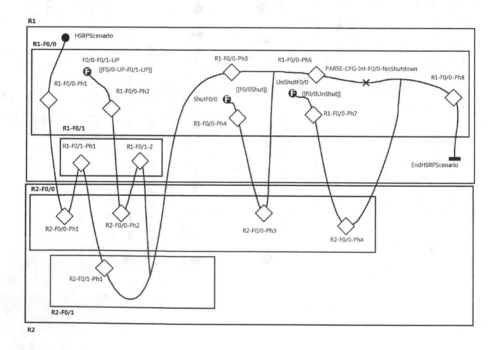

Fig. 9. UCM visualization of the recovery of the merged logs from routers R1 and R2

correlations. Another possible risk is log complexity. In the presented case study, we have used routers with simple configuration and limited sets of configured interfaces. In production networks, dozens of features and protocols are configured and interacts with each other. This issue can be mitigated by applying log customization based on a thorough understanding of the deployed protocols and their possible interactions.

In terms of *external validity*, there is some risk related to merging logs coming from different devices. This issue is more serious when we deal with equipments from different vendors. Indeed, depending on the device type and its configuration, discrepancies may arise in terms of the time reference and the event logger priority (e.g., an event logger can have a low priority on one device and a high priority on another), which may lead to a merged log with incorrect chronological order of events. The time reference issue can be mitigated by using the NTP (Network Time Protocol) protocol, which allows for clock synchronization between computer systems over packet-switched, variable-latency data networks.

As for the *construct validity*, scalability represents the most important limitation. As logs becomes more complex, the number of phases becomes difficult to manage and hence, difficult to visualize and to navigate through. Although, the UCM language offers a good encapsulation mechanism through the stub/plugin concept, models can rapidly become messy with overlapping paths and components. However, log customization (e.g., using abstraction techniques) and reduction (e.g., reduce the time stamp window) may help reduce the severity of the scalability issue.

6   Conclusions and Future Work

In this paper, we have proposed a novel UCM-based approach to recover and visualize availability requirements from execution traces. To this end, our proposed approach is built upon previous extensions of the UCM language with availability annotations covering the well-known availability tactics by Bass et al. [2]. Logs from various interacting components can be merged, customized, then segmented into execution phases. The resulting execution stages are then visualized using a combination of UCM regular and exception paths bound to the set of interacting components. Metadata of responsibilities and components implementing fault detection and recovery tactics are captured in an integrated UCM view.

As a future work, we aim to automate the proposed approach. Furthermore, we plan to investigate the design of semantic rules to better correlate the different execution phases. This would allow for more accurate UCM availability models.

Acknowledgements. The authors would like to acknowledge the support provided by the Deanship of Scientific Research at King Fahd University of Petroleum & Minerals (KFUPM) for funding this work through project No. IN131031.

References

1. Avizienis, A., Laprie, J.C., Randell, B., Landwehr, C.: Basic concepts and taxonomy of dependable and secure computing. IEEE Trans. Dependable Secur. Comput. 1(1), 11–33 (2004)
2. Bass, L., Clements, P., Kazman, R.: Software Architecture in Practice. Addison-Wesley Longman Publishing Co., Inc., Boston (2003)
3. Cisco Systems: Internetworking Technologies Handbook. Cisco Press networking technology series. Cisco Press (2004), http://bit.ly/1rr8b89
4. Cisco Systems: Hot Standby Router Protocol Features and Functionality (2006), http://www.cisco.com/c/en/us/support/docs/ip/hot-standby-router-protocol-hsrp/9234-hsrpguidetoc.pdf
5. Corbi, T.A.: Program understanding: Challenge for the 1990s. IBM Systems Journal 28(2), 294–306 (1989)
6. Cornelissen, B., Zaidman, A., van Deursen, A., Moonen, L., Koschke, R.: A systematic survey of program comprehension through dynamic analysis. IEEE Transactions on Software Engineering 35(5), 684–702 (2009)
7. GNS3: Graphical network simulator, gns3 v0.8.6 (2014), http://www.gns3.net/
8. Hassine, J.: Early availability requirements modeling using use case maps. In: ITNG, pp. 754–759. IEEE Computer Society (2011)
9. Hassine, J.: Describing and assessing availability requirements in the early stages of system development. Software & Systems Modeling, 1–25 (2013), http://dx.doi.org/10.1007/s10270-013-0382-0
10. Hassine, J., Gherbi, A.: Exploring early availability requirements using use case maps. In: Ober, I., Ober, I. (eds.) SDL 2011. LNCS, vol. 7083, pp. 54–68. Springer, Heidelberg (2011)
11. Hassine, J., Hamou-Lhadj, A.: Towards the generation of AMF configurations from use case maps based availability requirements. In: Khendek, F., Toeroe, M., Gherbi, A., Reed, R. (eds.) SDL 2013. LNCS, vol. 7916, pp. 36–53. Springer, Heidelberg (2013)
12. Hassine, J., Mussbacher, G., Braun, E., Alhaj, M.: Modeling early availability requirements using aspect-oriented use case maps. In: Khendek, F., Toeroe, M., Gherbi, A., Reed, R. (eds.) SDL 2013. LNCS, vol. 7916, pp. 54–71. Springer, Heidelberg (2013)
13. Hassine, J., Rilling, J., Dssouli, R.: Timed use case maps. In: Gotzhein, R., Reed, R. (eds.) SAM 2006. LNCS, vol. 4320, pp. 99–114. Springer, Heidelberg (2006)
14. ITU-T: Recommendation Z.151 (10/12), User Requirements Notation (URN) language definition, Geneva, Switzerland (2012), http://www.itu.int/rec/T-REC-Z.151/en
15. Jalote, P.: Fault Tolerance in Distributed Systems. Prentice-Hall, Inc., Upper Saddle River (1994)
16. Koskimies, K., Mössenböck, H.: Scene: Using scenario diagrams and active text for illustrating object-oriented programs. In: Proceedings of the 18th International Conference on Software Engineering, ICSE 1996, pp. 366–375. IEEE Computer Society, Washington, DC (1996)
17. Li, T., Cole, B., Morton, P., Li, D.: Cisco Hot Standby Router Protocol (HSRP). RFC 2281 (Informational) (March 1998), http://www.ietf.org/rfc/rfc2281.txt
18. Nadas, S.: Virtual router redundancy protocol (vrrp) version 3 for ipv4 and ipv6. RFC 5798 (Proposed Standard) (March 2010), http://www.ietf.org/rfc/rfc5798.txt

19. Reiss, S.P.: Visualizing program execution using user abstractions. In: Proceedings of the 2006 ACM Symposium on Software Visualization, SoftVis 2006, pp. 125–134. ACM, New York (2006), http://doi.acm.org/10.1145/1148493.1148512
20. jUCMNav v5.5.0: jUCMNav Project, v5.5.0 (tool, documentation, and meta-model) (2014), http://jucmnav.softwareengineering.ca/jucmnav (last accessed, June 2014)
21. Walker, R.J., Murphy, G.C., Freeman-Benson, B., Wright, D., Swanson, D., Isaak, J.: Visualizing dynamic software system information through high-level models. In: Proc. 13th ACM SIGPLAN Conference on Object-oriented Programming, Systems, Languages, and Applications, OOPSLA 1998, pp. 271–283. ACM, New York (1998)
22. Wright, H.K., Kim, M., Perry, D.E.: Validity concerns in software engineering research. In: Roman, G.C., Sullivan, K.J. (eds.) FoSER, pp. 411–414. ACM (2010)
23. Zaidman, A.: Scalability solutions for program comprehension through dynamic analysis. In: Proceedings of the Conference on Software Maintenance and Reengineering, CSMR 2006, pp. 327–330. IEEE Computer Society, Washington, DC (2006)

Architecture Framework for Software Safety

Havva Gülay Gürbüz[1], Nagehan Pala Er[2], and Bedir Tekinerdogan[1]

[1] Department of Computer Engineering, Bilkent University, Ankara 06800, Turkey
havva.gurbuz@bilkent.edu.tr, bedir@cs.bilkent.edu.tr
[2] ASELSAN MGEO, P.O. Box: 30 Etlik, Ankara 06011, Turkey
npala@aselsan.com.tr

Abstract. Currently, an increasing number of systems are controlled by software and rely on the correct operation of software. In this context, a safety-critical system is defined as a system in which malfunctioning software could result in death, injury or damage to environment. To mitigate these serious risks, the architecture of safety-critical systems needs to be carefully designed and analyzed. A common practice for modeling software architecture is the adoption of software architecture viewpoints to model the architecture for particular stakeholders and concerns. Existing architecture viewpoints tend to be general purpose and do not explicitly focus on safety concerns in particular. To provide a complementary and dedicated support for designing safety critical systems, we propose an architecture framework for software safety. The architecture framework is based on a metamodel that has been developed after a thorough domain analysis. The framework includes three coherent viewpoints, each of which addressing an important concern. The application of the viewpoints is illustrated for an industrial case of safety-critical avionics control computer system.

Keywords: Software Safety, Safety-Critical Systems, Architectural Modeling, Architecture Design, Architectural Viewpoints.

1 Introduction

Currently, an increasing number of systems are controlled by software and rely on the correct operation of software. In this context, a safety-critical system is defined as a system in which malfunctioning software could result in death, injury or damage to environment. Software can be considered safe if it does not produce an output that causes a catastrophic event for the system. Several methods, processes and models are developed in order to make the software safe. System safety engineering is the application of engineering and management principles, criteria, and techniques to optimize all aspects of safety within the constraints of operational effectiveness, time, and cost throughout all phases of the system life cycle [8][12].

Designing appropriate software architectures of a safety-critical system is important to meet the requirements for the communication, coordination and control of the safety-critical concerns. A common practice in the software architecture design

D. Amyot et al. (Eds.): SAM 2014, LNCS 8769, pp. 64–79, 2014.

community is to model and document different architectural views for describing the architecture according to the stakeholders' concerns. An architectural view is a representation of a set of system elements and relations associated with them to support a particular concern. Having multiple views helps to separate the concerns and as such support the modeling, understanding, communication and analysis of the software architecture for different stakeholders. Architectural views conform to viewpoints that represent the conventions for constructing and using a view. An architectural framework organizes and structures the proposed architectural viewpoints. Different architectural frameworks have been proposed in the literature [1][4][5][10].

For modeling the software architecture of safety-critical systems, we can consider the approaches of both the safety engineering domain and the software architecture modeling domain. From the safety engineering perspective, we can observe that many useful models such as fault trees and failure modes and effect analysis have been identified. In addition, several guidelines and patterns have been proposed to support the architecture design of safety critical systems. Unfortunately, the safety engineering domain does not provide explicit modeling abstractions for modeling the architecture of safety-critical systems. On the other hand, existing software architecture frameworks tend to be general purpose and do not directly focus on safety concerns in particular. However, if safety is an important concern, then it is important to provide explicit abstraction mechanisms at the architecture design level to reason about to communicate and analyze the architectural design decisions from an explicit safety perspective. In particular, this is crucial for safety-critical systems which have indeed demanding requirements.

To address the safety concern explicitly and assist the architect, we propose an architecture framework for modeling architecture for software safety. The architecture framework is based on a metamodel that has been developed after a thorough domain analysis. The framework includes three coherent viewpoints, each of which addressing an important concern. The framework is not mentioned as a replacement of existing general purpose frameworks but rather needs to be considered complementary to these. The application of the viewpoints is illustrated with an industrial case of safety-critical avionics control computer system.

The remainder of the paper is organized as follows. In Section 2, we describe the problem statement in more detail using a real industrial case study. Section 3 presents the metamodel on which the framework is based. Section 4 presents the three viewpoints of the architecture framework. Section 5 illustrates the application of the framework for the described industrial case study. Section 6 presents the related work and finally Section 7 concludes the paper.

2   Problem Statement

In this section, we describe the general approach for designing safety-critical systems that is adopted in safety engineering practices. For this purpose, we will use an industrial case study of an avionics control system project. Based on the case study, we illustrate the need for architecture viewpoints for safety.

The industrial case that we discuss is in the avionics domain. Several reported accidents show that the faults in avionics systems could lead to catastrophic consequences that cause loss of life, and likewise we can consider avionics as a safety-critical system. There are several standards, such as the DO-178B [11], used to regulate software development and certification activities for the avionics domain. Usually, avionics control systems have to meet hundreds of requirements related to safety concerns. Table 1 shows an example subset of the requirements that we have selected to describe our case study. In fact, each of these requirements needs to be properly addressed in order to avoid unsafe situations.

Table 1. Requirements of our case study

Requirement	Explanation
Display aircraft altitude data	Altitude is defined as the height of the aircraft above sea level. Altitude information is shown to pilots, as well as, also used by other avionics systems such as ground collision detection system. Pilots depend on the displayed altitude information especially when landing.
Display aircraft position data	Position is the latitude and longitude coordinates of the aircraft received from GPS (Global Positioning System). Route management also uses aircraft position. Aircraft position is generally showed along with the other points in the route. Pilots can see the deviation from the route and take actions according to the deviation.
Display aircraft attitude data	Attitude is defined with the angles of rotation of the aircraft in three dimensions, known as roll, pitch and yaw angles. For instance, the symbol, called as ADI (Attitude Direction Indicator), is used to show roll and pitch angles of the aircraft.
Display fuel amount	Fuel amount is the sum of fuel in all fuel tanks. Fuel amount is generally represented with a bar chart in order to show how much fuel remains in the aircraft.
Display radio frequency channel	The radio frequency channel is used to communicate with ground stations.

In practice, requirements such as those shown in Table 1 are used to identify possible hazards and define safety requirements from possible hazards. This overall activity is performed together with domain experts (avionics engineers and pilots), system engineers and safety engineers using several hazard identification methods such as defined in [8]. A hazard is a presence of a potential risk situation that can result or contribute to a mishap. Some of the identified hazards for our case study are given in Table 2 along with possible causes, consequences, severity classification, probability and risk definition. The severity class of the hazards numbered from *HZ1* to *HZ4* is identified as catastrophic since a possible consequence of these hazards is an aircraft crash. For instance, if a high altitude is displayed instead of its correct value, the pilots could assume that the aircraft is high enough not to crash to the ground especially when landing. This assumption could lead to aircraft crash that causes deaths, system loss, and in some cases severe environmental damage. When the consequence of *HZ5* is considered, its severity class is identified as negligible because this hazard results in only a communication error with ground station.

Hazard identification is followed by safety requirement identification. For example, Table 3 lists the safety requirements related with *HZ1*. Similarly various safety requirements can be defined for the other identified hazards.

Table 2. Hazard identification for the case study

Hazard	Possible Causes	Cons.	Severity	Probability	Risk
[HZ1] Displaying wrong altitude data	Loss of/Error in altimeter, Loss of/Error in communication with altimeter, Error in display	Aircraft crash	Catastrophic	Improbable	Medium
[HZ2] Displaying wrong position data	Loss of/Error in GPS, Loss of/Error in communication with GPS, Error in display	Aircraft crash	Catastrophic	Improbable	Medium
[HZ3] Displaying wrong attitude data	Loss of/Error in gyroscope, Loss of/Error in communication with gyroscope, Error in display	Aircraft crash	Catastrophic	Improbable	Medium
[HZ4] Displaying wrong fuel amount	Loss of/Error in fuel sensor, Loss of/Error in communication with fuel sensor, Error in display	Aircraft crash	Catastrophic	Improbable	Medium
[HZ5] Displaying wrong radio frequency	Loss of/Error in radio, Loss of/Error in communication with radio, Error in display	Communication error	Negligible	Occasional	Low

Table 3. Safety requirements derived from HZ1

ID	Definition
SR1	Altitude data shall be received from two independent altimeter devices.
SR2	If altitude data can be received from only one altimeter device, the altitude data received shall be displayed and a warning shall be generated.
SR3	If altitude data can be received from neither altimeter device, the altitude data shall not be displayed and a warning shall be generated.
SR4	If the difference between two altitude values received from two altimeter devices is more than a given threshold, the altitude data shall not be displayed and a warning shall be generated.
SR5	Altitude data shall be displayed on two independent display devices.

Figure 1 shows the component and connector view [1] of the architecture design of the case study, using a UML component diagram. *Altimeter1Mgr* and *Altimeter2Mgr* are the managers of altimeter device 1 and 2, respectively. Each altimeter manager receives the aircraft's altitude data from the specified altimeter device and provides it to *NavigationMgr*. *Gyro1Mgr* and *Gyro2Mgr* are the managers of gyroscope device 1 and 2, respectively. Each gyroscope manager receives the aircraft's attitude data from the specified gyroscope device and provides it to *NavigationMgr*. *Gps1Mgr* and *Gps2Mgr* are the managers of GPS device 1 and 2, respectively. Each GPS manager receives the aircraft's position data from the specified GPS device and provides it to *NavigationMgr*. *Fuel1Mgr* and *Fuel2Mgr* are the managers of fuel sensor 1 and 2, respectively, and each receives the aircraft's fuel data from the specified fuel sensor and provides it to *PlatformMgr*. *RadioMgr* is the manager of radio device. *RadioMgr* receives radio frequency data from the radio device and provides it to *CommunicationMgr*. *NavigationMgr* reads the aircraft's altitude, attitude and position data from the specified managers and provides them to graphics managers. *PlatformMgr* reads fuel data from the fuel managers and provides it to graphics managers. *CommunicationMgr* reads radio frequency data from *RadioMgr* and provides it to graphics managers. *Graphics1Mgr* and *Graphics2Mgr* read the aircraft's altitude, attitude, position, fuel and radio frequency data and show these on the graphics displays.

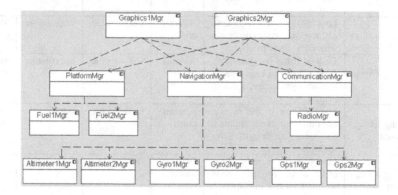

Fig. 1. Component and connector view of the case study

It should be noted that existing general purpose views including the component and connector view of Fig. 1 do not directly address the safety concerns. For example, the information about whether a component is safety-critical is not explicit. Safety-critical components implement safety-critical requirements but the general purpose views do not answer the question which safety requirements are implemented in which components. Another missing knowledge is about the tactics and patterns that are applied to handle safety requirements.

The goal of providing safety concerns in views is two-fold: (1) communicating the design decisions related with safety concerns through views (2) accomplishing safety analysis of the architecture from views. The first goal, communicating the design decisions related with safety concerns, is important for safety engineers, system engineers and software engineers. Safety and system engineers perform hazard identification and provide safety requirements, a subset of which is allocated to software. Then, the software engineers design and implement the software according to the safety requirements. Thus, these views would help bridge the gap between them by communicating safety information from the safety and system engineers to software engineers. The second goal, accomplishing safety analysis of the architecture, supports the safety assessment of the design. If safety-related information can be obtained from the views, the architecture can be properly analyzed. Typically, safety analysis is performed from the early stages of the design and the architecture can be updated after safety analysis, if deemed necessary. For example, an important guideline is not to include not-safety-critical software inside safety-critical software. If the safety-critical and not-safety-critical components can be differentiated, such an analysis can be performed. After the analysis is accomplished and if there is a safety-critical component which includes not-safety-critical components, then the architecture is reshaped.

To address the safety concerns at the architecture design level, we can now proceed in different ways. We could adopt the guidelines and tactics in the safety engineering domain to reshape the architecture of Fig. 1 using existing general purpose viewpoint approaches. In this case, all the applied knowledge on safety would be implicit in the architecture and it will be hard to communicate the design decisions and analyze the architecture with respect to safety concerns. In addition to the usage of existing general purpose viewpoints, we will define a framework that includes explicit viewpoints for addressing safety concerns.

3   Metamodel for Software Safety

In this section, we provide a metamodel for software safety to represent the safety-related concepts. The metamodel shown in Fig. 2 has been derived after a thorough domain analysis to safety design concepts and considering existing previous studies such as [2][14][17]. The metamodel in Fig. 2 reuses the common concepts of existing metamodels and provides an integrated model. It consists of three parts that form the basis for the architecture viewpoints. The bottom part of the metamodel includes the concepts related to hazards in the system. A *Hazard* describes the presence of a potential risk situation that can result or contribute to mishap. A *Hazard causes* some *Consequences*. *Safety Requirements* are *derived from* identified *Hazards*. We define *FTA Node, Operator* and *Fault* to conduct Fault Tree Analysis, which is a well-known method. Fault Tree Analysis [7] aims to analyze a design for possible faults that lead to hazard in the system using Boolean logic. *FTA Nodes, Faults* and *Operators* are the elements of a Fault Tree. *Faults* are the leaf nodes of the Fault Tree. *Operator* is used to conduct Boolean logic. *Operator* can be *AND* or *OR*. A *Hazard* is *caused by* one or more *FTA Nodes*.

The middle part of the metamodel includes the concepts related to applied safety tactics in the design. Different studies, such as [3] and [16], have proposed architectural tactics or patterns for supporting safety design. In [16], Wu and Kelly propose safety tactics by adopting the SEI's tactic work. Based on these studies we have identified well-known safety tactics: fault avoidance, fault detection and fault tolerance. The fault avoidance tactic aims to prevent faults from occurring in the system. When a fault has occurred, the fault is detected by applying fault detection tactics. Fault tolerance is the ability of the system to continue properly when the fault has occurred and maintain a safe operational condition. Therefore, applied *Safety Tactic* can be *Fault Avoidance Tactic, Fault Detection Tactic* or *Fault Tolerance Tactic* in order to deal with faults.

The top part of the metamodel includes the concepts that present elements in the architecture design. These elements are *Monitoring Element, Safety-Critical Element* and *Non-Safety Critical Element* where *Architectural Element* is their superclass. An *Architectural Element* can read data from another *Architectural Element,* write data to another *Architectural Element,* and command to another *Architectural Element. Monitoring Element monitors* one or more *Safety-Critical Elements* by checking their status. If there is a problem in a *Safety-Critical Element,* it can react by stopping/starting/restarting/initializing the related *Safety-Critical Element. Safety-Critical Element* presents the element that includes safety-critical operations. One *Safety-Critical Element* can *be element of* another *Safety-Critical Element. Safety-Critical Elements* can *report* occurred *faults* to other *Safety-Critical Elements.* A *Safety-Critical Element has States* to describe its condition. *Safe State* is one type of the *State*. If a *Fault* is detected that can lead to a *Hazard* and is there is a *Safe State* that can prevent this *Hazard*, the *Safety-Critical Element* can switch its state to that *Safe State*. *Safety-Critical Element*s should not include the elements that do not have safety-critical operations. Therefore, *Non-Safety-Critical Element* is defined to represent the elements that do not include safety-critical operations. One *Non-Safety-Critical Element* can *be element of* another *Non-Safety-Critical Element*. A *Monitoring Element* or *Safety-Critical Element* *implements* the *Safety Tactic*s in order to ensure the safety of the system. A *Safety-Critical Element* can *implement* one or more *Safety Requirement*s in order to provide the desired functionality.

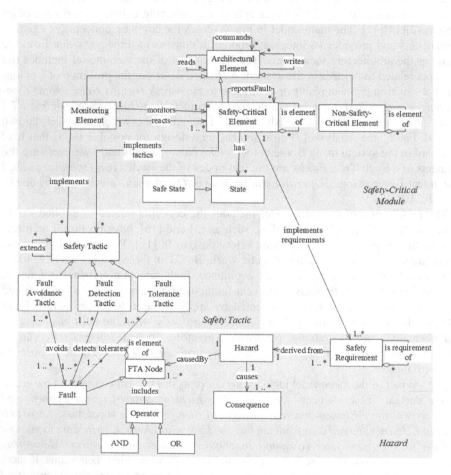

Fig. 2. Metamodel for software safety

4   Viewpoint Definition for Software Safety

Based on the metamodel discussed in the previous section, we derive and explain the viewpoints defined for software safety. We have identified three coherent viewpoints that together form the safety architecture framework: *Hazard Viewpoint*, *Safety Tactics Viewpoint* and *Safety-Critical Viewpoint*.

Table 4 shows the Hazard Viewpoint. It aims to support the hazard identification process and shows each hazard along with the fault trees that can cause the hazard, the derived safety requirements and the possible consequences of the hazard.

Table 4. Hazard viewpoint

Section	Description
Overview	This viewpoint describes the identified hazards, their possible causes and consequences, derived safety requirements from these hazards and possible faults in the system.
Concerns	Which safety requirements are derived from which hazards? Which faults can cause which hazards? What are the possible consequences of the identified hazards?
Stakeholders	Software Architect, Safety Engineer
Constraints	• One or more safety requirements can be derived from a hazard. • A hazard can cause one or more consequences. • A hazard can be caused by one or more FTA Nodes.
Elements	 Hazard Consequence Safety Requirement Fault FTA Node for AND FTA Node for OR
Relationships	derivedFrom causes causedBy ←———————— ————————→ ————————→ derived from causes caused by

Table 5 presents the safety tactics viewpoint that models the tactics and their relations to cope with the identified hazards. In general we can distinguish among fault avoidance, fault detection and fault tolerance tactics. In the metamodel definition, we define *avoids*, *detects* and *tolerates* relationship from *Safety Tactic* element to *Fault*. However, one *Fault* can be handled by different *Safety Tactics*, we define an attribute *handledFaults* in *Safety Tactic* element instead of presenting each handled faults as an element and constructing relationships between *Safety Tactics* and *Faults*. This approach improves the readability of the view and shows traceability between *Faults* and *Safety Tactics*.

Table 5. Safety tactics viewpoint

Section	Description
Overview	This viewpoint describes the safety tactics implemented in the system. Also it shows the faults handled by the safety tactics.
Concerns	What are the applied safety tactics? Which faults are handled by which safety tactics?
Stakeholders	Software Architect, Safety Engineer, Software Developer
Constraints	A safety tactic can extend different safety tactics.
Elements	<<Tactic>> name: type: handledFaults: Safety Tactic, Fault Avoidance, Fault Detection, Fault Tolerance
Relationships	──────▷ extends

Table 6. Safety-critical viewpoint

Section	Description
Overview	This viewpoint shows the safety-critical elements, monitoring elements, non-safety-critical elements and relations between them. It presents also the implemented safety tactics by related safety-critical elements and monitoring elements. Additionally it shows the implemented safety requirements by related safety-critical elements.
Concerns	What are the safety-critical elements and their relations? What are the monitoring elements and relations between monitoring and safety-critical elements? What are the implemented safety tactics and safety requirements by safety-critical elements and monitoring elements? What are the non-safety-critical elements and their relations?
Stakeholders	Software Architect, Software Developer, Safety Engineer
Constraints	• A safety-critical element can read data from one or more safety-critical elements. • A safety-critical element can write data to one or more safety-critical elements. • A safety-critical element can command one or more safety-critical elements. • A safety-critical element can report fault to one or more safety-critical elements. • A monitoring element can monitor one or more safety-critical elements. • A monitoring element can stop/start/init/restart one or more safety-critical elements.
Elements	<<SC>> implementedTactics: criticality level: implementedSReqs: <<NSC>> <<Monitor>> implementedTactics: Safety-Critical Element Non-Safety-Critical Element Monitoring Element
Relationships	reads → writes → commands → reads writes commands reportsFault → <<reaction>> → monitors → reports fault reacts monitors

Table 6 explains the safety-critical viewpoint. In the metamodel definition, we define an *implements* relationship from *Monitoring Element* and *Safety-Critical Element* to *Safety Tactic*. One *Safety Tactic* can be implemented by different *Monitoring Elements* or *Safety-Critical Elements*. Therefore, we define an attribute *implemented-Tactics* in both *Monitoring Element* and *Safety-Critical Element* instead of showing *Safety Tactics* as an element in this viewpoint. This modification is also done for the *implements* relationship between *Safety-Critical Element* and *Safety Requirement*. This relation is shown as an attribute *implementedSReqs* in *Safety-Critical Element*.

5   Application of the Architecture Framework

We have applied the viewpoints approach to the case study described in Section 2. The following subsections illustrate the application of defined viewpoints on the case study.

5.1   Hazard View

The hazard view for *HZ1* is shown in Fig. 3. Other hazards are excluded for the sake of simplicity. Such a filter can be implemented with a tool. The filter takes the hazards as a parameter and shows the faults and safety requirements related only with the specified hazards. This view answers the following questions for our case study.

- *Which safety requirements are derived from which hazards?*
The safety requirements derived from *HZ1* are displayed in Fig. 3. These safety requirements are defined in Table 3.
- *What are the possible consequences of the identified hazards?*
As shown in Fig. 3, aircraft crash is possible consequence of the HZ1
- *Which faults can cause which hazards?*

The faults that can cause HZ1 are shown as the leaf nodes of a fault tree generated by using Fault Tree Analysis, which is a well-known method [7]. The faults are numbered from F1 to F13. Their definitions are given in Table 7. The names of the FTA Nodes are enumerated from N1 to N9. N1 and N2 indicate "Loss of Altimeter1" and "Loss of Altimeter2". N3 and N4 represent "Error in Altimeter1" and "Error in Altimeter2". Wrong altimeter data can be displayed when one of the followings occur: when altimeter1 is lost and there is an error in altimeter2 (*N5*), when altimeter2 is lost and there is an error in altimeter1 (*N6*), when there is an error in both altimeters (*N7*) and the difference between them is not greater than the threshold, when there is an error in display device 1 and the graphics manager 2 fails (*N8*), when there is an error in display device 2 and the graphics manager 1 fails (*N9*), when the navigation manager fails.

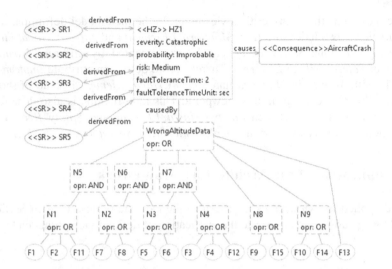

Fig. 3. Hazard view for HZ1

Table 7. Fault table

Fault	Description	Fault	Description
[F1]	Loss of altimeter device 1	[F9]	Error in display device 1
[F2]	Loss of communication with altimeter device 1	[F10]	Error in display device 2
[F3]	Loss of altimeter device 2	[F11]	Altimeter1Mgr fails
[F4]	Loss of communication with altimeter device 2	[F12]	Altimeter2Mgr fails
[F5]	Error in altimeter device 1	[F13]	NavigationMgr fails
[F6]	Error in communication with altimeter device 1	[F14]	Graphics1Mgr fails
[F7]	Error in altimeter device 2	[F15]	Graphics2Mgr fails
[F8]	Error in communication with altimeter device 2		

5.2   Safety Tactics View

The safety tactics view shows the tactics implemented in the architecture along with
the handled faults. This view answers the question *"Which tactics are applied to handle which faults?"*. Fig. 4 displays the implemented tactics to handle the faults related
with *HZ1*. Such a filter can be developed within a tool. The filter takes the hazards
that the user wants in order to see the tactics to handle the faults that can cause these
hazards.

The tactics named T1, T4, T5, T8 and T9 are generated as fault tolerance tactics.
T1 is a redundancy tactic for altitude data. Altitude data is received from two different
altimeter devices. By applying the tactic T1, the faults from F1 to F8 are handled. T5
is a redundancy tactic for displaying altitude data. Altitude data is displayed on
two different displays. The tactic T5 is applied to handle faults F9 and F10. T4 is a

warning tactic for altitude data. An altitude warning is generated when there is a difference between two altitude values received from two different altimeters, or when altitude data is received from only one of the altimeters, or when altitude data cannot be received from both altimeters (different warnings are generated to distinguish these cases). By applying the tactic T4, the faults from F1 to F8 are handled. T8 is a recovery tactic for navigation manager. When navigation manager fails, it is recovered. The tactic T8 is applied to handle faults F11, F12 and F13. T9 is a recovery tactic for graphics managers. When one of the graphics managers fails, it is recovered. The tactic T9 handles the faults F14 and F15.

The tactics named T2, T3, T6 and T7 are fault detection tactics. T2 is a comparison tactic and it compares the altitude values received from two different altimeter devices and detects if there is a difference. The tactic T2 is applied to handle faults from F5 to F8. T3 is a comparison tactic and it compares the received altitude value with its minimum and maximum values in order to detect out of range altitude value. By applying the tactic T3, the faults from F5 to F8 are handled. T6 is a monitoring tactic that monitors the graphics managers' failures. The tactic T6 handles the faults F14 and F15. T7 is a monitoring tactic that monitors the navigation manager's failure. The tactic T7 is applied to handle faults F11, F12 and F13.

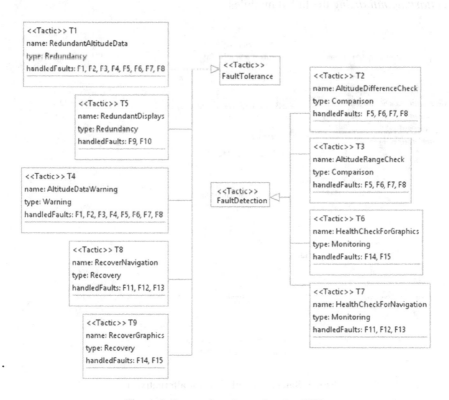

Fig. 4. Safety tactics view related to HZ1

5.3   Safety-Critical View

The safety-critical view for our case study is shown in Fig. 5. The figure shows the related modules with HZ1. A filtering approach can also be applied for this view. Safety-critical modules and their monitors are filtered according to the specified hazards. *CommunicationMgr* and *RadioMgr* modules are displayed in Fig. 5 in order to show an example of non-safety-critical modules.

As explained in Section 2 the *Altimeter1Mgr* and *Altimeter2Mgr* are the managers of the altimeter devices and the *Graphics1Mgr* and *Graphics2Mgr* are the managers of the graphics devices. *NavigationMgr reads* the altitude data from *Altimeter1Mgr* and *Altimeter2Mgr*. *Graphics1Mgr* and *Graphics2Mgr read* the altitude data from *NavigationMgr*. If a warning should be generated *NavigationMgr* notifies the *Graphics1Mgr* and *Graphics2Mgr* through *commands* relation. If a fault is occurred in *Altimeter1Mgr* and *Altimeter2Mgr*, they report the occurred fault to *NavigationMgr* through *reportsFault* relation. *NavigationMonitor monitors Altimeter1Mgr, Altimeter2Mgr* and *NavigationMgr*. It detects the failure when one of these managers fails and recovers from failures by *stopping/starting/initializing* the failed modules. Similarly, *GraphicsMonitor monitors* the *Graphics1Mgr* and *Graphics2Mgr*. It detects the failure when one of these managers fails and recovers from failures by *stopping/starting/initializing* the failed modules.

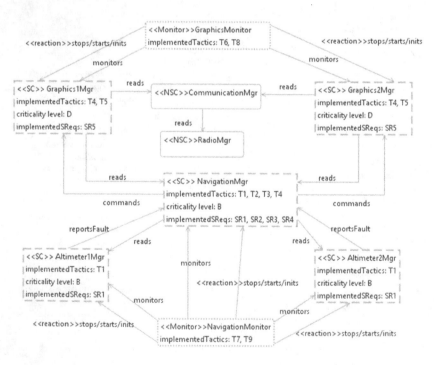

Fig. 5. Safety-critical view for alternative 1

As it can be observed from Fig. 5, *NavigationMgr* causes single-point of failure that can also be inferred from the fault tree shown in the hazard view in Fig. 3. In this particular case, the identification of the failures is easy to identify, but for more complex systems typically component dependency analysis is needed. The analysis of failures and the required design decisions is beyond the scope of this paper since we focus primarily on the modeling of the safety concerns. However, using the architectural views both the analysis and design of safety critical systems will be supported. For solving the single point of failure of Fig. 5, we can provide another design alternative, which is illustrated in Fig. 6. (Note that changing this view also affects hazard and safety tactics views. Since the changes are straightforward, they are not given.) In the second design alternative, (1) redundancy technique is also applied to navigation manager by defining two navigation managers, (2) navigation monitor controls only navigation managers, and (3) a new monitor called *AltimeterMonitor* is added to control altimeter managers. There are two new tactics implemented by altimeter monitor, which are called as *HealthCheckForAltimeter* (T10) and *RecoverAltimeter* (T11). By applying a redundancy tactic for navigation manager, the single-point of failure problem is solved. This design increases the safety of the system. However, addition of the new monitor and manager also increases the relations (function calls) between the related modules and this impacts the performance of the system.

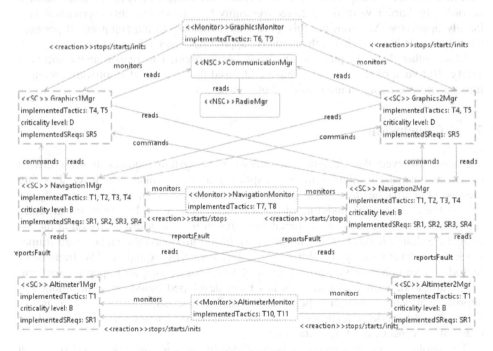

Fig. 6. Safety-critical view for alternative 2

6   Related Work

Various studies [2][14][17] propose a metamodel for safety. Douglas [2] provides a UML profiling for safety analysis including profiling for FTA (Fault Tree Analysis) diagrams. Taguchi [14] provides a metamodel that includes safety concepts expressed with the ISO/FDIS 26262 standard [5] from scratch. In [17], they define a metamodel that includes safety concepts extracted from the airworthiness standard, RTCA DO-178B [11], by extending UML.

In [10], Rozanski and Woods state that quality concerns are crosscutting concerns on the viewpoints and for each quality concern creating a new viewpoint seems less appropriate. Therefore, they propose a concept of *architectural perspective* that includes a collection of activities, tactics and guidelines that require consideration across a number of the architectural views. In this way, the architectural views provide the description of the architecture, while the architectural perspectives can help to analyze and modify the architecture to ensure that system exhibits the desired quality properties. Rozanski and Woods do not seem to have addressed the safety in their architectural perspective approach.

In our earlier work, we have considered the explicit modeling of viewpoints for quality concerns [13][15]. Hereby, each quality concern, such as adaptability and recoverability, require a different decomposition of the architecture. To define the required decompositions for the quality concerns, architectural elements and relations are defined accordingly. Earlier work on local recoverability has shown that this approach is also largely applicable. We consider this work complementary to the architectural perspectives approach. It seems that both alternative approaches seem to have merits.

Many other different publications have been provided to reason about software safety. But none of these seem to have addressed the solution at a software architecture perspective using an integrated set of viewpoints.

7   Conclusion

We have observed that designing a safety-critical system requires to show design decisions related to safety concerns explicitly at the architectural level. Existing viewpoint approaches tend to be general purpose and deliberately do not directly focus on the architectural modeling of software safety concerns. However, in particular for safety-critical systems, it is crucial to represent these concerns early on at the architecture design level. For this purpose, we have introduced the architecture framework for software safety to address the safety concerns explicitly. The framework includes three coherent viewpoints, each of which addressing an important concern. The framework with its viewpoints has been developed based on a metamodeling approach, which is a common practice. We did not encounter many problems in defining the metamodels, in particular because of the broad knowledge on safety and the reuse of concepts of existing metamodels.

The application of the viewpoints is illustrated for an industrial case on safety-critical avionics control computer system. These viewpoints have formed the basis for analysis and support for the detailed design of the safety-critical systems. Using the viewpoints we could (1) analyze the architecture in the early phases of the development life cycle,

(2) analyze the design alternatives, (3) increase the communication between safety engineers and software developers and (4) communicate the design decisions related with safety. We have shown how the architecture framework can be used for a real design of a safety critical system in the avionics domain. The framework appeared indeed to be useful to support architecture design of safety critical systems. We have focused on supporting explicit modeling of safety concerns. We believe that with the current framework, the design of safety critical systems can now be better supported. As future work, we will focus on design heuristics to define metrics and develop tools to analyze several design alternatives for safety-critical systems based on the proposed viewpoints.

References

1. Clements, P., Bachmann, F., Bass, L., Garlan, D., Ivers, J., Little, R., Nord, R., Stafford, J.: Documenting Software Architectures: Views and Beyond. Addison-Wesley, Boston (2003)
2. Douglass, B.P.: Analyze System Safety using UML within the IBM Rational Rhapsody Environment. IBM Rational White Paper, IBM Software Group (2009)
3. Gawand, H., Mundada, R.S., Swaminathan, P.: Design Patterns to Implement Safety and Fault Tolerance. International Journal of Computer Applications 18, 6–13 (2011)
4. Hofmeister, C., Nord, R., Soni, D.: Applied Software Architecture. Addison-Wesley, MA (2000)
5. ISO/DIS 26262, Road vehicles - Functional safety. International Organization for Standardization, Geneva, Switzerland (2009)
6. Kruchten, P.: The 4+1 View Model of Architecture. IEEE Software 12(6), 42–50 (1995)
7. Leveson, N.G., Harvey, P.R.: Analyzing Software Safety. IEEE Transactions on Software Engineering 9(5), 569–579 (1983)
8. Leveson, N.G.: Safeware: System Safety and Computers. Addison-Wesley, NY (1995)
9. Meta Object Facility (MOF), http://www.omg.org/mof/
10. Rozanski, N., Woods, E.: Software Architecture Systems Working with Stakeholders Using Viewpoints and Perspectives. Addison-Wesley (2005)
11. RTCA DO-178B, Software Considerations in Airborne Systems and Equipment Certification (1992)
12. Software Safety Guide Book, NASA Technical Standard, http://www.nasa.gov/
13. Sözer, H., Tekinerdogan, B., Aksit, M.: Optimizing Decomposition of Software Architecture for Local Recovery. Software Quality Journal 21(2), 203–240 (2013)
14. Taguchi, K.: Meta Modeling Approach to Safety Standard for Consumer Devices. Seminar on Systems Assurance & Safety for Consumer Devices (2011)
15. Tekinerdogan, B., Sözer, H.: Defining Architectural Viewpoints for Quality Concerns. In: Crnkovic, I., Gruhn, V., Book, M. (eds.) ECSA 2011. LNCS, vol. 6903, pp. 26–34. Springer, Heidelberg (2011)
16. Wu, W., Kelly, T.: Safety Tactics for Software Architecture Design. In: Proceedings of the 28th Annual International Computer Software and Applications Conference, pp. 368–375. IEEE Computer Society, USA (2004)
17. Zoughbi, G., Briand, L., Labiche, Y.: A UML Profile for Developing Airworthiness-Compliant (RTCA DO-178B), Safety-Critical Software. In: Engels, G., Opdyke, B., Schmidt, D.C., Weil, F. (eds.) MODELS 2007. LNCS, vol. 4735, pp. 574–588. Springer, Heidelberg (2007)

Search-Based Model Optimization Using Model Transformations

Joachim Denil[1,2], Maris Jukss[2], Clark Verbrugge[2], and Hans Vangheluwe[1,2]

[1] University of Antwerp, Belgium
[2] McGill University, Canada
{Joachim.Denil,mjukss,clump,hv}@cs.mcgill.ca

Abstract. Design-Space Exploration (DSE) and optimization look for a suitable and optimal candidate solution to a problem, with respect to a set of quality criteria, by searching through a space of possible solution designs. Search-Based Optimization (SBO) is a well-known technique for design-space exploration and optimization. Model-Driven Engineering (MDE) offers many benefits for creating a general approach to SBO, through a suitable problem representation. In MDE, model transformation is the preferred technique to manipulate models. The challenge thus lies in adapting model transformations to perform SBO tasks. In this paper, we demonstrate that multiple SBO techniques are easily incorporated into MDE. Through a non-trivial example of electrical circuit generation, we show how this approach can be applied, how it enables simple switching between different SBO approaches, and integrates domain knowledge, all within the modeling paradigm.

1 Introduction

Design-Space Exploration and optimization look for a suitable candidate solution, with respect to a set of quality criteria, by searching through a design space. Examples of quality metrics include performance and cost. Different approaches to design-space exploration are currently in common use in different engineering disciplines. Examples include mathematical optimization techniques such as Mixed Integer Linear Programming [27], Constraint-Satisfaction techniques [9,23] and Search-Based Optimization techniques (SBO) [1,26].

Applying SBO to an engineering problem requires four components: (a) a representation of the problem, (b) a method to create a candidate solution to the problem, (c) a goal-function or fitness metric to evaluate if a candidate solution is "good", and (d) an optimization method. The theory of SBO currently offers little guidance as to the choice of representation, fitness metric, and search method, therefore such choices are often made on a problem-by-problem basis [2].

Model-Driven Engineering (MDE) [22] uses abstraction to bridge the cognitive gap between the problem space and the solution space in complex system problems in general and in software engineering problems in particular. To bridge this gap, MDE uses models to describe complex systems at multiple levels of abstraction, using appropriate modeling formalisms. These suitable problem

D. Amyot et al. (Eds.): SAM 2014, LNCS 8769, pp. 80–95, 2014.

representations, in the form of models, form a strong basis for creating a general approach to SBO.

Burton and Poulding [2] propose models as a suitable problem and solution representation for SBO. Models indeed enable the representation of the problem in a highly structured and consistent way. This eliminates the need to find a suitable problem-specific representation amenable for search. Model-Driven Engineering also has a tool-set available for manipulating these models using systematic transformations of problem-level abstractions into their implementations. Model transformation is even regarded as the "heart and soul of model-driven software and system development [24]". Finally, MDE also allows one to visualize the obtained solutions without an additional translation cost from the problem-specific search representation to a representation in the problem domain.

Although model transformation is proposed as the tool for the manipulation of models, little work has been done in integrating search in model transformation models. The contributions of this paper can be summarized as follows:

- We propose a strategy for integrating multiple, common, single-state search techniques directly into a model transformation approach.
- Our design is demonstrated through a non-trivial running example of automatic electrical circuit construction. Through this example, we show how to easily apply different SBOs to the same problem space, and thus evaluate and explore, and potentially integrate different search strategies.
- A model transformation approach has the further advantage of naturally incorporating domain knowledge. We illustrate this by showing how an additional rule, encoding higher-level knowledge of circuit design, is easily added, and how this results in improved/optimal output.

The rest of this paper is organized as follows: Other motivations are discussed in Section 2 . Section 3 introduces the running example. Section 4 introduces the components of a rule-based model transformation language. In Section 5, model transformation models with search are created. The results of the experiments are shown in Section 6. In Section 7, we discuss the approach. Section 8 discusses related work. Finally, in Section 9, we conclude and look at future work.

2 Motivation

Including Search-Based Optimization techniques in model transformation models has multiple advantages over creating a search-specific representation of the same problem, avoiding out-of-paradigm translation, exposing and more easily integrating domain knowledge, and allowing for natural integration into MDE. Transformations used to create candidate solutions for the search method make domain knowledge explicit. Indeed, they show where the variation points in the model are and how we can create candidate solutions to the problem. In the proposed approach, the model remains at the center of the problem. Complex problems for searching are described in the natural language of the engineers since both the model and the transformation rules share a common (possibly visual) representation. This removes the difficult need to create a problem-specific search representation of the problem. No transformations need to be created to transform the model to and from this search representation.

There is however another advantage to the use of model transformation rules to explicitly model the variation points. Domain experts' knowledge can be easily integrated in the search problem by either adding another rule or augmenting the existing rules with extra constraints.

Using a transformation-based approach to search problems allows for the full integration of the optimization in the MDE-cycle. The Formalism Transformation Graph and Process Model (FTG+PM) [15] allows for the creation of complex model transformation chains with non-linear control- and data-flow. Model optimization can be entirely represented as an FTG+PM [16]. The FTG+PM as well allows for the creation of optimization chains, where the search problem is divided into different parts, to create complex, hybrid optimization chains [5]. Manual optimization steps are also possible in this approach, where a selection of steps can be done using human interaction. The overall approach allows for the full integration of search in the MDE cycle resulting in documented, reusable optimization models.

3   Running Example

The essential contribution of this paper is demonstrated using an example from the electronic circuit design community. The example focuses on the creation of an electrical signal filter from a given number of electrical components, each with specified parameter values. The signal filter's behavior should be as close as possible to a specified filter specification. Electronic filters are electronic circuits that remove unwanted frequency components and/or increase desired frequencies. We focus on the design of passive analog filters. This type of filter only uses passive components such as *Resistors* (R), *Inductors* (I) and *Capacitors* (C). They do not depend on external power supplies and/or active components such as transistors or operational amplifiers. Different types of passive filters can be constructed in various ways: low-pass filters, for example, let through low-frequency signals and attenuate signals with a frequency higher than the cutoff frequency (ω_c). Similarly, high-pass filters attenuate frequencies lower than the cutoff frequency while letting the frequencies higher than the cutoff frequency through. Other types include bandpass filters, band-stop filters, notch filters, etc. The frequency response of a filter is usually represented using a Bode plot. A Bode (magnitude) plot shows the magnitude of the signal response gain in decibels (db) versus the frequency, on a logarithmic scale. The Bode plot of a low-pass filter is shown in Fig. 1a. The example low-pass filter has a cutoff frequency of 5kHz. Frequencies above this point are attenuated with at least half of their power compared to the original power at that frequency. On the Bode plot this evaluates to the -3db point.

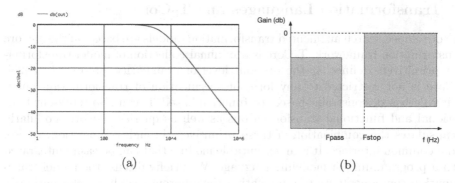

(a)   (b)

Fig. 1. (a) An example Bode plot of a low-pass filter with ω_c 5kHz; (b) A low-pass filter specification example

The specifications of filters are also expressed using a Bode plot. Figure 1b shows the specification of a low pass filter. The white areas show the attenuation ranges at the different frequencies. The grey areas show the no-go zones of the filter characteristic. Different well known techniques are available to create filters with different characteristics. In the running ex-

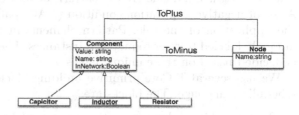

Fig. 2. Meta-model of the passive filter network

ample, we will use generative techniques with search to create a filter. Figure 2 shows the meta-model of our passive filter network. Three components can be used in a model: resistor, capacitor and inductor. Each component has a name, a value (for the resistor in Ohm, the capacitor in Farad and the inductor in Henry) and a boolean attribute that states whether the component is a mandatory part of the network or whether it is a spare component that can be used in the search problem. Components connect to a Node via a plus or minus connection. Three nodes should always be present in the network: the out-node, the ground-node and the in-node. In our start model for the exploration, these three nodes are present and connected via resistors.

The creation of filter circuits using generative techniques is a non-trivial problem appropriate for DSE because of the large solution space of physically realizable models. The problem has a clear specification and known solutions using traditional circuit design techniques, allowing us to validate our results. Finally, the circuit design community has a host of domain knowledge available that is readily usable in the model transformations.

4   Transformation Languages and T-Core

The developed search augmented transformation models are based on the T-Core transformation framework. T-Core is a minimal collection of model transformation primitives, defined at the optimal level of granularity, presented in [25]. T-Core is not restricted to any form of specification of transformation units, be it rule-based, constraint-based, or function-based. It can also represent bidirectional and functional transformations as well as queries. T-Core modularly encapsulates the combination of these primitives through composition, re-use, and a common interface. It is an executable module that can be easily integrated with a programming or modeling language. We briefly discuss the model transformation components we use in creating the different search transformations.

Rule-based model transformation languages work on typed, attributed and directed graphs that represent the model. A transformation rule represents a manipulation operations on the represented model. A rule consists of a left-hand side (LHS) pattern representing the precondition for the applicability of the rule. The right-hand side (RHS) pattern defines the outcome of the operation. A set of negative application condition (NAC) patterns can be defined to block the application of the rule. Pattern elements in the LHS, RHS and NAC are uniquely labeled to refer to matched instances. The transformation rule outcome is decided based on these unique labels.

We use several T-Core primitive building blocks and combine them using a scheduling language. The blocks are:

- Matcher: binds elements in the input model to the corresponding elements in the precondition pattern. The complete binding forms a "match". The different matches are stored in a match-set. The matcher can be parameterized to find a certain number of matches or all of the available matches in the model. Using graph-based models, the matching problem leads to the subgraph isomorphism problem that is known to be NP-complete [3]. Performance may be approved by providing an initial binding, often called a pivot.
- Iterator: gives the modeler explicit control to select a single match from the match-set, as input to the Rewriter. The iterator can be set up to always select the first match in the set or to randomly select a match in the set.
- Rewriter: rewrites the model using a match and the RHS pattern.
- Rollbacker: enables backtracking (typically to different matches in the match-set) in the transformation language.

A "scheduling language" is used to compose different transformation primitives. To execute a single transformation rule, a *matcher* first creates the match-set containing the matches that comply to the LHS pattern of the rule. One of these matches is chosen by the *iterator*. The *rewriter* adapts the model based on the chosen match and the RHS pattern. At a higher level, the scheduling language allows for composition of rules. Different kinds of scheduling languages can be used such as activity diagrams, DEVS, or a common procedural programming language [25].

5   Including Search in Transformation Models

To include search in model transformation models, the different components of
a search-based optimization techniques need to be present in the model transformation.

5.1   Problem Representation

The model itself is used as the problem representation without any augmen-
tations for search. Figure 3 shows an example start model for circuit design.
The search is finite because the number of components that can be used in the
problem is limited.

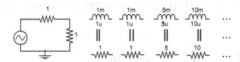

Fig. 3. Example start model for circuit design

5.2   Creation of Candidate Solutions

To create a single candidate solution, a model transformation or a set of model
transformations are used. Depending on the problem, the model transformation
rules create only feasible solutions or, because of the complexity of the problem,
feasible and non-feasible solutions. A non-feasible solution is a model that is
syntactically correct (i.e., conforms to the modeling language's meta-model), but
does not satisfy all the constraints of the search problem. Non-feasible candidate
solutions should be pruned on evaluation.

Some example rules to explore the design space of the electrical filters are:

- CreateSeries: The transformation selects a component from the set of unused
  components (denoted by an attribute of the component in the model) and
  adds this component in series with an already present component in the
  circuit. Figure 4a depicts the transformation rule.
- CreateParallel: The transformation rule adds a component from the set of
  unused components in parallel to a component already used in the network.
  The transformation rule is shown in Fig. 4b.
- AddRandom: An unused component is randomly added between two arbitrary different nodes in the circuit. This rule may create non-feasible solutions.
- ChangeComponent: A component in the circuit is replaced with another
  component from the set of unused components.

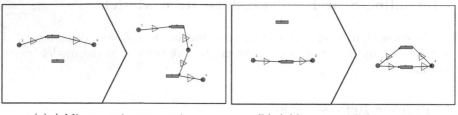

(a) Adding a series connection   (b) Adding a parallel connection

Fig. 4. Example transformation rules to create candidate solutions

Depending on the used optimization technique, not all operations may be used. The opposite operation of the transformation rules may also be available. Creation of a circuit, for example, could potentially use the creation rules alone, but optimization might need to remove components as well to traverse the entire design-space.

5.3   Evaluation of Candidate Solutions

A metric is needed to evaluate if a solution is first "feasible" and additionally "good." Metrics can be calculated depending on the domain using (a) a model transformation, when the metric is based on structural properties of the model or when the model transformations incrementally keep the metrics consistent with the model as in [6] or, by (b) transforming the model to another representation (e.g., a simulation model, algebraic equation, etc.) if the metric is based on the behaviour, structure or a derived property of the model. We explicitly make the distinction between a "feasible" and a "good" candidate solution. A feasible candidate solution is a model that is within all the constraints of the search problem. In our running example this means that the created network is correct with respect to the laws of circuit design. A "good" solution or "better" solution is a comparison of two feasible solutions with respect to the filter specification.

A design candidate of the exploration process is evaluated by transforming the model to a SPICE simulation model [17]. The SPICE simulator executes a frequency sweep on the created circuit and creates a Bode plot of the candidate as shown in Fig. 1a. The evaluation function compares this Bode plot (expressed in the SPICE trace language) with the filter specification and assigns a score based on the difference between the solution and the specification. The distance between the required characteristic and the number of components is used to define a metric on how "good" a candidate solution is. Infeasible solutions are candidate solutions that are not physically possible (for example, no path to ground). Infeasible solutions are detected by the SPICE simulator.

5.4   Optimization Technique

In the following paragraphs we show how to include different optimization processes in model transformation models. The optimization process is implemented using the scheduling language of the model transformation language. Four well-known search techniques that are used in optimization are constructed: *exhaustive search, randomized search, Hill Climbing and Simulated Annealing.* We define for each of the proposed search techniques what the requirements of the model transformation language are. Transformation rules are created for the running example to create the candidate solutions.

Exhaustive Search: While the exhaustive search is not practical for most problems, as a potentially huge search space needs to be explored, it can be used for the optimization of small problems. Exhaustive search will generate all solutions in the design space that are reachable by the defined transformations. Figure 5 shows an activity diagram of the implementation of the exhaustive search method. The transformation schedule performs a depth-first-search-like traversal of the search-space by exhaustively trying all possibilities. At each rule application, the search creates a checkpoint that is used by the Rollbacker component to implement the backtracking. The checkpoint contains (a) the model, (b) the selected match and (c) the match-set, without the chosen match. With each backtracking step, another match is used, creating a new branch in the search tree. Depending on the problem, each of the intermediate steps represents a candidate solution or only a partial solution (with a full solution on the leaf node of the tree).

Randomized Search: In randomized search, a set of solutions are created in a random way. The technique is used to get an overview of the search-space. It can also be used to create a starting point for other search techniques that require a candidate solution to start optimizing. Random search uses only the matcher, iterator and rewriter. After matching all occurrences of the pattern in the model, a random match is selected for rewrite. This requires a different iterator than in the exhaustive case. The rewriter applies the randomly chosen match on the model. Afterwards, another rule or the same rule can be executed until a solution point is obtained. The rules can be applied a random number of times or until no more matches can be found in the model. A loop is used to create multiple solution points.

Hill Climbing: Hill climbing is a local search technique that uses an incremental method to optimize a single solution. The algorithm starts with an arbitrary solution to the problem and iteratively optimizes this solution by changing a single element. If the change is a better solution to the optimization problem, the change is accepted. This procedure is repeated until no better result is found. Figure 5 shows the building blocks of the hill climbing transformation. After matching all occurrences in a (set of) rule(s), the iterator picks one match at random and rewrites this in the model. The solution is evaluated and compared with the original solution. In case the solution is not better, the original solution (with the matches) is restored and another match is randomly selected and evaluated. If the solution is a better one, it is accepted. The evaluator contains a set of transformation rules to calculate the metrics of the solution or to generate

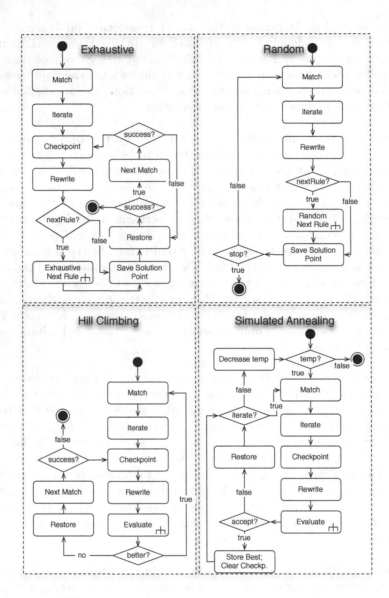

Fig. 5. Activity diagram of Exhaustive Search, Random Optimization, Hill climbing and Simulated Annealing using T-Core primitives

an analysis or simulation model that can be executed. The metrics obtained are used by the scheduling language to decide if the solution is more optimal than the previous solution. When a better solution has been found, the process is restarted until no more improvements can be found.

Simulated Annealing: Simulated annealing is a generic probabilistic optimization algorithm [13]. The algorithm is inspired by metallurgy where controlled cooling is used to reduce defects in the crystal structure of the metal. The controlled cooling is used in simulated annealing to decrease the probability in accepting not only a more optimal solutions but also a less optimal solution. By not only accepting better solutions, the search algorithm is able to escape a local optimal result. Again, all occurrences are matched where only a single one is picked for rewriting. Based on the difference between the previous solution and the candidate solution, and the temperature, the candidate solution is accepted or rejected (resulting in a backtracking step). At low temperatures only better and equal solutions are accepted. Backtracking is thus more intensive at lower temperatures. This process is iterated for a predefined number of times. Afterwards, the temperature is decreased and the optimization algorithm resumes with a new temperature. The best overall solution is stored during the optimization cycle.

6   Experimental Evaluation

In this section, we look at the results of the design-space exploration of the running example. A small optimization chain is created and domain knowledge is added to the transformations.

6.1   Optimization Results

Our experimental setup uses two start models to generate different types of filters. The first model has 25 spare components to create a filter. The second model has 38 spare components. The experimental setup uses three filter specifications (the first uses the first model, the second and third use the second model). The parameters of the search algorithms are chosen based on initial experiments, for example simulated annealing has 40 temperature drops with each 20 different changes (800 different solutions are examined). We repeat each experiment ten times and record the number of used components in the filter, the difference between the specification of the filter and the results and finally, the optimization time. Table 1 shows the results for hill climbing and simulated annealing. Both optimization methods have similar results. A filter within specification or very close to the specification is created from the available components. Figure 6 shows the application of a hill climbing on the generation of a filter. All the previously presented rules (and the opposite rules) are used in the optimization. The filter resulting from the search is entirely within the requested specification. Figure 7 shows the result of a Simulated Annealing experiment. On the left side, a filter with band-pass characteristics is shown. The search method finds a solution very close to the requested filter characteristic but not completely according to the specification. On the right side the evolution of the score is shown per temperature drop. The start score for the start model is 10^8 but is left out of the graph to better show the evolution.

Table 1. Results of the hill climbing (HC) and simulated annealing (SA) experiment. The difference from the specification at the sample points (dB per sample point) is used as a measure for the quality of the filter.

		Difference		Nr. of Components		Time (s)		Within Spec.
		Average	Std. Dev.	Average	Std. Dev.	Average	Std. Dev.	
Spec. 1	SA	0.0531	0.1596	4.1666	0.9374	312.9743	24.5175	70%
	HC	0.0594	0.097	4	1.154	49.449	17.2671	70%
Spec. 2	SA	0.063	0.1263	5.6	1.0749	527.0944	44.0954	60%
	HC	0.5325	0.8554	4.4	1.505	44.0690	21.2225	60%
Spec. 3	SA	5.087459	7.4341	8.4	2.3190	486.4568	80.8747	20%
	HC	1.4242	1.8716	9	3.0912	135.6770	64.0912	40%

6.2   Optimization Chains

As shown in [5], the FTG+PM allows us to combine different transformations, search-based transformations and Model-to-Model transformations, in sequence or in parallel, to optimize a system. In the running example, the created filter networks usually contain some components that do not have any effect on the characteristic of the filter. Removing these elements would benefit the architecture of our generated filter circuit as well as the production cost of our filter. The FTG+PM allows us to encode and operationalize this optimization chain. The first transformation creates the filter as described above. The resulting model is then optimized using hill-climbing with a single rule that tries to remove a component in the model. On certain occasions the transformation removes one to five components.

6.3   Adding Domain Knowledge

As already stated, model transformation rules allow for an elegant encoding of domain knowledge in the constraints and model transformation rules. For the design of passive filters, a well-known topology is the ladder network. A ladder network consists of cascaded asymmetrical L-sections. For a low-pass filter, the ladder would consist of series inductors and shunt (connected to the ground) capacitors. A model transformation rule can nicely capture the creation of this L-section to grow a ladder topology. Figure 8 shows a transformation rule to add a new L-section to a ladder topology.

The exhaustive and random search methods are used to create different ladder networks using only the presented rule (eight components are available). As expected, the exhaustive method finds the optimal ladder order and components to use in the ladder. The search created 62216 different solutions instead of the millions of solutions available if all rules would be used. Figure 9 shows a created ladder network and corresponding Bode plot for a low-pass filter requirement. Randomly sampling the design space is not performant for this application.

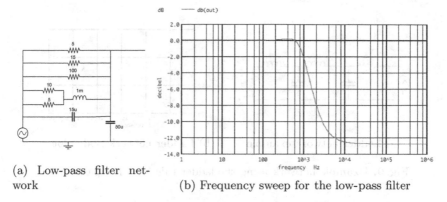

(a) Low-pass filter network

(b) Frequency sweep for the low-pass filter

Fig. 6. Hill climbing example results

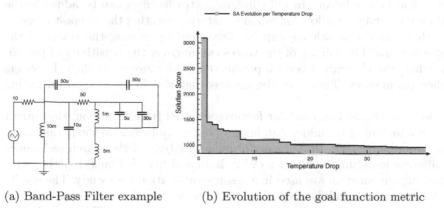

(a) Band-Pass Filter example

(b) Evolution of the goal function metric

Fig. 7. Simulated annealing example results

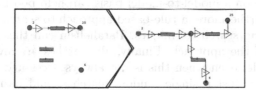

Fig. 8. Creation of an L-section for a ladder topology

7 Discussion

In this section, we discuss some of the issues and opportunities of using a rule-based model transformation approach to search-based optimization.

The proposed search algorithms can be used as a starting point for more advanced optimization techniques. Multiple variants of the presented algorithms are proposed in the literature. The exhaustive search, for example, can be converted to a branch-and-bound algorithm [14]. By adding an extra evaluation on partial candidates, solution branches can be pruned very early during search to

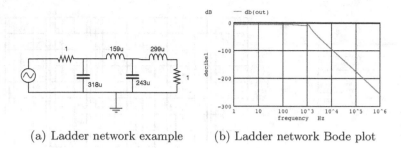

(a) Ladder network example   (b) Ladder network Bode plot

Fig. 9. Example network using the ladder rule for a low-pass filter

find the optimal solution when the branch is already less optimal than the currently found best solution. In hill-climbing, extra features can be added in the scheduling language to allow for random restarts, selecting the steepest descent, etc. Other domain knowledge can be discovered by mining the traces of the transformations. The mining of the traces can uncover the sensitivity of parameters, where the changes of certain parameters have more effect than the effects of other parameters. These are the choices that should be focused on during search.

Because matching is a modular feature of model transformation, the correct choice of a matching technique can have a positive influence on the performance of the overall approach. In [6], a performance analysis of the search techniques and different matching techniques (VF2, Rete and Search Plans) together with a coded implementation are used in a resource allocation case study. The results show that creating candidate solutions using model transformations is computationally more expensive compared to optimal representations. This is attributed to the complexity of finding of sub-graphs in the model. Using the correct type of matching technique on a model-to-model basis can help boost the performance of the approach. Furthermore, a rule-based approach to search exposes the parallelism in branching search techniques. Parallelism can thus further enhance the performance of the approach. Finally, all matches are always matched in the underlying model even when this is not always necessary. Using a random matcher that creates just a single random match should be more performant for random -and simulated annealing searches. Another approach to improving the performance of the matching is to use a divide and conquer strategy. Scoping [10] can be used to select subparts of the model to optimize. The scoping can dynamically change (and broaden over time) to reduce the cost of matching during hill climbing where all matches are required for the algorithm to work.

8   Related Work

Related work can be found in Search-Based Software Engineering (SBSE) and in Model-Driven DSE. To the best of our knowledge, the integration of single-state

SBO techniques in model transformations has not been previously explored in a structured way. SBSE solves software engineering problems using SBO. An example of the use of models and search can be found in [11]. The authors search for a model transformation to translate a sequence diagram into a colored Petri net. Simulated annealing as well as Particle Swarm Optimizations are used to search in the large design-space of such a problem. The authors use this experience in [12] to create a framework for using genetic algorithms with models. A generic encoding meta-model is proposed as well as the use of model transformations for encoding and decoding the domain specific models. Another approach is proposed in [1]. The authors introduce a MDE solution to solving acquisition problems. Model transformations are used to create an initial population for a genetic algorithm and to evaluate candidate solutions. Finally, evolutionary algorithms have been used before to search for optimized models [26]. Our approach does not require the model to be transformed to another representation for meta-heuristic search.

Two transformation-based approaches have been previously used for design-space exploration. In the first approach, models are transformed to another representation more suitable for exploration or having a dedicated solver for exploration. For example, the DESERT tool-suite [18] provides a framework for design-space exploration. It allows an automated search for designs that meet structural requirements. Possible solutions are represented in a binary encoding that can generate all possibilities. A pruning tool is used to allow the user to select the designs that meet the requirements. These can then be reconstructed by decoding the selected design. In [20], Saxena and Karsai present an MDE framework for general design-space exploration. It comprises an abstract design-space exploration language and a constraint specification language. Model transformation is used to transform the models and constraints to an intermediate language. This intermediate language can be transformed to a representation that is used by a solver. Model generation techniques can also be used to search in a design-space. The FORMULA tool is able to construct instances from a meta-model [9]. Sen et al. uses Alloy to generate models for testing purposes [23]. A second approach, similar to our approach, uses model transformation to search the design-space using the model itself. Schätz et al. developed a declarative, rule-based transformation technique [21] to generate the constrained solutions of an embedded system. The rules are modified interactively to guide the exploration activity. In [4], a transformation-based approach is proposed to generate the full design-space of a cyber-physical system. The transformation language is based on Answer-Set Programming. Different approximation levels are introduced where non-feasible solutions can be pruned. In [8], a framework for guided design-space exploration using graph transformations is proposed. The approach uses hints, provided by analysis, to reduce the traversal of states. Finally, Drago et al. introduce an extension to the QVTR transformation language to represent rational information about alternative designs, and to provide performance feedback to engineers while transforming [7]. In our work, meta-heuristics are added to search the design space.

9 Conclusions and Future Work

In this paper, we demonstrated that multiple SBO techniques are easily incorporated into MDE. Through a non-trivial example of electrical circuit generation, we showed how this approach can be applied and how it enables simple switching between different SBO approaches, and how it allows for the elegant integration of domain knowledge, all within the modeling paradigm. Our strategy can be easily extended to facilitate different search processes, taking advantage of the modular nature of the underlying model transformation systems.

Our next steps in including search in transformation models include improving the current performance of the approach. We will focus on creating a non-deterministic and random matcher, so a single non-deterministic or random match can be found in the model without the need to match all the possible neighbors of a solution.

References

1. Burton, F.R., Paige, R.F., Rose, L.M., Kolovos, D.S., Poulding, S., Smith, S.: Solving acquisition problems using model-driven engineering. In: Vallecillo, A., Tolvanen, J.-P., Kindler, E., Störrle, H., Kolovos, D. (eds.) ECMFA 2012. LNCS, vol. 7349, pp. 428–443. Springer, Heidelberg (2012)
2. Burton, F.R., Poulding, S.M.: Complementing metaheuristic search with higher abstraction techniques. In: Paige et al. [19], pp. 45–48
3. Cook, S.A.: The complexity of theorem-proving procedures. In: Proc. Third Annual ACM Symp. on Theory of Computing (STOC 1971), pp. 151–158. ACM, USA (1971)
4. Denil, J., Cicchetti, A., Biehl, M., De Meulenaere, P., Eramo, R., Demeyer, S., Vangheluwe, H.: Automatic Deployment Space Exploration Using Refinement Transformations. Electronic Communications of the EASST Recent Advances in Multi-paradigm Modeling 50 (2011)
5. Denil, J., Han, G., Persson, M., De Meulenaere, P., Zeng, H., Liu, X., Vangheluwe, H.: Model-Driven Engineering Approaches to Design Space Exploration. Tech. rep., McGill University, SOCS-TR-2013.1 (2013)
6. Denil, J., Jukss, M., Verbrugge, C., Vangheluwe, H.: Search-based model optimization using model transformation. Tech. Rep. SOCS-TR-2014.2, School of Computer Science, McGill University (January 2014)
7. Drago, M.L., Ghezzi, C., Mirandola, R.: QVTR2: A rational and performance-aware extension to the relations language. In: Dingel, J., Solberg, A. (eds.) MODELS 2010. LNCS, vol. 6627, pp. 328–328. Springer, Heidelberg (2011)
8. Hegedus, A., Horvath, A., Rath, I., Varro, D.: A model-driven framework for guided design space exploration. In: Proc. ASE 2011, pp. 173–182. IEEE CS, USA (2011)
9. Jackson, E.K., Kang, E., Dahlweid, M., Seifert, D., Santen, T.: Components, platforms and possibilities: Towards generic automation for mda. In: Proc. EMSOFT 2010, pp. 39–48. ACM, USA (2010)
10. Jukss, M., Verbrugge, C., Elaasar, M., Vangheluwe, H.: Scope in model transformations. Tech. Rep. SOCS-TR-2013.4, School of Computer Science, McGill University (January 2013)

11. Kessentini, M., Wimmer, M., Sahraoui, H., Boukadoum, M.: Generating transformation rules from examples for behavioral models. In: Proc. Second International Workshop on Behaviour Modelling Foundation and Applications, BM-FA 2010, pp. 1–7. ACM Press, New York (2010)
12. Kessentini, M., Langer, P., Wimmer, M.: Searching models, modeling search: On the synergies of SBSE and MDE. In: Paige et al. [19], pp. 51–54
13. Kirkpatrick, S., Gelatt, C.D., Vecchi, M.P.: Optimization by Simulated Annealing. Science 220(4598), 671–680 (1983)
14. Land, A., Doig, A.: An Automated Method of Solving Discrete Programming Problems. Econometrica 28(3), 497–520 (1960)
15. Lúcio, L., Mustafiz, S., Denil, J., Vangheluwe, H., Jukss, M.: FTG+PM: An integrated framework for investigating model transformation chains. In: Khendek, F., Toeroe, M., Gherbi, A., Reed, R. (eds.) SDL 2013. LNCS, vol. 7916, pp. 182–202. Springer, Heidelberg (2013)
16. Mustafiz, S., Denil, J., Lúcio, L., Vangheluwe, H.: The FTG+PM framework for multi-paradigm modelling: An automotive case study. In: Proc. MPM 2012, pp. 13–18. ACM, USA (2012)
17. Nagel, L., Pederson, D.: SPICE (Simulation Program with Integrated Circuit Emphasis). Tech. Rep. UCB/ERL M382, EECS Department, University of California, Berkeley (April 1973)
18. Neema, S., Sztipanovits, J., Karsai, G., Butts, K.: Constraint-based design-space exploration and model synthesis. In: Alur, R., Lee, I. (eds.) EMSOFT 2003. LNCS, vol. 2855, pp. 290–305. Springer, Heidelberg (2003)
19. Paige, R.F., Harman, M., Williams, J.R. (eds.): CMSBSE@ICSE 2013. IEEE CS (2013)
20. Saxena, T., Karsai, G.: Mde-based approach for generalizing design space exploration. In: Petriu, D.C., Rouquette, N., Haugen, Ø. (eds.) MODELS 2010, Part I. LNCS, vol. 6394, pp. 46–60. Springer, Heidelberg (2010)
21. Schätz, B., Hölzl, F., Lundkvist, T.: Design-Space Exploration through Constraint-Based Model-Transformation. In: 2010 17th IEEE International Conference and Workshops on Engineering of Computer-Based Systems, pp. 173–182. IEEE (2010)
22. Schmidt, D.C.: Guest Editor's Introduction: Model-Driven Engineering. IEEE Computer 39(2), 25–31 (2006)
23. Sen, S., Baudry, B., Vangheluwe, H.: Towards domain-specific model editors with automatic model completion. Simulation 86(2), 109–126 (2010)
24. Sendall, S., Kozaczynski, W.: Model transformation: the heart and soul of model-driven software development. IEEE Software 20(5), 42–45 (2003)
25. Syriani, E., Vangheluwe, H., LaShomb, B.: T-Core: a framework for custom-built model transformation engines. Software & Systems Modeling, 1–29 (2013)
26. Williams, J.R., Poulding, S., Rose, L.M., Paige, R.F., Polack, F.A.C.: Identifying desirable game character behaviours through the application of evolutionary algorithms to model-driven engineering metamodels. In: Cohen, M.B., Ó Cinnéide, M. (eds.) SSBSE 2011. LNCS, vol. 6956, pp. 112–126. Springer, Heidelberg (2011)
27. Zeng, H., Natale, M.D.: Improving real-time feasibility analysis for use in linear optimization methods. In: 22nd Euromicro Conference on Real-Time Systems (ECRTS), pp. 279–290. IEEE CS (2010)

Associativity between Weak and Strict Sequencing

Gregor v. Bochmann

School of Electrical Engineering and Computer Science, University of Ottawa,
Ottawa, Ontario, Canada
bochmann@eecs.uottawa.ca

Abstract. In this paper, we consider workflows (called collaborations) involving several system components (or roles) where different components may independently start their participation in the collaboration, or terminate their participation. We consider a global workflow that is composed out of several sub-collaborations which should be executed in a specified order. For sequential execution, strict and weak sequencing have been defined. With strict sequencing all actions of the first sub-collaboration must be completed before the second sub-activity may start. Weak sequencing was introduced for sequencing distributed activities, in particular sequence diagrams, and implies only local sequencing at each system component, but no global sequencing rule. We define the semantics of a collaboration in terms of the partial order among its internal actions, and we also use partial orders to define the semantics of strict and weak sequencing of sub-collaborations. Then we concentrate on the associativity between weak and strict sequencing. Based on the given definitions, it is shown that such associativity is satisfied in most situations, however, its validity depends on certain conditions about the participation of the different system components in the sequenced sub-collaborations and on the question whether they play an initiating or terminating role in these activities. The lack of associativity may lead to ambiguities when the dynamic behavior of complex workflows is developed and specified. These difficulties can be avoided by conventions for priorities between weak or strict sequencing, and/or some appropriate bracketing structure in the workflow notation.

1 Introduction

Execution in sequence is a basic structuring concept in programming languages and also for the definition of the dynamic system behavior in requirements specifications. At the requirement specification level, the behavior of the system is normally specified at a high level of abstraction. This means that the activities that are described as an individual action are relatively large. The **strict** sequencing requirement between two activities, say first A then B, means that activity A must be completely finished before any part of activity B may start. However, such a requirement may be too strong, since some limited form of concurrency may be allowable for performance reasons or for simplifying the design

D. Amyot et al. (Eds.): SAM 2014, LNCS 8769, pp. 96–109, 2014.
© Springer International Publishing Switzerland 2014

of the system. In particular, if the system is to be implemented in a distributed context and some of the activities are performed in collaboration by different system components, the implementation of strict sequencing may require a large number of coordination messages and therefore lead to ineffective implementations.

Lamport pointed out in 1978 [8] that the ordering of events in a distributed system is naturally described by a partial order. This led later to the definition of **weak** sequencing for the sequential execution of two collaborations, each defined by a sequence diagram [9]. The sequence diagrams identify the different system components that participate in the behavior, and weak sequencing means that each component imposes local sequencing, however, no global sequencing is enforced. This leads to some form of concurrency, since one system component may already start with the second collaboration while another component is still involved in the first. The ITU-T Message Sequence Chart notation that Mauw and Reniers described [9] is in most respects interchangeable with UML sequence diagrams, so that in this paper "sequence diagrams" refers to both.

UML allows strict and weak sequencing for defining the order of execution of different sequence diagrams, however, the semantics of UML activity diagrams is geared at strict sequencing of activities. In the context of describing requirements of distributed applications at a high level of abstraction, we have used the term "collaboration" to designate an activity that is performed by several components within a distributed system and where the different components may independently initiate or terminate their involvement in the collaboration [2]. The static aspect of such a "collaboration" can be described by a UML Collaboration. For describing the order in which the different sub-collaborations within a specified system should be executed, we proposed the notation of UML activity diagrams with slightly modified semantics allowing for strict and weak sequencing. Similar notations have also be used for deriving distributed system designs from global descriptions of service requirements [1, 3].

In this context, the requirements engineer may define some system behavior that includes several collaborations between various components which are scheduled in sequence, where some of the sequencing operators are weak and others strict. To our surprise, it turns out that strict and weak sequencing operators are not associative with one another, that is, the behavior of $((A \xrightarrow{s} B) \xrightarrow{w} C)$ is not necessarily equal to $(A \xrightarrow{s} (B \xrightarrow{w} C))$, where A, B and C are collaborations and "$\xrightarrow{w}$" and "$\xrightarrow{s}$" stand for weak and strict sequencing, respectively.

The purpose of this paper is to explore these issues in detail. In Section 2.1, we describe the nature of collaborations in more detail, define the meaning of strict and weak sequencing and give some examples. In Section 2.2, we give a formal meaning to these concepts by using the formalism of partial orders for describing the semantics. This formal definition is the basis for the analysis of the association rules discussed in Section 3.

Section 3 starts by proving that several consecutive weak sequencing operators are associative by showing that $((A \xrightarrow{w} B) \xrightarrow{w} C)$ and $(A \xrightarrow{w} (B \xrightarrow{w} C))$ give rise to the same partial order of events for the different parties involved (and similarly for strong sequencing). Then mixed sequencing, such as $(A \xrightarrow{s} B \xrightarrow{w} C)$ is considered and it is shown that associativity does not hold in general. It turns out that associativity is broken in certain cases depending on which collaborations the different parties are involved in. In addition, this question also depends on whether certain parties play an initiating or terminating role within the first or last collaboration, as explained in detail in Section 3. This means that the notation "$(A \xrightarrow{s} B \xrightarrow{w} C)$" is ambiguous if the associativity is not satisfied. The conclusion points out that a notational convention is needed to avoid such ambiguity either by giving priority to weak or strict sequencing or by using some notation equivalent to bracketing.

The section on related work discusses another sequencing operator, called *layered sequencing*, which imposes certain sequencing constraints in order to avoid conflicts with variables shared among the different sub-collaborations. Algebraic properties have been defined when this sequencing operator is combined with concurrency.

2   System Design with Collaborations and Partial Orders

2.1   Using Collaborations and Roles for Structuring Global Behaviors

For describing the structural as well as the behavioral aspects of complex activities in a hierarchical manner that allows the description of an activity in terms of its sub-activities and further its sub-sub-activities, we proposed in [2] a notation that combines the UML Collaborations for structural aspects with a variation of UML activity diagrams for the description of the behavior of an activity by describing the order in which its sub-activities would be executed. We note that UML allows already that several roles are involved in a single activity. However, we introduce three important modifications to the semantics of UML:

1. Within a given instance of an activity, several roles may independently start their sub-activities (often due to independent incoming data flows). We call these roles **initiating** roles and their starting sub-activities **initial** sub-activities. (Note that UML requires that all initial sub-activities of an activity be initiated simultaneously, which may be unrealistic if the activity is performed within a distributed system).
2. Within a given instance of an activity, several roles may independently terminate their sub-activities (which means that their output can be produced in any order). We call these roles **terminating** roles and their ending sub-activities **terminal** sub-activities. (Note that UML requires that all outputs of sub-activities be generated simultaneously which, again, is unrealistic if the activity is performed within a distributed system).
3. Besides the usual sequencing operators of activity diagrams, namely (strict) sequence, alternatives, concurrency and loops, we also allow for weak sequencing.

In the following, we call activities with this semantics "collaborations". An example of a collaboration with its sub-collaborations is shown in Fig. 1(a). The roles are indicated by the vertical lines, collaborations are represented by ovals, and local activities performed by a single role are represented as small circles. We show for each role the first and last sub-activity in which the role is involved and possibly some other local activities. The initial and terminal sub-activities are indicated by a dark circles. The basic ordering relationships between the sub-activities are indicated by dotted arrows. We see that the starting activity of *role-2* has to wait for the completion of the starting activity of *role-1* (the former is not initiating). The collaboration A shown in the figure has a sub-collaboration, called B, which has one initial and one terminal sub-activity. The diagram shows that the terminal sub-activity of *role-1* has to wait for the completion of the last sub-activity of *role-2* (because the latter is not terminal in collaboration B).

There is some similarity between our notation for collaborations and sequence diagrams. The sequence diagram of Fig. 1(b) represents the same ordering relationships as Fig. 1(a). However, it highlights exchanged messages and does not explicitly show the local sub-activities.

In many situations, we want to make abstraction from the inner workings of a collaboration. In that case, we only represent the starting and ending sub-activities and indicate whether they are initial or terminal, respectively, as shown in Fig. 1(c).

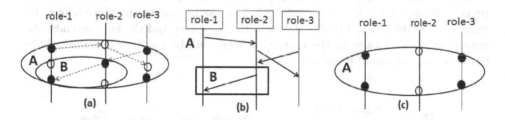

Fig. 1. (a) Example of a collaboration (dark circles are initial or terminal sub-activities); (b) corresponding sequence diagram; (c) abstracted view

For defining the sequential execution of two collaborations A and B, two important sequencing operators have been defined: strict (or strong) sequencing and weak sequencing. We note that the definition of weak sequencing requires the distinction of the different roles (or system components) that participate in the realization of the collaborations. In the case of sequence diagrams, these roles are the vertical "lifelines", and in UML activity diagrams, these are the swimlanes. Weak sequencing is the natural concept for sequencing of sequence diagrams and was introduced for the composition in Hierarchical Message Sequence Charts (H-MSC) [9] and was later included in UML.

These sequencing concepts can be defined as follows:

Strict Sequence: We write $(A \xrightarrow{s} B)$ to state that B is executed strictly after A, which means that all sub-activities of A must be completed before any sub-activity of B may start. This is, in a sense, the default meaning of "sequencing".

Weak Sequence: We write $(A \xrightarrow{w} B)$ to state that B is weakly sequenced after A, which means that each role participating in A must complete all the sub-activities of A in which it is involved before it may get involved in any sub-activity of B. This means that there is a local strict order enforced for each role, but no global ordering.

We give in the following a few examples of workflow activities that will be used for demonstration throughout the paper. The activity shown in Fig. 2(a) represents a construction project, where a product is built by a team and the project leader, and then delivered to the client after it has been checked out by the project leader. When the building of the product is completed, the team will also perform a clean-up of the workshop. The sequencing (strict or weak) between the different activities and sub-activities is indicated by annotated arrows (**s** stands for strict, **w** for weak sequencing). The roles are indicated by vertical lines, similarly as in sequence diagrams. We note that the *clean-up* can be performed concurrently with the *check* activity because they are performed by different roles and they are weakly sequenced.

The activity in Fig. 2(b) represents the organization of a concert for the king (an imagined process from the Middle Ages) where the king contracts an artist to prepare and produce a concert for the king and his court. The artist has to prepare himself for the concert, and a helper has to reserve the place where the concert will take place. Finally, the concert takes place and the king attends. We note that in this example, the activity *reserve* can be performed quite early in the process because of weak sequencing.

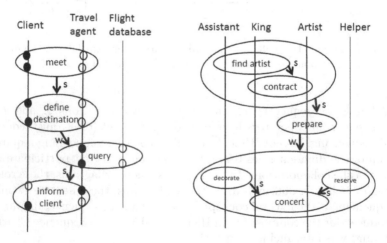

Fig. 2. (a) A construction project; (b) The king's concert

2.2   Defining Sequencing Operators Using Partial Orders

In his paper from 1978 [8], Lamport pointed out that partial orders are useful for understanding the meaning of sequence diagrams. In particular, he noted that two events are ordered in time if and only if this order can be derived from the basic ordering relationships of certain events. In the case of a sequence diagram, the basic ordering relationships are two-fold: (1) the reception of a message occurs after the sending of that message, and (2) an event on a vertical line (representing the actions of a single role) occurs after all events on that same line that lie above (at locally earlier times).

For a single activity, as shown in Fig. 1, we have a partial order for the execution of the sub-activities based on the following basic ordering relationship:

1. The sub-activities of a given role are executed in the given local order.
2. Basic ordering relationships between sub-activities of different roles are explicitly indicated by a dotted arrow and/or implied by the designation of certain local sub-activities as initial or terminal sub-activities.
3. Additional ordering relationships are implied by the transitivity rule of partial orders. For instance, the second action of *role-3* will be after the initial action of *role-1*.

It is important to note that we can give a formal definition of the initiating and terminating roles of a collaboration based on the partial order of its sub-activities.

Definition 1: Given a collaboration and the partial order among its sub-activities, a role r is **initializing (terminating)** if the first (last) sub-activity X of r is a minimal (maximal) element of the partial order, that is, there is no other sub-activity B in the collaboration that is earlier (later) in the partial order than X.

We will see that the initiating and terminating roles have a specific role to play in the definition of strict sequencing. Therefore, we often represent a collaboration abstractly as shown in Fig. 1(c), ignoring the internal sub-activities and the internal partial order of the collaboration, and representing only the first and last sub-activities of each role, and also indicating whether they are initial or terminal.

The concept of partial orders can also be used for defining strict and weak sequencing for collaborations, as proposed in [5,6]. Figures 3(a) and 3(b), adapted from [4], show the semantics of strict and weak sequencing, respectively. These diagrams show the general case where the collaborations A and B involve different subsets of roles - the roles with index A (B) are only involved in collaboration A (B), and the roles with index AB are involved in both collaborations. For the definition of the strong sequence, a virtual event (called **e** in the figure) is introduced which represents the moment when all sub-activities of A have been executed and the execution of B has not yet started. The representation of weak sequencing is straightforward.

For the implementation of complex workflows in a distributed environment, it is often useful to start out with a specification of the global system behavior

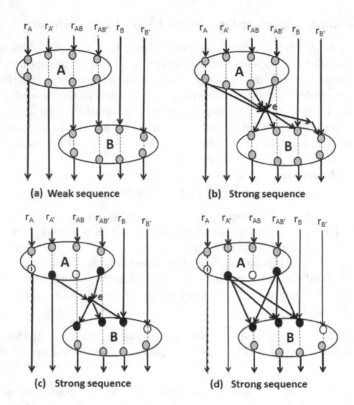

Fig. 3. Definition of sequencing through partial orders: (a) weak sequencing; (b) strict sequencing; (c) strict sequencing under consideration of initial and terminal sub-activities; (d) coordination messages for strict sequencing

in terms of the ordering of sub-activities and the involved roles, and later to allocate these roles to specific distributed system components and then derive the behavior of these system components, including their exchange of messages for the coordination of the global actions, from the given global system behavior. The difficulties in the design of these system components due to possible race conditions between the exchanged coordination messages was discussed in [2], and a derivation algorithm allowing for strict and weak sequencing is described in [1]. The coordination messages are required for imposing certain partial order relationships among the sub-activities that are implemented in the different components of the distributed system.

From the definition of weak sequencing shown in Fig. 3(a), it is clear that no coordination messages are required between the different roles, since only local ordering is imposed.

The definition of strict sequencing, as shown in Fig. 3(b) can be simplified when it is known which roles of A are terminating and which roles of B are initiating. It is easy to see that the simplified definition of Fig. 3(c) defines the same partial order as the one defined in Fig. 3(b). This can be seen as follows: For each last sub-activity x of A that is not terminal, there is an ordering relationship implied by transitivity to the event **e** because there is an ordering relationship from x to one of the terminal sub-activities of A (otherwise x would itself be terminal).

Coordination messages for strict sequencing of complex behaviors were first introduced in [3]. These messages correspond to the thick arrows in Fig. 3(d). It is clear that the ordering relationship between the terminating sub-activities of A and the initiating sub-activities of B is the same in Figs. 3(c) and 3(d), although Fig. 3(d) does not contain the artificial event **e**. These considerations provide a simple proof that the coordination messages introduced in [3] realize the definition of strict sequencing presented in Fig. 3(b).

3 Association Rules

3.1 Associativity of Strict and Weak Sequencing

Lemma: Weak (strict) sequencing is associative, which means that for three given activities A, B and C, we have $((A \rightarrow B) \rightarrow C) = (A \rightarrow (B \rightarrow C))$, where "$\rightarrow$" stands for "$\xrightarrow{w}$" ("$\xrightarrow{s}$").

In the following, we use the partial order sequencing definitions given in Section 2.2 in order to show that this lemma is indeed true. In order to decide this question, we consider the partial orders between the sub-activities of the three activities A, B and C implied by the two behavior expressions, and we say that the two behaviors are equal if and only if the corresponding partial orders are the same.

The partial orders implied by the expressions $((A \rightarrow B) \rightarrow C)$ and $(A \rightarrow (B \rightarrow C))$ are shown in Fig. 4, on the left for weak sequencing and on the right for strong sequencing. These diagrams are derived from the partial order definitions of Figs. 3(a) and 3(b), respectively. In these diagrams, a vertical line R_X represents all roles that are only involved in activity X ($X = A$, B or C), a line R_{XY} represents all roles that are involved in activities X and Y (but not the third activity), and R_{XYZ} represents all roles that are involved in all three activities.

Concerning the partial order defined for weak sequencing, the behaviors $((A \xrightarrow{w} B) \xrightarrow{w} C)$ and $(A \xrightarrow{w} (B \xrightarrow{w} C))$ give rise to the same partial order shown in Fig. 4 (on the left). Therefore these two behaviors are the same.

The corresponding expression $((A \xrightarrow{s} B) \xrightarrow{s} C)$ with strict sequencing gives rise to the partial order shown in Fig. 4 (on the right) including the dashed dependencies, but excluding the dotted dependencies. We note, however, that the dashed dependencies are redundant since they are implied by the other dependencies shown as full arrows. For instance, the dependency from the last sub-activity of A for the roles R_A to the synchronization event **e2** is already implied by the following dependencies: (1) from the last sub-activity of A for the roles R_A to the synchronization event **e1**, (2) from that event to the first sub-activity of B for the roles R_{AB} , (3) from that sub-activity to the last sub-activity

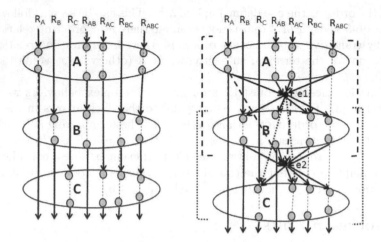

Fig. 4. Associativity of (a) weak and (b) strict sequencing

in B of those roles, and (4) from that sub-activity to the synchronization point **e2**. Therefore these dashed dependencies do not change the partial order, and they can be dropped. Similarly, we obtain for the behavior $(A \xrightarrow{s} (B \xrightarrow{s} C))$ the partial order shown in Fig. 4(b) including the dotted dependencies, but excluding the dashed dependencies. Again, the dotted dependencies are redundant and can be dropped. Therefore, we obtain the same partial order for both behaviors.

3.2   Association between Strong and Weak Sequencing

The situation is not so simple when we combine strict and weak sequencing within one expression. We ask in particular the following question: Is the behavior of $((A \xrightarrow{s} B) \xrightarrow{w} C)$ equal to the behavior $(A \xrightarrow{s} (B \xrightarrow{w} C))$? Again, we use the partial orders implied by these expressions to decide whether they represent the same behavior. The partial orders implied by these two expressions are shown in Fig. 5 using the same conventions as in Fig. 4. We see that these two partial orders are the same except that the behavior $(A \xrightarrow{s} (B \xrightarrow{w} C))$ has two additional dependencies (shown as dotted arrows in the figure):

1. **Additional Dependency for R_C:** The roles only involved in C have to wait for all roles to have completed activity A. In the case of $((A \xrightarrow{s} B) \xrightarrow{w} C)$, they can start immediately.
2. **Additional Dependency for R_{AC}:** The roles involved in A and C (but not in B) have to wait for all roles to have completed activity A. In the case of $((A \xrightarrow{s} B) \xrightarrow{w} C)$, they only have to wait that they have completed A themselves (weak sequencing).

As an example we consider the workflow of the Kings Concert shown in Fig. 2(b). It can be represented by the expression (*find-artist* $\xrightarrow{s}$ *contract*) $\xrightarrow{s}$

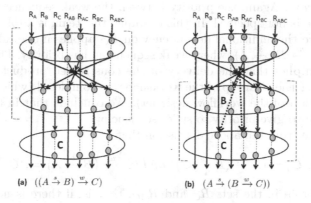

(a) $((A \xrightarrow{s} B) \xrightarrow{w} C)$ (b) $(A \xrightarrow{s} (B \xrightarrow{w} C))$

Fig. 5. Partial orders implied by two expressions

$prepare \xrightarrow{w} ((decorate \parallel reserve) \xrightarrow{s} concert)$ or by $(A \xrightarrow{s} B \xrightarrow{w} C)$ where $A = (find-artist \xrightarrow{s} contract)$, $B = prepare$, and $C = ((decorate \parallel reserve) \xrightarrow{s} concert)$. The diagram of Fig. 2(b) does not indicate in which order the strict and weak sequencing operators between A, B and C should be applied. If we give priority to the strict sequence, that is, we take the interpretation $((A \xrightarrow{s} B) \xrightarrow{w} C)$, then the assistant can start with the decoration as soon as he has found the artist, and the helper can reserve the place of the concert even before the artist has been identified. However, if we give priority to weak sequencing, that is, we take the interpretation $(A \xrightarrow{s} (B \xrightarrow{w} C))$, the additional dependencies for R_C and R_{AC} apply, and the decoration and reservation actions can only be started when the contract has been signed.

We now consider the case that the order of strict and weak sequencing is exchanged, that is, we consider the situation where weak sequencing is followed by strict sequencing. We note that the definitions of weak and strict sequencing given by Fig. 3 are symmetric in respect to the reversal of time. If we reverse the time we have simply to consider the arrows in the opposite direction. We also note that the expressions $(A \xrightarrow{s} B \xrightarrow{w} C)$ under time reversal becomes $(C \xrightarrow{w} B \xrightarrow{s} A)$. Therefore we can use the diagrams of Fig. 5 to determine whether the behavior of $(C \xrightarrow{w} (B \xrightarrow{s} A))$ is equal to the behavior $((C \xrightarrow{w} B) \xrightarrow{s} A)$. Similar to above, we see that $((C \xrightarrow{w} B) \xrightarrow{s} A)$ imposes two additional constraints, namely:

1. **Additional Dependency on R_C:** All sub-activities of A can only start after the last sub-activities in C by the roles R_C have completed. In the case of $(C \xrightarrow{w} (B \xrightarrow{s} A))$, there is no such dependency.
2. **Additional Dependency on R_{AC}:** All sub-activities of A can only start after the last sub-activities in C by the roles R_{AC} have completed. In the case of $(C \xrightarrow{w} (B \xrightarrow{s} A))$, the roles R_{AC} may start with activity A as soon as they have completed their sub-activities of C.

As an example, we may consider the construction project shown in Fig. 2(a). Its behavior may be represented by the expression $((build \xrightarrow{s} clean-up) \xrightarrow{w}$

check $\xrightarrow{s}$ *deliver*). Again, the priority between the weak sequence and the later strict sequence is not specified. In this example, the Team is a role belonging to R_C. Therefore the additional dependency on R_C applies if one takes the interpretation $((C \xrightarrow{w} B) \xrightarrow{s} A)$, where weak sequencing has priority. This additional dependency implies that the delivery of the constructed product can only be performed after the clean-up of the workshop was completed (which is probably not the intention of the workflow designer). We conclude that in this example, it is preferable to give priority to strict sequencing.

We conclude from the above discussion that

$$((A \xrightarrow{s} B) \xrightarrow{w} C) = (A \xrightarrow{s} (B \xrightarrow{w} C)) \ and \ (C \xrightarrow{w} (B \xrightarrow{s} A)) = ((C \xrightarrow{w} B) \xrightarrow{s} A)$$

if there is no role in the sets R_C and R_{AC}, that is, if there is no role that is involved in C and not involved in B.

However, this is not a necessary condition, as shown by the example of Fig. 6. Let us consider here the first three activities: (*meet* $\xrightarrow{s}$ *define-destination* $\xrightarrow{w}$ *query*). The Flight-database belongs to the roles R_C. Therefore the "additional dependency for R_C" would apply if we assume that weak sequencing has priority. However, this dependency is redundant in this example, since the Flight-database has no initiating role, but must wait for the query activity to be initiated by the Travel-agent. Therefore the "additional dependency for R_C" would not introduce any additional ordering constraint and therefore we obtain the same partial order whether we assume priority for weak or strict sequencing.

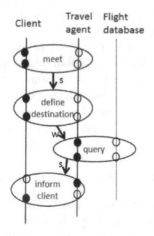

Fig. 6. Example: workflow for a travel agency

This example indicates how we can obtain an "if an only if" condition for associativity of weak and strict sequencing. We note that each arrow to the event **e** in Fig. 5 actually represents a set of order relationships, one for each role in the set R_X from where the arrow comes, and similarly each arrow from **e** represents a set of "arrows", one for each role in the set pointed to by the arrow.

If we use the strict sequencing definition of Fig. 3(c) (instead of Fig. 3(b)) in the construction of the diagrams of Fig. 5, then we retain among the "arrows" that enter **e** only those that come from a terminating role of A, and among the "arrows" that leave **e**, we only retain those that lead to an initializing role of B or C.

In particular, among the dotted arrows leaving **e** (which are of particular interest), we would only retain those that lead to initializing roles of C. This observation leads to the following proposition:

Proposition 1: The expressions $((A \xrightarrow{s} B) \xrightarrow{w} C)$ and $(A \xrightarrow{s} (B \xrightarrow{w} C))$ define the same behavior if and only if each initiating role of C is involved in B.

By considering the same situation with reversed direction of time (as discussed above), we obtain the following:

Proposition 2: The expressions $((C \xrightarrow{w} B) \xrightarrow{s} A)$ and $(C \xrightarrow{w} (B \xrightarrow{s} A))$ define the same behavior if and only if each terminating role of C is involved in B.

4   Related Work

Other algebraic laws, besides rules like associativity in the form $((A \xrightarrow{s} B) \xrightarrow{w} C) = (A \xrightarrow{s} (B \xrightarrow{w} C))$, have been discussed in other contexts with different sequencing operators. For instance, Olderog [10] considers the following operators:

Concurrency: This means there is no sequencing; the two activities are executed concurrently, independently from one another. We write $(A \parallel B)$ for the concurrent execution of two activities A and B.

Layered Sequence: In order to define this concept, one needs another extension of the model of "collaborations". In this case, one assumes that the sub-activities of a collaboration communicate through shared global variables that can be read or updated. We write $(A \xrightarrow{l} B)$ to state that B is executed in layered sequence after A, which means [10] that A and B are executed concurrently, except that a sub-activity of B which uses certain global variables can only be executed when all updates and read usages of these variables by A have already been completed.

It is interesting to note that layered sequencing can be used to model weak sequencing [11]. The weak sequence $(A \xrightarrow{w} B)$ can be modeled by $(A \xrightarrow{l} B)$ if one assumes that for each role associated with A or B (according to the weak sequence), there is a global variable used to define the layered sequence, and each sub-activity of A or of B that involves a given role will update or read the global variable associated with this role. Then the execution orders of the sub-activities of A and B allowed by weak sequencing are exactly the same as those allowed according to the corresponding layered sequencing.

In [10], the following so-called "communication closed layer" law is proven: Given four collaborations $A1$, $A2$, $B1$ and $B2$ with the property that $A1$ and $B2$ have no common global variable, and $B1$ and $A2$ have no common global variable, then the following two behaviors are equivalent:

$$(A1 \xrightarrow{l} A2) \parallel (B1 \xrightarrow{l} B2) = (A1 \parallel B1) \xrightarrow{l} (A2 \parallel B2)$$

Using the modeling of weak sequencing through layered sequencing mentioned above, we obtain a similar property for weak sequencing:

Lemma: Given four collaborations $A1$, $A2$, $B1$ and $B2$ with the property that $A1$ and $B2$ have no common role and $B1$ and $A2$ have no common role, the following two behavior definitions are equivalent:

$$(A1 \xrightarrow{w} A2) \parallel (B1 \xrightarrow{w} B2) = (A1 \parallel B1) \xrightarrow{w} (A2 \parallel B2)$$

Using this lemma with empty behavior for $A2$ and $B1$, we obtain $(A1 \parallel B2) = (A1 \xrightarrow{w} B2)$ if $A1$ and $B2$ have no common role (which is well known).

5   Summary and Conclusions

Strict and weak sequencing are two different sequencing concepts supported in UML. While the sequence of two activities A and B with strict sequencing means that all sub-activities of A must be completed before any sub-activity of B may start, weak sequencing allows for more concurrency in a distributed environment. With weak sequencing, the order is enforced only locally for each role participating in these activities, but not in the global context.

We have shown that the meaning of a workflow may be ambiguous if it contains several sequencing operators in sequence, some weak and some strong. The above two propositions define exactly under which conditions such ambiguity does not occur.

We have discussed these issues using a formal definition of weak and strong sequencing based on the partial order of the events that define the execution, by the different roles, of the different sub-activities included in the sequenced activities. In this context, it is also important to consider which roles are initiating and terminating for a given activity. We recall that a role is initiating (terminating) if its first (last) sub-activity in the collaboration is not preceded (followed) by another sub-activity of the same collaboration.

In order to resolve the ambiguity, if it arises in the specification of some workflow, one could adopt one of the following schemes:

1. Define a default priority between strict and weak sequencing. It is not clear whether weak or strict sequencing should obtain higher priority. Laamarti [7] suggested weak; our current intuition goes towards strict sequencing.
2. Use parenthesis to indicate the order in which the sequencing operations should be applied (as done in the text discussing the examples above). However, often graphical notations are used to define the workflows, and it is not clear how best to include parenthesis structures in graphical notations. In UML activity diagrams, the notation of regions may be used, or the region of a parenthesis may be represented as a separate abstract activity.

We note that it may be interesting to consider other algebraic properties involving the different sequencing operators considered in this paper, in particular the associativity between strong sequencing and layered sequencing.

Acknowledgements. I would like to thank Fedwa Laamarti for pointing out for the first time that weak sequencing does not always associate with strict sequencing. I would also like to thank Toqeer Israr for many discussions on the formalization of the semantics of weak and strong sequencing, and for useful comments on the draft of this paper. Finally, I would like to thank Ernst-Rüdiger Olderog and Mani Swaminathan from the University of Oldenburg for interesting discussions on layered sequencing.

References

1. Bochmann, G.V.: Deriving component designs from global requirements. In: Baelen, S.V., Graf, S., Filali, M., Weigert, T., Gérard, S. (eds.) Proceedings of the First International Workshop on Model Based Architecting and Construction of Embedded Systems (ACES-MB 2008). CEUR Workshop Proceedings, vol. 503, pp. 55–69 (2008)
2. Castejón, H., von Bochmann, G., Bræk, R.: On the realizability of collaborative services. Software & Systems Modeling 12(3), 597–617 (2013)
3. Gotzhein, R., Bochmann, G.V.: Deriving protocol specifications from service specifications including parameters. ACM Trans. Comput. Syst. 8(4), 255–283 (1990)
4. Israr, T.: Modeling and Performance Analysis of Distributed Services with Collaboration Behaviour Diagrams. Ph.D. thesis, EECS - University of Ottawa (2014)
5. Israr, T., Bochmann, G.V.: Performance modeling of distributed collaboration services. In: Kounev, S., Cortellessa, V., Mirandola, R., Lilja, D.J. (eds.) ICPE 2011, pp. 475–480. ACM Press (2011)
6. Israr, T., von Bochmann, G.: Performance modeling of distributed collaboration services with independent inputs/outpus. In: Bernardi, S., Boskovic, M., Merseguer, J. (eds.) NiM-ALP@MoDELS. CEUR Workshop Proceedings, vol. 1074, pp. 16–23. CEUR-WS.org (2013)
7. Laamarti, F.: Derivation of component designs from a global specification. Master's thesis, EECS - University of Ottawa (2010)
8. Lamport, L.: Time, clocks, and the ordering of events in a distributed system. Commun. ACM 21(7), 558–565 (1978)
9. Mauw, S., Reniers, M.: High-level message sequence charts. In: Cavalli, A., Sarma, A. (eds.) SDL 1997: Time for Testing - SDL, MSC and Trends, pp. 291–306. Elsevier Science B.V. (1997)
10. Olderog, E.-R., Swaminathan, M.: Structural transformations for data-enriched real-time systems. In: Johnsen, E.B., Petre, L. (eds.) IFM 2013. LNCS, vol. 7940, pp. 378–393. Springer, Heidelberg (2013)
11. Swaminathan, M.: Private communication (2013)

Efficient Representation of Timed UML 2 Interactions

Alexander Knapp[1] and Harald Störrle[2]

[1] Universität Augsburg, Germany
knapp@informatik.uni-augsburg.de
[2] Danmarks Tekniske Universitet, Denmark
hsto@dtu.dk

Abstract. UML 2 interactions describe system behavior over time in a declarative way. The standard approach to defining their formal semantics enumerates traces of events; other representation formats, like Büchi automata or prime event structures, have been suggested, too. We describe another, more succinct format, interaction structures, which is based on asymmetric event structures. It simplifies the integration of real time, and complex operators like alt and break, and leads to an efficient semantic representation of interactions. We provide the formalism, and a prototypical implementation highlighting the benefits of our approach.

1 Introduction

Among the many languages defined in UML 2, interactions are among the most widely used [2,3]. They describe system behavior over time in a declarative way, focusing on the message exchange between instances. Thus, interactions are well-suited to specify temporal constraints. A sample UML 2 interaction is shown in Fig. 1 below.

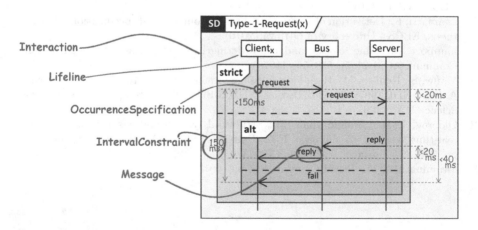

Fig. 1. A first example of a UML 2 interaction. Time constraints are highlighted in red, explanations of UML concepts are shown blue.

Equipped with a suitable formal semantics, UML 2 interactions can be used for rigorous analysis of system specifications, in particular, checking the consistency between

D. Amyot et al. (Eds.): SAM 2014, LNCS 8769, pp. 110–125, 2014.

different parts of a specification. In the context of run-time verification and online checking, it is particularly interesting whether a given interaction specifying a system's behavior is temporally sound. More precisely, are the temporal constraints logically consistent? Do they hold for a given trace? Do they hold for all traces?

Existing formal semantics for UML 2 interactions such as [14] already allow to answer such questions, though only in theory: simply compute the set of all traces and check for emptiness of the set (logical consistency) or inclusion of the target trace. So, clearly, we can decide the above consistency questions for all finite traces in principle. However, due to the existence of interaction operators like par, the number of traces is exponential in the size of the interaction, so we would have to enumerate a very large set of traces before we can answer the questions raised above. Clearly, this approach is of little practical value.

Unfortunately, all existing semantics that include real time and the interaction operators (which distinguish UML 2 from UML 1 interactions) suffer from this limitation (or use an exponentially sized semantic representation of the interaction to begin with). In contrast, the approach presented in this paper introduces a novel semantic representation that represents the set of all traces of an interaction in a format that grows linearly in the size of the underlying interaction. It allows to check whether a concrete run complies with an interaction and its temporal constraints, and it can be implemented efficiently, with very modest effort. This is reminiscent of the way binary decision diagrams (BDDs) improved model checking of propositional logic formulas.

Synopsis. After discussing related work in Sect. 2, we summarize the sub-language of UML 2 interactions that we consider in Sect. 3. Our format of symbolic representations of these interactions is introduced in Sect. 4, where we also discuss the resulting traces and the translation of UML 2 interactions into a symbolic representation. In Sect. 5, we give an overview of our prototypical implementation and its performance. We conclude and discuss future work in Sect. 6.

2 Related Work

A comprehensive survey of UML 2 interaction semantics is found in [9]. Among other things, the transition from UML 1 to UML 2 introduced a novel semantics for interactions, which is why the first investigations of UML 2 interactions [14,13] focused on understanding and interpreting the standard document. Since the UML specification informally suggests that the meaning of interactions are sets of sequences of so-called "interaction occurrences", this is what the first semantics defined formally.

While this point of view was well-suited to understand and formalize the prose specification of UML 2, it is less-well suited for the analysis of interactions and their possible traces, since interactions give rise to an exponential number of traces. The same problem is encountered by approaches using an automata-based representation (e.g., [7]), as they need to encode traces in states, which again leads to an exponential number of states. The declarative representation we propose in this paper, on the other hand, encodes UML 2 interaction as sets of constraints whose size is linear in the size of the interaction. Furthermore, it allows to include real-time annotations seamlessly. It is suitable for checking whether a given trace of time-stamped events is a valid trace according to the interaction without having to compute all its possible traces.

An approach similar to ours has first been pursued by Küster-Filipe [8]. While Küster-Filipe employed prime event structures, we propose to use a format inspired by asymmetric event structures [1], which yields a more compact symbolic representation by avoiding duplications that are required when using prime event structures. At the same time, asymmetric event structures also allow us to integrate UML 2's break operator for breaking scenarios, an important practical scenario not covered by Küster-Filipe.

There is a rich body of work on timed Message Sequence Diagrams and timed UML 1 interactions, but there are only three approaches to study timed UML 2 interactions according to [9]. None of these has been implemented; in contrast, we do present a prototypical implementation for checking the conformance of timed traces w.r.t. an interaction, and discuss its performance.

There have also been other approaches that focus on different aspects of interactions. For model checking against the automaton-based specification format of UML 2 state machines, a representation of an interaction as an additional observer Büchi automaton is a closer fit [7]; also, the relation of interactions to safety and liveness properties can be expressed when using Büchi automata [4]. For testing, a representation as a structured composite graph makes the decision structure more transparent, which can be used to derive test data [10]. For studying the concurrency inherent in an interaction, the use of (prime) event structures, a denotational framework for true concurrency, [8] or lattices [5] turned out to be fruitful.

3   UML 2 Interactions

The main building block is the basic interaction, which represents orderings of so-called "occurrence specifications" directly, as a partial order. An occurrence specification captures that an event (like the sending or receiving of a message) happens on an instance partaking in the interaction; the ordering relations define the sequences in which these events may happen. Basic interactions form an "interaction fragment" that may be combined by the "interaction operators" strict (strict sequential composition), seq (lifeline-wise sequential composition), par (parallel composition), alt (alternative composition), break (aborting composition), and ref (including a named interaction). Additionally, all fragments may be equipped with timing constraints. For later reuse by ref, interaction fragments can be given a name.

We assume three primitive, finite domains for *instances* $\mathcal{I}$, *messages* $\mathcal{M}$, and interaction *names* $\mathcal{N}$. We always assume that all identifiers of occurrence specifications are globally unique. An *occurrence specification* is of the form $o : \tau$, where o is the identifier of the occurrence specification and τ is its *type*. The type of an occurrence specification is of one of the forms $\mathrm{SND}(s, r, m)$ or $\mathrm{RCV}(s, r, m)$, representing the dispatch and the arrival of message m from *sender* instance s to *receiver* instance r, respectively. The set $\mathcal{O}$ comprises all occurrence specifications over $\mathcal{I}$ and $\mathcal{M}$. For an $o : \tau \in \mathcal{O}$, we write $\tau(o)$ for τ.

A *basic interaction* B is given by a directed acyclic graph $(O, \rightarrow)$ with $O \neq \emptyset$ and $O \subseteq \mathcal{O}$ a finite, non-empty set of occurrence specifications such that the identifiers of the occurrence specifications in O are all different, and $\to\ \subseteq\ O \times O$ such that the reflexive-transitive closure of $\to$ on O forms a partial order. The abstract syntax of our fragment of UML 2 interactions is given by the grammar in Fig. 2.

$$
\begin{aligned}
TimingConstraint \ni \Gamma &::= o_2 - o_1 \bowtie d \mid \ell \bowtie d \\
&\mid\ \text{true} \mid \Gamma_1 \wedge \Gamma_2 \mid \Gamma_1 \vee \Gamma_2 \\
Interaction \ni I &::= \text{sd}(name,\, T) \\
InteractionFragment \ni T &::= B \mid CF \mid \text{tmconstr}(T, \Gamma) \\
CombinedFragment \ni CF &::= \text{strict}(T_1, T_2) \mid \text{seq}(T_1, T_2) \mid \text{par}(T_1, T_2) \\
&\mid\ \text{alt}(T_1, T_2) \mid \text{break}(T_1, T_2) \mid \text{ref}(name)
\end{aligned}
$$

Fig. 2. Abstract syntax of timed interactions: $o_1, o_2 \in \mathcal{O}$, $\bowtie \in \{<, \leq, \geq, >\}$, and $d \in \mathbb{Q}_{\geq 0}$; B ranges over the basic interactions, *name* over the interaction names $\mathcal{N}$

For expressing timing constraints, we use clauses of the form Γ specified in Fig. 2. Intuitively, a timing constraint $o_2 - o_1 \bowtie d$ means that the difference in time between any occurrence of an event conforming to o_2 and any event conforming to o_1 is bounded by d w.r.t. to the relation $\bowtie$. A timing constraint $\ell \bowtie d$ means that the duration of the interaction fragment to which this timing constraint is attached is bounded by d w.r.t. to $\bowtie$. Furthermore, true represents the timing constraint that is always true, and $\Gamma_1 \wedge \Gamma_2$ and $\Gamma_1 \vee \Gamma_2$ respectively mean the conjunctive and disjunctive combination of the timing constraints Γ_1 and Γ_2. Though we have restricted ourselves to binary relations over occurrence specifications, this language can be extended easily for correlating an arbitrary number of occurrence specifications.

Example 1. Consider the following UML 2 interaction diagram:

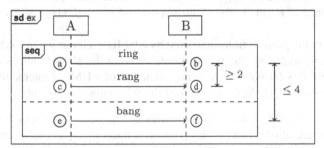

In the abstract syntax, this is represented by $\text{sd}(\text{ex}, \text{tmconstr}(\text{seq}(\text{tmconstr}(\mathsf{B}_1, \mathsf{T}_1), \mathsf{B}_2), \mathsf{T}_2))$ with basic interaction B_1 and B_2, and timing constraints T_1 and T_2 given by

$$
\begin{aligned}
\mathsf{B}_1 =\ &(\{\text{\textcircled{a}} : \text{SND}(A, B, \text{ring}), \text{\textcircled{b}} : \text{RCV}(A, B, \text{ring}), \\
&\ \ \text{\textcircled{c}} : \text{SND}(A, B, \text{rang}), \text{\textcircled{d}} : \text{RCV}(A, B, \text{rang})\}, \\
&\ \{\text{\textcircled{a}} \to \text{\textcircled{b}}, \text{\textcircled{c}} \to \text{\textcircled{d}}, \text{\textcircled{a}} \to \text{\textcircled{c}}, \text{\textcircled{b}} \to \text{\textcircled{d}}\}), \\
\mathsf{B}_2 =\ &(\{\text{\textcircled{e}} : \text{SND}(A, B, \text{bang}), \text{\textcircled{f}} : \text{RCV}(A, B, \text{bang})\}, \{\text{\textcircled{e}} \to \text{\textcircled{f}}\}), \\
\mathsf{T}_1 =\ &\text{\textcircled{d}} - \text{\textcircled{b}} \geq 2, \\
\mathsf{T}_2 =\ &\text{\textcircled{d}} - \text{\textcircled{b}} \leq 4.
\end{aligned}
$$

$\square$

The language of interactions can be extended by introducing syntactical abbreviations like, e.g., a finite upper-bounded $\mathsf{loop}(k, T)$ setting

$\mathsf{loop}(1, T) \equiv T$

$\mathsf{loop}(k + 1, T) \equiv \mathsf{alt}(T, \mathsf{seq}(T\rho_1, \mathsf{loop}(k, T\rho_2)))$

where the renamings ρ_1 with $\rho_1(o) = \mathsf{seq}.o$ and ρ_2 with $\rho_2(o) = \mathsf{loop}.o$, written in postfix notation, introduce consistently new names for the occurrence specifications of T.

4   Symbolic Representation of UML 2 Interactions

According to the UML 2 standard, (timed) UML 2 interactions describe "emergent behavior" [12], i.e., UML 2 interactions can be considered to specify which traces of events are allowed (or disallowed) to be observed from an implemented system. The occurrence specifications of a UML 2 interaction express the possible events. On the one hand, the orderings of these occurrence specifications, be they directly given by a basic interaction, or be they expressed by the interaction operators strict, seq, or par, restrict the possible sequences of events. On the other hand, compositions of interaction fragments via alt and break specify choices between different sequences. Usages of ref merely correspond to macro expansions. Finally, the timing constraints restrict timing distances between events for the occurrence specifications.

Formally, a (timed) *event* $e = \langle \tau, t \rangle$ consists of two parts: the type τ of an occurrence specification, saying whether it is a sending or receiving event, for which message, and between which instances; and the time point $t \in \mathbb{R}_{\geq 0}$ at which it occurs. We write $\tau(e)$ for τ, and $t(e)$ for t. We say that an event e *conforms to* an occurrence specification o, if $\tau(e) = \tau(o)$. A sequence of events $e_1 e_2 \ldots e_k$ is a *trace* if $t(e_1) \leq t(e_2) \leq \ldots \leq t(e_k)$.

We now want to capture the prescriptions mandated by a UML 2 interaction in a symbolic format that succinctly expresses the requirements on what the allowed traces of (timed) events are. We call this format an *interaction structure* of a UML 2 interaction. Such an interaction structure (O, R, X, Θ) consists of the following components:

- a finite set of occurrence specifications O; it specifies all the occurrence specifications for which events are allowed to be observed: in a trace $e_1 \ldots e_k$, all events e_i have to conform to one of the occurrence specifications in O. However, there may be several choices for conformance and we have to provide an injective map $\lambda : \{e_1, \ldots, e_k\} \to O$ with $\tau(e) = \tau(\lambda(e))$ for all $e \in \{e_1, \ldots, e_k\}$ in order to fix which event represents which occurrence specification.
- a binary relation $R \subseteq O \times O$ specifying a *causality relation* over O, i.e., a partial ordering on O. This relation says in which order the events conforming to O are allowed to occur, if they occur at all: if for a trace $e_1 \ldots e_k$ the events e_i and e_j with $i \leq j$ shall represent the occurrence specifications o_i and o_j in O, then it must not be the case that $o_j \preceq_R o_i$ in the partial order $\preceq_R$ generated by R.
- a binary relation $X \subseteq O \times O$ specifying an R-compatible *inhibition relation* over O, i.e., an irreflexive relation $\rhd_{(R,X)} \subseteq O \times O$ with $o_2 \rhd_{(R,X)} o_3$ iff there is an $o_1 \in O$

with $o_1 \preceq_R o_2$ and $(o_1, o_3) \in X$. This relation expresses which events inhibit others: if $o_1 \rhd_{(R,X)} o_2$, then an event e representing the occurrence specification o_1 excludes events conforming to o_2 from occurring after e in a trace.
- a timing constraint Θ, which is a conjunctive or disjunctive combination of timing constraints of the form true or $o_2 - o_1 \bowtie d$; it says which timing conditions the time-stamps of events have to obey (where duration constraints of the form $\ell \bowtie d$ are reduced to combinations of occurrence constraints).

For the traces of an interaction structure (O, R, X, Θ), we require that before each event on the trace a maximal, consistent set of events w.r.t. to R, X, and Θ occurs: All the causes of the event w.r.t. the causality relation $\preceq_R$ which are not present on the trace have to be excluded by the inhibition relation $\rhd_{(R,X)}$, and all timing constraints from Θ have to be satisfied for the chosen events; see Sect. 4.1.

Example 2. Consider the following UML 2 interaction diagram:

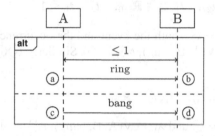

The traces of events allowed by this interaction are of one of the following two forms:

$$\langle \text{SND}(A, B, \text{ring}), t_1 \rangle \langle \text{RCV}(A, B, \text{ring}), t_2 \rangle, \quad t_1, t_2 \in \mathbb{R}_{\geq 0}, \quad t_2 - t_1 \leq 1 \, ;$$
$$\langle \text{SND}(A, B, \text{bang}), t_3 \rangle \langle \text{RCV}(A, B, \text{bang}), t_4 \rangle, \quad t_3, t_4 \in \mathbb{R}_{\geq 0} \, .$$

The requirements on the occurrence specifications themselves are: ⓐ is ordered before ⓑ, and ⓒ before ⓓ; either the upper operand can be observed, i.e., ⓐ and ⓑ occur, or the lower operand can be observed, i.e., ⓒ and ⓓ occur; at most a single time unit elapses between ⓐ and ⓑ. We can express these requirements by the following interaction structure:

$$O = \{ⓐ, ⓑ, ⓒ, ⓓ\} \, ,$$
$$R = \{ⓐ \rightarrow ⓑ, ⓒ \rightarrow ⓓ\} \, ,$$
$$X = \{ⓐ \leadsto ⓒ, ⓐ \leadsto ⓓ, ⓑ \leadsto ⓒ, ⓑ \leadsto ⓓ,$$
$$\qquad ⓒ \leadsto ⓐ, ⓓ \leadsto ⓐ, ⓒ \leadsto ⓑ, ⓓ \leadsto ⓑ\} \, ,$$
$$\Theta = ⓑ - ⓐ \leq 1 \, ,$$

where we write $o \leadsto o'$ for a pair $(o, o') \in X$. Relation R requires that ⓐ only may be observed before ⓑ, and that ⓒ may only be observed before ⓓ. The interpretation of X is that an observation of ⓐ or ⓑ must not be followed by an observation of ⓒ or ⓓ in the future, and, symmetrically, that the observation of ⓒ or ⓓ must not be followed by an observation of ⓐ or ⓑ in the future. In combination, R and X say that an observation of ⓑ not only cannot be followed by an observation of ⓒ or ⓓ but must be preceded by an observation of ⓐ, since ⓐ → ⓑ, and not ⓐ ⤳ ⓑ.

Thus the following non-empty sequences of occurrence specifications conform to both the ordering constraints R and the inhibition constraints X:

ⓐ,   ⓐⓑ,   ⓒ,   ⓒⓓ.

Generally, we would require that either the upper or the lower operand are observed completely, which then only leaves ⓐⓑ and ⓒⓓ.

For taking into account the timing constraints, we look for all traces of events for which we can find a bijective labeling from the set of events in the trace to a sequence of occurrence specifications conforming to the interaction structure such that the concrete time-stamps of the events satisfy the conditions of the timing constraints. For ⓐⓑ this results in

$$\langle \mathrm{SND}(A, B, \mathrm{ring}), t_1 \rangle \langle \mathrm{RCV}(A, B, \mathrm{ring}), t_2 \rangle, \quad t_1, t_2 \in \mathbb{R}_{\geq 0}, \quad t_2 - t_1 \leq 1$$

using the labeling $\lambda(\langle \mathrm{SND}(A, B, \mathrm{ring}), t_1 \rangle) = $ ⓐ (both the event and the occurrence specification have the same type), and $\lambda(\langle \mathrm{RCV}(A, B, \mathrm{ring}), t_2 \rangle) = $ ⓑ. Similarly, ⓒⓓ yields

$$\langle \mathrm{SND}(A, B, \mathrm{bang}), t_3 \rangle \langle \mathrm{RCV}(A, B, \mathrm{bang}), t_4 \rangle, \quad t_1, t_2 \in \mathbb{R}_{\geq 0}$$

using the labeling $\lambda(\langle \mathrm{SND}(A, B, \mathrm{bang}), t_3 \rangle) = $ ⓒ and $\lambda(\langle \mathrm{RCV}(A, B, \mathrm{bang}), t_4 \rangle) = $ ⓓ; here the timing constraint $\Theta = $ ⓑ $-$ ⓐ ≤ 1 is satisfied, since the labeling does not mention ⓐ and ⓑ.   □

For an interaction structure $S = (O, R, X, \Gamma)$, we write $O(S)$, $R(S)$, $X(S)$, and $\Gamma(S)$ for O, R, X, and Γ, respectively.

The format of interaction structures is inspired by the notion of *prime event structures* $(E, \leq, \sharp)$, where E is a set of *events*, $\leq \subseteq E \times E$ is a partial order describing the *causal relationship* of events, and $\sharp$ is an irreflexive, symmetric binary relation $\sharp \subseteq E \times E$, specifying which events are in *conflict* with each other [11]. In a *configuration* $C \subseteq E$ of the prime event structure, all causes of each event have to be present and any two events must not be in conflict.

Küster-Filipe [8] has suggested to capture a UML 2 interaction as a prime event structure, where its (partial) executions correspond to the configurations of the prime event structure. However, when expressing alt by the symmetric conflict relation of a prime event structure, it is necessary to duplicate all future events: Consider strict(alt(ⓐ, ⓑ), T), where ⓐ and ⓑ represent basic interactions of a single occurrence specification; here, ⓐ and ⓑ are in conflict. If all occurrence specifications of the interaction fragment T get ⓐ and ⓑ as their causes, no configuration containing ⓐ or ⓑ could also contain any occurrence specification from T, since then also all the causes of this occurrence specification, which are both ⓐ and ⓑ, would have to be present, which is impossible. Thus, the occurrence specifications of T are duplicated and one copy gets only ⓐ as its cause, the other copy ⓑ.

We circumvent this duplication process by using the notion of *asymmetric* conflicts taken from *asymmetric event structures* [1]. There, conflicts are expressed by *weak causes* saying that if an event e is a weak cause for another event e' and both events e and e' occur in a configuration then e has to precede e'; in fact, if e' also would be a weak cause for e, then e and e' could not occur simultaneously in one configuration. In our approach, we rely exclusively on such weak causes, i.e., both R and X of an interaction structure (O, R, X, Θ) are interpreted in this way. This makes the presentation more uniform, though at the expense of requiring that all possible weak causes of an occurrence specification have to be present in a trace.

4.1   Traces of an Interaction Structure

For an interaction structure (O, R, X, Θ), we now define its traces of events following the recipe of the last example. We proceed in two steps: First, we define all sequences of occurrence specifications (not events) that are allowed by the interaction structure. Then we take the timing constraints into account and define the traces of (O, R, X, Θ).

For the first step, let $o_1 \ldots o_k$ be a sequence of different occurrence specifications with $\{o_1, \ldots, o_k\} \subseteq O$. Let $\preceq_R$ be the partial order relation generated by R through taking the reflexive, transitive closure of R on O, and let $\rhd_{(R,X)}$ be the inhibition relation generated from R and X by taking the upwards closure of X w.r.t. $\preceq_R$. We say that $o_1 \ldots o_k$ *conforms to* the ordering constraints R and the inhibition constraints X if for all $1 \le j \le k$ the occurrence specification o_j is a minimal element of the partial order $(O_j, \preceq_R \cap (O_j \times O_j))$ with

$$O_j = O \setminus (\{o_1, \ldots, o_{j-1}\} \cup \{o \in O \mid \exists 1 \le i \le j - 1 . o_i \rhd_{(R,X)} o\}) .$$

The sequence of occurrence specifications $o_1 \ldots o_k$ is *allowed by* (O, R, X, Θ) if it conforms to R and X and is maximal w.r.t. conformance, i.e., there is no $o \in O \setminus \{o_1, \ldots, o_k\}$ such that also $o_1 \ldots o_k o$ conforms to R and X.

Example 3. Consider the following interaction structure (O, R, X, true) (where we omit the occurrence specification types):

$$O = \{ⓐ, ⓑ, ⓒ, ⓓ\} ,$$
$$R = \{ⓐ \to ⓑ, ⓒ \to ⓓ\} ,$$
$$X = \{ⓒ \rightsquigarrow ⓐ, ⓒ \rightsquigarrow ⓑ, ⓓ \rightsquigarrow ⓐ, ⓓ \rightsquigarrow ⓑ\} .$$

Here, every sequence of occurrence specifications allowed by (O, R, X, Θ) must not show ⓐ or ⓑ after ⓒ or ⓓ. On the other hand, ⓑⓒ is not allowed, since ⓐ $\to$ ⓑ, i.e., ⓑ is not a minimal element of $\preceq_R$. By the maximality condition, the allowed sequences of occurrence specifications are:

$$ⓒⓓ, \qquad ⓐⓒⓓ, \qquad ⓐⓑⓒⓓ . \qquad\qquad\qquad \square$$

For the second step, taking the timing constraints Θ into account, let $e_1 \ldots e_k$ be a trace of events. We say that $e_1 \ldots e_k$ *conforms to* a sequence of occurrence specifications $o_1 \ldots o_l$ allowed by (O, R, X, Θ) *via* a function $\lambda : \{e_1, \ldots, e_k\} \to$

$\{o_1, \ldots, o_l\}$ if λ is bijective and $\tau(e) = \tau(\lambda(e))$ for all $e \in \{e_1, \ldots, e_n\}$; we call such a function a *labeling*. Now, let $e_1 \ldots e_k$ conform to $o_1 \ldots o_l$ via the labeling λ. The trace of events $e_1 \ldots e_k$ *satisfies* a time constraint $o_2' - o_1' \bowtie d$ w.r.t. λ if either $\{\lambda(e) \mid e \in \{e_1, \ldots, e_k\}\} \neq \{o_1', o_2'\}$, i.e., at least one of the occurrence specifications mentioned by the timing constraint is not covered by the trace of events; or if $t(\lambda^{-1}(o_2')) - t(\lambda^{-1}(o_1')) \bowtie d$, i.e., the time difference between the events representing o_2' and o_1', respectively, is bounded by d w.r.t. $\bowtie$ (with its usual meaning on the real numbers). The trace *satisfies* a time constraint $\Theta_1 \wedge \Theta_2$ w.r.t. λ if it satisfies both Θ_1 and Θ_2 w.r.t. λ; and it *satisfies* a time constraint $\Theta_1 \vee \Theta_2$ w.r.t. λ if it satisfies Θ_1 or Θ_2 w.r.t. λ.

Summing up, a trace of events $e_1 \ldots e_k$ *satisfies* the interaction structure (O, R, X, Θ) if there is a sequence of occurrence specifications $o_1 \ldots o_l$ allowed by (O, R, X, Θ) such that $e_1 \ldots e_k$ conforms to $o_1 \ldots o_l$ via a labeling $\lambda : \{e_1, \ldots, e_k\} \to \{o_1, \ldots, o_l\}$ and $e_1 \ldots e_k$ satisfies Θ w.r.t. λ.

Example 4. Consider the interaction structure of the previous example where now the occurrence specification types are

> ⓐ : SND(A, B, ring) ,   ⓑ : RCV(A, B, ring) ,
>
> ⓒ : SND(A, B, ring) ,   ⓓ : RCV(A, B, ring) ;

and where we replace the timing constraint true by ⓑ − ⓐ $\leq$ 1. Then the trace of events $\langle$SND(A, B, ring), 0.2$\rangle$ $\langle$RCV(A, B, ring), 1.3$\rangle$ satisfies this interaction structure, since it conforms to the sequence of occurrence specification ⓒⓓ via the labeling $\lambda(\langle$SND(A, B, ring), 0.2$\rangle) = $ ⓒ and $\lambda(\langle$RCV(A, B, ring), 0.2$\rangle) = $ ⓓ; it satisfies the timing constraint ⓑ − ⓐ $\leq$ 1 trivially, since neither ⓐ nor ⓑ are part of ⓒⓓ. Also, the longer trace $\langle$SND(A, B, ring), 0.2$\rangle$ $\langle$RCV(A, B, ring), 0.9$\rangle$ $\langle$SND(A, B, ring), 1.1$\rangle$ $\langle$RCV(A, B, ring), 2.4$\rangle$ conforms to the sequence of occurrence specifications ⓐⓑⓒⓓ and satisfies the timing constraint ⓑ − ⓐ $\leq$ 1. □

4.2   Deriving an Interaction Structure

We now define a function $\mathcal{S}[\![-]\!]\,\Sigma$ that yields an interaction structure (O, R, X, Θ) for an interaction fragment given a context $\Sigma = \{\mathsf{sd}(name_1, T_1'), \ldots, \mathsf{sd}(name_k, T_k')\}$ of interactions, where the names $name_i$ are pairwise different. In the definition, we proceed recursively by the structure of our abstract syntax of UML 2 interaction fragments, where we always assume that the identifiers of occurrence specifications are globally unique. We write $\mathrm{Min}(O, \preceq)$ and $\mathrm{Max}(O, \preceq)$ for the set of minimal and maximal elements of a partial order $(O, \preceq)$.

Basic Interactions. For a basic interaction $B = (O, \to)$, the occurrence specifications O make up the occurrence specifications component of the resulting interaction structure, and the ordering relation $\to \subseteq O \times O$ yields the ordering constraints:

$$\mathcal{S}[\![(O, \to)]\!]\,\Sigma = (O, \to, \emptyset, \mathrm{true}) .$$

Note that for any interaction structure, we only need to record the skeleton of the partial ordering resulting from the order component which, in general, may reduce the number of pairs to be stored considerably.

Combined Fragments. We give the definitions for strict, seq, par, alt, break, and ref, abbreviating $\mathcal{S}[\![T_i]\!]\,\Sigma$ by $(O_i, R_i, X_i, \Theta_i)$:

A strict composition strict(T_1, T_2) of two timed fragments T_1 and T_2 requires that T_1 has to have completely finished before T_2 starts. For $\mathcal{S}[\![\text{strict}(T_1, T_2)]\!]\,\Sigma$ we therefore not only take the union (resp. conjunction) of all the components of the interaction structures for T_1 and T_2, but also add the constraint that any occurrence specification from $\mathcal{S}[\![T_1]\!]\,\Sigma$ has to occur before any occurrence specification from $\mathcal{S}[\![T_2]\!]\,\Sigma$:

$$\mathcal{S}[\![\text{strict}(T_1, T_2)]\!]\,\Sigma = (O_1 \cup O_2,$$
$$R_1 \cup R_2 \cup \{o_1 \to o_2 \mid o_1 \in O_1,\ o_2 \in O_2\},$$
$$X_1 \cup X_2, \Theta_1 \wedge \Theta_2)\,.$$

Example 5. Consider the following UML 2 interaction diagram:

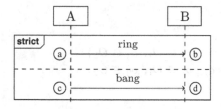

The two inner fragments have the interaction structure

$$(\{\text{ⓐ} : \text{SND}(A, B, \text{ring}), \text{ⓑ} : \text{RCV}(A, B, \text{ring})\}, \{\text{ⓐ} \to \text{ⓑ}\}, \emptyset, \text{true})\,,$$
$$(\{\text{ⓒ} : \text{SND}(A, B, \text{bang}), \text{ⓓ} : \text{RCV}(A, B, \text{bang})\}, \{\text{ⓒ} \to \text{ⓓ}\}, \emptyset, \text{true})\,.$$

Combining these strictly adds $\text{ⓐ} \to \text{ⓒ}$, $\text{ⓐ} \to \text{ⓓ}$, $\text{ⓑ} \to \text{ⓒ}$, and $\text{ⓑ} \to \text{ⓓ}$, thus the interaction structure is

$$(\{\text{ⓐ}, \text{ⓑ}, \text{ⓒ}, \text{ⓓ}\},$$
$$\{\text{ⓐ} \to \text{ⓑ}, \text{ⓐ} \to \text{ⓒ}, \text{ⓐ} \to \text{ⓓ}, \text{ⓑ} \to \text{ⓒ}, \text{ⓑ} \to \text{ⓓ}, \text{ⓒ} \to \text{ⓓ}\}, \emptyset, \text{true})\,,$$

where we have omitted the types of the occurrence specifications; taking the skeleton of the partial order specified in the order component, this can be expressed equivalently by

$$(\{\text{ⓐ}, \text{ⓑ}, \text{ⓒ}, \text{ⓓ}\}, \{\text{ⓐ} \to \text{ⓑ}, \text{ⓑ} \to \text{ⓒ}, \text{ⓒ} \to \text{ⓓ}\}, \emptyset, \text{true})\,. \qquad \square$$

A weak sequential composition seq(T_1, T_2) of two timed fragments T_1 and T_2 only requires that T_1 has to have finished before T_2 *lifeline-wise*, i.e., all occurrence specifications of T_1 on some lifeline have to happen before all occurrence specifications of T_2 on the same lifeline. Let us write $o_1 \gtrless o_2$ when o_1 and o_2 are *active* for the same lifeline where a $\text{SND}(s, r, m)$ is active for the sender s, and a $\text{RCV}(s, r, m)$ is active for the receiver r:

$$\mathcal{S}[\![\text{seq}(T_1, T_2)]\!]\,\Sigma = (O_1 \cup O_2,$$
$$R_1 \cup R_2 \cup \{o_1 \to o_2 \mid o_1 \in O_1,\ o_2 \in O_2,\ o_1 \gtrless o_2\},$$
$$X_1 \cup X_2, \Theta_1 \wedge \Theta_2)\,.$$

Example 6. Consider the UML 2 interaction diagram of the previous example but with strict replaced by seq. The two inner fragments have the same interaction structure as before, but the ordering constraints added now are only ⓐ → ⓒ and ⓑ → ⓓ.   □

A parallel fragment $par(T_1, T_2)$ allows for an arbitrary interleaving of the occurrence specifications in T_1 and T_2, as long as the constraints for T_1 and T_2 are satisfied separately; therefore we take the union resp. conjunction of all components of the respective interaction structures:

$$\mathcal{S}[\![par(T_1, T_2)]\!]\, \Sigma = (O_1 \cup O_2, R_1 \cup R_2, X_1 \cup X_2, \Theta_1 \wedge \Theta_2)\,.$$

An alternative fragment $alt(T_1, T_2)$ represents a choice of either T_1 or T_2. Here, we express the two possibilities by making the occurrence specifications of T_1 and T_2 mutually exclusive:

$$\mathcal{S}[\![alt(T_1, T_2)]\!]\, \Sigma = (O_1 \cup O_2, R_1 \cup R_2,$$
$$X_1 \cup X_2 \cup \{o_1 \rightsquigarrow o_2 \mid o_1 \in O_1,\, o_2 \in O_2\} \cup$$
$$\{o_2 \rightsquigarrow o_1 \mid o_1 \in O_1,\, o_2 \in O_2\},$$
$$\Theta_1 \wedge \Theta_2)\,.$$

An example for alt has been given in Ex. 2. However, the representation of the inhibition constraints $X = \{$ⓐ $\rightsquigarrow$ ⓒ, ⓐ $\rightsquigarrow$ ⓓ, ⓑ $\rightsquigarrow$ ⓒ, ⓑ $\rightsquigarrow$ ⓓ, ⓒ $\rightsquigarrow$ ⓐ, ⓓ $\rightsquigarrow$ ⓐ, ⓒ $\rightsquigarrow$ ⓑ, ⓓ $\rightsquigarrow$ ⓑ$\}$ given there can be reduced to $\{$ⓐ $\rightsquigarrow$ ⓒ, ⓐ $\rightsquigarrow$ ⓓ, ⓒ $\rightsquigarrow$ ⓐ, ⓓ $\rightsquigarrow$ ⓐ$\}$ using the ordering constraints $R = \{$ⓐ $\rightarrow$ ⓑ, ⓒ $\rightarrow$ ⓓ$\}$.

A break fragment $break(T_1, T_2)$ says that T_1 may be aborted at any time during its execution, and T_2 is performed on abortion. (Note that the UML 2 specification introduces break as a unary interaction operator showing only one interaction fragment as operand; it aborts its enclosing interaction fragment. We prefer to make break binary in order to clarify the two operands.) The translation of break is thus similar to the translation of alt; however, we only require that after T_2 has started, no occurrence specification of T_1 is allowed any more, and if T_1 has finished, no occurrence specification from T_2 is allowed:

$$\mathcal{S}[\![break(T_1, T_2)]\!]\, \Sigma = (O_1 \cup O_2, R_1 \cup R_2,$$
$$X_1 \cup X_2 \cup \{o_2 \rightsquigarrow o_1 \mid o_1 \in O_1,\, o_2 \in O_2\} \cup$$
$$\{o_1 \rightsquigarrow o_2 \mid o_1 \in Max(O_1, \preceq_{R_1}),\, o_2 \in O_2\},$$
$$\Theta_1 \wedge \Theta_2)\,.$$

Example 7. Consider the following UML 2 interaction diagram:

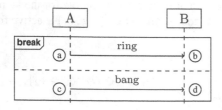

The resulting inhibition constraints are $\{ⓒ \leadsto ⓐ, ⓒ \leadsto ⓑ, ⓓ \leadsto ⓐ, ⓓ \leadsto ⓑ, ⓑ \leadsto ⓒ, ⓑ \leadsto ⓓ\}$. This is similar to Ex. 3, but $\{ⓑ \leadsto ⓒ, ⓑ \leadsto ⓓ\}$ is added. The resulting allowed sequences of occurrence specifications are ⓐⓑ, ⓐⓒⓓ, and ⓒⓓ. □

Finally, a reference fragment ref($name$) amounts to yielding the interaction structure of the interaction fragment T from sd($name$, T) $\in \Sigma$; in order keep all identifiers of occurrence specifications unique, we use a *renaming* ρ with $\rho(o) = name.o$ (where $name.o$ is assumed to be fresh), which we write in postfix notation:

$$\mathcal{S}[\![\mathsf{ref}(name)]\!]\, \Sigma = (O\rho, R\rho, X\rho, \Theta\rho) \quad \text{if sd}(name, T) \in \Sigma \text{ and}$$
$$\mathcal{S}[\![T]\!]\, \Sigma = (O, R, X, \Theta).$$

Timing Constraints. For a timed fragment tmconstr(T, Γ), we first reduce each duration constraint $\ell \bowtie d$ in Γ to an expanded form resulting in a timing constraint Θ, characterizing the duration of the interaction fragment T in terms of its occurrence specifications. Then we add this expanded Θ conjunctively to the timing constraints of the interaction structure $\mathcal{S}[\![T]\!]\, \Sigma$:

$$\mathcal{S}[\![\mathsf{tmconstr}(T, \Gamma)]\!]\, \Sigma = (O(\mathcal{S}[\![T]\!]\, \Sigma), R(\mathcal{S}[\![T]\!]\, \Sigma), X(\mathcal{S}[\![T]\!]\, \Sigma), \Theta(\mathcal{S}[\![T]\!]\, \Sigma) \wedge \Theta).$$

The expansion of an $\ell \bowtie d$ uses the partial order $(O, \preceq) = (O(\mathcal{S}[\![T]\!]\, \Sigma), \preceq_{R(\mathcal{S}[\![T]\!]\, \Sigma)})$ and has to distinguish between the two cases whether $\bowtie \in \{<, \leq\}$ and $\bowtie \in \{\geq, >\}$. In the case of an upper bound where $\bowtie \in \{<, \leq\}$, the expansion is the conjunction of upper bounds between the minimal and the maximal occurrence specifications of T; i.e., all occurrence specifications must happen within time bound d:

$$\bigwedge \{o_2 - o_1 \bowtie d \mid o_2 \in \mathrm{Max}(O, \preceq), o_1 \in \mathrm{Min}(O, \preceq)\}.$$

In the case of a lower bound where $\bowtie \in \{\geq, >\}$, the expansion is the disjunction of lower bound between the minimal and the maximal occurrence specifications of T; i.e., the difference in time between some occurrence specifications must be at least d:

$$\bigvee \{o_2 - o_1 \bowtie d \mid o_2 \in \mathrm{Max}(O, \preceq), o_1 \in \mathrm{Min}(O, \preceq)\}.$$

Example 8. Consider the following UML 2 interaction diagram:

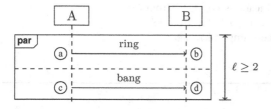

The duration of the par-fragment shall be at least 2. The minimal elements of the overall interaction structure are $\{ⓐ, ⓒ\}$, the maximal elements $\{ⓑ, ⓓ\}$. The expansion of $\ell \geq 2$ therefore is

$$(ⓑ - ⓐ \geq 2) \vee (ⓑ - ⓒ \geq 2) \vee (ⓓ - ⓐ \geq 2) \vee (ⓓ - ⓒ \geq 2). \quad □$$

5   Validation

We validate our approach by a prototypical implementation with a large number of test cases, and an extended example, where we check whether given traces comply with an interaction *without* computing all the traces of the interaction first. The transformation of interactions into interaction structures is straightforward and directly follows the definitions given in Sect. 4 above. Algorithm 1 shows how trace prefixes of arbitrary length can be checked for conformance against a given interaction structure. The *successor* function simply takes an ordering or time constraint and extracts the event occurrence with a higher time-stamp. The *choose*-operation is necessary since it is possible that concurrent fragments start with event occurrences with the same signature, as our example shows. In this situation, all alternative paths have to be explored; using Prolog's built in backtracking features allows straightforward handling of this situation. While one can construct abnormal cases where this is indeed occurring, leading to deterioration of performance, it may be argued that this is a modeling mistake, so that most practical scenarios will not suffer from this drawback. Without it, the computational effort of this algorithm is linear in the size of the interaction and the trace.

Algorithm 1. Check whether a trace conforms to an interaction structure

---

Input: an interaction structure IS and a trace of events $e_1 \ldots e_k$
for $i = 1..k$ **do**
$\quad$ // *Compute unconstrained (i.e., enabled) occurrence specifications*
$\quad U_i \leftarrow O(IS)$;
$\quad$ **for** $c \in R(IS) \cup constraints(\Theta(IS))$ **do**
$\quad\quad\lfloor\ U_i \leftarrow U_i \setminus successor(c)$;
$\quad$ // *Choose enabled, conforming occurrence specification, if possible*
$\quad O_i \leftarrow \{o \in U_i \mid e_i$ conforms to $o\}$;
$\quad$ **if** $O_i = \emptyset$ **then**
$\quad\quad\mid$ **abort** "trace does not conform";
$\quad$ **else**
$\quad\quad\lfloor\ o_i \leftarrow$ **choose** O_i;
$\quad$ // *Propagate choice removing irrelevant occurrence specifications and constraints*
$\quad X_i \leftarrow conflicting(o_i, X)$;
$\quad IS \leftarrow$ remove occurrence specifications $\{o_i\} \cup X_i$ from IS;
$\quad IS \leftarrow$ remove constraints related to $\{o_i\} \cup X_i$ from IS;
$\quad\lfloor\ IS \leftarrow$ simplify $\Theta(IS)$ with time-stamp $t(e_i)$ for o_i;
// *Check all timing constraints*
evaluate $\Theta(IS)$;

We have also implemented the symbolic representation and the above algorithm to demonstrate its feasibility. We used SWI-Prolog [15] for this purpose to be able to align the implementation closely with the definitions of this paper. The implementation consists of 5 modules with less than 800 lines of code/1000 clauses, plus a few generic auxiliary libraries. The implementation allows to check interactions for well-formedness, transform them into timed event structures, expand them to trace sets, and, of course, check traces against interaction structures. Another set of modules (approx. 300 lines of code) defines approx. 100 test cases and run-time measurement scaffold. We have used this implementation to analyze the sample interaction shown in Fig. 1 and Fig. 3. We have defined ten examples and counter-examples of valid traces manually, and checked them for compliance against the interaction, validating that our implementation does indeed truthfully implement our approach. The smallest of these samples for Client(1)-Server is shown in Fig. 3 (bottom, left).

In order to validate the scalability of our approach, we created a loop wrapping a simple elementary interaction (see Fig. 4, top), and checked it against traces of increasing length. In Fig. 4, bottom, we show the length of traces as the x-axis (corresponds to the number of occurrence specifications in the interaction structure), the number of constraints arising from it (y-axis, grey bar chart/graph), and the time used for converting an interaction to an interaction structure (y-axis, red graph). The time to check a trace against an interaction structure was too small to be measured. All measurements are the average of ten runs, to cancel out delays due to garbage collection and similar issues. All measurements were taken on an outdated sub-notebook computer (Intel Core Duo, 1.2GHz, 2GB RAM).

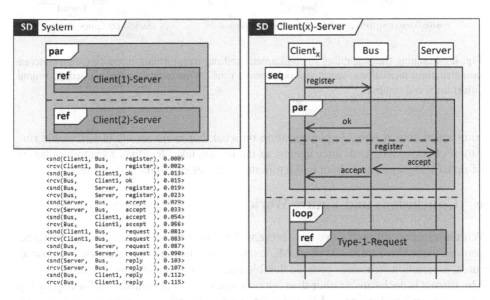

Fig. 3. An extended example for validating our approach and implementation. Observe, that the interaction shown in Fig. 1 is re-used.

The measurements clearly show that, with increasing length of loop unrolling and trace length, the number of constraints increases linearly, while the conversion times increase polynomially. Recall, that this translation occurs only once, at model compile time; afterwards, all checks are executed in constant time. Even when including the

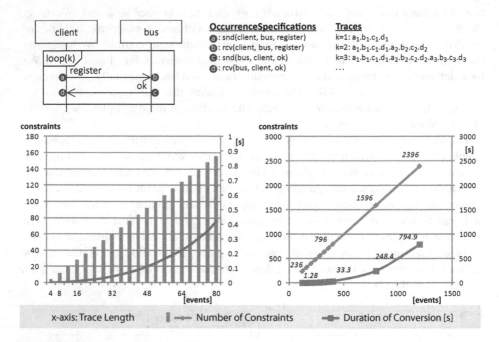

Fig. 4. Measuring the scalability of the implementation: transforming interactions into interaction structures takes linear space and polynomial time. "Constraints" include ordering, timing constraints, and conflicts.

translation time, a naive implementation on weak hardware results in acceptable runtimes: checking a (timed) trace against an interaction takes less than a second for traces of up to 100 events, and about half a minute for traces of around 500 events.

6   Conclusions and Future Work

With interaction structures, we have presented a compact and versatile format for representing the positive trace sets of a UML 2 interaction. Based on asymmetric event structures, interaction structures provide flexible means for specifying alternative scenarios. The format is declarative rather than operational; it relies on constraints for expressing orderings and exclusions and includes timing constraints for expressing real-time requirements in interactions. We have also described a prototypical implementation for translating a UML 2 interaction into an interaction structure and checking the conformance of a trace with the interaction structure.

The approach presented in this paper is the first to cover time for UML 2 interactions in an efficient way, including the major interaction operators. This is essential for practical tool support, which we demonstrate with a proof-of-concept implementation. Previous approaches either suffered from exponential blow-up of the representations, or considered only a much smaller language fragment.

One of the open issues is the inclusion of interaction fragments with empty traces, like opt. This would require a small extension of the notion of interaction structures with "virtual" occurrence specifications that indicate the beginning and ending of an interaction fragment and which can be interpreted as "silent actions" [8], though we would like to minimize their number. A proper integration of the notorious negative behavior specification operators neg and assert is more challenging, where, e.g., modal sequence diagrams may be an interesting approach [6]. We would also like to investigate the use of our algorithm for checking the conformance of a trace to an interaction for run-time verification.

References

1. Baldan, P., Corradini, A., Montanari, U.: Contextual Petri Nets, Asymmetric Event Structures, and Processes. Inf. Comput. 171(1), 1–49 (2001)
2. Dobing, B., Parsons, J.: How UML Is Used. Comm. ACM 49(5), 109–113 (2006)
3. Dobing, B., Parsons, J.: Dimensions of UML Diagram Use: Practitioner Survey and Research Agenda. In: Siau, K., Erickson, J. (eds.) Principle Advancements in Database Management Technologies: New Applications and Frameworks, pp. 271–290. IGI Publishing (2010)
4. Grosu, R., Smolka, S.A.: Safety-Liveness Semantics for UML 2.0 Sequence Diagrams. In: Proc. 5th Conf. Appl. of Concurrency to System Design (ACSD 2005), pp. 6–14. IEEE Computer Society (2005)
5. Hammal, Y.: Branching Time Semantics for UML 2.0 Sequence Diagrams. In: Najm, E., Pradat-Peyre, J.-F., Donzeau-Gouge, V.V. (eds.) FORTE 2006. LNCS, vol. 4229, pp. 259–274. Springer, Heidelberg (2006)
6. Harel, D., Maoz, S.: Assert and Negate Revisited: Modal Semantics for UML Sequence Diagrams. J. Softw. Syst. Model. 7(2), 237–252 (2008)
7. Knapp, A., Wuttke, J.: Model Checking of UML 2.0 Interactions. In: Kühne, T. (ed.) MoD-ELS 2006. LNCS, vol. 4364, pp. 42–51. Springer, Heidelberg (2007)
8. Küster-Filipe, J.: Modelling Concurrent Interactions. Theo. Comp. Sci. 351(2), 203–220 (2006)
9. Micskei, Z., Waeselynck, H.: The Many Meanings of UML 2 Sequence Diagrams: A Survey. J. Softw. Syst. Model. 10(4), 489–514 (2011)
10. Nayak, A., Samanta, D.: Automatic Test Data Synthesis using UML Sequence Diagrams. J. Obj. Techn. 9(2), 75–104 (2010),
    http://www.jot.fm/issues/issue201003/article2/
11. Nielsen, M., Plotkin, G., Winskel, G.: Petri Nets, Event Structures and Domains, Part I. Theo. Comp. Sci. 13, 85–108 (1981)
12. Object Management Group: OMG Unified Modeling Language (OMG UML), Superstructure. Version 2.4.1. OMG Document Number: formal/2011-08-06. Tech. rep., Object Management Group (August 2011), http://www.omg.org/spec/UML/2.4.1/
13. Störrle, H.: Assert, Negate and Refinement in UML-2 Interactions. In: Jürjens, J., Rumpe, B., France, R., Fernandey, E.B. (eds.) Proc. Ws. Critical Systems Development with UML. Technical report TUM-I0317. pp. 79–94 (2003)
14. Störrle, H.: Semantics of Interactions in UML 2.0. In: Hosking, J., Cox, P. (eds.) Proc. IEEE Symp. Human Centric Computing Lang. and Env., pp. 129–136. IEEE Computer Society (2003)
15. Wielemaker, J., Schrijvers, T., Triska, M., Lager, T.: SWI-Prolog. Theory and Practice of Logic Programming 12(1-2), 67–96 (2012)

Integrating Graph Transformations and Modal Sequence Diagrams for Specifying Structurally Dynamic Reactive Systems

Sabine Winetzhammer[1], Joel Greenyer[2], and Matthias Tichy[3]

[1] Chair of Applied Computer Science 1, Software Engineering
Universität Bayreuth, Universitätsstraße 30, 95440 Bayreuth, Germany
sabine.winetzhammer@uni-bayreuth.de
[2] Software Engineering Group
Leibniz Universität Hannover, Welfengarten 1, 30167 Hannover, Germany
greenyer@inf.uni-hannover.de
[3] Software Engineering Division
Chalmers, University of Gothenburg, 412 96 Gothenburg, Sweden
matthias.tichy@cse.gu.se

Abstract. Software-intensive systems, for example service robot systems in industry, often consist of multiple reactive components that interact with each other and the environment. Often, the behavior depends on structural properties and relationships among the system and environment components, and reactions of the components in turn may change this structure. Modal Sequence Diagrams (MSDs) are an intuitive and precise formalism for specifying the interaction behavior among reactive components. However, they are not sufficient for specifying structural dynamics. Graph transformation rules (GTRs) provide a powerful approach for specifying structural dynamics. We describe an approach for integrating GTRs with MSDs such that requirements and assumptions on structural changes of system resp. environment objects can be specified. We prototypically implemented this approach by integrating MOD-GRAPH with SCENARIOTOOLS. This allows us not only to specify MSDs and GTRs in Eclipse, but also to simulate the specified behavior via play-out.

Keywords: scenario-based specification, reactive systems, embedded systems, automotive, simulation, validation, testing.

1 Introduction

In many areas, such as industry and transportation, we find increasingly complex, interconnected, software-intensive systems. In industry, for example, service robots support workers and decentralized control components control complex production processes; advanced driver assistance systems in cars rely on the inter-vehicle communication to realize collision avoidance or vehicle platooning.

D. Amyot et al. (Eds.): SAM 2014, LNCS 8769, pp. 126–141, 2014.

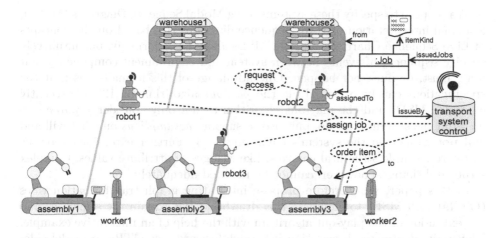

Fig. 1. Example of an autonomous robot transport system in a production plant

As an example, Fig. 1 shows an autonomous robot transport system in a production plant. Workers at assembly stations can order items to be delivered to them by a transport system. Upon receiving an order, the transport system control assigns a job to a robot, which executes it by requesting access to the given location (a warehouse), picking up the item, and delivering it.

These systems often consist of multiple, physically distributed mechatronic components that comprise hardware, mechanical parts, and software. It is the software that mainly realizes the systems' complex functionality. The software processes environment events, performs the coordination of the components, handles interactions with users, and acts on the physical environment via actuators. We therefore view these systems as distributed reactive systems.

The challenge in the design of these systems is that the requirements often span multiple components, and components may have to satisfy multiple requirements at the same time. To exemplify this, consider a worker that orders an item: the worker inputs the order via a terminal at the assembly station, the terminal then notifies the transport system control, which then assigns a job to a service robot, etc. At the same time, the transport system may receive notification of a robot's malfunction and must notify service personnel.

Moreover, the requirements often relate to the system's structure, which can be its physical structure or logical structures within or shared among its software components. For example, which robot the transport system control assigns a job to depends on the robot's availability and proximity to the pick-up location (physical structure). Which warehouse the robot requests access to depends on the job it received (logical structure). In turn, reactions of the software can change physical or logical structures. For example, when ordering the robot to move to a certain location, we can assume that it will eventually arrive there (physical structure). An example for changes in the logical structure would be the transport system control creating a job object and assigning it to a robot.

We propose to specify these systems using Modal Sequence Diagrams (MSDs), a formal interpretation of UML sequence diagrams [10] based on the concepts of Live Sequence Charts (LSCs) [4]. MSDs allow us to formally, but intuitively specify sequences of events between system and environment components that may, must, or must not happen. One advantage of this formalism is that the specifications can be executed via the *play-out* algorithm [11,12]. We recently extended MSDs and the play-out algorithm to not only consider *requirements* on what the system must do, but also to support *assumptions* on what will and will not happen in the system's environment [3]. Further extensions allow us to express simple structural changes, like changes of attribute values. Complex structural changes, however, cannot be modeled adequately.

In this paper, we therefore propose integrating graph transformation rules (GTRs) with MSDs to eliminate this drawback. We explain the semantics and the extension of the play-out algorithm with the help of an illustrative example. The main idea of the integration is straightforward: use GTRs to model side-effects that messages have on the system structure. However, our integration goes further: GTRs can also constrain in which structural contexts the system is allowed to perform certain actions (requirements) and in which structural contexts certain events can occur in the environment (assumptions). We implemented our approach prototypically by integrating MODGRAPH[1] [19], a tool for modeling and executing GTRs, and SCENARIOTOOLS[2] [3], a tool suite that supports the modeling and play-out of MSDs.

The resulting modeling and analysis approach supports an iterative and incremental specification of message-based interaction behavior and structural system reconfiguration behavior. The advantage of the scenario-based approach is that adding single scenarios to a specification can extend as well as constrain previously specified behavior [13]. Integrating GTRs adds intuitive means for expressing structural changes. The declarative style of specifying rules with object-patterns as pre- and post-conditions, combined with the graphical, color-coded notation, makes complex changes on the object system easy to understand.

This paper is structured as follows. Section 2 provides the foundations. Section 3 then describes the concepts of the integration, and Sect. 4 describes the tool integration. We discuss related work in Sect. 5 and conclude in Sect. 6.

2   Foundations

In the following, we describe the basics of MSDs and graph transformation rules.

2.1   Modal Sequence Diagrams

MSDs [10] are a formal interpretation of UML sequence diagrams, based on the concepts of LSCs [4,12]. An MSD specification consists of a set of MSDs. MSDs can be either *existential* or *universal*. Existential MSDs describe sequences of

---

[1] http://btn1x4.inf.uni-bayreuth.de/modgraph/homepage
[2] http://scenariotools.org

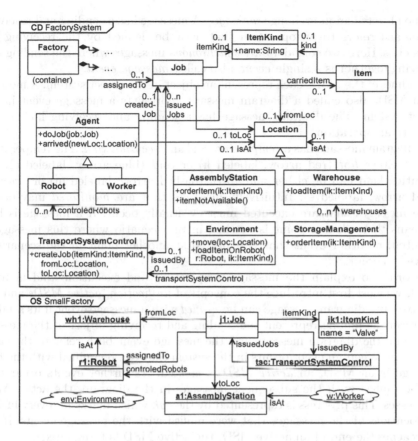

Fig. 2. Class diagram of production plant systems and an object diagram of a small instance system (cf. Fig. 1)

events that must be possible to occur, whereas universal MSDs describe properties that must hold for all sequences of events. Here, we focus on universal MSDs only.

The lifelines of an MSD represent *objects* in an *object system*. The objects are either controllable *system objects* or uncontrollable *environment objects*. The set of environment objects is also called the *environment*; the set of system objects is also called the *system*.

We consider the object system to be a valid instance of a class model that can define associations and attributes. Objects then carry attribute values according to the attribute definitions and there can exist *links* among the objects according to the associations. As an example, Fig. 2 shows the class diagram of our factory system and a possible object system; the object system represents a very simple plant with one assembly station, one robot, and one warehouse. Environment objects have a cloud-like shape; system objects have a rectangular shape.

The objects can interchange *messages*. A message has a sending and receiving object and refers to an operation that must be defined by the receiving object's class. Here, we consider only *synchronous* messages where the sending and receiving together is a single *event*, also called *message event*.

Lifelines of the MSDs each represent an object in the object system. A message in an MSD, also called a diagram message, represents a message event in the object system. The diagram message has a sending and receiving lifeline and refers to an operation.

A diagram message has a *temperature* and an *execution kind*. The temperature can be either *hot* (red arrow, labeled h) or *cold* (blue arrow, labeled c); the execution kind can be either *monitored* (dashed arrow, labeled m) or *executed* (solid arrow, labeled e). Intuitively, messages that are *monitored* may occur, while messages that are executed must eventually occur. If a message is hot, it means that when a point is reached in the scenario where this message is expected, no other event that is expected at another point in the scenario is allowed to occur.

In order to explain the message temperature and execution kind in more detail, we must first introduce the concepts of *unification, active MSDs* and the *cut*. We say a diagram message can be *unified* with a message event if its sending and receiving lifeline represent the sending and receiving object of the message event and the diagram message and the message event both refer to the same operation. When an event occurs in the system that can be unified with the first message in an MSD, an *active MSD* is created. As further events occur that can be unified with the subsequent messages in the diagram, the active MSD progresses. This progress is represented by the *cut*, which marks for every lifeline the locations of the messages that were unified with the message events. If the cut reaches the end of an active MSD, the active MSD is terminated.

The semantics of the messages temperature and execution kind is as follows. If the cut is in front of a message on its sending and receiving lifeline, the message is *enabled*. If a hot message is enabled, the cut is also *hot*. Otherwise the cut is *cold*. If an executed message is enabled, the cut is also *executed*. Otherwise the cut is *monitored*. A *violation* of an MSD occurs if a message event occurs that can be unified with a message in the MSD that is not currently enabled. If the cut is hot, it is a *safety violation*; if the cut is cold, it is called a *cold violation*. Safety violations must never happen, while cold violations are allowed to occur and result in terminating the respective active MSD. If the cut is executed, this means that the active MSD must progress and it is a *liveness violation* if it does not. Instead, an active MSD is not required to progress in a monitored cut.

A (universal) MSD *accepts* an infinite sequence of message events in an object system, also called a *run* of an object system, if it does not lead to a safety or liveness violation of that MSD. An object system *satisfies* an MSD specification (consisting of a set of universal MSDs), iff all possible runs of the object system are accepted by all universal MSDs. We assume that at some point the specification will be implemented by a software *controller* for the system objects. This controller can be a single, centralized control program for all system objects, or

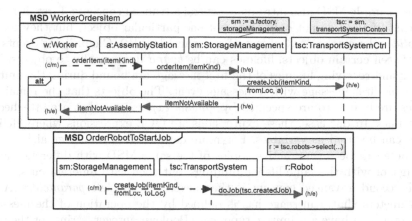

Fig. 3. MSDs to order an item

it can be a set of distributed controllers, e.g., one controller per system object. We say that a controller for the system objects *implements* an MSD specification if the closed system formed of the system controller with any possible environment are accepted by all universal MSDs in the specification. Additionally it is assumed that the system is always fast enough to take any finite number of steps before the next environment event occurs [12]. Note that an MSD specification can contain contradictions and then no implementation exists [2,7,8,9].

For more details on the MSD semantics, we refer to Harel and Maoz [10]. Note, however, that our interpretation of the message modalities differs slightly from the original definition where hot messages also encode the liveness requirement (must eventually occur). In our interpretation, the execution kind defines whether a message may or must eventually occur. Hot messages are typically also executed and cold messages are monitored, but there are also cases where hot monitored messages (may occur but must not be violated) or cold executed ones (must eventually occur but may be violated) are used.

As an example of MSD, consider the MSD WorkerOrdersItem in Fig. 3. It says that when a worker tells the assembly station to order an item of a particular kind, the assembly station must send an order to the storage management. Then the storage management can reply that the item is not available; in that case the assembly station must then forward this information to the worker. Alternatively, the storage management can command the transport system to create a job (for some robot) to pick up an item of the given kind a certain location and deliver it to another location. When the message `createJob` is sent, this activates a copy of the MSD OrderRobotToStartJob, which requires then that a robot be ordered to do the job[3].

---

[3] Here, the job sent to the robot is the one that the transport system control points to via its createdJob link. We assume that this link points to the job that was created last. However, how we model the creation of a job will be explained in Sect. 3, where we also introduce a more elegant way of assigning the new job to the robot.

This example MSD also introduces several advanced concepts. First, it is possible that lifelines do not only represent one particular object, but they can be *symbolic* and represent any object of a certain class [12, Chap. 7]. As events occur between certain objects, lifelines can be *bound* dynamically to objects. The sending and receiving lifelines of the first message are bound during the unification of the first message with a message event. The objects that the remaining lifelines are bound to are specified by *binding expressions* that are attached to the lifelines. In our case, these expressions are OCL expressions where lifelines names can be used as variables. For more details, see Brenner et al. [3]. Note that there can be several active copies of the same MSD with different lifeline bindings, or with the same lifeline bindings, but then with different cuts.

The second advanced concept is that messages can have *parameters*. A list of parameters that a message has is defined by the operation of the message. Parameters can have a primitive type, e.g., Boolean, integer, string, or they can by typed by classes. A message event must carry *values* for each parameter that the operation defines, which are thus concrete primitive values or, in the case that the parameter is typed by a class, pointers to objects. A diagram message in an MSD can specify values for message parameters, either by defining constant values or by referring to lifeline names, or other variables.

For example, by referring to the lifeline a in the MSD WorkerOrdersItem, we specify that the destination of the transport job should be the assembly station where the worker placed the order initially (observe that the third parameter of the operation TransportSystemControl.createJob(...) is toLoc).

An MSD can also contain further variables, called *diagram variables*, which are only visible in the scope of an active MSD. They can be *bound* or *unbound* if no value was yet assigned to them. In the MSD WorkerOrdersItem, for example, the variable itemKind specifies the parameter value for the two `orderItem` messages. Initially, the variable is unbound and in that case the diagram message can be unified with any `orderItem` message sent between a worker and an assembly station, regardless which item kind object it carries as parameter value. After unification, the variable itemKind is bound to the item kind object carried by the unified message event. For the next `orderItem` message sent from the assembly station to the storage management, the diagram variable itemKind is bound and, in that case, the diagram message can only be unified to a message event when the carried parameter value matches the specified value.

If a message event occurs that can be unified with the diagram message, but only carries a parameter value that does not match the specified value, this is a violation of the MSD (cold violation or safety violation, depending on the cut temperature). In the MSD WorkerOrdersItem, this means that the item kind transmitted to the storage management (msg. 2) and the item kind for the creation of the job (msg. 3) must be the same item kind as originally sent by the worker to the assembly station (msg. 1). For more details on message parameters, see Harel and Marelly [12, Chap. 7] and Brenner et al. [3].

The third advanced concept is the alt-fragment, which allows us to specify decisions or non-deterministic choices. Here, there is a non-deterministic choice as to whether to create a job or to reply that an item is not available. What this decision depends on can be modeled in another MSD that, for example, checks whether an item of that kind is available in a warehouse. We omit this for brevity.

An MSD specification can be executed by the *play-out* algorithm, which provides an operational semantics to MSD/LSC specifications [12,15]. It roughly works as follows: when an environment event occurs that activates or progresses one or multiple MSDs into cuts where executed system messages are enabled, then a system event is executed that can be unified with one of the enabled executed system messages and does not lead to a safety violation.

We recently extended the play-out algorithm to execute not only MSD specification consisting of MSDs that describe what the system objects are *required* to do, but we also support *assumption MSDs* that describe assumptions on what the environment can, will or will not do. We can think of the set of assumption MSDs, also called *environment assumptions*, as the dual to the requirements: a system is expected to satisfy its requirements as long as the environment satisfies the assumptions [8]. This extension of play-out is implemented in SCENARIO-TOOLS [3]. We give an example of an assumption MSD in Sect. 3.

The SCENARIOTOOLS play-out supports messages that can have simple side-effects on the objects in the object system. For example, by convention, if a class defines an attribute a:⟨Type⟩ and an operation setA(a:⟨Type⟩) (with a parameter of the same type), then message events referring to that operation will change the attribute value of the receiving object according to the value carried by the message event. This also works for single-valued references. Maoz et al. describe an implementation of the play-out algorithm that supports the creation of objects [16]. Complex changes, for example, the creation of a job object as shown in Fig. 2, with its links to other objects, are currently very difficult to express; they require one message per creation of an object or link.

2.2   Graph Transformation Rules

Graph transformation rules (GTRs) [6] describe changes on a typed graph in a declarative way. Since software models can be considered graphs, typed by their meta-model, GTRs can be used to describe changes on models.

An existing graph, called *host graph*, is changed into a *target graph* using a graph transformation rule, which consists of a left-hand and a right-hand side as shown on the left of Fig. 4. They are marked with LHS and RHS, respectively. The figure shows the GTR arrived that describes the movement of an agent from one location oldLoc to another location newLoc.

The left-hand side defines a pattern for which a *match*, an isomorph subgraph, needs to exist in the host graph in order to apply the rule. The right-hand side defines the replacement to be performed on the host graph that changes it into the target graph. Hence, the two sides of the rules can be interpreted as follows: (1) nodes and edges occurring on the left-hand and right-hand side are kept in the host graph, (2) nodes and edges occurring on the left-hand but not the

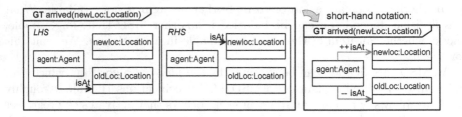

Fig. 4. Two representations of a GTR for an agent arriving at a new location

right-hand side are removed from the host graph, and (3) nodes and edges occurring only on the right-hand side are added to the host graph.

In our example, the left hand side requires the agent to be at a location. The right-hand side defines that the agent must be at another location after the transformation.

We use a short-hand notation for GTRs as shown on the right of Fig. 4. Elements marked red and with "−−" belong to the right-hand side whereas element marked green and with "++" belong to the left-hand side. Unmarked elements belong to both sides.

There exists a range of tools that support the modeling and execution of graph transformations. They often add concepts like positive and negative *conditions*. Positive conditions are additional conditions that must hold in order to apply the rule. Conversely, negative conditions, also called *negative application conditions* (NACs), must not hold in order to apply the rule. Conditions can be specified using additional graph patterns or expressions, for example in OCL.

MODGRAPH [20] is a tool for model-driven software engineering with GTRs. It is based on and built for the Eclipse Modeling Framework (EMF) [18]. The vision of MODGRAPH is to provide a model-driven software engineering tool that combines the advantages of EMF, Xcore[4] and MODGRAPH's GTRs. EMF, with its meta-modeling language Ecore, supports the modeling of object-oriented structures. Xcore is a textual language for Ecore, extended with the programming language Xbase. On top, MODGRAPH's GTRs provide a higher level of abstraction for operations that involve complex matching and transformation.

A MODGRAPH GTR implements an operation defined in an Ecore or Xcore class model. A rule comprises a rule pattern in short-hand notation (as shown in Fig. 4) and, optionally, textual pre- and post-conditions and graphical NACs. If the operation is called on an object, the rule, if applicable, will be applied. If the rule is not applicable, an exception is thrown.

A graph pattern can consist of several kinds of nodes. First, there is a special node, called the *current node*, which is named this. This node represents the object on which the operation is called. When the operation is called on an object, this node is *bound* to the called object, which means that, in order to apply the rule, a match of the LHS-pattern must be found in the model where the this-node maps to the called object.

---

[4] http://wiki.eclipse.org/Xcore

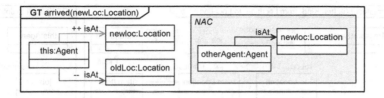

Fig. 5. The GTR for Agent.arrived(newLoc:Location) with a current node and NAC

Also, other nodes in the rule can have a pre-defined binding. If a node's name equals the name of an accordingly typed parameter of the operation, these nodes, when the operation is called, will be bound to the objects that are provided as parameter values by the call. Again the match for the rule's LHS must respect these pre-defined node bindings. Parameter names can also be used in conditions and nodes with pre-defined bindings can also appear in graphical NACs.

All other nodes are *unbound* and can be mapped to any object in a match.

Figure 5 shows a modified version of the GTR arrived. We suppose that arrived(...) is an operation of the class Agent. The agent node is now the this-node. The node newLoc has a pre-defined binding due to the operation's corresponding newLoc-parameter. The node oldLoc is unbound and will be bound to whatever location the agent is at the time the operation is called. The figure also shows a NAC that says that the rule can only be applied when there is currently no (other) agent at the new location. This expresses that, in our factory example, only one robot may be at a warehouse or assembly station at a time; we can think of each location having only one loading/unloading apparatus.

Technically, for execution, MODGRAPH GTRs are transformed into Java code or Xcore operations. The transformation to Xcore enables the indirect interpretation of the GTRs [20].

3   Integration of MSDs and GTRs

The basic idea of our integration of MSDs and GTRs is straightforward. As before, we use GTRs to describe implementations of operations. As message events occur during a system run, GTRs are executed as side-effects. More specifically, for each message event referring to an operation that is implemented by a GTR, that GTR is executed. The execution is synchronous, which means that the next message event occurs only after the execution of the GTR is completed.

In addition, GTRs can also constrain the allowed sequences of events: We define that, if the *precondition* for applying a GTR is *not satisfied*, that is, there is no match for the LHS, a positive precondition is not satisfied, or there is a match for a NAC, then this implies that *the corresponding event must not occur*. In other words, an occurrence of an event that demands the execution of an inexecutable GTR leads to a *safety violation*. If the event is a message sent by a system object, then it is a safety violation of the *requirements*; if it is a message sent by an environment event, it is a safety violation of the *assumptions*.

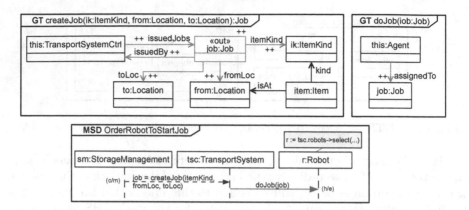

Fig. 6. GTRs for creating a job and assigning it to an agent with a more elegant version of MSD OrderRobotToStartJob

In the following, we illustrate the integration by two examples:

As a first example, consider the two GTRs that implement the operations TransportSystemControl.createJob(...) and Agent.doJob(job:Job) shown in Fig. 6. While the second could be modeled equally with a message referring to an operation Agent.setAssignedTo(job:Job) (see the convention for set-messages explained in Sect. 2.1), the structural change intended by TransportSystemControl.create-Job(...) is much more elaborate and the GTR provides a concise, visual way for modeling the creation of a job object and the setting of the all the links.

Furthermore, the LHS of the rule also contains an item node. This node will not be connected to the job via any link—its only purpose is to constrain the application of the rule in such a way that the rule will be applied only if at least one item of the specified kind is at the the specified pick-up location. If this is not the case, sending the respective message event would be a safety violation of the requirements.

We furthermore extend the integration so that now an operation's return value can be assigned to a MSD diagram variable. We extend the example so that now the operation TransportSystemControl.createJob(...) returns the newly created job. In the MSDs, we then use the return value. In the new version of the MSD OrderRobotToStartJob shown on the right of Fig. 6, we use the reference to the newly created job to more easily model that the newly created job must be assigned to a robot (cf. Fig. 3). This way, we no longer require the association TransportSystemControl.createdJob to point to the newly created job (see the class diagram in Fig. 2).

Figure 7 shows the MSD RobotMoveToPickUpLocation. It specifies that the Robot, after being ordered to perform the job, must move to the pick-up location as indicated by the job (Job.fromLoc). This is modeled as a message

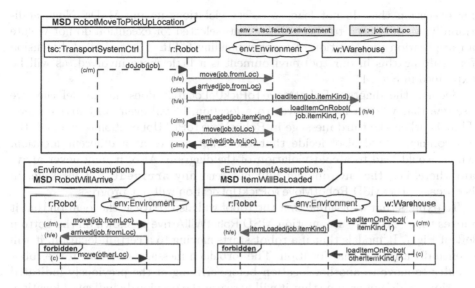

Fig. 7. MSD for a robot to execute a job

to the environment, which abstracts from the robot's software controller ordering its drives to physically move to the location. The arrival is modeled as a message from the environment to the robot, which abstracts from the robot's sensors telling the robot that it arrived at the desired location.

Upon arrival at that location, which is a warehouse that will be bound to the w:Warehouse lifeline, the robot must order the warehouse to load an item of the kind specified by the job onto the robot. Again, we abstract by a message to the environment that the warehouse's software orders some physical/mechanical loading mechanism (maybe even a human worker) to load an item onto the robot. Also, the effective loading of the item onto the robot, which will be recognized by a sensor of the robot, is again modeled as a message from the environment to the robot. After the item is loaded, the robot moves to the destination as specified by the job (Job.toLoc). The unloading of the item is modeled in another MSD that we omit here for brevity.

There are two aspects about the process modeled in the MSD RobotMoveTo-PickUpLocation that are not expressed in this diagram.

The first missing aspect is that arriving at a certain location is a *spatial change* of the robot in the factory. It should be accompanied with a structural change in the object system. We model this with the GTR arrived that we discussed previously (see Fig. 5). Note that, due to the NAC, this rule is only applicable if no other agent is currently at the target location. Since arrived(...) is an environment message (sent by an environment object), an occurrence of that message in this case would lead to a safety violation of the environment assumptions. It means that we assume that this will never happen.

Extending the play-out algorithm to consider the safety properties implied by GTRs is conceptually quite simple: The play-out algorithm selects only events for execution that do not lead to safety violations in any MSDs. Now, additionally, we only need to check that events selected for execution do not violate an application precondition of a corresponding GTR. The technical dimension for realizing this in our tool environment is a little more involved, as will be explained in Sect. 4.

Second, the diagram RobotMoveToPickUpLocation does not model that we *assume* that when a robot moves to a location, it will eventually arrive there. That is, when the third message in RobotMoveToPickUpLocation is enabled, the environment could also decide that the robot arrives at a different location, which would lead to a cold violation of the diagram. Also, it may never arrive anywhere, i.e., the environment will not send any arrived(...) message. In both cases, the MSD RobotMoveToPickUpLocation will not progress.

To express that we assume that the robot will also arrive at the location that it moves to, we need the assumption MSD RobotWillArrive as shown on the bottom left of Fig. 7. It models that if a robot starts moving to a certain location, it will eventually arrive at that location. The forbidden message says that if the robot decides to move to another location before arriving at the previously indicated location, we do not assume that it will arrive at the previously indicated location. The idea behind the assumption MSD ItemWillBeLoaded is very similar.

4   Integrating ScenarioTools and ModGraph

In the following, we describe how we implement the integration of MSDs and GTRs by integrating the tools MODGRAPH and SCENARIOTOOLS.

The interaction between both tools is shown in Fig. 8. In SCENARIOTOOLS, MSD specifications are modeled in UML, using the Papyrus editor (see step 1 in Fig. 8). UML is extended with a profile to add modalities to sequence diagram messages, for example. The UML class model is then transformed into an Ecore class model (step 2), from which an object system can be instantiated (step 5). Based on the object system, SCENARIOTOOLS can interpret the MSDs and perform play-out (step 6) [3].

When integrating MODGRAPH with SCENARIOTOOLS, before performing play-out, we model GTRs and compile them into an executable Xcore model. The basis for modeling GTRs with MODGRAPH is the Ecore model created in step 2. The behavior of the operations in the Ecore class model can be specified by GTRs (step 3). These GTRs are then compiled into an Xcore model (step 4). The Xcore implementation of the GTRs can now be called by SCENARIOTOOLS when corresponding message events are executed during play-out.

In the Xcore model, for each GTR, two Xcore operations are generated, a *check-operation* and a *do-operation*. The check-operation is used to check the precondition for the applicability of the rule; the do-operation executes the transformation. When the SCENARIOTOOLS play-out selects possible messages events for execution, it first calls the check-operation. Only if this message returns a valid match of the precondition, play-out may choose to safely execute the corresponding message event. Otherwise, as described in Sect. 3 executing the message leads to a safety violation.

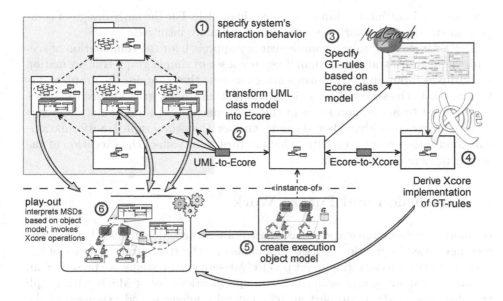

Fig. 8. Overview of the ScenarioTools-ModGraph-integration

One limitation of our tool integration is that currently SCENARIOTOOLS only supports messages with one parameter. We plan to extend SCENARIOTOOLS so that multiple parameters will be supported. For realizing our example with the current limitation, we use multiple messages to transmit each parameter individually. This complicates the current example implementation, but conceptually, the tool integration demonstrates a successful integration of the two modeling paradigms.

5   Related Work

While there is extensive work on scenario-based specification and analysis approaches based on LSCs/MSDs or other kinds of sequence diagrams, e.g., STAIRS [14], to the best of our knowledge, none of the them rigorously supports the reconfiguration of the participating objects or components at run-time.

Thus, we will in the following discuss two different approaches that combine models for structural reconfiguration behavior and message-based interaction behavior.

The MechatronicUML [1] is a design method for self-adaptive mechatronic systems. This method consists of a family of languages for modeling real-time behavior and architectural reconfiguration [17]. The behavior of the components is specified using state machines with real-time annotations. The architectural reconfiguration is specified using graph transformations on the component structure. Similar to our approach, the execution of graph transformation changes the structure of the active components and their behavior. However, in MechatronicUML, the message based interaction is defined by intra-component state machines and not inter-component scenario models. For the early design of complex interaction behavior, the latter are much more intuitive.

Diethelm et al. [5] take a complementary approach for the combination of scenarios and graph transformation. They use a set of simple graph transformation scenarios as input and synthesize a state machine that contains the graph transformations in the states. The basic idea is that all similar graph transformations are mapped to a common state in the state machine. An additional difference to our approach is that they do not consider that the graph transformations can change the object structure, which in turn would affect the execution of the scenarios as in our approach.

6   Conclusion and Future Work

In many software-intensive systems, there is a tight interdependency between the message-based interaction of its components and the structural dynamics of the system. In order to intuitively, yet precisely design such systems, we presented an approach that integrates scenario-based specifications using MSDs with graph transformation. MSDs support an incremental refinement and extension of the message-based interaction behavior and GTRs offer easy-to-understand, declarative, pattern-oriented means for expressing structural change. The integration of the two formalisms works in two ways: structural transformations are executed as side effects of messages, but GTRs can also constrain when certain actions can be performed.

One interesting direction of future research is how to systematically and efficiently analyze the resulting specification for realizability. Simulation via play-out is, of course, a first method to search for contradictions, but one can hardly be sure to simulate all possible sequences of events in all structural configurations. We are working on an extension of the SCENARIOTOOLS realizability-checking capabilities [7] to be able to explore different object system reconfigurations.

Acknowledgments. We thank Fabian Schmidt for his work on the factory example.

References

1. Becker, S., Dziwok, S., Gerking, C., Schfer, W., Heinzemann, C., Thiele, S., Meyer, M., Priesterjahn, C., Pohlmann, U., Tichy, M.: The MechatronicUML design method – process and language for platform-independent modeling. Tech. Rep. tr-ri-14-337, Heinz Nixdorf Institute, University of Paderborn, version 0.4 (March 2014)
2. Bontemps, Y., Heymans, P.: From live sequence charts to state machines and back: A guided tour. Transactions on Software Engineering 31(12), 999–1014 (2005)
3. Brenner, C., Greenyer, J., Panzica La Manna, V.: The ScenarioTools play-out of modal sequence diagram specifications with environment assumptions. In: Proc. 12th Int. Workshop on Graph Transformation and Visual Modeling Techniques (GT-VMT 2013), vol. 58, EASST (2013)

4. Damm, W., Harel, D.: LSCs: Breathing life into message sequence charts. In: Formal Methods in System Design, vol. 19, pp. 45–80. Kluwer Academic (2001)
5. Diethelm, I., Geiger, L., Maier, T., Zündorf, A.: Turning collaboration diagram strips into storycharts. In: Workshop on Scenarios and State Machines: Models, Algorithms, and Tools (SCESM 2002) ICSE Workshop, Florida, Orlando, USA (2002)
6. Ehrig, H., Ehrig, K., Prange, U., Taentzer, G.: Fundamentals of Algebraic Graph Transformation. Springer, Berlin (2006)
7. Greenyer, J., Brenner, C., Cordy, M., Heymans, P., Gressi, E.: Incrementally synthesizing controllers from scenario-based product line specifications. In: Proceedings of the 2013 9th Joint Meeting on Foundations of Software Engineering, ESEC/FSE 2013, pp. 433–443. ACM, New York (2013)
8. Greenyer, J., Kindler, E.: Compositional synthesis of controllers from scenario-based assume-guarantee specifications. In: Moreira, A., Schätz, B., Gray, J., Vallecillo, A., Clarke, P. (eds.) MODELS 2013. LNCS, vol. 8107, pp. 774–789. Springer, Heidelberg (2013)
9. Harel, D., Kugler, H.: Synthesizing state-based object systems from LSC specifications. International Journal of Foundations of Computer Science 13(01), 5–51 (2002)
10. Harel, D., Maoz, S.: Assert and negate revisited: Modal semantics for UML sequence diagrams. Software and Systems Modeling (SoSyM) 7(2), 237–252 (2008)
11. Harel, D., Marelly, R.: Specifying and executing behavioral requirements: The play-in/play-out approach. Software and System Modeling (SoSyM) 2(2), 82–107 (2002)
12. Harel, D., Marelly, R.: Come, Let's Play: Scenario-Based Programming Using LSCs and the Play-Engine. Springer (August 2003)
13. Harel, D., Marron, A., Weiss, G.: Behavioral programming. Commun. ACM 55(7), 90–100 (2012)
14. Haugen, Ø., Husa, K., Runde, R., Stølen, K.: STAIRS towards formal design with sequence diagrams. Software & Systems Modeling 4(4), 355–357 (2005)
15. Maoz, S., Harel, D.: From multi-modal scenarios to code: Compiling LSCs into AspectJ. In: Proc. 14th Int. Symp. on Foundations of Software Engineering, SIGSOFT 2006/FSE-14, pp. 219–230. ACM, New York (2006)
16. Maoz, S., Harel, D., Kleinbort, A.: A compiler for multimodal scenarios: Transforming LSCs into AspectJ. ACM Trans. Softw. Eng. Methodol. 20(4), 18:1–18:41 (2011)
17. Priesterjahn, C., Steenken, D., Tichy, M.: Timed hazard analysis of self-healing systems. In: Cámara, J., de Lemos, R., Ghezzi, C., Lopes, A. (eds.) Assurances for Self-Adaptive Systems. LNCS, vol. 7740, pp. 112–151. Springer, Heidelberg (2013)
18. Steinberg, D., Budinsky, F., Paternostro, M., Merks, E.: EMF: Eclipse Modeling Framework, 2nd edn. Addison-Wesley, Boston (2009)
19. Winetzhammer, S.: ModGraph – generating executable EMF models. In: Margaria, T., Padberg, J., Taentzer, G., Krause, C., Westfechtel, B. (eds.) Proc. 7th Int. Workshop on Graph Based Tools (GraBaTs 2012). Electronic Communications of the EASST, vol. 54, pp. 32–44. EASST, Bremen (2012)
20. Winetzhammer, S., Westfechtel, B.: Compiling graph transformation rules into a procedural language for behavioral modeling. In: Pires, L.F., Hammoudi, S., Filipe, J., das Neves, R.C. (eds.) Proc. 2nd Int Conf. on Model-Driven Engineering and Software Development (MODELSWARD 2014), pp. 415–424. SCITEPRESS Science and Technology Publications, Portugal (2014)

A Systematic Approach to Automatically Derive Test Cases from Use Cases Specified in Restricted Natural Languages

Man Zhang[1], Tao Yue[2], Shaukat Ali[2], Huihui Zhang[1], and Ji Wu[1]

[1] Software Engineering Institute, Beihang University, Beijing, China
{zhangman1126,pkuzhhui}@cse.buaa.edu.cn,
wuji@buaa.edu.cn
[2] Simula Research Laboratory, Oslo, Norway
{tao,shaukat}@simula.no

Abstract. In many domains, such as avionics, oil and gas, and maritime, a common practice is to derive and execute test cases manually from requirements, where both requirements and test cases are specified in natural language (NL) by domain experts. The manual execution of test cases is largely dependent on the domain experts who wrote the test cases. The process of manual writing of requirements and test cases introduces ambiguity in their description and, in addition, test cases may not be effective since they may not be derived by systematically applying coverage criteria. In this paper, we report on a systematic approach to support automatic derivation of manually executable test cases from use cases. Both use cases and test cases are specified in restricted NLs along with carefully-defined templates implemented in a tool. We evaluate our approach with four case studies (in total having 30 use cases and 579 steps from flows of events), two of which are industrial case studies from the oil/gas and avionics domains. Results show that our tool was able to correctly process all the case studies and systematically (by following carefully-defined structure coverage criteria) generate 30 TCSs and 389 test cases. Moreover, our approach allows defining different test coverage criteria on requirements other than the one already implemented in our tool.

Keywords: Use Cases, Restricted Use Case Modeling, Test Case Specification, Restricted Test Case Specification, Natural Language, Test Generation, Test Cases, Transformation and Automation.

1   Introduction

Test cases in many critical domains such as avionics and maritime are derived manually by domain experts from requirements specified in natural language (NL) and domain experts manually execute test cases. Such a process has the following drawbacks: 1) The overall process is largely dependent on domain experts; 2) Requirements and test cases written in NL are often ambiguous and are interpreted differently by different domain experts; 3) The process of deriving test cases from NL is not

D. Amyot et al. (Eds.): SAM 2014, LNCS 8769, pp. 142–157, 2014.

systematic since the process does not follow any systematic process; and 4) Traceability links from requirements to test cases and vice versa, which serve several purposes such as verifying tests against requirements, are not systematically established.

To overcome the above-mentioned drawbacks of the current practice, an ideal situation should be deriving textual, easy-to-understand, and manually-executable test cases from textual, informal requirements automatically and at the same time establish traceability links between requirements and tests. Moreover, a more systematic process, e.g., considering coverage criteria, is required to generate effective test cases. To deal with these drawbacks of the current process, we propose an automated approach based on the Restricted Use Case Modeling approach (RUCM) [1] and the Restricted Test Case Modeling approach (RTCM) [2], to systematically and automatically derive Test Case Specifications (TCSs) (in RTCM) and test cases (in RTCM) from requirements (in RUCM), based on structural test coverage criteria.

RUCM is based on a template and a set of restriction rules for textual Use Case Specifications (UCSs). Using template and restriction rules is a common feature of NL analysis approaches for reducing imprecision and incompleteness in UCSs. The main factor to consider is that the restricted NL should be expressive and convenient enough for use by developers. Experimental results [1] further suggest that RUCM has enough expressive power, is easy to apply, helps achieve better understandability of use cases and improves the quality of manually-derived analysis models.

Inspired and based on RUCM, RTCM was proposed to specify TCSs. TCSs are a common way of documenting a set of test cases for a System Under Test (SUT) at a high level. TCSs are commonly written in NL and the transition to executable test cases requires much test engineer effort regarding test coverage criteria to implement. Moreover, the quality of manually developed test cases might not be satisfactory, as test engineers might not systematically apply test coverage criteria. In the context of our industrial partners, test cases are implemented manually; therefore, it is important to have a language that has sufficient expressive power and is easy to apply to specify TCSs and test cases. This particularity motivates us to design RTCM.

All the concepts of RTCM are formalized in TCMeta [2], a metamodel defining the language by extending the *UCMeta* metamodel [3] formally defining RUCM. The editors for RUCM and RTCM have been implemented in a modeling framework called Lightweight Modeling Framework (LMF [4]), similar to Eclipse Modeling Framework (EMF) except that LMF reduces the tight coupling with Eclipse to ease transformations to other platforms.

In this paper, we propose an automated solution to derive TCSs and test cases by implementing carefully-defined structure test coverage criteria on TCSs. Notice that our transformation is divided into two steps: generating TCSs and generating test cases. The rationale behind this is that when introducing different test coverage criteria, generating TCSs can remain untouched.

To assess our approach, we evaluated it with four case studies: Crisis Management Systems, Banking System, Subsea Production Systems and Autopilot System. The last two are industrial case studies. There are in total 30 use cases with 579 steps of flow of events collected for the case studies, which lead to the automated and systematic generation of 30 TCSs and 389 test cases.

The rest of the paper is organized as follows: Section 2 presents the background necessary to understand the paper and Section 3 describes the transformation from

RUCM to RTCM. Section 4 presents the evaluation of the transformation, and related work is presented in Section 5. Last, we conclude the paper in Section 6.

2   Background

In this section, we summarize the key features of RUCM for use case modeling and RTCM for specifying TCSs and test cases, respectively.

2.1   Restricted Use Case Modeling (RUCM)

Previously, we have devised the RUCM methodology, which encompasses a use case template and 26 restriction rules for the textual UCSs [1]. The goal of RUCM is to be easy to use, to reduce ambiguity and improve understanding, and to facilitate automated analysis. We therefore performed a controlled experiment to evaluate RUCM in terms of its ease of use [1]. The results showed that RUCM is overall easy to use, and that it leads to significant improvements over the use of a standard use case template [5] (without restrictions to the use of NL) in terms the UCS understandability.

A RUCM UCS has one basic flow and can have one or more alternative flows. An alternative flow always depends on a condition occurring in a specific step in a flow of reference, called reference flow, which is either the basic flow or an alternative flow. We classify alternative flows into three types: A specific alternative flow refers to a specific step in the reference flow; A bounded alternative flow refers to more than one step (consecutive or not) in the reference flow; A global alternative flow (called general alternative flow in [6]) refers to any step in the reference flow. The different types of alternative flows specify precisely the interactions between the reference flow and its alternative flows. For specific and bounded alternative flows, a RFS (Reference Flow Step) section specifies one or more (reference flow) step numbers. We also classify action sentences of steps of flows of events according to their semantic functions into five types: 1) Initiation: the primary actor sends a request and data to the system; 2) Validation: the system validates a request and data; 3) Internal Transaction: the system alters its internal state (e.g., recording or modifying something); 4) Response2PrimaryActor: the system replies to the primary actor with a result; and 5) Response2SecondaryActor: the system sends requests to a secondary actor. These five types can be automatically identified using our tool.

RUCM also defines a set of keywords to specify conditional logic sentences (IF-THEN-ELSE-ELSEIF-ENDIF), concurrency sentences (MEANWHILE), condition checking sentences (VALIDATES THAT), and iteration sentences (DO-UNTIL). These keywords limit opportunities for ambiguities in UCSs. They also greatly facilitate the automated generation of other models such as UML sequence diagrams and test cases. Keywords ABORT and RESUME STEP are used to describe an exceptional exit action and where an alternative flow merges back in its reference flow, respectively. An alternative flow ends either with ABORT or RESUME STEP, which means that the last step of the alternative flow should clearly specify whether the flow returns back to the reference flow and where (using keywords RESUME STEP followed by a returning step number) or terminates (using keyword ABORT).

One example is provided in Fig. 1, where use case WithdrawFund is specified using RUCM, implemented in an editor we developed, named as RUCMEditor.

Fig. 1. Use case Withdraw Fund specified using RUCM (in RUCMEditor)

2.2   Restricted Test Case Modeling (RTCM)

RTCM is inspired by RUCM by reusing the core part of RUCM, that is, specifying scenarios. The essential idea of Scenario Specification is that a flow of events is composed of a sequence of steps (Sentences) and a Post Condition. Flows of events are further classified into Basic Flow and Alternative Flow, which are further classified into four types: Specific Alternative, Bounded Alternative, Global Alternative and Oracle Verification Flow. The first three types were inherited from RUCM and Oracle Verification Flow is a newly proposed for RTCM.

Test Case Specification	
Name	Test_Withdraw Fund
Brief Description	This test case specification is for testing use case specification that ATM customer withdraws a specific amount of funds from a valid bank account.
Precondition (Test Data Specification)	The system is idle. The system is displaying a Welcome message.
Tester	None
Dependency	None

Basic Flow (Test Sequence) (Untitled) ▼	Steps	
	1	INCLUDE TEST CASE SPECIFICATION Test_Validate PIN
	2	Test System or Tester selects Withdrawal through the system
	3	Test System or Tester enters the withdrawal amount through the system
	4	Test System or Tester selects the account number through the system
	5	Test System or Tester VERIFIES THAT the validation that the account number is valid is <True or False>.
	6	Test System or Tester VERIFIES THAT the validation that ATM customer has enough funds in the account is <True or False>.
	7	Test System or Tester VERIFIES THAT the validation that the withdrawal amount does not exceed the daily limit of the account is <True or False>.
	8	Test System or Tester VERIFIES THAT the validation that the ATM has enough funds is <True or False>.
	9	Test System or Tester VERIFIES THAT The system dispenses the cash amount.
	10	Test System or Tester VERIFIES THAT The system prints a receipt.
	11	Test System or Tester VERIFIES THAT The system ejects the ATM card.
	12	Test System or Tester VERIFIES THAT The system displays Welcome message.
	Postcondition (Test Oracle)	ATM customer funds have been withdrawn.

Specific Alt. Flow (Test Sequence) "alt1" ▼	RFS 8	
	1	Test System or Tester VERIFIES THAT The system displays an apology message MEANWHILE Test System or Tester VERIFIES THAT the system ejects the ATM card
	2	Test System or Tester VERIFIES THAT The system shuts down.
	3	ABORT.
	Postcondition (Test Oracle)	ATM customer funds have not been withdrawn. The system is shut down.

Bounded Alt. Flow (Test Sequence) "alt2" ▼	RFS 5-7	
	1	Test System or Tester VERIFIES THAT The system displays an apology message MEANWHILE Test System or Tester VERIFIES THAT the system ejects the ATM card
	2	ABORT.
	Postcondition (Test Oracle)	ATM customer funds have not been withdrawn. The system is idle. The system is displaying a Welcome message.

Global Alt. Flow (Test Sequence) "alt3" ▼	Test System or Tester enters Cancel.	
	1	<- internal transaction ->
	2	Test System or Tester VERIFIES THAT The system ejects the ATM card.
	3	ABORT.
	Postcondition (Test Oracle)	ATM customer PIN number has not been withdrawn. The system is idle. The system is displaying a Welcome message.

Fig. 2. TCS corresponding to use case WithdrawFund (Fig. 1)

Test Item is a concept borrowed from the international ISO/IEC/IEEE 29119 standard [7], where *Test Item* (an alternate to commonly used term SUT) is defined as "work product that is an object of testing. The test item is composed of a set of *Test Setup* and *TCS*, both of which should be specified using the *Scenario Specification* template. *Test Setup* can be shared/reused across TCSs. We define *Test Setup* as a set of steps to get the test item ready for executing flows of events defined in a TCS. *TCS*, as defined in the ISO 29119 standard [7], is "documentation of a set of one or more test cases". A tester interacts with a test setup or TCS by either manually performing or verifying steps specified in the test setup or the TCS. In both cases, it is impossible to execute test cases on the test item and hence steps specified in either the test setup or the TCS have to be run manually, which is very common in many domains involving both software and (mechanical and electrical) hardware components.

In addition to the RUCM keywords, RTCM introduces a set of keywords including: INCLUDE TCS and VERIFIES THAT.

We define the keyword INCLUDE TEST CASE SPECIFCATION to specify that a TCS includes another one with the objective to facilitating reuse of specification fragments. This keyword, from the perspective of tooling, corresponds to the Include semantics of the UML use case diagram notation and can therefore be formalized in *TCMeta* to facilitate automated transformations to test cases.

We define the keyword VERIFIES THAT to provide the capability for testers to manually verify a test sequence step and, therefore, subjects of sentences with this keyword must be Tester. This keyword will be used during the generation of test cases as an indication of manual steps that have to be performed. Sentences with this keyword only appear in Oracle Verification Flows. We provide an example of the TCS corresponding to use case WithdrawFund in Fig. 2. We will discuss in Section 3 how such a TCS can be derived from a UCS automatically.

3   Transformation

Fig. 3 shows an overview of the transformation from RUCM specifications to TCSs in RTCM and test cases in RTCM using a set of transformations implemented in our tool called aToucan4Test. In the section, we discuss its main components.

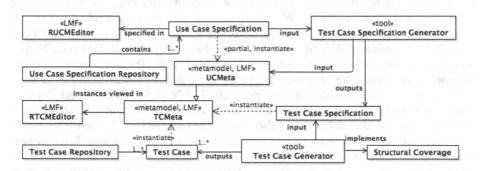

Fig. 3. An overview of aToucan4Test

3.1   RUCMEditor and RTCMEditor

UCSs and TCSs are specified in the RUCM editor and RTCM editor, respectively implemented in our modeling framework called Lightweight Modeling Framework (LMF [4]). The framework implements similar kinds of functionalities as the Eclipse Modeling Framework (EMF), but with a lightweight design that aims to reduce tight coupling with Eclipse to facilitate easier transformations to other platforms. For example, RUCM and RTCM can be easily deployed to different platforms such as Java Web Applications and C++ in the future.

Both LMF and EMF have two editors: reflective model and metamodel editors. The Reflective Editor is a simple model editor that can automatically adapt metamodel changes based on the LMF metamodel reflection mechanism. When a user registers a domain-specific metamodel extension (e.g., *UCMeta* and *TCMeta* in our context) to the framework, the reflective editor is instantly ready for editing model instances that conform to the newly registered metamodel. The LMF metamodel editor allows users to implement UCMeta extensions easily (*TCMeta* in our case). With this editor, users can create new packages, new metaclasses and enumerations and it is also possible to append new attributes to existing metaclasses in UCMeta. The editor can also automatically generate Java code for the newly introduced metamodel or extension. Moreover, the framework predefines a set of extension points to ease the process of extending the graphical notations such as adding a new keyword and highlighting it with a different color. We utilized this facility of LMF to implement *TCMeta*.

Based on LMF, we implemented *RUCMEditor* and *RTCMEditor* and it was used to conduct the industrial case studies reported in this paper. Built-in and domain-specific keywords (can be embedded additionally) are automatically highlighted in both editors. Keywords can be enabled or disabled depending on the application.

3.2   TCS Generator (TCSG)

This transformation automatically generates a TCS for each use case. Here, the generated TCS mostly keeps the control flow of the use case but with additional testing information such as having sentences with Tester and Test System as subjects of test steps. For example, the TCS in Fig. 2 is automatically generated from the UCS of WithdrawFund given in Fig. 1. We summarize the transformation rules in Table 1, where one can see that the transformation is straightforward. This is because RTCM itself is an extension of RUCM. In addition, the formalization of RTCM (i.e., TCMeta) is an extension of the formalization of RUCM: UCMeta. The transformation keeps the control flow structure of a use case in the generated TCS. For example, as indicated in R1.1.1.2.1, conditional sentences (IF-THEN-ELSE-ENDIF) and iterative sentences (DO-UNTIL) remain the same during the transformation. The structure of the basic flow and alternative flows also remain the same (R1.1.1.2.3 and R1.1.1.2.4). However, the transformation changes simple sentences in a UCS into different sentences of the corresponding TCS, depending on sentence semantics of the simple sentences (Section 2.1). For example, as shown in R1.1.1.2.1, for a simple sentence, when it is with semantics of type Initiation, its subject is changed from the name of an actor that initiated the use case to "Tester or the test system".

Table 1. Transformation rules from UCSs to TCSs

Rule#	Description
R1	Transform a UCMeta instance to a TCMeta instance
R1.1	UseCase → SUT, which groups a set of TCSs
R1.1.1	UseCaseSpecification → TestCaseSpecification
R1.1.1.1	Precondition → TestDataSpecification
R1.1.1.2	FlowOfEvents → FlowOfEvents for TestScenarios
R1.1.1.2.1	\<Sentence> steps -> \<Sentence> steps
R1.1.1.2.1	Sentence → Sentence4Test
Simple Sentence	1. Initiation: Test System or Tester < the predicate of the sentence> 2. InternalTransaction: None 3. Response2PrimaryActor and Response2SecondaryActor: Test System or Tester VERIFIES THAT < the predicate of the sentence>
Complex Sentence	1. ConditionalSentence, IterativeSentence and Parallel-Sentence remain the same. 2. ConditionCheckSentence: Test System or Tester VERFIES THAT \<internal condition> is \<True or False>
Special Sentence	1. ResumeStepSentence and AbortSentence remain the same. 2. IncludeSentece → IncludeTCSpecNature 3. ExtendSentence → ExtendTCSpecNature
R1.1.1.2.2	Postcondition -> TestOracle
R1.1.1.2.3	Structure of the basic flow remains the same.
R1.1.1.2.4	Structures of the alternative flows remain the same.
R1.2	See R1.1.1.2.1, special sentence for handling Include and Extend. We did not see the need to transformation Generalization between two use cases.
R1.3	Test Setup cannot be automatically generated since such information is not contained in use case models. Users are required to manually add them if needed.

3.3 Test Case Generator (TCG)

The second step transformation is to generate test cases from the generated TCSs in TCSG. During this transformation, each test case scenario is transformed into a set of test cases, each of which defines a unique set of test steps without containing any

Test Case Specification

Name	Test_Withdraw Fund_test4_include_Test_Validate PIN_test7
Brief Description	None
Precondition (Test Data Specification)	The system is idle. The system is displaying a Welcome message.
Tester	None
Dependency	None

Basic Flow (Test Sequence) (Untitled) ▼	Steps	
	1	INCLUDE TEST CASE SPECIFICATION Test_Validate PIN_test7
	2	Test System or Tester selects Withdrawal through the system
	3	Test System or Tester enters the withdrawal amount through the system
	4	Test System or Tester selects the account number through the system
	5	Test System or Tester VERIFIES THAT The system displays an apology message MEANWHILE Test System or Tester VERIFIES THAT the system ejects the ATM card
	6	Test System or Tester VERIFIES THAT The system shuts down.
Postcondition (Test Oracle)		ATM customer funds have not been withdrawn. The system is shut down.

Fig. 4. One test case generated from the TCS in Fig. 2

condition and branch. The transformation is based on the structural coverage. Below, we provide a brief description of the structure coverage criteria implemented in TCG inspired from traditional software testing coverage criteria [8,9].

Structural coverage criteria focus on covering certain structural features of RTCM specifications. We implemented the following two types of structural coverage criteria: *Branch Coverage Criteria* and *Loop Coverage Criterion*. The former focus on traversing branches (Alternative Flow) in TCSs specified using RTCM. We implemented the following criteria: 1) *All Branch Coverage*: This coverage criterion generates a set of test cases that cover all branches of RTCM specifications at least once; 2) *All Condition Coverage*: This coverage criterion ensures that all conditions of all branches are covered at least once. As for the *Loop Coverage Criterion*, it ensures that each loop (DO UNTIL) is exercised exactly *one*, *none*, and *x* number of times, where *x* can be specified by a user beforehand. In our current implementation of the Loop Coverage Criterion, we exercise each loop exactly once.

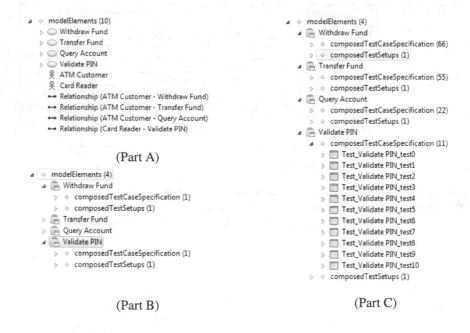

(Part A)

(Part B)

(Part C)

Fig. 5. Structures of the RUCM Model (Part A), generated RTCM TCS model (Part B) and generated RTCM test case model (Part C) for use case WithdrawFund

Moreover, from the perspective of UCSs (requirements), our current implementation of TCG achieved *All Sentence Coverage* and *All FlowOfEvents Coverage*. *All Sentence Coverage* generates a set of test cases that covers all sentences of RTCM TCSs at least once. *All FlowOfEvent Coverage* ensures that the basic flow and all the alternative flows are covered at least once. During the transformation, all three types of alternative flows are properly handled. For a specific or bounded alterative flow, one or more branches are derived based on the information in the RFS sentence, where the location (one or more steps in the reference flow) that the flow should branch from is defined. For a global alternative flow, we derive branches for one se-lected step of the reference flow of events, from which the global alternative flow branches. Of course, depending on their needs, users can provide input on which cri-terion to apply when generating test cases.

During the transformation, we also systematically handled all complex and special sentences to ensure that for each flow of events (either basic or alternative flows), we achieved *All Sentence Coverage* and *All Condition Coverage*. With this implementa-tion, for use case WithdrawFund, aToucan4Test generated in total 154 test cases including the proper handling of the special sentence of INCLUDE USE CASE Vali-date PIN. One of these generated use cases is provided in Fig. 4 for illustration pur-pose. In Fig. 5, we provide the structures of the model elements (in our RUCMEditor and RTCMEditor) of three models: the RUCM model for the WithdrawFund use cas-es, the automatically generated RTCM TCS model from the RUCM model, and the automatically generated RTCM test case model from the RTCM TCS model.

4   Evaluation

4.1   Description of Case Studies

Banking System: Gomma [10] defined this case study by providing UCSs on how a user interacts with an Automated Teller Machine (ATM) to, for example, withdraw money and transfer money. We rewrote the UCSs provided in the book using RUCM for our previous experiments [11] and this one.

Crisis Management System: Capozucca et al. [12] defined requirements of a soft-ware product line of Crisis Management Systems (CMS), called bCMS-SPL, with the aim to manage car crash crises. We modeled one key use case named *Communicate with other coordinator* using RUCM and results were presented in the CMA@MODELS2013 workshop [13]. The RUCM model was evaluated by modeling experts and was deposited to the ReMoDD repository for public access. In this paper, we used the modeled specifications to generate the TCS and test cases.

Autopilot: Autopilot System (AS) is an industrial case study that we used to assess our test case generation approach. AS controls and guides an aircraft, based on control law computation that takes data sampled from sensors as input and sends commands to actuators. The AS has two operating modes: Auto mode (that does not need any instruction from a pilot) and Manual mode (that needs instructions from a pilot). A pilot can switch the modes during flight. We modeled 11 use cases for this case study using RUCM, including Start, Synchronize, Handle Faults, Power-up Build-in-Test (PUBIT), Sample Data, Transmit Input Data, Vote Input Data, Calculate Control Rate, Transmit Output Data, Vote Output Data and Output Flight Data. The modeling inputs of these 11 use cases are real requirements from our industrial partner in the avionics domain. Our industrial partner is a company that provides commercial aero-nautical computing techniques to the market in China. We do not provide the name of the company due to confidentiality issues (this restriction applies to the next one too).

Subsea Control: Subsea Production Systems (SPSs) are used for managing the exploitation of oil and gas production fields. These systems consist of hundreds of mechanical, hydraulic, electrical and software components that are typically geo-graphically distributed and connected through networks. Subsea control systems are a very important part of subsea production systems, with configurable software deployed to monitor and control various types and large number of sensors and actuators. For this case study, based on given requirements, we derived 14 use cases and specified them using RUCM, which covers functionalities of waking up the control system, handling sensors, handling various types of actuators such as chokes and handle communication loss.

In Table 2, we provide the descriptive statistics of the key elements of the RUCM models we derived for the case studies, in total with 30 use cases specified and 579 sentences captured as the steps of the flows of events of all the use cases.

Table 2. Descriptive Statistics of the RUCM Models

Case Studies	# UCSs	# Dependencies	# Flows	# Flow steps	# Condition sen.	# Validation sen.	# Resume
ATM	4	3	14	70	3	10	1
CMS	1	0	8	60	13	1	5
AS	11	5	34	212	11	16	3
SPS	14	6	28	237	28	15	2
Total	30	14	84	579	55	42	11

4.2 Results of TCS and Test Case Generation

Table 3 summarizes the results of TCS and test case generation from the RUCM specifications of the case studies (Table 2). Notice that each UCS in RUCM is mapped to exactly one TCS and thus we have in total 30 UCSs (Table 2) and correspondingly 30 TCSs in RTCM as shown in Table 3. In total, we generated 389 test cases for the four case studies based on the structure test coverage criteria discussed in Section 3.

Table 3. Results of the Generation of TCSs and Test Cases

Case Studies	TCS (30 in total)			# Test Cases
	# Condition sentences	# Validation sentences	# Resume sentences	
ATM	3	10	1	154
CMS	7	1	5	60
AS	11	16	3	69
SPS	28	15	2	106
Total	49	42	11	389

4.3 Discussion

We summarize below the benefits of using our approach in practice.

Systematic and Automated. In many organizations, a common practice is to write UCSs and TCSs in NL. Using RUCM, one is forced to specify specifications systematically in a restricted NL, thus enabling precision and facilitating automation. With our approach, UCSs can be specified more systematically and thoroughly and test cases can be generated automatically based on systematic coverage criteria.

Precise and Easy to Understand Specifications. Using RUCM/RTCM, use cases/TCSs can be specified precisely and are understandable by various stakeholders. Compared to the common practice, where use cases and TCSs are specified in free text, the latter may not be understandable by everyone because of the high ambiguity inherent to free text. By specifying use cases/TCSs in RUCM/RTCM, the specifications should be more understandable by different stakeholders since it combines restricted NL, templates and keywords specifying use cases/TCSs.

Easier than Modeling Behavioral Models for Testing. While working with model-based testing, the most difficult activity is the development of complex UML models such as UML state machines, which are commonly used for supporting model-based testing as we experienced in our previous works [14]. On the other hand, practitioners are more comfortable with writing textual specifications than developing UML models. Therefore, specifying use cases/TCSs with RUCM/RTCM provides an alternative way for test case generation for model-based testing using behavioral models. However, we need to conduct more systematic empirical studies in the future to come to a definitive conclusion.

Reducing Reliance on Domain Experts. Our tool support, i.e., aToucan4Test, generates test cases in a unified format, namely RTCM. This means that these test cases are understandable by anyone familiar with RTCM and thus can be executed by different testers. In contrast, test cases written by a tester in NL might not be precisely understandable by different testers and thus execution of a particular set of test cases is dependent on the availability of a particular domain expert. With our proposed approach, the use of a standardized format for TCSs reduces the reliance on the availability of domain experts.

Traceability. Our proposed approach maintains traceability among three different types of artifacts, i.e., UCSs, TCSs, and test cases. Maintaining such traceability facilitates automated change impact analysis, which we plan to investigate in the future.

Easier Test Case Maintenance. Using RUCM/RTCM, use case/test case maintenance is much easier as compared to the common practice, where every change in a specification has to be reflected manually in all the impacted specifications. With our approach, changes must be reflected in UCSs and test cases can be generated again.

Separation of Concerns. Our approach is implemented in a two-step transformation, where the first transformation maintains control structure of RUCM specifications in RTCM specifications. In the second step, various structural and data coverage criteria are implemented to generate test cases in RTCM. Such separation facilitates integrating more sophisticated coverage criteria in the future in the second transformation without changing the first transformation.

Conformance to Existing Standards. RTCM borrows some concepts from [7] such as *Test Item*, *Test Case Specification* and *Test Data Specification*. Future extensions of RTCM will be designed to conform to existing standards as much as possible.

Notice that we did not assess the effectiveness of the generate test cases, which require much support from our industrial partners since test cases have to be manually executed. This will be investigated in the future.

5   Related Work

We classified the related work into three research streams: requirements-based testing, keywords-based testing and behavior-based testing.

5.1   Requirements Based Testing

A controlled NL, named ucsCNL, was proposed by Barris et al. in [15] for UCSs with the objective of facilitating automated generation of test cases by taking use cases written with this controlled NL as input. To compare with RUCM, the proposed method does not include a use case template, which is commonly required when documenting a UCS and considered as an important means to structure textual requirements. RUCM however includes a comprehensive and well-evaluated use case template, which is also the foundation for structuring RTCM TCSs. In addition, both RUCM and RTCM rely on the keyword mechanism to enhance the precision of specifications and enable automation. uscCNL, however, defines a rather comprehensive list of grammars for using English. RUCM/RTCM specifications can be automatically formalized as instances of UCMeta/TCMeta. Therefore, the identification of English sentence patterns and grammar can be automated.

In [16], Badri et al. have proposed a methodology to generate test cases using use cases and collaboration diagrams. Their process starts with constructing use cases for the system, which are realized by constructing a sequence diagram corresponding to each use case. In order to manipulate the collaboration diagram for test case generation, a customized formal language known as Collaboration Description Language was used. This language represents description of the collaboration diagram in a textual format. Our approach directly takes RUCM specifications as input to automatically generate test cases. No additional modeling notations are required in between.

In [17], Nebut et al. have proposed a methodology to generate test cases for system testing by taking use cases with associated contracts and parameters as input. Once use cases are parameterized (with inputs defined), the contracts including pre- and post-conditions of the use case are defined. These conditions are defined in the form of logical expressions. In addition, the system and application properties are also specified using these contracts. The relationships between the use cases (e.g., include, exclude, and extend) are also defined within logical expressions. Finally test cases were generated by instantiating the use case parameters. Notice that no detailed steps of UCSs are exercised to generate test cases in their approach. We, however, generate test cases by taking into account flows of events and their steps of each TCS while applying coverage criteria.

In [18], Ryser et al. have proposed a methodology to generate test cases for system testing from the scenarios, which represent requirements in NL. Therefore, scenarios tend to be more ambiguous, so a formal model was needed in which scenarios are converted. Test cases are then generated from the generated model. In this approach state machines were used as converted models to generate test cases. RTCM is rigorous to compare with free style NL. Moreover, we have an automated solution to formalize RTCM specifications as instances of TCMeta. Further derivation of test cases based on the formalized representation becomes easy to achieve.

Tahan et al. [19] proposed a requirements-based, black-box test generation approach to generate test cases from requirements specified using the System Description Language (SDL) [20,21,22,23]. Each individual SDL requirement is first automatically transformed into a SDL system model. Manual combination of individual SDL system models to an integrated one is required. The combined SDL model is then automatically transformed into Extended Finite State Machine (EFSM), which is provided as input to a test generator for generating test cases. To compare our work with this approach, which takes three transformation steps (with manual intervention in between), our approach provides a direct transition from RUCM to test cases.

5.2   Keyword Driven Testing

Tang et al. [24] propose a keyword driven automated testing framework to support the conversion of the keyword-based test cases into different kinds of test scripts. Keywords are used to identify operations or atomic actions in test execution and they are very specific to applications such as 'Click' for GUI applications. Test engineers use these keywords (via a GUI) to specify test cases, which are then transformed into test scripts. Notice that each test case defines a sequence of actions or operations. Therefore, there is no branch or loop in each test case description. Our approach, however, aims to generate test cases from use cases.

Hametner et al. [25] proposed a keyword-driven testing approach for industrial automation systems, with the aim to specify test cases in a high abstraction level and enable non-programmers to read and write test cases. Test engineers write test cases manually, in a tabular format using predefined keywords, but automated generation of executable tests from the tabular format is not supported.

5.3   Behavior Driven Development (BDD)

BDD [26] is a software development process based on Test Driven Development (TDD) [27], which describes the cycle of writing a test first before writing the code being tested. For TDD, to write a test, the developer must clearly understand the requirements specification of a feature to be implemented. Such a requirements specification is often written as use cases and user stories, which essentially describes the behavior of the feature. BDD however concentrates on specifying desired behavior (e.g., business requirements) of SUT, which leads to the derivation of tests.

BDD chooses to use a semi-formal format for specifying behavior, which is similar to user story specifications. During the process, BDD specifies that business analysts and developers should collaborate and specify behavior in terms of user stories. Similarly to our approach, BDD aims to become a communication medium among all stakeholders in a project. Some templates have been proposed to specify user stories. For example, North [28] suggested a textual format template including keywords like 'in order to', 'given' and 'when'. Based on this textual format, North proposed a number of frameworks that support BDD, including JBehave [29] for Java and RBehave [29] for Ruby, which was the basis for Cucumber [30], recently proposed. There also exist other BDD-based tools (e.g., Fitnesse [31]), which use different formats such as decision tables. All these BDD tools do not support the automated generation of test cases from requirements like what we do. They instead aim to achieve agile development of software applications, including facilitating software design, specifying software behavior and documenting code. Our framework however can generate test cases to test not only software but also software-intensive systems.

6   Conclusion and Future Work

TCSs document a set of test cases for a SUT and are commonly used to either manually code executable test cases in a test scripting language or execute TCSs manually. Such TCSs are usually derived from requirements specified in NL and require transitions from requirements to TCSs and to test cases. The overall process of these transitions has several drawbacks such as: ambiguity in NL, lack of systematic approach due to a manual process, and the whole process largely dependent on domain experts. To overcome these drawbacks, we proposed an approach where requirements are specified in restricted NL and TCSs and test cases are generated automatically by applying systematic coverage criteria. We extended our existing Restricted Use Case Modeling (RUCM) approach that was developed to specify requirements in restricted NL and developed a TCS language called Restricted Test Case Modeling (RTCM) that is used to specify TCSs in restricted NL. Both RUCM and RTCM have easy-to-use editors for specifying requirements and TCSs. We reported an automated transformation from requirements specified in RUCM into corresponding TCSs and test cases in RTCM by applying systematic coverage criteria on RTCM.

To assess the applicability of our proposed approach, we modeled four systems, including two that are industrial systems from the avionics and oil/gas domains. Using our test generation tool, called aToucan4Test, which implements structure coverage criteria on RTCM specifications, we managed to systematically and automatically generate TCSs and test cases from the RUCM specifications.

References

1. Yue, T., Briand, L.C., Labiche, Y.: Facilitating the Transition from Use Case Models to Analysis Models: Approach and Experiments. ACM Trans. Softw. Eng. Methodol. 22 (1), Article 5 (2011)
2. Zhang, M., Yue, T., Ali, S.: A Keyword and Restricted NL Based TCS Language for Automated Testing. Simula Research Laboratory, Norway, Technical Report (2014-01)
3. Yue, T., Briand, L., Labiche, Y.: Automatically Deriving a UML Analysis Model from a Use Case Model. Simula Research Laboratory, Norway, Technical Report (2013)
4. Zhang, G., Yue, T., Wu, J., Ali, S.: Zen-RUCM: A Tool for Supporting a Comprehensive and Extensible Use Case Modeling Framework. In: Liu, Y., et al. (eds.) Demos/Posters/StudentResearch@MoDELS. CEUR-WS, vol. 1113, pp. 41–45 (2013)
5. Bruegge, B., Dutoit, A.H.: Object-Oriented Software Engineering Using UML, Patterns and Java. Prentice Hall (2004)
6. Bittner, K.: Use Case Modeling. Addison-Wesley, Boston (2002)
7. Reid, S.: Software and systems engineering Software testing Part 1: Concepts and definitions. ISO/IEC/IEEE 29119-1, pp. 1–64 (2013)
8. Myers, G.J., Sandler, C., Badgett, T.: The art of software testing. John Wiley & Sons (2011)

9. Binder, R.: Testing object-oriented systems: models, patterns, and tools. Addison-Wesley Professional (2000)
10. Gomaa, H.: Designing Concurrent, Distributed, and Real-Time Applications with UML. In: 23rd International Conference on Software Engineering, pp. 737–738. IEEE CS (2001)
11. Briand, L., Falessi, D., Nejati, S., Sabetzadeh, M., Yue, T.: Traceability and SysML Design Slices to Support Safety Inspections: A Controlled Experiment. ACM Trans. Softw. Eng. Methodol. 23 (1), Article 9 (2014)
12. Capozucca, A., et al.: Requirements Definition Document for a Software Product Line of Car Crash Management Systems. ReMoDD (2011), http://bit.ly/1jUkIhN
13. Zhang, G., Yue, T., Ali, S.: Modeling Crisis Management System with the Restricted Use Case Modeling Approach. In: Moreira, A., et al. (eds.) CMA@MODELS. CEUR-WS, vol. 1079, paper 2 (2013)
14. Ali, S., Hemmati, H.: Model-based Testing of Video Conferencing Systems: Challenges, Lessons Learnt, and Results. In: IEEE International Conference on Software Testing, Verification, and Validation (ICST), pp. 353–362. IEEE CS (2014)
15. Barros, F.A., Neves, L., Hori, E., Torres, D.: The ucsCNL: A Controlled Natural Language for Use Case Specifications. In: SEKE, pp. 250–253 (2011)
16. Badri, M., Badri, L., Naha, M.: A use case driven testing process: Towards a formal approach based on UML collaboration diagrams. In: Petrenko, A., Ulrich, A. (eds.) FATES 2003. LNCS, vol. 2931, pp. 223–235. Springer, Heidelberg (2004)
17. Nebut, C., Fleurey, F., Le Traon, Y., Jézéquel, J.M.: Requirements by contracts allow automated system testing. In: ISSRE 2003, pp. 85–96. IEEE CS (2003)
18. Ryser, J., Glinz, M.: A scenario-based approach to validating and testing software systems using statecharts. In: Proc. 12th International Conference on Software and Systems Engineering and their Applications (1999)
19. Tahat, L.H., Vaysburg, B., Korel, B., Bader, A.J.: Requirement-based automated blackbox test generation. In: COMPSAC 2001, pp. 489–495. IEEE CS (2001)
20. Algayres, B., Lejeuhe, Y., Hugonnet, F.: GOAL: Observing SDL Behavior with Object Code. In: Braek, R., Sarma, A. (eds.) SDL 1995 with MSC in CASE, pp. 26–29. Elsevier (1995)
21. Bochmann, G., Petrenko, A., Bellal, O., Maguiraga, S.: Automating the process of test derivation from SDL specifications. In: Cavalli, A., Sarma, A. (eds.) SDL 1997: Time for Test-ing: SDL, MSC and Trends, pp. 261–276. Elsevier (1997)
22. Brömstrup, L., Hogrefe, D.: TESDL: Experience with generating test cases from SDL specifications. In: Linn, R.J., Uyar, Ü. (eds.) Conformance Testing Methodologies and Architectures for OSI Protocols, pp. 455–467. IEEE CS (1995)
23. Dssouli, R., Saleh, K., Aboulhamid, E., Bourhfir, C.: Test development for communication protocols: towards automation. Computer Networks 31(17), 1835–1872 (1999)
24. Tang, J., Cao, X., Ma, A.: Towards adaptive framework of keyword driven automation testing. In: Automation and Logistics, ICAL 2008, pp. 1631–1636. IEEE CS (2008)
25. Hametner, R., Winkler, D., Zoitl, A.: Agile testing concepts based on keyword-driven testing for industrial automation systems. In: IECON 2012, pp. 3727–3732. IEEE CS (2012)
26. Chelimsky, D., et al.: The RSpec book: Behaviour driven development with RSpec, Cucumber, and friends. Pragmatic Bookshelf (2010)
27. Beck, K.: Test-driven development: by example. Addison-Wesley Professional (2003)
28. North, D.: What's in a story (2009), http://dannorth.net/whatsin-a-story
29. North, D.: Introducing BDD. Better Software (2006)
30. Cucumber, http://cukes.info/
31. FitNesse, http://fitnesse.org/FitNesse

Acceptance Test Optimization

Mohamed Mussa and Ferhat Khendek

Electrical and Computer Engineering Department, Concordia University,
Montreal, Quebec, Canada
{mm_abdal,khendek}@ece.concordia.ca

Abstract. Test case generation and execution may be time and effort consuming. At a given testing phase, test case execution can be optimized by avoiding the consideration of test cases that have already been exercised in a previous phase. For instance, one can avoid test case redundancy between integration testing and acceptance testing. Characterizing this redundancy is not straightforward since some integration test cases are applied on an incomplete system with test stubs emulating system components and therefore cannot be substituted to acceptance test cases. In this paper, we propose an approach that maps acceptance test cases to integration test cases and eliminates test cases that have already been exercised on the system during the integration testing phase.

Keywords: Acceptance testing, Integration testing, Test optimization, Model Based Testing, Sequence diagrams.

1   Introduction

Testing improves the quality of software products. It aims to detect software defects before deployment. Large software systems are generally composed of several components that are developed separately and then integrated. On the other hand, tests are designed and applied on individual components, subsystems and complete systems during component testing, integration testing and system/acceptance testing, respectively. There are many software testing approaches and tools that cover a wide spectrum of domains. However, they target specific testing phases: component, integration, system or acceptance testing. To the best of our knowledge, there is no a systematic testing approach/tool that links the different testing phases. The lack of such connections hampers the efficiency of the testing process. In [1], we proposed a Model Based Testing (MBT) [2] framework that links three testing phases: component, integration and acceptance testing. The framework re-utilizes the test models of a testing phase to generate/optimize the test model(s) of the subsequent testing phase. In this framework, the UML testing profile (UTP) [3] is used for the specification of test models, which consist of a set of test cases and of a test architecture. Test cases describe the test behavior, while the test architecture specifies the identity of the participated test objects and relations among them.

In this paper, we propose an approach that optimizes the acceptance test model by relating it to the integration test models. We aim to reduce the acceptance test execution

D. Amyot et al. (Eds.): SAM 2014, LNCS 8769, pp. 158–173, 2014.

time by reducing the number of acceptance test cases. This can be achieved by eliminating acceptance test cases that have already been exercised on the system during integration testing. The approach maps the acceptance test cases to the integration test cases and excludes the ones that have already been exercised during the integration phase.

Mapping two or more models to identify differences and similarities is not new. Text/Code comparison has been investigated for a long time [4, 5]. Several mature approaches exist to solve the problem of software versioning and code-cloning [6, 7]. However, these approaches cannot be applied to graphical models, since they do not consider model hierarchy and model semantics [7-9]. Different approaches have been proposed to handle graphical models [7-9]. Some are domain specific or modeling notation specific while others are more general and domain independent [8]. These approaches target different aspects of the software development lifecycle: Version Control Systems (VCS) [10], Model-Cloning [6, 11], and Model Transformation Testing [12, 13]. One characteristic is common to all these approaches: the assumption that all models have evolved from the same source model/fragment, called the base model. These approaches are actually classified into two categories depending on the required information for the comparison: three-way comparison and two-way comparison [5]. Three-way comparison techniques require the existence of a base model, or changes log, in addition to the two models to compare. Two-way comparison techniques compare two models without external references; however, they are also based on the assumption of the existence of the base model. In this paper, the acceptance test model is compared to the integration test model(s). In our approach, we cannot assume that test models evolved from the same base model since they are built independently. Our approach eliminates acceptance test cases that have been exercised during the integration testing phase. However, not all integration test cases are applied on complete systems during integration testing. Integration test cases may be applied on subsystems with test stubs for system components that are not yet realized at the time of the test execution. Such integration test cases cannot be substituted to acceptance test cases to be applied on a complete system. Therefore, we need to analyze the integration test cases and select those that have been applied on the complete system and compare them to the acceptance test cases.

The structure of this paper is as follows. We present the acceptance test case optimization approach in Section 2. An example for illustration purposes is discussed in Section 3. Section 4 reviews and discusses related work. We conclude in Section 5.

2   Acceptance Test Case Optimization Approach

Acceptance testing is about validating the software product against user requirements. Acceptance test models are generated from the user requirement specifications. There are two steps in acceptance testing: Alpha & Beta. They usually consist of the same set of test cases, but they are applied at different locations and times. Alpha is performed on the development platform before the deployment of the product; while

Beta is executed on the target platform at the user site during the deployment of the product and mostly performed by the user. In this work, we are concerned more with the optimization of the Alpha acceptance testing. The approach can be applied to the Beta too; if the development platform and environment are identical to the user platform and environment.

Integration testing focuses on the interoperability between the integrated system components. It is performed during the integration phase of the development process. Different integration strategies and orders can be adopted to build the system. Test stubs, dummy components, are used to emulate the system environment and/or system components that are not realized yet during an integration round. Since integration testing is performed before acceptance testing, our goal is to develop an approach to optimize the acceptance test model to avoid the redundant execution of test cases that have already been exercised during integration testing.

Our approach maps the acceptance test cases against the integration test cases. Test cases are specified with UML sequence diagrams. The ones that match are removed from the acceptance test model. However, syntax and semantic matching are not sufficient for elimination of acceptance test cases as the corresponding integration test cases may have been exercised on systems that contain test stubs as system components. To eliminate an acceptance test case, the matching integration test case should have been applied to a system without stubs representing components. The optimization approach consists of two algorithms:

1. Selection algorithm: to analyze and select integration test cases that do not use test stubs as system components.

2. Mapping algorithm: to compare acceptance test cases to the selected integration test cases and remove any acceptance test case that is contained in an integration test case.

Before introducing these two algorithms, we provide some preliminary definitions. A test case is specified with a UML sequence diagram. It is composed of a set of instances and a set of events. Instances represent test objects, which interact with each other through messages. The role of each instance, in a test model, is identified using UTP stereotypes. UTP *TestContext* is used to identify the test control. UTP *SUT* is used to identify the implementation under test (IUT); it can be a component under test (CUT) or a system under test (SUT). UTP *TestComponent* is used to identify a test stub. In a well-formed test case, there must be a test control and one or more IUTs. Test controls exercise test cases on the IUT and provide verdicts. Test stubs emulate the system environment and/or system components that are not yet realized during the test execution. Test stubs can be specified explicitly or implicitly by embedding their behavior within the test control. Each instance, in a UML sequence diagram, is represented by a vertical lifeline that represents the time progress from top to bottom. Events are specified on lifelines. With the exception of UML co-regions and UML combined-fragments, events are in total order along the lifeline of each instance.

Definition 1 (Test case): A test case T is a tuple (I, E, R), where

I : a set of instances

E : a set of events (defined further in Definition 2)

$R \subseteq (E \times E)$: a partial order reflecting the transitive closure of the order relation between events on the same axis and the sending and reception events of the same message.

We will use the test cases in Fig. 1 to illustrate our definitions throughout this section. Event names are in italic. The test case *tcase1* is formally defined as:

$tcase1 = (I, E, R)$,
$I = \{ TC, C1 \}$
$E = \{ e_1, e_2, e_3, e_4, e_5, e_6, e_7 \}$
$R = \{ (e_1,e_2), (e_1,e_3), (e_1,e_4), (e_1,e_5), (e_1,e_6), (e_1,e_7), (e_2,e_3), (e_2,e_4), (e_2,e_5), (e_2,e_6), (e_2,e_7), (e_3,e_4), (e_3,e_5), (e_3,e_6), (e_3,e_7), (e_4,e_5), (e_4,e_6), (e_4,e_7), (e_5,e_6), (e_5,e_7), (e_6,e_7) \}$

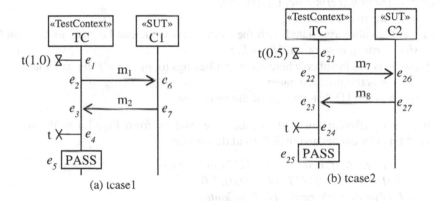

(a) tcase1   (b) tcase2

Fig. 1. Examples of test cases

We classified events into three categories: message events, time events and miscellaneous events. Message events, the sending event and receiving event, represent the two ends of messages exchanged between two instances referred to as the sender and the receiver, respectively. Time events represent events related to timers. Each timer is associated with one instance. We classify the rest of event types, such as instance termination and UTP verdict, into the third category. Notice that the association between events and instances is part of the event definition in this work.

Definition 2 (Event): An event is defined as a tuple. We have three different kinds of events and therefore three definitions:

1. A message event E_{msg} is a tuple (*ty, nm, owner, msg, oIns*), where
   (a) $ty \in \{$ send, receive $\}$
   (b) *nm* is the event name
   (c) *owner* is the instance where the event belongs to. *owner* = (*nm, st*) where

   (i) *nm* is the instance name

   (ii) *st* is the UTP stereotype of the instance

  (d) *msg* is the message the event is related to

  (e) *oIns* is the other instance related to msg, *oIns* = (*nm, st*) where

   (i) *nm* is the instance name

   (ii) *st* is the UTP stereotype of the instance

2. A time related event E_{time} is a tuple (*ty, nm, tm, owner, pd*), where

  (a) *ty* ∈ {*TimeOut, SetTimer, ResetTimer, StopTimer*}

  (b) *nm* is the event name

  (c) *tm* is the timer name

  (d) *owner* is the instance where the event belongs to, *owner* = (*nm, st*) where

   (i) *nm* is the instance name

   (ii) *st* is the UTP stereotype of the instance

  (e) *pd* is the timer value;it is used by *SetTimer* events and set to zero for the other
      two events (*TimeOut, ResetTimer*)

3. A miscellaneous event E_{misc} is a tuple (*ty, nm, v, owner*) , where

  (a) *ty* ∈ {*Action, Terminate, UTPverdict*}

  (b) *nm* is the event name

  (c) *v* is the value associated with the event. This value can be *pass, fail, inconclu-
      sive, err*or in case *ty* = *UTPverdict*.

  (d) *owner* is the instance where the event belongs to, *owner* = (*nm, st*) where

   (i) *nm* is the instance name

   (ii) *st* is the UTP stereotype of the instance

We use three different kinds of events, e_6, e_1 and e_5, from Fig. 1.a to illustrate the
different types of events and their formal definitions:

e_6 = (*receive, e6, (C1,SUT), m1, (TC,TestContext)*)

e_1 = (*SetTimer, e1, t, (TC,TestContext), 1.0*)

e_5 = (*UTPverdict, e5, pass, (TC,TestContext)*)

2.1   Test Case Selection Algorithm

Software integration goes through several rounds starting from the first two components until the integration of all system components. In parallel, the integration test
model, composed of a set of test cases, is generated for each integration round to test
the compatibility of the integrated system component with the rest of the system.
Integration test cases exercised during the last round of integration are performed on
the complete system, so they can be directly selected for the mapping algorithm discussed in the next section. The rest of integration test cases, from the other rounds, are
passed to the selection algorithm to check if they do not contain test stubs for system
components. We need to analyze these test cases and the identities of the potential test
stubs they may contain and compare them to identities of the system components.

The comparison is based on event of the same type comparison. For this we need
to define the concept of event matching. The easiest way is to match event names.
Störrle [11] shows the effectiveness of such an approach on UML models. This may

be applicable in other domains such as clone-detection, but it may not work well in our case. While we strongly recommend the usage of a consistent naming convention, at least, across the same project, test developers may use different naming conventions for different test models. Moreover, modeling tools may use/generate the same names to different events of different models. Furthermore, test stubs can be embedded in the test control; in this case, name matching is irrelevant. Hence, we use event attributes to define event matching $Match_{msg}$, $Match_{time}$ and $Match_{misc}$, for the case of E_{msg}, E_{time} and E_{misc}, respectively.

Definition 3 (Event matching): Let e_1 and e_2 be two events of the same type from two different test cases, then e_1 and e_2 match (and noted $e_1 = e_2$) if and only if:

1. $Match_{msg}(e_1, e_2) = \{ e_1 \in E_{msg}, e_2 \in E_{msg} / (e_1.ty = e_2.ty) \wedge (e_1.msg = e_2.msg) \wedge ((e_1.nm = e_2.nm) \vee (((e_1.owner.nm = e_2.owner.nm) \vee (e_1.owner.st \neq SUT) \vee (e_2.owner.st \neq SUT)) \wedge ((e_1.oIns.nm = e_2.oIns.nm) \vee (e_1.oIns.st \neq SUT) \vee (e_2.oIns.st \neq SUT)))) \}$.

2. $Match_{ime}(e_1, e_2) = \{ e_1 \in E_{time}, e_2 \in E_{time} / (e_1.ty = e_2.ty) \wedge (e_1.tm = e_2.tm) \wedge (e_1.pd = e_2.pd) \wedge ((e_1.nm = e_2.nm) \vee (e_1.owner.nm = e_2.owner.nm) \vee (e_1.owner.st \neq SUT) \vee (e_2.owner.st \neq SUT)) \}$.

3. $Match_{misc}(e_1, e_2) = \{ e_1 \in E_{misc}, e_2 \in E_{misc} / (e_1.ty = e_2.ty) \wedge (e_1.v = e_2.v) \wedge ((e_1.nm = e_2.nm) \vee (e_1.owner.nm = e_2.owner.nm) \vee (e_1.owner.st \neq SUT) \vee (e_2.owner.st \neq SUT)) \}$.

Let us consider again the test cases in Fig. 1. We compare the events of test case *tcase1* to events of the same type in test case *tcase2*. The results of the comparison of message events are negative, false, since they are associated to different sets of messages. The term $(e_1.msg = e_2.msg)$ is evaluated to false; thus the whole expression is evaluated to false. The results of the comparison of time related events are negative too. The events belong to the same instance, *TC*, and timer *t*, but they have different periods, 1.0 and 0.5. The term $(e_1.pd = e_2.pd)$ is evaluated to false, therefore the whole expression is evaluated to false. The comparison of the UTP verdicts, e_5 and e_{25}, is positive since they have the same type, $ty=UTPVerdict$, the same value, $v=pass$, belong to the same instance, $e1.owner.nm = TC$, and their owner instance is not an *SUT*. The term $(e_1.nm = e_2.nm)$ is evaluated to false but it does not affect the expression.

An integration test case has to be free of stubs of system components in order to be considered for mapping to acceptance test cases. To select these test cases, integration test cases at a given integration round have to be mapped to integration test cases of subsequent integration rounds in order to examine whether they hold test stubs of subsequently integrated system components. The last integration round builds the complete system. Hence, integration test cases applied in the last integration round are exercised on complete systems and selected for the mapping algorithm. Integration test cases from other integration rounds have to be investigated. We adopted a mapping approach, which depends on the behavior of the test stubs. Since the components under test (CUTs) are the system components, the approach compares the behavior of the components under test (CUTs) against the behavior of test stubs, i.e., it compares the events located on CUT lifelines and the events located on the test stubs lifelines. We compare the behavior of each CUT with the behavior of the test stubs that are specified in the integrated test cases of the preceding integration rounds. In case of a match, we conclude that a test stub is emulating a system component in that test case. Therefore, we exclude that test case. Event matching (Definition 3) is used to compare events. The selection algorithm maps each integration test case to test cases of subsequent integration rounds and stops as soon as the selection condition fails as expressed in line 11 of the algorithm shown in Algorithm 1.

Definition 4 (Selection condition): Let $T_{kh} = (I_{kh}, E_{kh}, R_{kh})$ be the integration test case h at integration round k and $T_{ij} = (I_{ij}, E_{ij}, R_{ij})$ be the integration test case j at integration round i, where $i > k$, then T_{kh} does not use a test stub for the CUT of T_{ij} if and only if:

$$Sel_{kh} = \begin{array}{l} \forall (e_j, e_h). e_j \in E_{ij}, e_h \in E_{kh} | (e_j \neq e_h) \vee \\ \left((e_j = e_h) \wedge (e_j. owner. st \neq SUT) \right) \end{array} .$$

```
1 read integration test models: TM[1..n]
2 initialize the set of selected test cases:
            SelectionSet = {}
3 for k = 1 to n-1 do
4    traverse through test cases of test model TM[k]:
            T[ h = 1..m ]
5      isSelected = true
6      for i = k+1 to n do
7          traverse through test cases of test model
                  TM[i]: T[ j = 1..w ]
8          evaluate Sel_kh
9          isSelected = Sel_kh
10         if isSelected = false then
11            exit
12         endif
13     endfor
14     if isSelected = true then
15        SelectionSet.add( TM[k].T[h] )
16     endif
17 endfor
```

Algorithm 1. The selection algorithm

Informally, a test case T_{kh} does not contain a test stub for a component integrated/tested at round i if and only if in case of event matching, these events do not belong to the CUT at stage i. The integration test cases selection algorithm is outlined in Algorithm 1. It is based on Definition 3 and Definition 4. To illustrate this algorithm, let us consider the example in Fig. 2. We have two integration test cases, T_k and T_i, from two different integration rounds, k and i. Round k is performed before round i. In round k, we are testing the integration of component C_k; while in round i, we are testing the integration of component C_i. The subsystem sbSys represents the system components, including C_k, integrated prior to C_i. In this example, we want to examine if the test case T_k in round k, Fig. 2.b, contains a test stub for C_i. By inspecting the test case alone, we cannot reach a conclusion especially that we do not have the specifications of the components. We apply our algorithm and use test cases of the subsequent integration rounds, in this example T_i, to examine the test case T_k. The algorithm compares the events e_{i1} to e_{i10} of the test case T_i to the events e_{k1} to e_{k8} of the test case T_k using Definitions 3 and 4. Events e_{i9} and e_{i10} do not match any events of test case T_k since they correspond to a different message msg_5. Events e_{i1}, e_{i2}, e_{i3}, e_{i4}, e_{i6} and e_{i7} do match events e_{k1}, e_{k2}, e_{k3}, e_{k4}, e_{k6} and e_{k7} respectively, and these events do not belong to the CUT C_i. However, events e_{i5} and e_{i8} match events e_{k5} and e_{k8}, respectively, and they fail the selection condition Sel_{kh} of Definition 4 since the events belong to the CUT C_i. We conclude that the test control TC_k of the integration test case T_k emulates the system component C_i. Therefore, the integration test case T_k is excluded by the selection algorithm since it contains a stub for a system component. The selection algorithm stops with the comparison of events e_{i5} and e_{k5}, which evaluates Sel_{kh} to false.

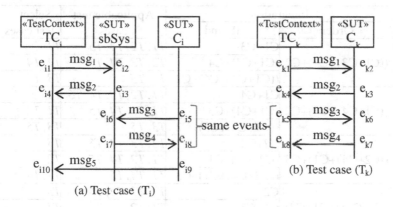

(a) Test case (T_i)

(b) Test case (T_k)

Fig. 2. Test cases from different integration rounds

The results of the selection algorithm depend on the integration order. The usage of test stubs of system components depends on the integration order. We may not require any test stub when we choose the right integration order. There is a lot of research work being done on the selection of the right integration order [14-16]. Our algorithm selects different sets of intermediate integration test cases for different integration orders. However, the same number of test cases is selected whatever is the order. We use the example in Fig. 3 to illustrate this. The system in this example is composed of four components, C1, C2, C3 and C4, and provides five services, S1, S2, S3, S4 and S5. Each component contributes to some of these services as shown in the figure with the dotted rectangles. We selected a set of integration test cases T1, T2, T3, T4 and T5 to target the different services S1, S2, S3, S4 and S5 respectively. We apply these test cases on subsystems composed of components that contribute to the corresponding services. To be able to execute these test cases, we used test stubs for the components that are not available at the time of test execution. Table 1 shows the results of the selection algorithm for different integration orders. As shown in the table, the selected test cases differ from an integration order to the other. However, for each integration order, all test cases T1, T2, T3, T4 and T5 are selected at different rounds.

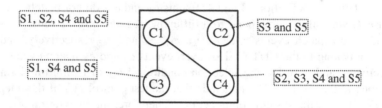

Fig. 3. System specification

Table 1. Selection algorithm for different integration orders

#	Integration		Applicable test	Selected
	Order	Round	cases	test cases
1		C1+C3	*T1, T2, T4, T5*	*T1*
2	((C1+C3)+C4)+C2	(C1+C3)+C4	*T2, T3, T4, T5*	*T2, T4*
3		((C1+C3)+C4)+C2	*T3, T5*	*T3, T5*
4		C1+C4	*T1, T2, T3, T4, T5*	*T2*
5	((C1+C4)+C3)+C2	(C1+C4)+C3	*T1, T3, T4, T5*	*T1, T4*
6		((C1+C4)+C3)+C2	*T3, T5*	*T3, T5*
7		C2+C4	*T2, T3, T4, T5*	*T3*
8	((C2+C4)+C1)+C3	(C2+C4)+C1	*T1, T2, T4, T5*	*T2*
9		((C2+C4)+C1)+C3	*T1, T4, T5*	*T1, T4, T5*
10		C2+C4	*T2, T3, T4, T5*	*T3*
11	(C2+C4)+(C1+C3)	C1+C3	*T1, T2, T4, T5*	*T1*
12		(C2+C4)+(C1+C3)	*T2, T4, T5*	*T2, T4, T5*

2.2   Test Case Mapping Algorithm

The integration test cases, selected by the previous algorithm, are mapped to the acceptance test cases. The mapping algorithm has to examine if the acceptance test cases are contained (identical to or part of) in the selected integration test cases. It is given in Algorithm 2. We have to take into account that the events specified on an axis of an acceptance test case may be distributed over several entities in the integration test case as shown in Fig. 4. Acceptance test cases are usually composed of two test objects: the test control (TCa) and the system under test (SUT) while integration test cases are composed of at least three test objects: the test control (TCi), the CUT and the subsystem (SbSys). Hence, the behavior of the two test objects, TCa and SUT, in the acceptance test cases is distributed over three test objects, TCi, CUT and SbSys, in the integration test cases. Moreover, integration test cases may have extra behaviors that reflect internal interactions between the CUT and SbSys. In other words, we should not expect the acceptance test case to be a complete fragment/block within the integration test case. To illustrate this, let us consider the test cases shown in Fig. 4. We can compare the behavior of the test controls, TCa and TCi, as block since they have identical sets of events, (e1, e10). However, the behavior, (e2, e9), of the system, SUT, is distributed among two test objects. The event e2 belongs to the integrated component CUT while event e9 belongs to the subsystem SbSys. Furthermore, the behavior of the integration test case (e1, e2, e3, e4, e5, e6, e7, e8, e9, e10) contains internal events e3, e4, e5, e6, e7 and e8 that are not specified in the acceptance test case and divide the behavior of the acceptance test case (e1, e2, e9, e10) into two fragments. The first fragment consists of e1 and e2, and the second fragment consists of e9 and e10. Therefore, the mapping algorithm checks for the behavior of the acceptance test cases in the behavior of the integration test cases. Test case inclusion is defined hereafter.

Definition 5 (Test case inclusion): Let $T_a = \{I_a, E_a, R_a\}$ be an acceptance test case and $T_i = \{I_i, E_i, R_i\}$ be an integration test case, then the acceptance test is included in the integration test case if and only if the following conditions are satisfied:

(1) $E_a \subseteq E_i$

(2) $R_a \subseteq R_i$

The first condition states that the events specified in the acceptance test case are all specified in the integration test case. The second condition checks that all the order relations among the events of the acceptance test case are respected in the integration test case specification. There is no mapping between the instances of the acceptance test cases and the instances of the integration test cases as they are usually different. Actually, the integration subsystem is different from one integration round to the other. On the first round, the subsystem is composed of one system component. On the second integration round, the subsystem is composed of two system components, and so on. On the last integration round, the subsystem is composed of all the system components except one that to be integrated on this round. Acceptance test cases that meet the two conditions are removed from the acceptance test model as this is done with the mapping algorithm given in Algorithm 2. This comparison is possible as test cases have finite behaviors.

```
1 read acceptance test cases: TCa[1..n]
2 read selected integration test cases: TCi[1..m]
3 for i = 1 to n do
4   for j = 1 to m do
5     isContained = true;
6     isContained = isContained AND (TCa[i].E⊆TCi[j].E)
7     isContained = isContained AND (TCa[i].R⊆TCi[j].R)
8     if isContained = true then
9       remove TCa[i]
10      exit interior for loop "for j = ..."
11    endif
12  endfor
13 endfor
```

Algorithm 2. The mapping algorithm

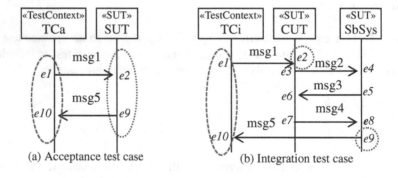

(a) Acceptance test case   (b) Integration test case

Fig. 4. Matching test cases

3   Illustration Example

We use the system specification shown in Fig. 5 as our case study. The system is composed of three components, *C1*, *C2* and *C3*, and provides three services, *S1*, *S2* and *S3*. Messages are named with three different letters, *A*, *B* and *C*, to relate them to the aforementioned services provided by the system, *S1*, *S2* and *S3*, respectively.

In this case study, we focus on the behavioral part of the test model. A subset of the acceptance test cases are shown in Fig. 6. There are four test cases. There is a test case for each provided service. The fourth test case, test case 4, is for the combination of the three services in a certain order. Please notice that the UTP stereotypes are not present in the test behavior because they are omitted, for the time being, in the UTP metamodel.

The system components are integrated according to the following integration order: (*C1* + *C2*) + *C3*, i.e., in the first round, we integrate *C1* and *C2* and in the second round, we add the third component, *C3*. A subset of the integration test cases are shown in Fig. 7. Two test cases, *Ti1* and *Ti2*, are generated during the first integration round while the third one, *Ti3*, is generated during the second integration round.

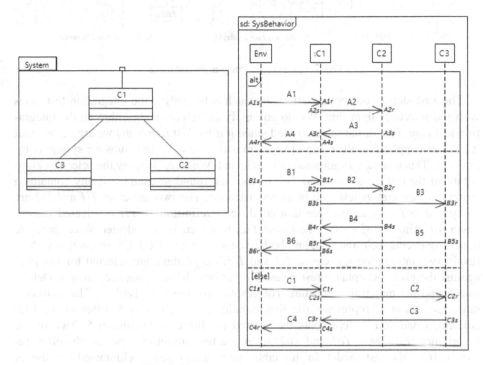

Fig. 5. Case study: system specification

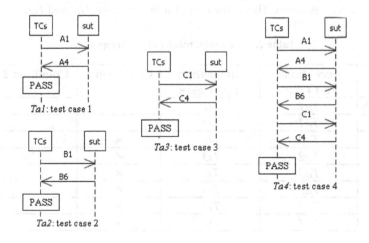

Fig. 6. Case study: acceptance test cases

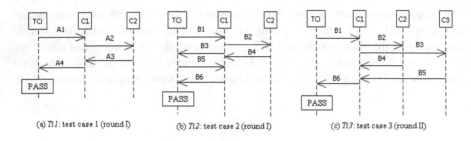

(a) *Ti1*: test case 1 (round I)   (b) *Ti2*: test case 2 (round I)   (c) *Ti3*: test case 3 (round II)

Fig. 7. Case study: integration test cases

The first step in our optimization approach is to analyze the integration test cases with the selection algorithm. We do not apply the selection algorithm on the integration test case, *Ti3*, of the second round since it is the last round and we are certain that it has been applied on the complete system and there is no test stubs for system components. This test case is automatically selected. We have to apply the selection algorithm on the test cases, *Ti1* and *Ti2*, of the first round to examine if any contains a system component as test stub in its specification. The two test cases *Ti1* and *Ti2* are compared to *Ti3* using the selection condition (Definition 4). *Ti1* is selected since it has a different set of events. Test case *Ti2*, however, is not selected since there are matching events, *B3r* and *B5s*, and both events belong to CUT *C3*, respectively. As a result, two integration test cases, *Ti1* and *Ti3*, out of three are selected for mapping against the given acceptance test cases. We perform the mapping according to Definition 5 and the mapping algorithm. The results are shown in Table 2. The forth column, Condition 1, represents the first condition of Definition 5, whereas the fifth column, Condition 2, represents the second condition of Definition 5. Two of the acceptance test cases, *Ta1* and *Ta2*, meet the two conditions and are therefore removed from the test model. In this table, when a test case is eliminated because of successful mapping with an integration test case, other mappings for this acceptance test case are not considered. This is the case, for instance, for *Ta1* and *Ti3*.

Table 2. Case study: results of the mapping

#	Acceptance Test Cases	Integration Test Cases	Condition 1	Condition 2
1	*Ta1*	*Ti1*	✓	✓
2	*Ta1*	*Ti3*		
3	*Ta2*	*Ti1*	✗	
4	*Ta2*	*Ti3*	✓	✓
5	*Ta3*	*Ti1*	✗	
6	*Ta3*	*Ti3*	✗	
7	*Ta4*	*Ti1*	✗	
8	*Ta4*	*Ti3*	✗	

4 Related Work

Model comparison is an important research stream in Model-Driven Engineering (MDE) [17], especially for version control systems, model-cloning and model transformation testing. It targets a variety of model types: structural, behavioral and data-flow. For UML models, the research focused more on structural diagrams [9, 18, 19], particularly the class diagram, than on behavioral diagrams [20, 21]. As far as we know, there is no test model comparison in the testing domain. We are not aware of a systematic testing approach that compares test models taking into account their specific characteristics. The nearest approach to our work is proposed by Liu et al. [21]. Their work was on model-cloning using UML sequence diagrams. The approach converts the sequence diagrams into an array. This array is represented as a suffix tree. Duplication is detected by traversing the tree and applying the longest common prefix algorithm. Our approach is different in two aspects. First, this approach handles only synchronous messages; while ours handles asynchronous messages as well. More importantly, the approach in [21] is restricted to contiguous behavior.

Much work has been done for the comparison of Message Sequences Charts (MSCs) [22, 23]. This work tackled the basic MSCs (bMSCs) and high-level MSCs (HMSCs) from a theoretical perspective considering more complex and infinite behaviors while we focused on finite behaviors for test case cases. Genest et al. [24] propose a pattern matching approach. The approach considers nested MSCs (bMSCs and HMSCs). The matching method relies on the FIFO order of the received events for the processes/instances. Thus, events are linearized for each process and can be compared. The approach considers asynchronous message and non-contiguous behavior too. However, it requires the existence of the same set of instances in both MSCs, which limits its applicability for our purposes as the numbers of instances and the instances may be different in the compared test cases. Tallam et al. [25] propose a test suite reduction algorithm. The algorithm requires a set of test cases and a set of test requirements. Each test case covers a set of test requirements. This information is provided as input in a table. They process the table to select the minimum set of test cases that covers all the test requirements. This approach can be used as a first step in our approach to select the set of acceptance test cases that covers all the test requirements, if provided, before comparing them to integration test cases. The approach proposed in [25] does not relate acceptance test cases to integration test cases.

5 Conclusion

We proposed an optimization approach that eliminates acceptance test cases that have been already applied during integration testing, hence leading to fewer acceptance test cases without sacrificing quality. Integration test cases are examined in order to be selected for the optimization process. Selected integration test cases have to be exercised on the actual system components and not only on test stubs of the system components. Our approach has been implemented in a prototype tool. We are currently experimenting with this prototype. On the other hand, some theoretical aspects of our approach need to be investigated further, for instance the complexity of the selection algorithm. We may also define some heuristics to improve this selection algorithm. Furthermore, our approach can be extended to include the test stimuli. Test stimuli consist of both test inputs and their corresponding expect outputs. UTP specification facilitates the design of the test stimuli within the test model. It can be specified in the test architecture and/or the test behavior.

Acknowledgements. This work has been partially supported by the Natural Sciences and Engineering Research Council of Canada (NSERC), Concordia University and the Libyan-North American Scholarship Program.

References

1. Mussa, M., Khendek, F.: Towards a Model Based Approach for Integration Testing. In: Ober, I., Ober, I. (eds.) SDL 2011. LNCS, vol. 7083, pp. 106–121. Springer, Heidelberg (2011)
2. Utting, M., Legeard, B.: Practical Model-Based Testing:A Tools Approach. Morgan Kaufmann Publishers, Amsterdam (2007)
3. Baker, P., Dai, Z.R., Grabowski, J., Schieferdecker, I., Williams, C.: Model-Driven Testing: Using the UML Testing Profile. Springer (2008)
4. Roy, C.K., Cordy, J.R., Koschke, R.: Comparison and Evaluation of Code Clone Detection Techniques and Tools: A Qualitative Approach. Science of Computer Programming 74(1), 470–495 (2009)
5. Fortsch, S., Westfechtel, B.: Differencing and Merging of Software Diagrams: State of the Art and Challenges. In: Proc. Second Intl. Conf. Software and Data Technologies (ICSOFT 2007), pp. 90–99. INSTICC Press (2007)
6. Roy, C.K., Cordy, J.R.: A Survey on Software Clone Detection Research. Technical Report 2007-541.Queen's University, Canada (2007)
7. Stephan, M., Cordy, J.R.: A Survey of Model Comparison Approaches and Applications. In: 1st International Conference on Model-Driven Engineering and Software Development (MODELSWARD 2013), pp. 265–277. INSTICC Press (2013)
8. Mens, T.: A State-of-the-Art Survey on Software Merging. IEEE Transactions on Software Engineering 28(5), 449–462 (2002)
9. Stephan, M., Cordy, J.R.: A Survey of Methods and Applications of Model Comparison. Technical Report2011-582, Queen's Univ., Canada (2011)
10. Brosch, P., Kappel, G., Langer, P., Seidl, M., Wieland, K., Wimmer, M.: An Introduction to Model Versioning. In: Bernardo, M., Cortellessa, V., Pierantonio, A. (eds.) SFM 2012. LNCS, vol. 7320, pp. 336–398. Springer, Heidelberg (2012)
11. Störrle, H.: Towards clone detection in UML domain models. In: Proceedings of the Fourth European Conference on Software Architecture: Companion, pp. 285–293. ACM, New York (2010)
12. Kolovos, D.S., Paige, R.F., Polack, F.A.C.: Model comparison: A foundation for model composition and model transformation testing. In: Proceedings of the 2006 International Workshop on Global Integrated Model Management, pp. 13–20. ACM, USA (2006)
13. Stephan, M., Cordy, J.R.: Application of model comparison techniques to model transformation testing. In: 1st International Conference on Model-Driven Engineering and Software Development (MODELSWARD 2013), pp. 307–311. INSTICC Press (2013)

14. Wang, Z., Li, B., Wang, L., Li, Q.: A brief survey on automatic integration test order generation. In: SEKE 2011 - Proceedings of the 23rd International Conference on Software Engineering and Knowledge Engineering, pp. 254–257. Knowledge Systems Institute Graduate School, Miami (2011)

15. Abdurazik, A., Offutt, J.: Using Coupling-Based Weights for the Class Integration and Test Order Problem. The Computer Journal 52(5), 557–570 (2009)

16. Briand, L.C., Labiche, Y., Wang, Y.: An Investigation of Graph-Based Class Integration Test Order Strategies. IEEE Transactions on Software Engineering 29(7), 594–607 (2003)

17. Schmidt, D.C.: Guest Editor's Introduction: Model-Driven Engineering. Computer 39(2), 25–31 (2006)

18. Xing, Z., Stroulia, E.: UMLDiff: An algorithm for object-oriented design differencing. In: Proceedings of the 20th IEEE/ACM International Conference on Automated Software Engineering, pp. 54–65. ACM, New York (2005)

19. Maoz, S., Ringert, J.O., Rumpe, B.: A manifesto for semantic model differencing. In: Dingel, J., Solberg, A. (eds.) MODELS 2010. LNCS, vol. 6627, pp. 194–203. Springer, Heidelberg (2011)

20. Nejati, S., Sabetzadeh, M., Chechik, M., Easterbrook, S., Zave, P.: Matching and merging of statecharts specifications. In: 29th International Conference on Software Engineering, pp. 54–64. IEEE CS (2007)

21. Liu, H., Niu, Z., Ma, Z., Shao, W.: Suffix Tree-Based Approach to Detecting Duplications in Sequence Diagrams. IET Software 5(4), 385–397 (2011)

22. Klein, J., Caillaud, B., Hélouët, L.: Merging scenarios. In: Proc. Ninth International Workshop on Formal Methods for Industrial Critical Systems (FMICS 2004), vol. 133, pp. 193–215. Elsevier, Amsterdam (2005)

23. Hélouët, L., Hénin, T., Chevrier, C.: Automating Scenario Merging. In: Gotzhein, R., Reed, R. (eds.) SAM 2006. LNCS, vol. 4320, pp. 64–81. Springer, Heidelberg (2006)

24. Genest, B., Muscholl, A.: Pattern Matching and Membership for Hierarchical Message Sequence Charts. Theory Comput. Syst. 42, 536–567 (2008)

25. Tallam, S., Gupta, N.: A Concept Analysis Inspired Greedy Algorithm for Test Suite Minimization. In: Proc. 6th ACM SIGPLAN-SIGSOFT Workshop on Program Analysis for Software Tools and Engineering, pp. 35–42. ACM, USA (2005)

Verifying Hypermedia Applications
by Using an MDE Approach

Delcino Picinin Júnior[1,4], Cristian Koliver[2], Celso A.S. Santos[3],
and Jean-Marie Farines[4]

[1] Federal Institute of Santa Catarina, Brazil
delcino.junior@ifsc.edu.br
[2] Catarinense Federal Institute, Brazil
ckoliver@ifc-camboriu.edu.br
[3] Federal University of Espirito Santo, Brazil
saibel@inf.ufes.br
[4] Federal University of Santa Catarina, Brazil,
picinin@das.ufsc.br, j.m.farines@ufsc.br

Abstract. Authoring tools for editing hypermedia documents should
be able to describe temporal and spatial relationships among objects,
and user interactions as well. These tools can also support modifications
in the document structure during the exhibition time. In all these situations, hypermedia document correctness should be guaranteed. In this
paper, we describe an approach supporting the formal verification of documents in the Nested Context Language (NCL) and Synchronized Multimedia Integration Language (SMIL) standards. Using usual authoring
tools, NCL and SMIL models are generated and, though an MDE design
environment, transformed into formal verification models to be used following a method proposed in this paper and supported by an appropriate
tool. A designer-oriented interface allows an easy and understandable description of properties to be checked and of required observers for more
complex properties. The results of the verification are also presented
in a comprehensive way for designers (as counterexamples) or executed
step-by-step in a common displaying tool. Our approach allows designers
to deal with the validation of their documents, built in a rigorous and
consistent way, without prior knowledge of verification models and tools.

Keywords: MDE, Hypermedia, IDTV, Verification, Model checking.

1 Introduction

Technological advances in computers and electronics have led to the emergence of
new ways of document communication, such as the Interactive Digital Television
(IDTV) and the Interactive Television over IP (IPTV). IDTV must reach a broad
audience of users, not always covered by the Web and often with little technical
knowledge. In this context, the TV application becomes a hypermedia document,
and the user does not just watch TV passively, but he/she can interact with its
content.

D. Amyot et al. (Eds.): SAM 2014, LNCS 8769, pp. 174–189, 2014.
© Springer International Publishing Switzerland 2014

A hypermedia document, commonly written in languages such as the Nested Context Language (NCL)[1] and the Synchronized Multimedia Integration Language (SMIL)[2], is composed of different media objects[3] with different exhibition times and characteristics. An object can interact with other objects and application user's devices and must be executable on various target platforms. Moreover, interactions (such as starting, pausing, and stopping a video presentation) are dynamic and can occur at any time. Consequently, if the document structure is not already verified, the synchronization among different objects may not be achieved properly during the presentation. This characterizes a time conflict, defined by Yu et al. [21] as conflicting attribute values in a temporal document specification.

Two types of time conflicts are possible: (1) intra-object and (2) inter-objects time conflicts. The first type corresponds to the case of conflicting attributes within a single object. For example, the difference between start and stop times does not match its specified duration. The second type is the case of conflicting attributes among different objects. An inter-objects time conflict is more difficult to identify because it can depend on the interactions between objects and users. The difficulty increases when the begin or the end of an object presentation is related to some event triggered by another object, or by a user's event, i.e., the event is not associated with a prefixed time [6].

In the development of hypermedia applications, usually the editing phase occurs before the presentation. However, in more recent scenarios involving document live editing (with IDTV and IPTV [8,13]) such phases can be concomitantly performed. As described by Asnawi et al. [2], beyond IDTV and IPTV applications, there exist other domain areas requiring that processes of authoring and presentation occur on-the-fly. For instance, classrooms, training, surveillance security, and entertainment often need a real time or live presentation. The temporal conflict analysis in live applications has real-time constraints, so a quick scan is needed. That is also a relevant issue to be dealt with in the multimedia domain.

Guaranteeing temporal and spatial consistency of hypermedia documents requires special attention during the design process and leads to improvements to existing hypermedia authoring tools [19]. Two approaches are differentiated: (1) *authoring tools* [7,16]) are based on visual inspection and commonly use a structured timeline view to edit and show the hierarchical structure from which timing constraints are derived. When the complexity of hypermedia applications increases, visual inspection becomes very complex for analysis by human eyes. (2) *formal verification methods* (model checking), integrated to the application design process, verify correctness of hypermedia documents against properties (mainly temporal properties), with good results as shown in [10,12].

Model checking uses formal languages for representing the hypermedia document structures and the set of properties to be checked. Nevertheless, the use of

---

[1] http://www.itu.int/ITU-T/recommendations/rec.aspx?rec=H.761
[2] http://www.w3.org/TR/SMIL/
[3] Hereafter, we will simply use the word "object" for media object.

model checking in the domain of hypermedia document design is difficult since designers do not have sufficient knowledge and expertise for using languages to specify and code correct formulas to be checked.

In this paper, we describe a design method based on model-checking in which the designer continues to use his/her well-known languages for hypermedia authoring. The system model designed with these languages is translated using a Model Driven Engineering (MDE) [20] approach to an appropriate language to be used for property verification. We also present an environment intended for non-expert users, bringing facilities to specify properties and to use verification tools. Our approach has the following contributions: (1) the use of MDE in a toolchain that allows to obtain formal models (input of verification tools) from hypermedia applications by successive translations; (2) the reduction of formal models by slicing, making possible the use of formal verification in live applications; (3) a comprehensive way for the designer to specify properties; and (4) the presentation of counterexamples in an understandable way, helping the designer with the correction of the spatial and temporal structure of the application.

This paper is organized as follows. Section 2 describes the proposed method for developing hypermedia documents, highlighting the main challenges for hypermedia document design and the phases of the proposed method. Section 3 focuses on the formal model used as input to the model-checking tool. Section 4 presents the design environment with its verification toolchain associated with the proposed method. Section 5 shows how the method and the toolchain are used by means of a short example. Section 6 reviews previous work and compares it with the proposed approach. Conclusions are presented in Section 7.

2   Proposed Design Method

The goal of our method is to aid designers build hypermedia applications free of temporal and spatial inconsistencies. More specific objectives include: (1) the validation of temporal and spatial relationships among objects, considering external interactions; (2) the reduction of the formal model of the application by slicing techniques, allowing a live application verification in an acceptable time; and (3) the use of the environment by users non expert in formal verification.

2.1   Main Challenges

Verification for hypermedia applications – particularly for the IDTV context – poses some interesting issues:

Time Relationships Verification. In IDTV, objects can be presented when: (1) the application starts; (2) a message is sent from another running object; or (3) the user triggers the presentation by using the remote control. Likewise, an object can be stopped when: (1) it receives a message from another object or from the remote control, or (2) the presentation time runs out. Unexpected temporal behavior, e.g., an object presented endlessly, can occur due timing errors.

Spatial Relationships Verification. In IDTV, visual objects (e.g., image, video, and text) must be presented in predefined regions of the screen. The placement of an object in the full screen and of other object regions defines spatial relationships. Unexpected placement, such as an important part of video content overlapped by a static image on the screen, should be identified.

Live Editing of the Application Spatio-temporal Structure. Verification requires a significant computational effort due to state explosion. Whereas this is often not a critical problem for pre-recorded applications, in which authoring and presentation are disjoint phases, the full scan of a new version and the correction of errors of a live IDTV application, edited on-the-fly, may be impractical due to real-time constraints.

Application Designer Facilities. Verification of IDTV applications also requires an environment that can be used easily by designers without expertise in formal models. Such environment should include facilities to define desired properties, and to identify and correct errors of the application.

2.2 Design Method

When developing a hypermedia application, the designer expects that it follows the planned behavior regarding relationships among objects, user interactions, and the placement of objects on display devices. Verification by model-checking allows one to identify and correct undesired behaviors from design or coding errors. However, this requires the translation of the hypermedia application to a formal model and the specification of the properties to be verified in a suitable language. A manual translation may introduce errors and is not viable in the case of live IDTV applications. In addition, an application designer who is also expert in formal modeling is uncommon. To avoid the need for knowledge about formal languages from designers, and to limit the possibility of creating erroneous formal models during translation, our work proposes a method to perform model transformations based on MDE, hence ensuring a correct translation. Our design method is divided into three phases, as follows:

Modeling Phase. The designer writes the application using hypermedia languages (e.g., NCL or SMIL) as usual. Also, by using the proposed high-level language, he/she creates a set of behavior properties to be checked.

Transformation Phase. The NCL or SMIL application and the set of properties are automatically translated into a model coded in a formal verification language by means of transformation rules defined in the MDE approach.

Verification Phase. Using model-checking principles, properties are verified and, when a property is not satisfied, a counterexample is generated. Such counterexample corresponds to a sequence of actions that led to the violation of the property and, consequently, it helps the designer fix the application errors.

3   Formal Verification

Once the application has been translated to a language suitable for use by a model-checker tool, the designer must define what behaviors must be verified. Most approaches (see Section 6) check only the end of an object exhibition. Our approach defines a set of behaviors, selected by the designer, that should be verified, represented through the use of formal properties expressed in Linear Temporal Logic (LTL) formulas, or by observers when a property requires checking some elapsed time.

An observer is a state machine in which the change from one state to another occurs upon the arrival of messages or elapsed time. Messages have as source or target observed object, and are also received by the observer. In comparison with formulas, observers have two drawbacks: they increase the size of the formal model, and they do not present counterexamples. The problem caused by the model growth can be tackled by means of a reduction approach. Moreover to obtain a counterexample for all properties not satisfied, we adopted LTL formulas to check the reachability of the same states, when using observers.

The sequence of actions representing a counterexample does not indicate the time when each action occurred. To add such information, a global time observer discretizes the passage of time in seconds, thus each change of state of this observer indicates the passage of one second in the global time.

3.1   Mapping Hypermedia Application to Fiacre

The formal verification is performed from a Fiacre model generated for SMIL or NCL applications using MDE. Fiacre [4] is a verification-oriented language, developed in the TOPCASED project[4], to represent temporal and behavioral aspects of systems for verification and simulation purposes. The language is strongly typed and its basic syntactic constructors are the *process*, used to describe sequential behavior, and the *component*, used to represent the system through the composition of processes and other components. Process behavior is defined from a set of states and transitions. For each state, expressions specify transitions towards the next state. These expressions depend on: (1) deterministic and non-deterministic constructors, as in a programming language; (2) communication events through ports; and (3) time delays (*wait*). The *main* component is the parallel composition of components or processes commnicating via synchronous ports and shared variables. Asynchronous communication is performed by adding a special process called *glue*, which allows one to desynchronize sender and receiver ports. Time in Fiacre code can progress in communication ports or in processes as delays. Non-determinism can be represented in the body of the process.

As shown in Fig. 1, the application language-to-Fiacre translation takes into account: the hypermedia document, the possible interactions of the user, the player features, and the behavior to be checked. As represented in the figure,

---

[4] http://www.topcased.org/

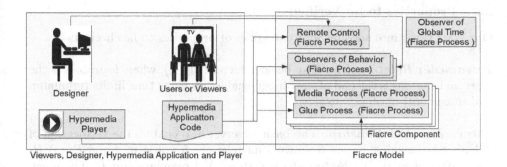

Viewers, Designer, Hypermedia Application and Player   Fiacre Model

Fig. 1. Environment for the transformation of hypermedia applications to Fiacre

for each object, a Fiacre component is created considering characteristics of the presentation platform and the media. Each component has a media process and an associated glue process. A media process represents the object behavior, whereas its glue process represents the player features where the object will be displayed (such as asynchrony in sending messages with discard behavior). In addition, a Fiacre process named Remote Control is created for each interactive object. For each object, the translator also creates another Fiacre process whose role is to observe the object behavior based on information from the object and properties. Finally, there is an observer for the global time. The internal structure of these Fiacre processes (except the global time observer) depends directly on the characteristics of the existing objects in the application. Example of characteristics described by Fiacre processes are: interactivity, end by message, end by time, multiple types of end, and use of temporal anchors.

3.2 Observers

Observers aim to verify temporal intramedia and intermedia relationships. Figure 2 shows the basic observer, which allows the identification of the elapsed time between the arrival of the *begin_obs* and *end_obs* messages. It supports three possible time intervals: (1) *elapsed time* $< t_{min}$; (2) $t_{min} \leq$ *elapsed time* $\leq t_{max}$; and (3) *elapsed time* $> t_{max}$. This basic observer captures all the well-known relationships between medias proposed by Allen [1]. Such observers can be automatically built to be used for verification purpose.

Fig. 2. Basic observer

3.3   Properties to be Verified

Our work takes into account four categories of properties to be checked:

Intramedia Relationship. The basic observer (Fig. 2), where *begin_obs* is the start and *end_obs* is the end of the object, enables checking time limits (minimum and maximum) of object display.

Intermedia Relationship. The basic observer also enables the verification of Allen's relationships. Figure 3 shows some relations for objects A and B: (a) B-start **after** A-start: (b) B-stop **after** A-stop (c) A **overlapping** B. These can be used to observe full or partial time overlapping in object presentation.

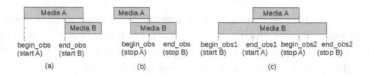

Fig. 3. Allen's relationships

Causal Relationship. Links between A and B represent causal relationships indicating that an event in object A results in an action on B. Checking the activation of a link allows verification of this relationship.

Spatial Relationship. Full or partial spatial overlap of objects on regions of the presentation device (screen area, audio channel, etc.) are generally unwanted when they occur in conjunction with time overlap. In our approach, we can identify when two or more objects are in this situation. To identify overlapping regions, we adopt an esthetic analysis of the Cartesian coordinates of each region. As for identifying temporal overlap, we use observers.

4   The Toolchain Associated with the Proposed Method

As described in Section 2, our method is composed of three phases: modeling, transformation and verification. A toolchain supports this design method as explained in this section by means of an example.

4.1   A Case Study

In this section, we use a hypermedia application to exemplify how our approach works. The application is coded in the Nested Context Language (NCL) [9], an XML application language standardized as ITU-T Recommendation H.761 for IPTV services in 2009 [15]. NCL is the standard declarative language of the Brazilian terrestrial IDTV system. NCL is a causal language in which each action is preceded by another one and triggered by an NCL condition, such as: user interaction (*onSelection*), beginning (*onBegin*) or end (*onEnd*) of media presentation. NCL Connectors and Links are used to define these conditions and actions. A condition is satisfied when an event occurs; an event can be triggered by actions such as user interaction(*selection action*), start object (*start action*) or stop object (*stop action*). Connectors and links are defined by the designer, as well as by the device and the presentation regions. In NCL documents, time features are associated with object duration, object anchors and delays on the connectors. Finally, the non-determinism due to user interactions can be also represented in NCL.

Our case study is the Live Longer ("Viva Mais" in Portuguese) application[5]. Such application is concerned with several subjects related to health and welfare and it offers opportunities for an active participation of the TV viewer. The "Healthy Food" interactive part asks the TV viewer to choose her/his preference among four different dish options. Once a dish is chosen, the TV viewer is informed of the quality of his/her choice in terms of excess or lack of nutrients. Code 1 is a fragment of the application as written by the actual designer. The designer decided to use the *RED* button for two purposes in different moments. The selection of the button *RED* (lines 1 and 2 of the code) enables interactive objects *dish1*, *dish2*, *dish3*, and *dish4* (line 4). If the viewer selects the button *RED* again (lines 6 and 7), corresponding to the choice of *dish1*, objects *dish2*, *dish3*, and *dish4* are disabled (line 8).

Code 1. NCL - part of the original code, developed by the designer

```
1 <link id="l1" xconnector="x1"><bind component="icon" role="onSelection">
2   <bindParam name="keyCode" value="RED"/></bind>
3   <bind component="icon" role="stop"/>
4   <bind component="dish1","dish2","dish3","dish4" role="start"/>
5 </link>
6 <link id="l2" xconnector="x2"><bind component="dish1" role="onSelection">
7   <bindParam name="keyCode" value="RED"/></bind>
8   <bind component="dish2","dish3","dish4" role="stop"/>
9   <bind component="dish1-quality" role="start"/>
10 </link>
```

Indeed, when the *icon* is enabled, the selection of the *RED* button enables objects *dish1*, *dish2*, *dish3* and *dish4*, and disables *icon*. Then, four alternative selection buttons ("RED", "BLUE", "YELLOW" and "GREEN") are presented. If the button *RED* is selected again in a short time (e.g., less than one second), the objects are enabled and disabled so fast that the viewer cannot see the set of alternatives and consequently *dish1* (corresponding to *RED* button) will always

---
[5] http://clube.ncl.org.br/node/29

be selected. This situation comes from a design error that permits dishes to be displayed too fast for human visual senses (this situation is different from not displaying the dishes). This error is due to to use of the same *RED* button for two sequential interactive selections. It can be easily corrected when detected, but detection is difficult via testing.

4.2   Translating Hypermedia Language to Intermediary Graph (IG)

In our toolchain, initially an MDE transformation of type model-to-model (M2M) translates the application from the hypermedia language (NCL) to the Intermediary Graph (IG) representation, as shown in Fig. 4. Transformation rules of the NCL2IG translator were coded in the model transformation language ATL [3]. Note that the use of IG enables the integration of different hypermedia languages (SMIL for example) in the toolchain, needing only the construction of a specific translator from the source language to IG.

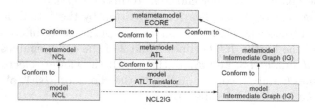

Fig. 4. NCL2IG transformation

Figure 5 shows an IG corresponding to Code 1. In IG, edges are labeled by ($< event, action >$) and states represent object presentations.

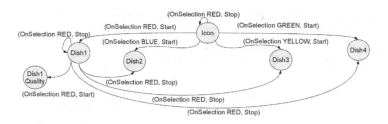

Fig. 5. IG of the fragment of code of the NCL application

4.3   Property Editor

Developed in Java, the Property Editor (PE) is used to define the properties to be checked, which were described in Section 3.3: Intramedia, Intermedia, Causal and Spatial Relationships.

To allow the definition of Causal and Spatial Relationships, PE analyzes IG and identifies the links between medias in a causal module and as a spatial overlay in a spatial module, as represented in Fig. 6. The results are presented in a *Graphical User Interface* (GUI) to assist the designer.

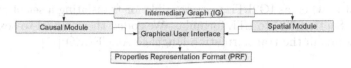

Fig. 6. Properties modules

Figure 7 illustrates the information provided to designer by the GUI. The behaviors list shows behaviors to be checked by formulas or observers. The designer then selects medias and behaviors to be used through this GUI. In the example of Fig. 7, the designer has selected the behavior 5, the *dish2* media and minimum time 2 for property checking: *when presented, dish2 always reaches the minimum time 2.*

Intra-media	Inter-media (General)	Inter-media (Causal)	Spatial			
Medias	**Behaviors List**			**Selected Behaviors, Medias and Times**		
				Behaviors	Medias	Times
video	[1] The media will always be presented			1	icon	-
dish2	[2] The media will never be presented			1	dish2	-
dish1result	[3] The media will always finish its exhibition			2	dish2	-
dish2result	[4] When presented the media never reach a minimum time			4	icon	1
dish3result	[5] When presented the media always reach a minimum time			4	icon	11
dish4result				4	icon	12
backdish				4	dish2	1
dish1				5	dish2	2
icon						
Minimum Time: 2	Create			Delete		

Fig. 7. Properties Editor (GUI)

4.4 Reducing IG Graph Sizes

In order to reduce the computational cost of the verification process, a very important requirement for live editing, our toolchain uses a module named *S*licer. Developed in Java, the slicer receives as inputs an IG and a set of properties, and performs a reduction for each associated media and property. This phase produces a reduced slice graph named IG'. The slicer follows a set of rules whose main goals are: (1) to eliminate parts of the model unnecessary to check the desired properties, and (2) to join multiple elements into a single one, if possible. The slicer aims to reduce the size of IG that represents the document presentation, without changing the original presentation behavior, and preserving the relevant parts of this graph for checking the desired properties.

4.5   Translating the IG to Formal Representations

From the IG, two MDE transformations lead to a verification domain represented by Fiacre and LTL models. They are shown in Fig. 8(a) and Fig. 8(b): IG2Fiacre involves the analysis of application semantics, properties to be verified, as well as the environment in which the application is inserted (detailed in Section 3.1) whereas IG2LTL is responsible for translating a set of properties (detailed in Section 3.3) to LTL formulas. We coded these model-to-text (M2T) transformations in the transformation language ACCELEO [17].

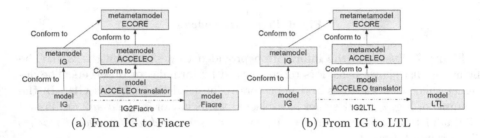

(a) From IG to Fiacre   (b) From IG to LTL

Fig. 8. Transformations from IG to formal languages

4.6   Verification

The code in Fiacre is compiled by the FRAC tool, hence generating equivalent code in Time Transition Systems (TTS) [14], which is the input format of the Time Petri Net (TPN) Analyzer (TINA) tool [5]. TINA is a toolbox to edit and analyze TPNs, with an extension to handle TTS data. SELT is the model checker tool of the TINA toolbox and allows the verification of formulas written in LTL. A LTL formula is formed by: (1) a finite set of atomic propositions; and (2) temporal operators: O (next), U (until), $true$, $\square$ (always), $\lozenge$ (in the future).

The result of verification for a given formula can be true or false (when not satisfied). When false, a counterexample is generated to help the designer. Since the counterexample is expressed in a rather unclear language, our approach transforms it into a more user-friendly representation, as shown in Section 5.

4.7   General Structure of Toolchain

Figure 9 presents the general view of the method and its toolchain. In this representation, rectangular elements represent the software that performs tasks. The other elements are files generated during the process. Elements with multiple layers indicate the existence of multiple instances.

5   Design Method and Environment in Practice

As we highlighted, the erroneous behavior of the "Live Longer" application permits dishes to be displayed outside human visual perception. Aiming to identify

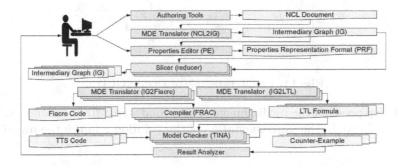

Fig. 9. A general view of the method and its toolchain

and avoid such undesirable behavior, the designer uses PE to specify a property to be verified: when presented, media *dish*2 always remains visible for a minimum time allowing human vision, as show in Fig. 7. We considered two seconds as an acceptable minimum time for human vision (in future work, we will make further pratical experiments on this issue). The property to check the elapsed time is represented by an observer (as presented in Fig. 2). The following LTL formula allows the verification of the observed behavior:

$$(\sqcup(ob\_dish2\_running1 \longrightarrow (\neg(\Diamond(ob\_dish2\_end1)))))). \tag{1}$$

This formula verifies that when *dish*2 is presented (*ob_dish2_running*1 observer state), the *dish*2 end will be never observed in the future before a minimum time (*ob_dish2_end*1 observer state). The non-reachability of the *end*1 state indicates that the exhibition time of the observed media *dish*2 always meets the minimum time. Figure 10 contains part of the interface listing the verification results. The last line corresponds to the verification of Eq. 1.

> (1) The media (icon) always be presented
> (4) The Media (icon) when presented never reaches the minimum time 12
> (4) Exists situations where the media (dish2) reaches the minimum time 1
> (5) Exists situations where the media (dish2) not reaches the minimum time 2

Fig. 10. List of results (Graphical User Interface)

The counterexample, which is the sequence of actions which leads to this property non-satisfaction, is show in Fig. 11. It also allows to obtain the time of action occurence and consequently the designer can know the residence time in *Running* state and compare it with requirements for human vision. From this information (in our case, the time is below the required minimum), the designer must modify the application code to avoid this erroneous situation.

The code correction requires human intervention since an automatic change could cause an unwanted change in its semantics. One possible solution to correct this situation consists in dividing the display of interactive media in two steps.

Line	Time	Media	States
1	74	Dish2	Stopped
2	74	Dish2	Running
3	75	Dish2	Stopped

Fig. 11. Counterexample of *Dish2* (GUI)

The first step presents the media image. The second step, after 2 seconds, allows interaction. In NCL, the implementation of this solution requires the use of two medias.

Performance Analysis: one of the main issues that we faced was how the designer verifies some formal properties in a hypermedia application, using observers (and in an acceptable response time). To deal with this issue, we propose an initial performance analysis, comparing IG with its IG' version, which represents the document presentation dynamics.

Table 1 shows a comparison of six cases. To get a fair comparison, in all cases, the target media to verifiy was always *dish2*. In all cases, LTL formulas were verified; the formula presented in Eq. 1 refers to case 4.

The results indicated that in all cases, the slicing resulted in a decrease in the size of the model, as well as in lower response times, which makes the approach suitable for on-the-fly checking (live applications). Note that case 6 is bigger than case 1, but its response time is smaller, possibly due to the low connectivity and absence of cycles in observers.

These results was obtained running on a AMD Phenom II P820 triple-core processor with 4 Gigabytes of RAM on Ubuntu Linux. These experiments were performed sequentially, but the proposed approach can be easily extended to allow verification of various model slices in the same time, by using a cluster of computers in a parallel way.

Table 1. Complete model (IG) vs. sliced model (IG')

Case	Description	States	Transitions	Response Time
1	Complete model without observer	26448	94454	18 seconds
2	Sliced model without observer	18576	66198	3 seconds
3	Complete model with 1 observer	33678	120688	29 seconds
4	Sliced model with 1 observer	22830	79928	4 seconds
5	Complete model with 2 observers	44105	161067	37 seconds
6	Sliced model with 2 observers	29017	101235	5 seconds

6 Related Work

Some approaches, techniques and tools have been proposed in recent years to support the verification of temporal consistency properties of hypermedia applications. The following presentation is not exhaustive, but provides a good idea of the state of the art on the temporal validation of hypermedia applications.

In [18], the SMIL application is mapped to an RT-LOTOS specification. Reachability analysis is adopted to verify that the end of all views is achieved. It defines consistency of documents, where the end state is always achieved for all media. This approach considers non-deterministic events, and the reachability analysis allows correction by eliminating inconsistent paths. A different approach is adopted by Gaggi and Bossi [12] where the SMIL application must by described through inference rules in accordance with Hoare's semantics. In this work, the analysis of consistency identifies conflict in parameters "begin", "end" and "duration", where all values must be deterministically defined previously. In the work of Bouyakoub and Belkhir [6], the SMIL application is described through the SMIL Builder tool, which uses a hierarchical SMIL Petri Net model. In this approach, the designer describes the application in SMIL and the tool automatically translates it to Petri Nets. SMIL Builder does not adopt model-checking tools; the analysis of consistency is static, and it identifies conflicts in parameters "begin", "end" and "duration" without considering non-deterministic values. Yu et al. [23] define a formalism called Software Architecture Model (SAM). Synchronization elements of SMIL are systematically modeled by Petri Nets. Useful QoS properties such as safety and liveness are specified using LTL formulas. A reachability tree technique is used to compute the reference timelines of object presentation. Deductive proof, structural induction, as well as model checking techniques are applied to verify synchronization requirements of SMIL documents.

As for the verification of applications in NCL, Santos et al. [19] described the translation of this hypermedia language to RT-LOTOS, where reachability analysis is adopted to verify that the end of all views is achieved. This approach considers non-deterministic events. In the work of Felix et al. [11], a NCL application is converted to an *Objects Representation Language* model, which is translated into a *Broadcaster Timed Automaton*. After the transformation, the UPPAAL model-checker is used to check properties such as reachability. Finally, Tovine et al. [22] propose an approach where the application is modeled in TPNs and properties in Visual Timed Scenarios, a graphical language for describing events, which also generates a TPN model. It uses model-checking and properties to verify, including: freshness, bounded response and event correlation.

Almost all approaches, excepting those presented in [6,12], do not consider non-deterministic events. The work of [6,12] does not adopt formal verification, instead they make the comparison of static temporal attributes of objects and structures. No approach has an environment for specifying properties developed to be usable by designers, or allows the association of temporal and spatial verification. Only the approach described in [6] allows incremental verification, eliminating the need for a full scan of the application, but it does not take into account non-deterministic events. Also, despite the identification of temporal conflicts, not all proposals provide facilities to correct them. When using model checking, the counterexamples are presented in the language of the formal model, usually unknown by the application designer. Our approach aims to overcome these limitations by checking temporal and spatial properties in an incremental way, offering a graphical environment for specifying good behaviors, considering non-deterministic events and aiding the designer to correct documents through an understandable counterexample containing an indication of the times corresponding to events leading to the undesired behavior.

7   Conclusion

This paper presented a method and a toolchain, based on formal verification, to deal with temporal and spatial relationships among objects of applications coded in the NCL and SMIL hypermedia authoring languages. Our approach uses MDE as a software development methodology, a rigorous approach to define transformations between models.

Although our focus is on NCL/SMIL hypermedia applications, our approach can be extended to support other high-level languages. Moreover, it is not tied to any authoring tool.

The experiment presented in this article, and other experiments, showed the efficiency and effectiveness of the proposed approach, because it allowed to identify several undesired behaviors indicating the paths that lead to such behaviors, with an acceptable computational cost. The results obtained by slicing indicate that the proposed method is suitable for the use in on-the-fly verification.

The proposed method and toolchain covered the intended goals: the verification of spatial and temporal behaviors; the reduction of the model, allowing its use in live editing; the use of formal verification effectively by users with no knowledge or expertise; and aid to the designer to correct undesirable behaviors in the document.

Acknowledgements. We are thanful to the CAPES and CNPq Brazilian Federal Research Funding agencies.

References

1. Allen, J.F.: Maintaining knowledge about temporal intervals. Commun. ACM 26, 832–843 (1983)
2. Asnawi, R., Ahmad, W.F.W., Rambli, D.R.A.: Formalization and verification of a live multimedia presentation model. International Journal of Computer Applications 20(2), Article 6 (2011)
3. ATLAS group: ATL user manual, version 0.7 (2006)
4. Berthomieu, B., Bodeveix, J.P., Farail, P., Filali, M., Garavel, H., Gaufillet, P., Lang, F., Vernadat, F.: FIACRE: an intermediate language for model verification in the topcased environment. In: 4th European Congress on Embedded RT Software - ERTS (2008)
5. Berthomieu, B., Ribet, P.O., Vernadat, F.: The tool TINA - construction of abstract state spaces for Petri Nets and Time Petri Nets. Int. Journal of Production Research 14(42), 2741–2756 (2004)
6. Bouyakoub, S., Belkhir, A.: SMIL builder: An incremental authoring tool for SMIL documents. ACM Trans. Multimedia Comp. Comm. Appl. 7, 2:1–2:30 (2011)

7. Bulterman, D., Hardman, L.: Structured multimedia authoring. ACM Trans. Multimedia Comput., Commun. and Appl. 1(1), 89–109 (2005)
8. Bulterman, D.C.A., Brailsford, D.F. (eds.): Proc. 2006 ACM Symposium on Document Engineering, Amsterdam, The Netherlands. ACM (2006)
9. Costa, R.M.D.R., Moreno, M.F., Soares, L.F.G.: Ginga-NCL: supporting multiple devices. In: Proc. of the XV Brazilian Symp. on MM and the Web, WebMedia 2009, pp. 6:1–6:8. ACM, USA (2009)
10. Courtiat, J.P., Santos, C.A.S., Lohr, C., Outtaj, B.: Experience with RT-LOTOS, a temporal extension of the LOTOS formal description technique. Computer Communications 23(12), 1104–1123 (2000)
11. Felix, M., Haeusler, E., Soares, L.: Validating hypermedia documents: a timed automata approach. Monografias em Ciência da Computação, PUC-RioInf.MCC21/02, PUC-Rio, Brazil (2002)
12. Gaggi, O., Bossi, A.: Analysis and verification of SMIL documents. Multimedia Syst. 17(6), 487–506 (2011)
13. da Graça, C., Pimentel, M., Cattelan, R.G., Melo, E.L., do Prado, A.F., Teixeira, C.A.C.: End-user live editing of itv programmes. IJAMC 4(1), 78–103 (2010)
14. Henzinger, T., Manna, Z., Pnueli, A.: Timed transition systems. In: Huizing, C., de Bakker, J.W., Rozenberg, G., de Roever, W.-P. (eds.) REX 1991. LNCS, vol. 600, pp. 226–251. Springer, Heidelberg (1992)
15. ITU-T Recommendation H.761: Nested Context Language (NCL) and Ginga-NCL for IPTV Services (April 2009)
16. Laiola Guimarães, R., Monteiro de Resende Costa, R., Gomes Soares, L.F.: Composer: Authoring tool for iTV programs. In: Tscheligi, M., Obrist, M., Lugmayr, A. (eds.) EuroITV 2008. LNCS, vol. 5066, pp. 61–71. Springer, Heidelberg (2008)
17. Obeo: Acceleo user guide (2008), http://www.acceleo.org
18. Sampaio, P., Courtiat, J.P.: An approach for the automatic generation of RT-LOTOS specifications from SMIL 2.0 documents. J. Braz. Comp. Soc. 9(3), 39–51 (2004)
19. Santos, C.A.S., Soares, L.F.G., Souza, G.L., Courtiat, J.-P.: Design methodology and formal validation of hypermedia documents. In: Proc. of the 6th ACM Intl. Conf. on MM, pp. 39–48. ACM, USA (1998)
20. Schmidt, D.C.: Model-driven engineering. IEEE Computer 39(2), 25–31 (2006)
21. Yang, C.-C.: Detection of the time conflicts for SMIL-based multimedia presentations. In: Workshop on Computer Networks, Internet, and Multimedia, pp. 57–63. National Chung Cheng University, Taiwan (2000)
22. Yovine, S., Olivero, A., Monteverde, D., Cordoba, L., Reiter, G.: An approach for the verification of the temporal consistency of NCL applications. In: II Workshop de TV Digital Interativa (WTVDI) - Colocated with ACM WebMedia 2010 (2010)
23. Yu, H., He, X., Gao, S., Deng, Y.: Modeling and analyzing SMIL documents in SAM. In: Proc. 4th IEEE Int. Symp. on Multimedia Software Engineering, pp. 132–139. IEEE CS (2002)

Revisiting Model-Driven Engineering
for Run-Time Verification of Business Processes

Wei Dou, Domenico Bianculli, and Lionel Briand

SnT Centre, University of Luxembourg, Luxembourg, Luxembourg
{wei.dou,domenico.bianculli,lionel.briand}@uni.lu

Abstract. Run-time verification has been widely advocated in the last
decade as a key technique to check whether the execution of a business
process and its interactions with partner services comply with the application requirements. Despite the substantial research performed in this
area, there are very few approaches that leverage model-driven engineering (MDE) methodologies and integrate them in the development process
of applications based on business process descriptions. In this position
paper we describe our vision and present the research roadmap for adopting MDE techniques in the context of run-time verification of business
processes, based on our early experience with a public service partner
in the domain of eGovernment. We maintain that within this context,
the adoption of MDE would contribute in three ways: 1) expressing, at
a logical level, complex properties to be checked at run time using a
domain-specific language; 2) transforming such properties in a format
that can leverage state-of-the-art, industrial-strength tools in order to
check these properties; 3) integrating such property checker in run-time
verification engines, specific to a target run-time platform, without user's
intervention.

1 Introduction

Enterprise information systems are usually realized leveraging the principles of
service-oriented architecture [18] and business process modeling. These paradigms
foster the design of systems that rely on composition mechanisms, like service
orchestrations defined in BPEL [23] or BPMN [24], where added-value applications are obtained by integrating different components, possibly from different
divisions within the same organization or even from third-party organizations.
This emerging scenario is highly dynamic, open, and decentralized. The global
system is not under control and coordination of a single authority. In principle, and according to an extreme viewpoint, multiple autonomous stakeholders
contribute to the wealth of available resources [5].

Run-time verification has been widely advocated as a key technique to check
whether the execution of a business process and its interactions with partner services comply with the application requirements [1]. Run-time verification becomes
very important in the dynamic scenario described above, since it complements

D. Amyot et al. (Eds.): SAM 2014, LNCS 8769, pp. 190–197, 2014.

traditional design-time verification, which cannot deal with the unexpected changes of the system and its environment, typical of open-world software [3].

In the last decade, substantial research has been performed in the areas of design- and run-time verification (see, for example, the surveys in [2,9,25]) of business-process-driven, service-based applications. However, we notice there are very few approaches that leverage model-driven engineering (MDE) methodologies and integrate them in the development process of applications based on business process descriptions. We contend that MDE techniques should be revisited in the context of run-time verification of business-process-driven, service-based applications. More specifically, we argue that in this context the adoption of MDE would contribute in three ways: 1) expressing, at a logical level, complex properties to be checked at run time using a domain-specific language; 2) transforming such properties in a format that can leverage state-of-the-art, industrial-strength tools in order to check these properties; 3) integrating such property checker in run-time verification engines, specific to a target run-time platform, without user's intervention.

In this paper, we outline a research roadmap for performing run-time verification of business processes using MDE techniques. This research roadmap is based on the early experience gained in the context of a project in collaboration with a public service partner in the domain of eGovernment.

The rest of this paper is structured as follows. Section 2 introduces our vision of model-driven run-time verification of business processes, and Sect. 3 describes the challenges we face and our research roadmap to tackle them. Section 4 discusses related work, and Sect. 5 concludes the paper.

2 Our Vision

In this section, we describe our long-term vision of a model-driven developement methodology for run-time verification of business processes. As depicted in Fig. 1, the methodology encompasses both the design-time and run-time phases for business processes. In addition, there is an additional layer, called *meta*, which virtually sits in between the design-time and the run-time ones. These three layers are described below.

Design-Time Layer

At this layer, the analyst designs the business process, based on requirements specifications. The analyst defines different models, such as use cases, business process models, and data models. Use cases and process models should be annotated with *properties* to be checked at run time. We envision these properties to be expressed in *Restricted Natural Language (RNL)*, using some predefined templates based on property specification patterns (such as the systems defined in [6,13,16,20]).

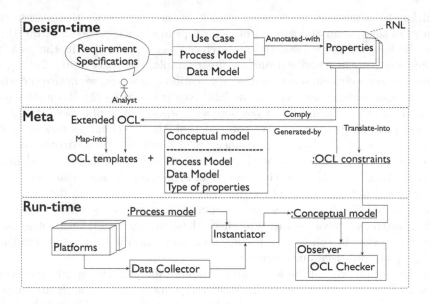

Fig. 1. Our vision of model-driven, run-time verification of business processes

Meta Layer

This layer captures the modeling information that is needed to develop a model-driven approach for run-time verification. Internally to the run-time verification "machinery", we plan to represent the properties to verify at run time using OCL (Object Constraint Language), since it is the standard language in the MDE community and is supported by industrial-strength tools. We then need to translate properties expressed in RNL and defined at the upper design-time layer into plain *OCL constraints*. This translation can be defined by introducing an intermediate language, in the form of an extended version of OCL, which maps RNL templates into corresponding OCL templates.

This layer also defines a *conceptual model* that captures the information that is needed for performing run-time checking: this includes the process model, the data model, the kind of properties to check (e.g., temporal or quality-of-service properties), and the information to be collected at run time at the infrastructure level.

Run-Time Layer

This layer defines the actual environment in which run-time checks happen. We assume there are different run-time *platforms* (e.g., business process execution engines, JavaEE application servers) on which a *process model* is deployed (possibly, after several model transformations) and operated. Each platform contains a platform-specific *data collector* that probes and gathers various kinds of run-time information. The process model instance and the information available from the data collector are given as input to an *Instantiator*, which builds a run-time instance of the conceptual model defined at the *meta* level. This instance is kept alive (and updated) at run time, based on the information coming from the process execution and the platform. The instance is fed into an *Observer*, which receives from the *meta* level also the *OCL constraints* to check. The Observer includes an *OCL checker*, which performs a check of the constraints against the model instance, possibly in an *incremental way*, responding to changes in the model instance. The output of the Observer, in case of violation of a property, can then be used to perform activities such as *root cause analysis*, *debugging*, and *adaptation* (in the form of corrective actions).

3   Research Roadmap

In this section, we present our research roadmap for the development of the methodology presented above, and briefly discuss the challenges faced through it and how MDE could contribute to tackle them.

3.1   Requirements Specification Language

Specifications play a significant role in the realm of business-process-driven applications implemented as service compositions. In practice, services are developed by independent parties and are exposed as black boxes that can only be invoked by clients. Their specifications are the only information available to clients, while their implementations are normally inaccessible. A well-designed specification language is thus required to capture and constrain the requirements that a composite business process and its partner services should guarantee. More importantly in the context of run-time verification, these requirements specifications represent the properties to be checked at run time, to assess the correct behavior and quality-of-service (QoS) provided both by the composite business process and by its partner services.

Our initial experience with our public service partner shows that such a requirements specification language should support the specification of functional and non-functional requirements that include the characterization of quantitative aspects of the system, possibly involving temporal constraints. Examples of these requirements are QoS attributes like response time, throughput, which can be expressed as bounds on the sequence and/or number of occurrences of system events, conjuncted with constraints on the temporal distance of events. More in general, the specification language should support the well-known property specification patterns, including temporal [13], real-time [20], and service provisioning [6] patterns.

One of the challenges in the design of such a specification language is to find the right balance between expressiveness and usability, while guaranteeing efficiency for the verification of the properties expressed in this language.

Following this direction, we have developed *OCLR* (OCL for Runtime Verification) [12], a novel temporal extension of OCL based on common property specification patterns, and extended with support for referring to a specific occurrence of an event in scope boundaries, and for specifying the distance between events and/or from boundaries of the scope of a pattern. *OCLR* extends OCL in a minimal fashion, complementing it to express temporal properties based on Dwyer et al.'s property specification patterns [13]. Moreover, the syntax is very close to English to foster its adoption among practitioners.

3.2 Property Checking

The second step related to run-time verification is how to efficiently verify the properties that can be expressed in the language detailed in the previous subsection.

The efficiency of the verification depends on the expressiveness of the specification language, on the formal model underlying the language, and on the tool support for the verification of the corresponding formal models.

In our case, since *OCLR* is based on OCL, our formal model is actually OCL itself and the tools that can be used for checking *OCLR* properties are represented by existing OCL checkers, such as Eclipse OCL.

Our idea is to recast the problem of the verification of *OCLR* properties at run time in terms of the checking of OCL constraints on instances of a model (kept alive at run time, as described in Sect. 2) corresponding to the actual execution of a business process. This approach leverages existing MDE techniques and technologies and we believe it is a safer and more efficient choice, with respect to developing a dedicated checker for *OCLR* from scratch.

In this regards, we have started assessing the feasibility of checking *OCLR* constraints over execution traces by proposing a mapping of *OCLR* constraints into OCL, based on a conceptual model for traces. The trace checking problem has been re-casted in terms of a check of OCL invariants [11]. The results of our preliminary evaluation using a proof-of-concept tool are encouraging, since the verification of traces with up to 10 million events takes only a few minutes, depending on the complexity of the properties.

The trace checking approach reported in [11] focuses on *offline checking*. The next research steps will focus on tuning up the checking procedure to provide adequate performance when used for *run-time* trace checking of *OCLR* properties. We will also consider the use of incremental checking techniques of OCL constraints (see, for example [7,8,14,21,26], possibly following a syntactic-semantic approach [4]) as well as techniques for efficiently managing the history of monitored events [10].

3.3 Integration with Run-Time Platforms

The last step of our research roadmap is the integration of the property checking procedure outlined in the previous section within the actual run-time execution platforms of business process applications. We plan to support at least two main execution platforms, which correspond to the ones adopted by our public service partner: a) JavaEE for business processes delivered as Web applications; b) executable BPMN 2.0 process description executed on a process execution engine. In both cases, the idea is to embed the property checker (based on an OCL checker) within the run-time platforms. While the checker is the same across the platforms, the data collection architecture used to feed the checker will be different and platform-specific. Based on the expected inputs (and outputs) of the checker, a data collector should be put in place, for example using message interceptors in the business process engine or a dedicated middleware component (for example, implemented with EJB) for the case of JavaEE applications.

4   Related Work

The research on design- and run-time verification of business-process driven, service-based applications spans for more than a decade (see, for example, the surveys in [2,9,25]). However, to the best of our knowledge, the solutions proposing a complete model-driven approach to run-time verification for this application domain are very few. In the rest of this section, we review them and comment on their limitations.

The model-driven approach presented in [27] relies on a graph-based model that includes *Key Performance Indicators (KPIs)* (e.g., process execution time, server availability); *correlation rules* that specify event patterns to be matched; and *action policies* defining the actions to be taken when a certain event occurs and when the KPIs have certain values. Based on the correlation rules, this graph is then decomposed and transformed into several BPEL processes, which are extended with a logic to monitor KPIs and execute action policies. This approach focuses on generating business processes with (KPIs) monitoring capabilities, but it does not provide any mechanisms to link back to high-level requirements and embeds the monitoring code directly within the process structure.

A fully integrated approach for design and implementation of monitored web service compositions is presented in [22]. The approach proposes a set of meta-models for defining performance indicators and their calculation rules, as well as a set of model transformations that are used to generate an executable implementation on top of IBM WebSphere Business Monitor. Although the approach promotes the adoption of reusable calculation templates for specifying custom indicators, the ones that can be expressed are still limited by the basic properties of the process activities (e.g., start time) that can be referenced within the templates.

Reference [19] proposes the ProGoalML language as an extension of BPMN with additional modeling elements for metrics, KPIs, and goals. Based on these elements, monitoring CEP (Complex Event Processing) rules are generated to collect the proper information, which is then used to assess the fulfillment of the goals. However, the approach allows for only simple metrics and does not support a temporal dimension for goal fulfillment.

A model-driven approach for transformation from regulatory policies to event correlation rules is presented in [15]. Policies are expressed using real-time temporal logic and then transformed into IBM ACT rules using some parameterized temporal patterns. The definition of the policies is disconnected from the models of the business processes; moreover, the type of policies is limited by the restricted set of temporal patterns supported during the transformation phase.

The model-aware monitoring approach presented in [17] is also related to policy compliance checking. The approach correlates low-level monitoring events with high-level business events by means of traceability information inserted into business process models. This information is then used at run time by a business intelligence component to perform the actual check on the process model instance to which the events refer to. However, the paper does not indicate which kind of policies can be checked using this approach.

5 Conclusion

In this paper we have presented our vision and the research roadmap to follow for run-time verification of business processes. This vision is currently being developed in collaboration with our public service partner CTIE (Centre des technologies de l'information de l'Etat, the Luxembourg national center for information technology), which has developed in-house a model-driven methodology for designing eGovernment business processes. Our goal is to complement this methodology with the model-driven run-time verification techniques discussed in this paper. At the time of writing this paper, CTIE has already started using *OCLR* [12] for specifying the requirements of business processes. Our next steps will focus on the integration of our model-driven trace checking technique [11] for *OCLR* within their business process execution platforms.

Acknowledgments. This work has been supported by the National Research Fund, Luxembourg (FNR/P10/03).

References

1. Baresi, L., Bianculli, D., Ghezzi, C., Guinea, S., Spoletini, P.: Validation of web service compositions. IET Softw. 1(6), 219–232 (2007)
2. Baresi, L., Di Nitto, E.: Test and Analysis of Web Services. Springer, Heidelberg (2007)
3. Baresi, L., Di Nitto, E., Ghezzi, C.: Toward open-world software: Issue and challenges. IEEE Computer 39(10), 36–43 (2006)
4. Bianculli, D., Filieri, A., Ghezzi, C., Mandrioli, D.: Syntactic-semantic incrementality for agile verification. Sci. Comput. Program (2013) (in press), doi:10.1016/j.scico.2013.11.026
5. Bianculli, D., Ghezzi, C.: Towards a methodology for lifelong validation of service compositions. In: SDSOA 2008, pp. 7–12. ACM (May 2008)
6. Bianculli, D., Ghezzi, C., Pautasso, C., Senti, P.: Specification patterns from research to industry: a case study in service-based applications. In: ICSE 2012, pp. 968–976. IEEE (2012)
7. Cabot, J., Teniente, E.: Incremental evaluation of OCL constraints. In: Martinez, F.H., Pohl, K. (eds.) CAiSE 2006. LNCS, vol. 4001, pp. 81–95. Springer, Heidelberg (2006)

8. Cabot, J., Teniente, E.: Incremental integrity checking of UML/OCL conceptual schemas. J. Syst. Softw. 82(9), 1459–1478 (2009)
9. Canfora, G., Di Penta, M.: Service-oriented architectures testing: A survey. In: De Lucia, A., Ferrucci, F. (eds.) ISSSE 2006-2008. LNCS, vol. 5413, pp. 78–105. Springer, Heidelberg (2009)
10. Chomicki, J.: Efficient checking of temporal integrity constraints using bounded history encoding. ACM Trans. Database Syst. 20, 149–186 (1995)
11. Dou, W., Bianculli, D., Briand, L.: A model-based approach to trace checking of temporal properties with OCL. Tech. Rep. TR-SnT-2014-5, SnT Centre - University of Luxembourg (March 2014)
12. Dou, W., Bianculli, D., Briand, L.: OCLR: a more expressive, pattern-based temporal extension of OCL. In: Cabot, J., Rubin, J. (eds.) ECMFA 2014. LNCS, vol. 8569, pp. 51–66. Springer, Heidelberg (2014)
13. Dwyer, M.B., Avrunin, G.S., Corbett, J.C.: Patterns in property specifications for finite-state verification. In: ICSE 1999, pp. 411–420. IEEE (1999)
14. Garcia, M., Möller, R.: Incremental evaluation of OCL invariants in the essential MOF object model. In: Modellierung 2008. LNI, vol. 127, pp. 11–26 (2008)
15. Giblin, C., Müller, S., Pfitzmann, B.: From regulatory policies to event monitoring rules: Towards model-driven compliance automation. Tech. Rep. Research Report RZ-3662, IBM Research GmbH (2006)
16. Gruhn, V., Laue, R.: Patterns for timed property specifications. Electron. Notes Theor. Comput. Sci. 153(2), 117–133 (2006)
17. Holmes, T., Mulo, E., Zdun, U., Dustdar, S.: Model-aware monitoring of SOAs for compliance service engineering. In: Service Engineering, pp. 117–136. Springer Vienna (2011)
18. Josuttis, N.: SOA in Practice: The Art of Distributed System Design. O'Reilly Media, Inc. (2007)
19. Koetter, F., Kochanowski, M.: Goal-oriented model-driven business process monitoring using proGoalML. In: Abramowicz, W., Kriksciuniene, D., Sakalauskas, V. (eds.) BIS 2012. LNBIP, vol. 117, pp. 72–83. Springer, Heidelberg (2012)
20. Konrad, S., Cheng, B.H.C.: Real-time specification patterns. In: ICSE 2005, pp. 372–381. ACM (2005)
21. Menet, L., Lamolle, M., Le Dc, C.: Incremental validation of models in a MDE approach applied to the modeling of complex data structures. In: Meersman, R., Dillon, T., Herrero, P. (eds.) OTM 2010. LNCS, vol. 6428, pp. 120–129. Springer, Heidelberg (2010)
22. Momm, C., Gebhart, M., Abeck, S.: A model-driven approach for monitoring business performance in web service compositions. In: ICIW 2009, pp. 343–350. IEEE (2009)
23. OASIS: Web Services Business Process Execution Language Version 2.0 (2007)
24. OMG: BPMN 2.0 specification (January 2011), http://www.bpmn.org
25. Salaün, G.: Analysis and verification of service interaction protocols - a brief survey. In: TAV-WEB 2010. EPTCS, vol. 35, pp. 75–86 (2010)
26. Vajk, T., Mezei, G., Levendovszky, T.: An incremental OCL compiler for modeling environments. ECEASST 15 (2008)
27. Yu, T., Jeng, J.J.: Model driven development of business process monitoring and control systems. In: Chen, C.-S., Filipe, J., Seruca, I., Cordeiro, J. (eds.) ICEIS 2005, pp. 161–166 (2005)

Model-Based Testing:
An Approach with SDL/RTDS and DIVERSITY

Julien Deltour[1], Alain Faivre[2], Emmanuel Gaudin[1], and Arnault Lapitre[2]

[1] PragmaDev, 18 rue des Tournelles, 75004 Paris, France
{julien.deltour,emmanuel.gaudin}@pragmadev.com
[2] CEA LIST, Point Courrier 174, 91191 Gif-sur-Yvette, France
{alain.faivre,arnault.lapitre}@cea.fr

Abstract. The objective of the PragmaList Lab, a joint laboratory between PragmaDev and CEA LIST, is to integrate the test generation tool DIVERSITY in the SDL modeling environment Real Time Developer Studio (RTDS). The resulting environment aims to extend RTDS with a Model-Based Testing approach. After briefly describing the characteristics of RTDS and DIVERSITY, this paper presents the work done to integrate these two environments. Then, it highlights the main principles of DIVERSITY based on symbolic execution, which enables the generation of test cases in TTCN-3 format. The paper then presents the existing coverage criteria in the integrated generation of test cases. It concludes with the open strategy of the PragmaList approach to work together with industrial actors based on the definition and integration of new specific coverage criteria consistent with their validation constraints.

Keywords: Model-based testing, Test generation, SDL, TTCN-3.

1   Introduction

PragmaList[1] is a joint laboratory resulting from the collaboration between the PragmaDev company and the CEA LIST national research center. The objective of this laboratory is to integrate CEA LIST's automatic test generation tool, namely DIVERSITY [2], with PragmaDev's Real Time Developer Studio (RTDS[2]), a modeling environment for SDL [5]. The resulting environment allows extending the current features of RTDS with a Model-Based Testing (MBT) approach in order to ensure compliance of the developed systems with their corresponding higher-level models written in SDL.

Indeed, MBT is an approach to system testing in which handwritten tests are replaced by tests automatically generated from a test model. This has several advantages: a huge number of tests can be generated from a test model in a short time while ensuring that the set of tests is the minimum set needed to cover all or a part of the

---

[1] http://www.pragmalist.org/
[2] http://www.pragmadev.com/

D. Amyot et al. (Eds.): SAM 2014, LNCS 8769, pp. 198–206, 2014.
© Springer International Publishing Switzerland 2014

model. Moreover, in the case of requirements changes, the update of a test model is much less time consuming than the update of a database of individual test cases.

After briefly describing the characteristics of the two separate environments, this paper presents the main translation rules used for the transformation of SDL models into the internal language of DIVERSITY called XLIA. Then, it gives the main principles of the core of DIVERSITY based on symbolic execution, which leads to the generation of test cases in the TTCN-3 format [6]. Afterwards, the paper presents the predefined coverage criteria in the integrated environment for test case generation that the user can parameterize. It concludes with the open strategy of the PragmaList approach to working together with industry actors. This approach should enable better compliance with the specific requirements of the different domains, working on both the development of SDL models and the integration of new specific coverage criteria consistent with their validation constraints.

2   PragmaDev's Modeling Technology

RTDS is a modeling and testing tool for the development of real time and embedded communicating systems. It was initially based on SDL-RT[3], a mix of SDL and C languages, and evolved to finally also support the SDL international standard [5]. This raised the tool abstraction level from code to an abstract but executable model. In order to offer the corresponding testing technologies, TTCN-3 was introduced in RTDS. It is therefore possible to simulate an SDL model against a TTCN-3 test case, or to generate code from an SDL model as well as from a TTCN-3 test case.

In the last few years, PragmaDev worked on verifying model properties and on how to generate test cases from a model. A first, an export to the Verimag[4] Intermediate Format (IF) was implemented and, more recently, an export to the FIACRE[5] pivot language was added to be able to run academic model checkers on the SDL model.

The basic principle of these technologies is to try to go through all possible cases. Industrial experimentation on real systems showed their limitations. The number of cases is so huge that the exploration is very time consuming and does not conclude.

For these reasons, PragmaDev was looking for another approach that could tackle real industrial systems. After investigation, it turned out CEA owned a promising technology that a few experiments proved to be very efficient. PragmaDev and CEA, hence, started a shared laboratory to enable using CEA technology transparently from and back to the PragmaDev modeling and testing environment.

3   CEA LIST's V&V Technology

The DIVERSITY tool [2], developed by CEA LIST, is a validation and verification platform based on model analysis. Models may be described with the help of

---

[3] http://www.sdl-rt.org/
[4] http://www-verimag.imag.fr
[5] http://projects.laas.fr/fiacre/

stateflow-type languages, describing potentially concurrent and communicating automata. They can also be characterized using dataflow languages such as the one used in MATLAB/Simulink.

DIVERSITY analyzes these models in order to generate test scenarios. In a first step, these scenarios may be used by a simulator associated with the modeling environment, like the one in RTDS, as simulation scenarios to validate the input model. In a second step, these scenarios may be used to verify the compliance of the implementation with the model.

For both uses, the DIVERSITY process consists of three steps:

1. Firstly, the input model is analyzed and translated into DIVERSITY's internal representation, called XLIA.
2. Then, an exhaustive symbolic exploration of nominal behaviors is performed (symbolic, in order to avoid numerical combinatorial explosion). This symbolic execution can highlight application-independent unexpected behaviors such as deadlocks or over-designing (parts of model never activated). Moreover, in order to guarantee termination or to limit the number of generated test cases, several basic structural criteria may be used during the symbolic execution.
3. Finally, DIVERSITY associates each generated behavior with one (or more) numerical test cases.

The deterministic approach of DIVERSITY differs from the random approaches commonly used by other industrial tools. The deterministic approach has the advantage of producing, in a systematic way, all test cases associated with the coverage criteria but with a computation time that can vary widely. The probabilistic approach, generally more efficient in terms of execution time, may not generate all test cases for low probabilistic behaviors. Moreover, for a given objective, our deterministic approach allows to generate smaller sets of tests than those generated by random approaches.

4   SDL and DIVERSITY

DIVERSITY provides an internal language called XLIA, which aims to capture all semantic elements of all languages for modeling complex, distributed and interconnected systems.

This language offers the necessary elements to describe different types of simulation semantics: interleaving or with the help of specific operators to define partial order of execution. It also offers elements to describe semantics of synchronous communication (e.g., with *rendezvous*) or asynchronous communication (e.g., with *FIFO message stacks*). It also contains all the concepts that take into account the structural elements used to describe the architecture of the modeled systems.

To specify the SDL to XLIA translator, we defined translation rules. These rules describe, for each element of SDL, which counterparties in XLIA to use.

As examples of rules, the translation rules of elements that structure SDL models like *SYSTEM*, *BLOCK*, and *PROCESS* are defined in Table 1.

Table 1. Examples of translation rules for SDL structural elements

SDL	XLIA

SYSTEM system_name	**@xfsp<system , 1.0 >:**
	 input_enabled system< and > system_name {
	 ...
	 @machine:
	   // *definition of machines (block / process)*
	 ...
	 } // *end system_name*

BLOCK block_name	**machine< and >** block_name {
	 ...
	 @machine:
	   // *definition of machines (block / process)*
	 ...
	 } // *end block_name*

PROCESS process_name
 (initial_nb, max_nb)
 	
 // *with states and links*
 // *between states*
	statemachine< or , *instance*: (*init*:<int>, *max*:<int>) **>** process_name {
	 ...
	 @machine:
	 state< initial > #init {
	   transition {
	     // statements
	     ...
	   } --> state1_name;
	 }
	 state state1_name {
	   ...
	 }
	 ...
	 } // *end process_name*

The SDL concept of "process instance", with its associated variables *SELF* and *PARENT*, has direct semantics equivalence in XLIA. On the other hand, the predefined variable *OFFSPRING* must be explicitly declared as a new variable in XLIA. Similarly, SDL concepts of "continuous signal" and "priority consumption", as well as mechanisms for managing signals, have direct counterparts in XLIA.

However, a number of SDL elements did not have an equivalent in XLIA, which was subsequently extended to take these elements into account. For example, the concept of multi-state did not exist in XLIA and the language has been extended to take into account this new element. This was also the case for the more complex concept of timer, which has been introduced in XLIA. Its associated translation rules are presented in Table 2.

In the same way, a number of operators were also added that did not exist in XLIA, e.g., the operators that handle strings.

To conclude on this point, all SDL concepts seem translatable into XLIA except object-oriented constructs and macros. For the last missing elements, they will be treated as and when the need arises in future industrial models considered.

Table 2. Translation rules associated to timer

Global preliminary to the system	var time NOW = 0 {
	　@on_write(T) { guard(T >= NOW); }
	}

TIMER myclock;
 	
SET(NOW+15,myclock)
	const time TIMER#UNSET = -1;
	var time myclock#endtime = TIMER#UNSET;
	signal myclock;
	myclock#endtime = (: NOW *newfresh*) + 15;
	output myclock;

INPUT myclock	// In the source state, an internal action :
	@irun{ (: NOW *newfresh*); }
	
	guard(myclock#endtime =/= TIMER#UNSET);
	input myclock;
	tguard(NOW >= myclock#endtime);

RESET myclock	myclock#endtime = TIMER#UNSET; (: buff remove myclock);

5　Test Case Generation and TTCN-3

The kernel of DIVERSITY generates a symbolic execution graph that characterizes all symbolic behaviors of the system. The two main formal techniques used for this calculation are:

- *Symbolic Execution*: The major problem with numerical approaches is the combinatorial explosion due to the value fields associated with system parameters. These value fields can be very large or even infinite. Symbolic computation can handle such fields, because it characterizes all behaviors that are not equivalent, but without making redundant calculations when different values of the variables correspond to the same behavior. The input parameters are not evaluated numerically, but appear as symbolic constants in guards of executed transitions. The guards of executed transitions in an execution path are integrated in a constraint that is the associated condition of the path. This path condition is simply the logical conjunction of all transition guards of the path. Its satisfiability is checked using external constraint solvers, like CVC4[6], to ensure that the corresponding path is executable. In that case, the resolution of this path condition by means of the constraint solvers produces a sequence of numeric system inputs which corresponds to a concrete test.

[6] http://cvc4.cs.nyu.edu/web/

- *Constraint Solver*: When the execution tree is built, all calculated symbolic behaviors of the system can be accessed by consulting the tree. Then, constraint solvers may be used to obtain numerical values for the system parameters by resolution of path conditions. Each condition gives way to an input sequence of the system.

After the symbolic execution phase, each symbolic path generated corresponds to a behavior of the system that must be tested. It consists of an input/output sequence interacting with the system environment. The chosen format for the test cases is TTCN-3 with the following four files:

- *TTCN_Declarations.ttcn*: This file contains declarations of types, numerical parameters associated with input/output messages, and the input/output ports corresponding to SDL channels.
- *TTCN_Templates.ttcn3*: This file defines the numerical value of all input and output messages and their associated parameters.
- *TTCN_TestCases.ttcn3*: This file specifies the sequence of inputs and outputs for each test case.
- *TTCN_ControlPart.ttcn3*: This file defines the sequence of execution of predefined test cases.

6   Stop Criteria and Coverage Criteria

In order to deal with the combinatorial explosion of behaviors and to select the most efficient test cases, DIVERSITY offers several coverage criteria [3,4]. The first ones are basic coverage criteria that enable the control of the number of generated test cases with a large coverage of the entire system or selected sub-systems. The last ones are more "intelligent" and comply with industrial V&V standards or are guided by properties given by users to obtain more relevant test cases with regard to system functionalities.

- *Structural Stop Criteria*: These criteria allow DIVERSITY to limit the symbolic execution in depth and width, which corresponds to limiting the length and number of test cases without further characterization. These criteria are generally used with other coverage criteria and thus can limit the symbolic execution, if other criteria appear not to be achievable within a reasonable time.
- *State/Transition Coverage*: This is the more conventional structural test coverage criterion to be used on an input model. It can be adapted in order to cover other types of basic elements of the model according to user needs such as internal/external signals coverage for example. It should be noted, this criterion can be parameterized in order to only target a subset of states or transitions.
- *Inclusion Criterion – Symbolic Behavior Coverage*: This is the most sophisticated coverage criterion proposed by DIVERSITY. In its basic form, the symbolic execution stops only if it has previously encountered a symbolic state that takes into account the current one. This means that this criterion, if reached, can characterize all possible symbolic system behaviors and provide the associated tests. Its interest

is to provide a set of tests with a very high level of confidence. Its disadvantage is that it requires an additional level of complex calculations during symbolic execution, which makes this approach inoperable from a certain size/complexity of the input model.

- *Test Case Generation Constrained by Properties*: All previous coverage criteria may be used to generate test cases in a particular context defined by properties expressed with the help of the model variables.

Adaptability of the Tool

It is important to note that the architecture of DIVERSITY allows one to easily integrate new criteria for selecting tests. This is done by means of "filters" to be defined jointly with the users. This highly scalable nature of the tool permits the design of coverage criteria or combination of criteria adapted to different levels and types of models. This also enables the generation of test sets conform to the expected level of assurance and standards.

Whatever the coverage criteria selected, the tool interface dynamically shows the evolution of the covered items using a "SpiderGraph" view, as shown in Fig. 1.

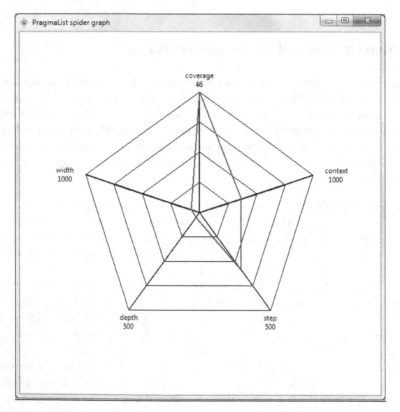

Fig. 1. SpiderGraph to view the analysis progress in the tool

Verification of Properties with Observers

DIVERSITY can also be used to try to determine if a property (a safety property, for example) may be violated. The negation of the property defined by the user is automatically encoded into an observer. Then, at each symbolic execution step, DIVERSITY will verify whether this negation is verified or not. DIVERSITY is not a real proof tool, but it will ensure that the security property is checked for symbolic behavior of the system of a given depth/width.

Preliminary Results

The resulting integration has been tested with very simple systems. The very first measures have been done on a system with two processes and a few messages with integers as parameters. The measures have been compared with Verimag's IFx toolbox, which runs exhaustive simulations on the model. Even though they cannot be directly compared, the coverage resolution time with DIVERSITY without any modification in the system is equivalent to the exploration time with Verimag if the input parameters range is restricted to the minimum set of values. This suggests that the symbolic DIVERSITY approach is optimal in that case. These results must be confirmed in real use cases in the future.

7   Conclusion

In this paper, we have presented the work undertaken in the PragmaList shared laboratory to integrate CEA LIST's automatic test generation technology with Pragma-Dev's RTDS platform. This work mainly focused on the translation of the SDL language into XLIA, and on formatting generated tests in the TTCN-3 format. It also focused on the specificities of the semantics of SDL, especially temporal aspects of the language, in the symbolic execution on which DIVERSITY is based.

With this integrated platform, we proposed a number of strategies for generating tests that allow users to run the tool on their SDL models to obtain a first set of tests at lower cost. However, on one hand, these strategies do not necessarily meet the needs of users according to their specific industrial field. On the other hand, the complexity of systems and associated SDL models will not necessarily enable the tool to complete with the proposed criteria coverage.

Therefore, our next step is to work closely with industrials to explore with them the specificities of their models and their requirements for the validation of their systems. This work should allow establishing a methodology for the elaboration of models that serve as references for testing the developed systems. It must also offer to industrials new criteria that will be integrated into DIVERSITY as new filters.

The results obtained from handling industrial models will then be compared to those obtained by the existing industrial tools based on deterministic or random test generation. More specifically, the proposed methodology could be compared to those proposed as part of MBT, e.g., the approach described by Baranov et al. [1] and based on three types of coverage criteria.

The proposed approach needs to involve both industrials, for writing models to be "executed" by tools, and tool suppliers, who must be able to quickly adapt the proposed strategies. This is, from our point of view, the best way to integrate this type of formal tools in the development chain of complex systems.

References

1. Baranov, S., Kotlyarov, V., Weigert, T.: Verifiable Coverage Criteria for Automated Testing. In: Ober, I., Ober, I. (eds.) SDL 2011. LNCS, vol. 7083, pp. 79–89. Springer, Heidelberg (2011)
2. Gaston, C., Le Gall, P., Rapin, N., Touil, A.: Symbolic execution techniques for test purpose definition. In: Uyar, M.Ü., Duale, A.Y., Fecko, M.A. (eds.) TestCom 2006. LNCS, vol. 3964, pp. 1–18. Springer, Heidelberg (2006)
3. Faivre, A., Gaston, C.: Test generation methodology based on symbolic execution for the Common Criteria higher levels. In: 2nd Workshop on Model Development and Validation (MoDeVa), Montego Bay, Jamaica (2005)
4. Faivre, A., Gaston, C., Le Gall, P.: Symbolic Model Based Testing for Component Oriented Systems. In: Petrenko, A., Veanes, M., Tretmans, J., Grieskamp, W. (eds.) TestCom/FATES 2007. LNCS, vol. 4581, pp. 90–106. Springer, Heidelberg (2007)
5. International Telecommunication Union: Recommendation Z.100 (12/11), Specification and Description Language - Overview of SDL-2010, http://www.itu.int/rec/T-REC-Z.100/en
6. International Telecommunication Union: Recommendation Z.161 (07/13), Testing and Test Control Notation version 3: TTCN-3 core language, http://www.itu.int/rec/T-REC-Z.161/en

On Bringing Object-Oriented Software Metrics into the Model-Based World – Verifying ISO 26262 Compliance in Simulink

Lukas Mäurer[1], Tanja Hebecker[1], Torben Stolte[2], Michael Lipaczewski[1], Uwe Möhrstädt[3], and Frank Ortmeier[1]

[1] Chair of Software Engineering,
Otto-von-Guericke University of Magdeburg,
Germany
lukas.maeurer@st.ovgu.de,
{tanja.hebecker,michael.lipaczewski,frank.ortmeier}@ovgu.de
[2] Institute of Control Engineering,
Technische Universität Braunschweig,
Germany
stolte@ifr.ing.tu-bs.de
[3] Porsche Engineering,
Bietigheim-Bissingen,
Germany
uwe.moehrstaedt@porsche.de

Abstract. For ensuring functional safety of electrical/electronic systems, it is necessary to exclude malfunctions from hardware and software as well as from the interaction of both. In today's passenger vehicles, more and more safety critical functionalities are implemented in software. Thus, its importance for functional safety increases. The dominating safety standard for the automotive domain (ISO 26262) considers the software part and defines requirements for safety critical software. However, applying and fulfilling the standard is a major problem in industry. In this context, the paper presents a novel metric-based approach to evaluate dataflow-oriented software architectures used in many model-driven processes regarding the fulfillment of requirements defined by ISO 26262 (in particular part 6). The core idea is to derive metrics for model-based software from already existing, well-performing metrics elaborated for other programming paradigms. To link metrics to requirements fulfillment of ISO 26262, we briefly sketch the factor-criteria-metrics paradigm for this problem. Technically, this paper presents a generic meta-model for dataflow systems, which is used to define the metrics. We implemented this meta-model and the metrics as a prototype for Matlab Simulink. As examples, two models of a 400 kW full Drive-by-Wire experimental vehicle with all-wheel-steering, all-wheel-drive, and electro-mechanical brakes are analyzed using this prototype.

Keywords: safety analysis, ISO 26262, formal verification, software metrics, Simulink.

D. Amyot et al. (Eds.): SAM 2014, LNCS 8769, pp. 207–222, 2014.
© Springer International Publishing Switzerland 2014

1 Introduction

In line with the increasing utilization of electronics, more and more software intensive systems are introduced in today's passenger vehicles. Many of these functions either are directly safety functions or their failure is often safety critical. This increases the need for well designed software.

In this context, the international standard ISO 26262 *"Road vehicles - Functional safety"* [9], officially published in November 2011, describes a holistic procedure to ensure functional safety of electrical and/or electronic (E/E) systems. Altogether, ISO 26262 provides requirements and processes regarding the whole safety lifecycle of a system under development including development, production, operation, service, decommissioning, as well as management. In this paper, we only consider issues related to the software development phase.

In ISO 26262, the processes and requirements regarding the actual software development are described in part 6 whereby solely systematic failures are considered on the software level. Thus, part 6 of ISO 26262 describes generic measures for software design, implementation, and testing. One central aspect during software development in ISO 26262 is the software architectural design. In order to avoid systematic failures, ISO 26262 proposes necessary properties of a software architecture [9, part 6 - 7.4.3]: *modularity, encapsulation,* and *simplicity.*

Apart from these abstract principles, no information is given how the fulfillment of these requirements can be verified. One approach might be an architectural design review. However, the results of such a review heavily depends on the experience of the reviewer. Thus, this paper proposes objective measures which should not replace design reviews by experts but might be used as an extra input for these. The core idea is to develop metrics for the evaluation of software architectural designs.

Another constraint to be considered is that model-driven software development is state-of-the-art in the automotive industry. As a consequence, the metrics must be applicable to model level instead of code level. After discussing some related approaches in Sect. 2, the paper briefly introduces requirements of ISO 26262 in Sect. 3. In Sect. 4, we sketch a meta-model for dataflow oriented systems and, using this meta-model, we formally define the metrics. Finally, we present the results of these metrics for the example of Simulink models stemming from an experimental vehicle at Technische Universität Braunschweig.

2 Related Work

Determining the quality of software has a long history. One commonly used method is to apply source code metrics. The core idea is to formalize knowledge about "good" code and compute a quality value automatically by parsing and analyzing the source code.

One of the first metrics suited for object oriented design was developed by Abreau und Carapuça in 1994 [1]. They introduced seven criteria for metrics in conjunction with a set of metrics. To assess the quality of object oriented designs, they focus on inheritance, encapsulation, and polymorphism that have to be evaluated for quantifying external quality attributes such as functionality, reliability, and maintainability.

In embedded software engineering, model-driven development is state-of-the-art. The most common tools are Matlab Simulink, SCADE, and ASCET. These three modeling languages are all based on some dataflow semantics. Thus, traditional object-oriented metrics cannot be applied directly. Assessing quality of such software may be done at two layers. One can either analyze the generated C/C++ code with traditional metrics or one can analyze the dataflow model itself. We only focus on the latter option. The reason is that metrics are most often used to judge maintainability and understandability of a code. This means they have to analyze the level of abstraction a programmer uses; not the generated low level code.

Analyzing dataflow models automatically is a hot topic. In 2012, Scheible [16] introduces a method for quality assessment of Simulink models for automatic code generation for *engine control units (ECUs)* in the automotive domain. He develops a quality model with respect to feasibility for code generation, efficiency, correctness, robustness, testability, comprehensibility, and maintainability. For each quality factor, he defines static model metrics on a graph representation of the Simulink metric leading to 84 different metrics. Comparing the results of his framework with the judgment of experts at Daimler-Chrysler, he concludes that his framework outputs a reasonable assessment of the general quality of a Simulink model. We take this work as a basis for a formalization. However, he does not explicitly address the requirements of ISO 26262 – the dominating standard in automotive industry.

Another approach is INProVE ("Indicator-based Non-functional Property-oriented eValuation and Evolution of software design models") [10], an Eclipse-based application to support quality evaluation and monitoring of modeling languages. It is based on a meta-model for dataflow modeling languages and configurable for company specific languages or metrics. The concept of INProVE's model assessment consists of indicators. Indicators can be combined and thus range from simple count measurements to complex pattern searches. The INProVE authors emphasize pattern searches heavily, arguing that expert knowledge can intuitively be represented in patterns. The good thing about this approach is its flexibility. On the downside, it lacks the definition of broadly accepted, standardized metrics as well as a connection to safety standards like ISO 26262.

Aiming at the support of Failure Mode and Effects Analysis (FMEA), the Simulink Model Metrics Calculator by Menkhaus and Andrich [13] is another tool to be mentioned here. Menkhaus and Andrich apply metrics to Simulink and use the results to guide the FMEA expert through the analysis of the software. Thereby, the application of metrics is only used as an aid for further methods, as the metrics are not sufficient for stand alone model analysis. However, the Calculator is a good technical starting point for building an implementation, as it also parses and analyzes Matlab Simulink models.

3 Metrics to Fulfill Requirements of ISO 26262

In this section, we present the core requirements of ISO 26262 part 6 for software architectures and reason the choice of metrics that we apply for checking the fulfillment of these requirements.

3.1 Architectural Design Requirements of ISO 26262

Part 6, chapter 7 of ISO 26262 describes the process for developing and verifying the architectural design of the software in automotive applications. The main three requirements – modularity, encapsulation, and simplicity – are stated in paragraph 7.4.3 of the standard.

Modularity of a software system describes according to Meyer [14] that the software system consists of autonomous software elements ordered in a coherent, simple structure. *Simplicity* often relates to two concepts: the pure size of one functionality as well as the complexity of a functionality. *Encapsulation*, according to Mayer and Hall [12], is the combination of privacy and unity.

To fulfill these abstract requirements, ISO 26262 introduces seven principles stated in Table 1.

Table 1. Principles for software architectural design according to ISO 26262 [9, part 6 - 7.4.4]

Methods		ASIL			
		A	B	C	D
1a	Hierarchical structure of software components	++	++	++	++
1b	Restricted size of software components	++	++	++	++
1c	Restricted size of interfaces	+	+	+	+
1d	High cohesion within each software component	+	++	++	++
1e	Restricted coupling between software components	+	++	++	++
1f	Appropriate scheduling properties	++	++	++	++
1g	Limited use of interrupts	+	+	+	++

The table indicates the necessity of the principles for the respective Automotive Safety Integrity Level (ASIL). As seen, all methods are either recommended (+) or highly recommended (++) for all ASIL. For the definition of the ASIL levels, we refer to the standard [9].

In this work, we focus on model (and source code) quality only. The principles 1f and 1g are aimed at dynamic/execution behavior and are thus outside the scope of this paper.

3.2 Applied Metrics

For the choice of metrics to evaluate the requirements of ISO 26262, we follow the Factor-Criteria-Metrics approach of Cavano and McCall [5]. Cavano and

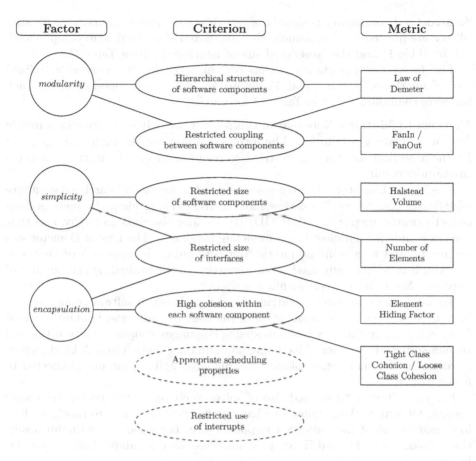

Fig. 1. Derivation of metrics

McCall introduce a principle to refine abstract requirements, called *factors*, to specify demands, called *criteria*, and map those to metrics. This approach was chosen because the structure of *factors* and *criteria* matches the structure of the three main requirements (*factors*) with the seven principles (*criteria*) of ISO 26262. Figure 1 shows the Factor-Criteria-Metrics approach applied to ISO 26262 software quality requirements.

Factors to Criteria: The *factor* modularity is assigned to the two *criteria* "hierarchical structure of software components" (1a in Table 1) and "restricted coupling between software components" (1e in Table 1). The criterion of hierarchical structure is related to the property of a coherent, simple structure, while restricted coupling increases autonomy of software elements. If a software element can fulfill its task autonomously, it does not rely on the functionality of other software elements and thus is less coupled to them.

Simplicity without further information is a rather imprecise requirement. In the context of this paper, we consider simplicity solely as a demand for low complexity.

As structural complexity is already assessed by modularity, the *criteria* for simplicity are limited to size, namely the "restricted size of software components" (1b in Table 1) and the "restricted size of interfaces" (1c in Table 1).

The *factor* encapsulation can thus be supported by the *criteria* "restricted size of interfaces" (1c in Table 1) for privacy and "high cohesion within each software component" (1d in Table 1) for unity.

Criteria to Metrics: Note that in this section, we only motivate why a metric fits for estimating a criterion. The formal definition of the metric are given in the next section. In general, we tried to avoid simple count metrics, to get a profounder result.

The Law of Demeter [11] was chosen as a metric for the "hierarchical structure of software components", because most of the existing hierarchy metrics from object-oriented metric suits (MOOD) [1] consider the class hierarchy, and thus are not usable for dataflow-based modeling languages. The Law of Demeter was originally used as a coupling metric, but continuing the approach of Oesterreich [15], it is additionally used as an hierarchy metric evaluating the number of bypassed hierarchical levels within a model.

To assess the criterion of "restricted coupling between software components" in more detail, we use an adaptation of the metrics FanIn and FanOut (derived from [8]). For our dataflow-based modeling languages, coupling can be estimated by measuring the number of incoming and outgoing connections. A block, which is connected to many other blocks, has higher coupling than one connected to fewer blocks.

For the criterion "restricted size of software components", two metrics were chosen. Of course, the Number of Elements metric was chosen to provide a first look assessment of the software component size. For a more meaningful result, the well-known and tested Halstead Volume was used as adapted and argued for by Stürmer et al. [7,17].

The "restricted size of interfaces" criterion for the *privacy* part of *encapsulation* is measured by the Element Hiding Factor. This metric was derived from "Attribute Hiding Factor" and "Method Hiding Factor" (both part of the standard set of metrics in MOOD [1]). These two were already stated as *privacy* metrics by Mayer and Hall when describing the nature of encapsulation [12] for object-oriented software.

Finally, we associated "high cohesion" with the metrics Tight Block Cohesion and Loose Block Cohesion as presented in [3]. Already Briand et al. named them as sound cohesion measurements [4]. Again, the key challenge was to re-define the object-oriented concept of finding direct and indirect connections between elements to abstract, dataflow-oriented software.

4   Formal Model

This section describes the underlying semantic model for defining object-oriented metrics on dataflow models. Note, that although we did all our experiments on

Matlab Simulink models, the concept may easily be transferred to other similar tools or languages like ASCET or SCADE.

4.1 Meta-Model of a Dataflow Model

For defining the metrics, a static model of the software is sufficient. A static model only contains structural information (e.g., hierarchies) as well as dependencies (e.g., input/output flows). Dynamic aspects like behavior of execution are not necessary for defining most object-oriented (OO) metrics. We base the definitions of our metrics on a meta-model, which is inspired by the meta-model of Scheible [16], and use a set of directed multi-graphs as semantics. In contrast to Scheible, we do not abstract from solely Simulink, to be able to evaluate additional languages. In the following, the term "software architecture" is used for denoting this static, graph-based model.

A **software architecture** $a\langle B, E, K \rangle$ is defined by a 3-tuple consisting of a set of blocks B, elements E, and edges K. A **block** $b\langle B, E, K \rangle$ is defined by a 3-tuple consisting of a set of (sub-)blocks B, elements E, and edges K. From a pure semantic point of view, blocks and architectures are the same. However, we use the term "architecture" to always denote the topmost view of our system, while "blocks" are used to refer to individual functionalities (i.e., sub-views). An **element** $e\langle P \rangle$ represents a single functional piece of a block where a set of **ports** $p\langle e \rangle$ provides an interface for edges. An **edge** $k\langle p_{start}, p_{end} \rangle$ is a 2-tuple of a starting and an ending port. The semantics of a block (and a software architecture) is a directed multi-graph, where nodes are in B or E and edges are in K. We further introduce the following functions:

- $P(e)$: Set of all ports of element e
- $e(p)$: Element e to which port p belongs
- $IP(e)$: Set of all incoming ports of element e
- $OP(e)$: Set of all outgoing ports of element e
- $D(e)$: Set of all edges starting or ending at some port $p \in P(e)$
- $D_+(e)$: Set of all edges starting at some port $p \in P(e)$
- $D_-(e)$: Set of all edges ending at some port $p \in P(e)$
- $EOP(e)$: Set of all elements on one path starting/ending from e
- $EOP^+(e)$: transitive closure of EOP(e)
- $N(b)$: Set of all successors of block b such that $\exists k(b, b_n) : b_n \in N(b)$
- $N^+(b)$: transitive closure of $N(b)$

Furthermore, all (sub-)blocks in a given block are also considered as elements (of this block); i.e., $B \subseteq E$. Intuitively, this means for example, that the (visual) complexity of a a single Matlab Simulink model is defined by the number of visual elements in this view. The only part visible of the (sub-)block are its (external) ports. Note, that the defining sets of a (sub-)block (i.e., blocks, elements, and edges) are typically not part of B, E and K of the super-block. We use $B^*(b)$, $E^*(b)$ and $K^*(b)$ to denote this transitive set of all sub-blocks, sub-elements and edges.

4.2 Redefining OO Metrics

We now use this meta-model to redefine the most wide-spread OO metrics on dataflow models. In particular, we will consider the following six metrics: "Number of Elements","Element Hiding Factor", "FanIn/FanOut", "Law of Demeter", "Halstead Volume", and "Block Cohesion". For each metric, we will briefly sketch the idea, then present the formalization and later discuss, how this metric helps in estimating properties of good model-based architecture. Due to the lack of space, we cannot give the full definition of these metrics in their traditional form for object-oriented software. Hence, we only sketch differences and extensions informally. For a definition of the underlying metrics for object-oriented systems, we refer to the corresponding references. For each metric, we define it for measuring a single block or the block including all its sub-blocks. In practice, the latter is typically used for assessing a software architecture or estimating the overall complexity of a larger functionality. However, the first helps in deciding which individual parts in an dataflow model are most difficult or should be re-engineered first.

Number of Elements (N_e): The "number of elements" metrics is the equivalent to the *Lines of Code* metrics in text-based programming languages. Just as a source code line represents the smallest functional entity, elements within the meta-models of this work are the smallest representation of a functionality.

$$N_e(b) = |E(b)| \tag{1}$$

$$N_e(a)^* = |E^*(a)| \tag{2}$$

Thus, the count of all elements within one block resp. one architecture gives an overview of the model's complexity. To indicate the desired low complexity, the value of this counting metric should be as small as possible.

Element Hiding Factor (EHF): The rational of this metrics (also in the related object-oriented metrics) is to hide as many details of the implementation of a block/class. The only visible (to the outside) parts of a block are its incoming and outgoing ports. This has to be seen in relation to the internal complexity of the block. The Element Hiding Factor (EHF) metrics determines this property in a block and it is defined as a quotient of the number of invisible elements and the total number of elements of a block.

$$EHF(b) = \frac{|E(b)| - |P(b)|}{|E(b)|} \tag{3}$$

For an architecture a the EHF is the average of all blocks in B.

$$EHF^*(a) = \frac{\sum_{b_i \in B(a)} EHF(b_i)}{|B(a)|} \tag{4}$$

The EHF value should be as high as possible. The upper (but not achievable) bound of this metrics is 1 (for a block without inputs/outputs). The lower bound is 0 for a block, which only passes information without any internal processing. Intuitively, blocks with an EHF under 0.5 should be checked manually, as more inports and outports than other elements indicate a bad implementation.

FanIn/FanOut (FI/FO): These metrics measure how highly coupled a block is. The key idea is to count the number of incoming and outgoing connections. This may be seen as an indicator of how difficult it is to re-engineer the block, as each connection implies having to have a look at the neighboring block.

$$FI(b) = |D_-(b)| \tag{5}$$

$$FI^*(a) = \frac{\sum_{b_i \in B(a)} FI(b_i)}{|B(a)|} \tag{6}$$

$$FO(b) = |D_+(b)| \tag{7}$$

$$FO^*(a) = \frac{\sum_{b_i \in B(a)} FO(b_i)}{|B(a)|} \tag{8}$$

An alternative definition could be to count connected blocks instead of connections. Based on practical experiments, we decided against this. The reason is that if there are multiple connections between two blocks they often refer to different functionalities or address different information. As a consequence, during re-engineering the number of connection better estimates the complexity then only the number of connected blocks.

Architecture values of FanIn and FanOut equal to 1 imply a very linear structure, while values higher than 3 are not observed in models considered well structured and with low coupling, therefore the preliminary threshold was set to 3. Single block values might differ from these values, depending on the purpose of the block.

Range of Demeter (RoD): Oesterreich describes an approach to apply the Law of Demeter in model-based development [15]. Even if the UML class diagrams differ in the most aspects from the model in this work, it is possible to transfer the underlying idea to our meta-model. The idea is illustrated in Fig. 2.

Let us say a block b_1 is *used* by another block b_2 if there is an edge $e(b_1, b_2)$. Now, assume there exists another block b_3, which is used by block b_2 and is using block b_1. It is then possible to decouple blocks b_1 and b_2 with a simple re-engineering (i.e., passing the information from b_1 to b_2 not directly but rather via block b_3). This is depicted in Fig. 2 with the dashed arrows. Hence, b_1 and b_2 can be changed independently from each other as long as the requirements of the interface of b_3 are fulfilled. In informal words, one could describe this metrics as: "Do not skip your neighbors.". Formally, RoD is defined as:

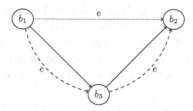

Fig. 2. Example: Range of Demeter

$$RoD(b) = \sum_{b_m \in B(b)} \sum_{p \in P(b_m, b_n)} |p(b_m, b_n)| - 1, (b_n \in N(b_m)) \wedge (b_n \in N^+(N(b_m)))$$

(9)

where $P(b_m, b_n)$ are all paths starting in block b_m and ending in block b_n.

$$RoD^*(a) = \sum_{b_i \in B(a)} RoD(b_i)$$

(10)

Consequently, RoD measures the number of "skipped" blocks. Therefore, we call it "Range of Demeter" instead of "Law of Demeter". The optimal value of RoD is 0, as it counts violations of a design rule.

Halstead Volume (HV): The Halstead Volume dates back to 1977. HV was developed to assess the complexity of algorithmic functions (back then mainly in Cobol and Algol). The core idea is to count the number of different operators (n_1) and different arguments (n_2) as well as the number of all operators (n_3) and number of all arguments (n_4).

In 2010, Stürmer et al. [17] gave a definition of the Halstead metric to Simulink, which we re-use in our approach directly. To define this metrics, a set of element types T has to be added to the meta-model and exactly one $t \in T$ is referred to each element e. Hence, we extend the definition of Sect. 4.1 with functions for types of elements:

- $T(a)$: Set of all different element types applied in the architecture a
- $T(b)$: Set of all different element types in $E(b)$
- $T^+(b)$: Set of all different element types in $E^*(b)$

The Halstead Volume is then defined as:

$$HV(b) = (n_1(b) + n_2(b)) * log_2(n_3(b) + n_4(b))$$

(11)

where $n_1(b) = |E(b)|$, $n_2(b) = |T(b)|$, $n_3(b) = |\bigcup_{e \in E(b)} IP(e)|$ and $n_4(b) = |\bigcup_{e \in E(b)} OP(e)|$

$HV(b)$ does not consider the lower levels of a block, therefore the Halstead Volume calculated with these values is used for an evaluation of the *local complexity*. For *local complexity*, Stürmer et al. [17] give the boundary value 300 for low complexity and 750 for normal complexity. For global complexity, the analogous definition is:

$$HV^*(a) = (n_1^*(a) + n_2^*(a)) * log_2(n_3^*(a) + n_4^*(a)) \qquad (12)$$

where n_i^* is derived from n_i by replacing $E()$ with $E^*()$ and $T()$ with $T^*()$.

However, this value is often only of limited interest as it has to be considered with caution. The main reason is, that the resulting value is very hard to interpret. On the one hand, it combines logarithmic and linear scales, while on the other hand, for example, the height of the hierarchy also plays a vital role (as at least in Matlab Simulink, in-port and out-ports are individual elements as well as types). As a consequence, it is not meaningful to give any generic advice for $HV^*(a)$.

Tight Block Cohesion (TBC) / Loose Block Cohesion (LBC): Cohesion is one of the most often mentioned aspects, when arguing about the quality of an object-oriented software design. Classes should be as loosely coupled as possible and as highly cohesive as possible. Cohesion is a property, which informally means: "Pieces of functionality highly depend on each other". Following this generic idea, we define cohesion of a block as a property, which measures whether the block can be easily separated or not. Bieman and Kang used the same idea 1995 [3] for object oriented systems. Of course, we have to restrict ourselves to method cohesion (as other cohesion metrics like inheritance cohesion are not applicable to dataflow models). For defining this on dataflow models, we first introduce the notion of "number-of-directly-connected-blocks (NDC)", "number- of-not-directly-connected-blocks (NIC)", and the "total-number-of-pairs-of-blocks (NP)":

$$NDC(b) = \sum_{e_i \in E(b)} |EOP(e_i)| \qquad (13)$$

$$NIC(b) = \sum_{e_i \in E(b)} |EOP^+(e_i)| \qquad (14)$$

$$NP(b) = |E(b)|^2 \qquad (15)$$

One might wonder, why the computation path (and not only the direct neighbor) is used in the definition of NDC. The argumentation is simple: a path in a dataflow model describes how inputs are (successively) transformed into outputs. The whole computation fails, if any(!) of the intermediate operators is removed from the chain. For NIC, we take the transitive closure. Meaning, that if some block b_i is on the current computation path and this block also gets input/produces output from/to some other block b_j then block b_j is in $NIC(b)$. Tight and loose block cohesion can then be formalized as:

$$TBC(b) = \frac{NDC(b)}{NP(b)} \tag{16}$$

$$LBC(b) = \frac{NIC(b)}{NP(b)} \tag{17}$$

$$TBC^*(a) = \frac{\sum_{b_i \in B(a)} TBC(b_i)}{|B(a)|} \tag{18}$$

$$LBC^*(a) = \frac{\sum_{b_i \in B(a)} LBC(b_i)}{|B(a)|} \tag{19}$$

The optimum value for TBC and LBC is 1. Values smaller than 1 indicate, that some blocks could either be split into sequentially connected sub-blocks, parallel sub-blocks, or a combination of both. Nevertheless, always aiming at the optimum value leads to a very large depth in the hierarchy and might not be useful. Following the threshold of Biemann and Kang [3] for their original metric, we declare a value of at least 0.75 for TBC as cohesive. However, LBC should have a value of 1 if there are no hard design constraints preventing it.

5   Evaluation

To evaluate the defined metrics, they were applied to model-based software utilized in the project MOBILE of the Institute of Control Engineering at Technische Universität Braunschweig. The experimental vehicle MOBILE features full Drive-by-Wire capability with all-wheel-steering, 400kW all-wheel-drive, and electromechanical brakes. Another main characteristic is the completely accessible software of all ECUs, which are programmed utilizing a Matlab Simulink tool chain.

The meta-model and the metrics were implemented in Java to be able to evaluate other languages than Simulink with a proper model-importer. To parse the Simulink model examples, our implementation relies on the Simulink Library provided by the TU Munich [6].

In the following, the application software of two ECUs of MOBILE is compared with respect to the model-based metrics proposed in Sect. 3.2 resp. 4.2. Thereby, both ECUs are considered as highly safety critical due to the strong distributed characteristic of the implementation of the overall vehicle functionalities on MOBILE. Neither of the models has been developed according to ISO 26262. However, an additional diagnostic and decision making system was developed for MOBILE to guarantee proper reconfiguration of the overall vehicle in case of failures of individual control units [2].

As its name already implies, the *Battery Management System (BMS)* ECU is responsible for all functionalities related to the battery package, such as charging, balancing, and surveillance of the batteries. The *Steering Controller* ECU serves as interface to control the vehicle. First of all, it evaluates the normal driver inputs coming from steering wheel, accelerator pedal, as well as brake pedal and outputs the target values for the actuators to MOBILE's network. Additionally, commands stemming from an overall vehicle control system can be fed into the vehicle network via the *Steering Controller (SC)*. Moreover, both ECUs require several information from different ECUs, e.g., the rotational speed of the wheel or the actual steering angle, to validate the plausibility of state transitions.

From a programmers perspective, the selected models possess different qualities concerning understandability and maintainability. The *BMS* has a comparably clear structure by separating input signals, data processing, and output signals in different high level blocks. Furthermore, the sub-blocks are also arranged in a hierarchically logical manner. On the contrary, the structure of the *Steering Controller* is less well designed. It can be described as what one would call "historically grown". Thus, it is expected that the application of the metrics suggested in Sect. 3.2 resp. 4.2 will yield better results for the model of the *BMS* than the *Steering Controller*.

Table 2 shows the results of the metrics for the two example models. A comparison of the model values with the target values for the metric gives a first indication of the fulfillment of the requirements of ISO 26262 regarding the software architecture. Here, the model of the *BMS* shows acceptable values for all metrics, whereas the *Steering Controller* model shows unacceptable values for Tight Block Cohesion and the Range of Demeter. The bad value for Tight Block Cohesion is supported by the rather poor value of Loose Block Cohesion, so the model should be revised with the goal to improve cohesion. The bad value for the Range of Demeter might also occur because of some special properties of the model, that make a better value impossible, e.g., four edges leading from a steering to a simulation block for the signals of each single wheel.

Table 2. Global metric results for example models

Metric	Target Value	SC	BMS
Halstead Volume	minimal	16554.93	53904.34
Number of elements	minimal	2411	8099
Loose Block Cohesion	1	0.84	0.96
Tight Block Cohesion	>0.75	0.57	0.77
Element Hiding Factor	>0.5	0.51	0.55
Range of Demeter	0	14	0
FanIn (FI)	1<=FI<=3	2.18	1.83
FanOut (FO)	1<=FO<=3	1.94	1.57

Additionally, we want to state that the metrics are calculated in very acceptable time. The *BMS* model was processed in under 20 seconds on a common computer with a Core i5 processor (3210m, 8GB RAM, Samsung 840SSD). The smaller model of the *Steering Controller* was evaluated within 10 seconds and tests on other models revealed no unreasonable growth of computation time.

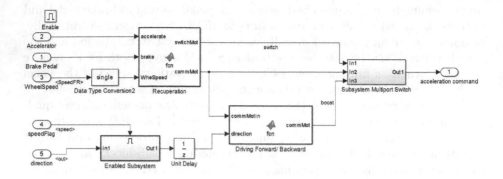

Fig. 3. Part of the *Steering Controller* model

The global value of the metric alone does not necessarily support an improvement of the software architecture. A bad global metric value at least indicates that some rework is needed. However, in a huge model manually searching for the weak spots is not desirable. Therefore, in addition to the global value of the model, a metric value for each block is computed by the prototype. Subsequent to the calculation, it highlights blocks with bad metric values such that they can easily be detected and reworked.

To make our approach clear, the sub-block of the *Steering Controller* demonstrated in Fig. 3 is evaluated as an example. It implements the generation of a target torque for the front left motor of MOBILE supporting driving forward and reversing as well as recuperative braking. For that reason, it obtains the actual positions of brake and accelerator pedal together with the actual velocity of the front left wheel. The speed flag is required as switching between forward driving and reversing is only permitted in standstill.

The values for the applied metrics of the sub-block are given in Table 3. The EHF value is minimally lower than 0.5, therefore it should be considered to minimize the interface. The FanOut value is equal to 1, but should be higher, and the FanIn value is higher than 3. Therefore, especially the FanIn value shows the violation of the requirement for restricted coupling. The low TBC and LBC values indicate bad cohesion in this model part. The Range of Demeter has the value 1 meaning that one block is skipped. The Halstead volume is lower than 300, which implies low complexity.

Comparing the block result with the results for the whole model, it can be noticed that the flaws detected by the global metrics match the flaws of the single block. Especially cohesion should be improved, and removing the one Range of Demeter violation in the presented block would directly improve the global Range of Demeter value.

Together, the global metric value and the block metric value provide an objective evaluation of the model quality with respect to ISO 26262 requirements and highlight model components which need to be improved. The short computation time of the metrics compared to a manual analysis of the model makes it

Table 3. Metrics for drive-control-front-right block

Metric	Target Value	Drive Control Front Left Model
Halstead Volume	minimal (<750)	88.23
Number of elements	minimal	13
Loose Block Cohesion	1	0.86
Tight Block Cohesion	>0.75	0.55
Element Hiding Factor	>0.5	0.46
Range of Demeter	0	1
FanIn (FI)	1<=FI<=3	6
FanOut (FO)	1<=FO<=3	1

possible to monitor the model quality during the development and to compare different maturity levels of the software model.

Again, we want to point out that the approach cannot improve the model quality by itself. An expert is required to look at the weak spots of the model and make suggestions for design improvements. Besides, specialized domains with partly special requirements may require manual adaptions of the metrics to match the characteristics of the model under evaluation.

6 Conclusions and Further Work

In this paper we presented an approach to evaluate dataflow-oriented software architectures regarding the requirements of ISO 26262. For that reason, we adapted existing metrics from other programming paradigms and used them as quality indicators. The metric results on model level for two example models in Simulink reveal general weaknesses of the software, e.g., a tendency for low cohesion software elements. The metric results on block level provide information about where to refine the software to improve the quality. The application to the example models confirms that metrics are useful during the development process, as they can be computed in a very short time and give a first evaluation of the fulfillment of ISO 26262 requirements.

For applying the presented approach directly for verification of software architectures according to ISO 26262, a definition of threshold values for the different metrics is necessary. These thresholds have to be determined in future case studies. To receive more precise statements about weak spots in software architectures, the metrics could be defined more precisely in future works, e.g., by introducing more metrics.

Acknowledgments. The authors wish to thank Porsche Engineering for its cooperation and support by giving initial ideas and further helpful comments.

References

1. Abreu, F.B., Carapuça, R.: Object-oriented software engineering: Measuring and controlling the development process. In: 4th Int. Conf. on Software Quality (1994)
2. Bergmiller, P., Maurer, M., Lichte, B.: Probabilistic fault detection and handling algorithm for testing stability control systems with a drive-by-wire vehicle. In: 2011 IEEE International Symposium on Intelligent Control (ISIC), pp. 601–606 (2011)
3. Bieman, J.M., Kang, B.K.: Cohesion and reuse in an object-oriented system. In: Proceedings of the 1995 Symposium on Software Reusability, SSR 1995, pp. 259–262. ACM (1995)
4. Briand, L.C., Daly, J.W., Wüst, J.: A unified framework for cohesion measurement in object-oriented systems. Empirical Software Engineering 3(1) (1998)
5. Cavano, J.P., McCall, J.A.: A framework for the measurement of software quality. In: Proceedings of the Software Quality Assurance Workshop on Functional and Performance Issues, pp. 133–139. ACM (1978)
6. Deißenböck, F.: Simulink Library for Java, https://www.cqse.eu/en/products/simulink-library-for-java/overview/
7. Halstead, M.H.: Elements of Software Science (Operating and programming systems series). Elsevier Science Inc. (1977)
8. Henry, S., Kafura, D.: Software structure metrics based on information flow. IEEE Transactions on Software Engineering SE-7(5), 510–518 (1981)
9. International Organisation for Standardization: ISO 26262 (11/11): Road vehicles - functional safety, http://www.iso.org/iso/catalogue_detail?csnumber=43464
10. Kemmann, S., Kuhn, T., Trapp, M.: Extensible and Automated Model-Evaluations with INProVE. In: Kraemer, F.A., Herrmann, P. (eds.) SAM 2010. LNCS, vol. 6598, pp. 193–208. Springer, Heidelberg (2011)
11. Lieberherr, K., Holland, I., Riel, A.: Object-oriented programming: an objective sense of style. In: Conference Proceedings on Object-oriented Programming Systems, Languages and Applications, OOPSLA 1988, pp. 323–334. ACM (1988)
12. Mayer, T., Hall, T.: Measuring OO systems: a critical analysis of the MOOD metrics. In: Proceedings of Technology of Object-Oriented Languages and Systems, pp. 108–117 (1999)
13. Menkhaus, G., Andrich, B.: Metric suite for directing the failure mode analysis of embedded software systems. In: ICEIS 2005 - Proceedings of the Seventh International Conference on Enterprise Information Systems, pp. 266–273 (2005)
14. Meyer, B.: Object-Oriented Software Construction. Prentice Hall (1998)
15. Oesterreich, B.: Analyse und Design mit der UML 2.5: Objektorientierte Softwareentwicklung. Oldenbourg Verlag (2012)
16. Scheible, J.: Automatisierte Qualitätsbewertung am Beispiel von MATLAB Simulink-Modellen in der Automobil-Domäne. Ph.D. thesis, Universität Tübingen (2012)
17. Stürmer, I., Pohlheim, H., Rogier, T.: Berechnung und Visualisierung der Modellkomplexität bei der modellbasierten Entwicklung sicherheitsrelevanter Software. Automotive–Safety & Security, 69–82 (2010)

Insights on the Use of OCL
in Diverse Industrial Applications

Shaukat Ali[1], Tao Yue[1], Muhammad Zohaib Iqbal[2,3],
and Rajwinder Kaur Panesar-Walawege[1]

[1] Simula Research Laboratory, P.O. Box 134, Lysaker, Norway
[2] National University of Computer & Emerging Sciences, Islamabad, Pakistan
[3] SnT Luxembourg, Luxembourg
{shaukat,tao,rpanesar}@simula.no,
zohaib.iqbal@nu.edu.pk

Abstract. The Object Constraint Language (OCL) is a widely accepted language, standardized by OMG, for specifying constraints at various meta levels (e.g., meta-models and models). Despite its wide acceptance, there is a lack of understanding about terminology and purposes for which OCL can be used. In this paper, we aim to reduce this gap and provide guidance for applying OCL in practical contexts and we report our experience of applying OCL for different industrial projects in diverse domains: Communications and Control, Oil and Gas production, Energy Equipment and Services, and Recycling. Based on our experience, first, we unify the commonly used terminology in the literature for applying OCL in different ways for addressing diverse industrial problems. Second, we report the key results of the industrial application of OCL. Finally, we provide guidance to researchers and practitioners for choosing an appropriate meta level and purpose for their specific industrial problem at hand.

Keywords: Object Constraint Language, Industrial Applications, Constraint Solving, Constraint Parsing.

1 Introduction

The Object Constraint Language (OCL – http://www.omg.org/spec/OCL/2.3.1/) is the Object Management Group's (OMG) standard language for specifying constraints on models. Constraints can be specified at all the meta levels provided by the Meta-Object Factory (MOF – http://www.omg.org/mof/)—the OMG's framework for meta-modeling. Thus, constraints can be specified on meta-meta models (e.g., an implementation of MOF), meta-models (e.g., UML meta-model), customized profiles on meta-models (e.g., MARTE profile for UML – http://www.omgmarte.org/), and models (e.g., UML models).

The OCL has been used in industrial projects for various purposes, such as for configuration management in energy and maritime and seismic acquisition [1] and test case generation in communication and control [2, 3]. OCL is also being used as the

D. Amyot et al. (Eds.): SAM 2014, LNCS 8769, pp. 223–238, 2014.

language for writing constraints on models in many commercial Model-Based Testing (MBT) tools such as CertifyIt[1] and Fokus!MBT[2].

For the past several years, we have used OCL in several industry-driven research projects. The most significant projects include: model-based functional and robustness testing of embedded systems and communication and control systems, configuration of product lines of large-scale integrated control systems, and certification of subsea production systems according to safety standards. In this paper, we present our experience of applying the OCL in these domains. Our key findings are: 1) a small subset of OCL can be sufficient for a given industrial application; 2) specification and enforcement of constraints at the different MOF meta levels works in the same way; 3) evaluation of constraints was the most common purpose for the use of OCL. Based on our findings, we present guidelines for practitioners to choose the right meta level and purpose to apply OCL for their particular problem. Notice that all the definitions and discussions presented in this paper are within the context of our industrial applications, and may need to be adapted to other contexts.

The contributions of this paper can be summarized as follows: 1) clear and precise definitions of commonly used terminology related to the use of OCL; 2) a clear relationship among the different purposes (e.g., OCL solving and evaluation) that OCL can be used for; 3) key results from our industrial applications of OCL; 4) a detailed discussion that can guide practitioners in choosing when to apply OCL for a particular purpose and at which meta level. These contributions are aimed at reducing the gap between the academic understanding of OCL and its industrial application.

The rest of the paper is organized as follows: Section 2 presents various classifications of our OCL applications, Section 3 reports results from our industrial applications, Section 4 provides discussion, and Section 5 concludes the paper.

2   Classification of Various OCL Applications

This section provides an overview of our industrial applications (Section 2.1), definitions and examples in Section 2.2 and Section 2.3, and the relationships between various purposes for which OCL can be used in Section 2.3.

2.1   Overview

We use a conceptual model to discuss the overall picture of our experience of applying OCL in various projects (Fig. 1). We characterize our applications mainly from two aspects: 1) *Purpose* of applying OCL: e.g., *Constraint Solving* and *Constraint Evaluation*, and 2) *Meta Level*, at which OCL constraints are applied. Moreover, we discuss each application (e.g., *TestDataGeneration*) based on the type(s) of models on which OCL was used (e.g., *Structural* and *Behavioral* model) and the types of diagrams used for each type of model (e.g., UML class diagrams as structural models).

---

[1] http://www.smartesting.com/en/product/certifyit
[2] http://www.fokusmbt.com/index.html

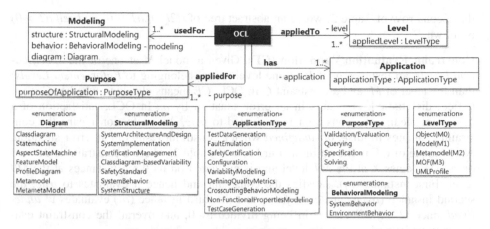

Fig. 1. Conceptual model of OCL applications

2.2   Definitions

This section presents definitions of the terms that we use in the rest of the paper.

Meta Levels. Meta-Object Facility (MOF) is a standard defined by Object Management Group (OMG) for model-driven engineering. MOF is designed as a four-level architecture, which allows modeling at four levels: meta-meta level (*M3*), meta level (*M2*), model level (*M1*), and Object level (*M0*). In other words, we define the term *Meta Levels* as a set of these four levels: *Meta Levels = {M3, M2, M1, M0}*.

Specification Levels. Specification levels are a subset of *Meta Levels*, on which OCL constraints can be specified: *Specification Levels = {M3, M2, M1}*.

Enforcement Levels. Enforcement levels are a subset of *Meta Levels*, at which OCL constraints are enforced (e.g., evaluated, solved). An enforcement level is one level lower than the level at which constraints are specified. It is defined as *Enforcement Level = {M2, M1, M0}*.

Purposes of Using OCL. In this section, we provide definitions and examples of the various purposes for which we have used OCL.

Constraint Specification (CSpec). Given a model *M* at one of the *Meta Levels*, *CSpec* means defining a constraint *C* on *M*. Based on the example given in the first row of Table 2, we define a constraint *((2/self.a1 > 0) and self.a2 > 0)* on class *X* (at *M1* level). We also show examples of OCL constraints at each meta level in Table 1. For example, in the third column of Table 1, we define a constraint on the definition of stereotype *MyStereotype (self.name = '')* in a profile diagram at the *M2* level.

Constraint Parsing (CP). Given a model *M* at one of the *Meta Levels* and a constraint *C* specified on *M*, *CP* means parsing *C* and obtaining an abstract syntax tree of *C* for further manipulation (e.g., calculating branch distances to generate test data from OCL constraints using a search algorithm [4]). An example of *CP* is shown in the second row of Table 2, where an abstract tree of $((2/self.a1 > 0)$ *and self.a2 > 0)* is shown.

Constraint Evaluation/Validation (CE). Given a model M at one of the *Specification Levels*, an instance o_i of M at one level lower (belonging to *Enforcement Levels*) than the level of M, and a constraint C in OCL, *CE* means checking whether C is satisfied, dissatisfied, or results in an error situation by o_i. In OCL, satisfaction of a constraint means, the constraint is evaluated to *true*, dissatisfaction means the constraint evaluates to *false*, or *undefined* when a constraint results in an error situation. An example of *CE* is shown in the third row of Table 2, where a constraint is defined on a UML class X at the *M1* level and is evaluated on its three instances at the *M0* level. First instance (o_1), satisfies the constraint and hence it evaluates to *true*, the second instance (o_2) evaluates to *false*, and the third instance (o_3) evaluates to *undefined* since $(2/self.a1)$ results in being divided by 0, and overall the constraint evaluates to *undefined*.

Table 1. Examples of OCL constraints at various levels

Level	Example	Constraint
M3	EAttribute [name : EString] * ← - eAttribute ◆ EClass [name : EString]	**Specification:** context EClass inv: self.name <> ''
M2	«metaclass» **Class** [isAbstract : Boolean, isActive : Boolean]	**Evaluation/Validation:** true
		Specification: context Class inv: self.isActive
	MyStereotype [name : String] → «metaclass» **Class** [isAbstract : Boolean, isActive : Boolean]	**Specification:** context MyStereotype inv: self.name = ''
M1	«MyStereotype» **Y** [a1 : Integer] «MyStereotype» name = "MyStereotype"	**Evaluation/Validation:** false
		Specification: context EClass inv: self.a1 > 0
M0	**YInstance : Y** [a1 = 1] «MyStereotype» name = "MyStereotype"	**Evaluation/Validation:** true

Constraint Solving (CSolv). Given a model M at one of the *Specification Levels*, an instance O of M at one meta level lower than M, i.e., belonging to *Enforcement Levels*, and a constraint C defined on M, *CSolv* means finding at least one instance of M, which evaluates C to be *true*, *false*, or *undefined*. An example of *CSolv* is shown in Table 2, row 5. Given the constraint $C= (2/self.a1 > 0)$ *and self.a2 > 0* defined on class X (at *M1* level), a constraint solver provides an instance o_i (at *M0* level) satisfying C. In this particular example, o_i can be instance $x4$ shown in the table. Notice that the constraint solver may provide multiple instances depending on the application.

Table 2. Examples of various purposes of OCL

Example	Model (M)	Instance (o_1)	Instance (o_2)	Instance (o_3)
A class X with two Integers $a1$ and $a2$, and with three instances available: $x1, x2,$ and $x3$.	**X** a1 : Integer a2 : Integer	**x1 : X** a1 = 1 a2 = 2	**x2 : X** a1 = 3 a2 = -2	**x3 : X** a1 = 0 a2 = 3
Specification		N/A		
Parsing				
Evaluation/Validation	context X inv: $(2/$**self**$.a1 > 0)$ and **self**$.a2 > 0$	true	false	undefined
Solving		**x4 : X** a1 = 2 a2 = 4		
Querying		**x1 : X** a1 = 1 a2 = 2		

OCL Querying (OQ). Given a model M at one of the *Specification Levels*, a set of its instances $O = \{o_1, o_2, o_3, ..o_n\}$ at one meta level lower (belonging to *Enforcement Levels*), OCL querying OQ returns one or more instances of M, which satisfy the constraint specified in OQ. An example is shown in Table 2, row 6, where given a constraint $C= (2/self.a1 > 0)$ and $self.a2 > 0$ and a set of instances $O = \{o_1, o_2, o_3\}$, a constraint querying returns instances from O that satisfies C. In this particular example, such an instance is o_1 $(x1)$.

2.3   Relationships between Various Purposes of Using OCL

OCL Querying. Fig. 2 shows the relationship among OCL querying, evaluation, and specification. The first step is specification of a constraint C at $M3$, $M2$, or $M1$ level. A query in OCL then returns a model at one meta level lower ($M2$, $M1$, or $M0$) level using OCL evaluation.

OCL Solving. Fig. 3 shows the relationship of how OCL solving is related to the purposes for which OCL can be used. The first step in OCL solving is to specify a constraint C on a model at $M3$, $M2$, or $M1$ level. OCL solving then starts with a random instance of a model at one meta level lower, i.e., $M2$ (C is specified at $M3$), $M1$ (C is specified at $M2$) or $M0$ (C is specified at $M1$) level. This instance is then evaluated using OCL evaluation. If the instance satisfies C the OCL solving stops. Otherwise OCL solving is guided towards another instance (using OCL parsing and OCL querying) using for example a search algorithm (see [4] for details) and a new instance is generated, which is again evaluated by OCL evaluation. OCL solving continues until an instance is found that satisfies C.

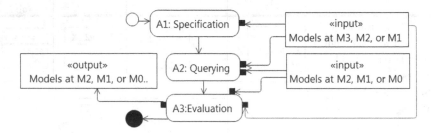

Fig. 2. OCL querying

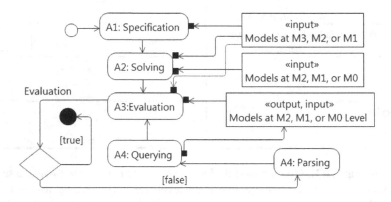

Fig. 3. OCL solving

3   Industrial Applications

In this section, we present our industrial applications of OCL based on the concepts and definitions presented in Section 2.

3.1   Model-Based Testing of Video Conferencing Systems

In this section, we discuss six applications of OCL, which are related to testing a commercial Video Conferencing System (VCS) developed by Cisco Systems.

Case Study Description. Our first case study is a VCS called *Saturn* developed by Cisco Systems Inc, Norway. The core functionality of *Saturn* manages establishing and disconnecting video conferences. In total, *Saturn* consists of 20 subsystems such as audio/video subsystems [5]. Each subsystem can run in parallel to the subsystem implementing the core functionality. *Saturn's* implementation consists of more than three million lines of C code. Our second case study is about a product line of VCSs called *Saturn Product Line*, developed in Cisco Systems Inc, Norway. The Saturn family consists of various hardware codecs ranging from C20 to C90. C20 is the lowest end product with minimum hardware and has lowest performance in the family.

Table 3. Mapping of applications to various aspects of OCL

#	Application	Case Study	Model Elements	#Constraints	Constructs/ Operations	Types of Attributes
A1	Test Data Generation	VCS	Guards	144	-	Enumeration, Integer, Boolean, String
		MSM	(Guards,	(11, 3)	select, forAll,	Integer, Boolean,
		BRE	Change Events)	(11,1)	implies, oclInState	String, Enumeration, NFP_Real
A2	Test Oracle Generation	VCS	State Invariants	100	select, collect, forAll, exists, includes, excludes	Enumeration, Integer, Boolean, String
		MSM/ BRE	Guards	3	select, forAll, oclInState	Integer, Boolean, NFP_Real
A3	Fault Emulation	VCS	Change Events	57	select, collect	Enumeration, Integer, Boolean, NFP_Real, NFP_Percentage
A4	Crosscutting Behavior Modeling	VCS	Change Events	57	select, collect	Enumeration, Integer, Boolean, NFP_Real, NFP_Percentage
			State Invariants	10	-	Enumeration, Integer, Boolean, NFP_Real, NFP_Percentage
A5	Specifying Non-Functional Properties	VCS	Pointcuts	12	-	Enumeration, Integer, Boolean, String
			Advice	144	-	Enumeration, Integer, Boolean, String
A6	Variability Modeling	VCS	Configuring UML State Machine	52	select, forAll, exists, includes, excludes	Enumeration, Integer, Boolean, String
			Configuring Aspect State Machines	44	select, forAll, exists, includes, excludes	Enumeration, Integer, Boolean, String, NFP_Real, NFP_Percentage
A7	Safety Certification	SPCS	Stereotypes	218	select, collect, forAll, exists, includes	No variables used.
A8	Configuration	SCM	Package, Stereotype, Class, TemplateSignature, Dependency	6	select, forAll, allInstances,	Integer, Boolean, String

Problem Description. The first problem in this project is about supporting automated, model-based robustness testing of *Saturn*. *Saturn* should be robust enough to handle the possible abnormal situations that can occur in its operating environment and invalid inputs. For example, *Saturn* should be robust against hostile environment conditions (regarding the network and other communicating VCSs), such as high percentage of packet loss and high percentage of corrupt packets. Such behavior is very important for a commercial VCS and must be tested systematically and automatically to be scalable. More details on the robustness behavior of *Saturn* and its modeling can be found in [5]. The second problem in this project emerged while working with model-based robustness testing discussed in the last paragraph. We wanted to significantly reduce the amount of modeling effort required for MBT by devising a product line modeling and configuration methodology since Video Conferencing Systems (VCSs) are product lines.

Objectives. 1) *Test Data Generation (A1)* aims to solve OCL constraints to generate data required to generate executable test cases. 2) *Test Oracle Generation (A2)* has the objective of evaluating OCL constraints to determine if the execution of a test case passed or failed. 3) *Fault Emulation in Environment (A3)* is to solve OCL constraints defined on the environment of a real-time embedded system with the goal of generating the data that violates the constraints so that various faults can be emulated in the environment to test the robustness of a system. 4) *Specifying Non-Functional Properties (NFPs) with MARTE (A4)* aims to specify constraints on NFPs defined in the UML MARTE profile using OCL. 5) *Crosscutting Behavior Modeling (A5)* was proposed to model crosscutting behavior using Aspect State Machine (ASM) [2, 5, 6]. OCL queries are used to model Pointcuts [7] (a feature in Aspect-Oriented Modeling)— modeling elements of a standard UML state machine, on which an ASM should be weaved. 6) *Behavioral Variability Modeling (A6):* The objective of this application is to model and resolve various types of variability that exist in UML state machines with the ultimate aim of reducing the modeling effort required for MBT of different products in a product line.

Solution. Saturn consists of 20 subsystems. To model the functional behavior, for each subsystem, we modeled a class diagram to capture APIs and state variables. In addition, we modeled one or more state machines to capture the behavior of each subsystem. On average each subsystem has five states and 11 transitions, with the biggest subsystem having 22 states and 63 transitions. Note that, though an individual subsystem may not look complex in terms of number of states and transitions, all subsystems run in parallel to each other and therefore the space of system states and possible execution interleaving are very large.

Saturn's robustness behavioral models consist of five aspect class diagrams and five aspect state machines. An ASM is a UML state machine extended with a UML profile for AOM called AspectSM [5]. The largest ASM specifying robustness behavior has three states and ten transitions, which would translate into 1604 transitions in standard UML state machines without having AspectSM applied. The modeling of ASM is systematically derived from a fault taxonomy [5] categorizing different types of faults (faults in the environment such as communication medium and media streams that lead to faulty situations in the environment). Each ASM has a corresponding aspect class diagram modeling different properties of the environment using the MARTE profile, whose violations lead to faulty situations in the environment.

Saturn Product Line family also consists of 20 subsystems and each subsystem has at least one configurable state machine specifying its functionality and on average such state machine has five states and 11 transitions. Saturn product line family models also consist of 124 hardware configuration parameters and 99 software configuration parameters.

Results. Table 3 provides a summary of the key results of applying OCL for all the applications of all the projects. For each application, we report on which model elements OCL was specified and how many constraints were there in our industrial case studies. In addition, for each application we provide OCL constructs and operations used and also types of attributes used in the constraints. For example, for *A3*, we modeled 57 change events with OCL *Select* and *Collect* operations. In addition, we used attributes of types: *Enumeration*, *Integer*, *Boolean*, and a couple of *NFPs* from MARTE. In all the applications, we used relational and logical operations, and hence we do not mention them explicitly in the table.

3.2   Safety Certification

Case Study Description. This case study concerns the certification of the software used in a subsea production control system (SPCS) developed by a large energy company in Norway. SPCS is a complex safety-critical system consisting of a myriad of equipment types. An oil field consists of subsea oil wells that have an assembly of control valves, pressure gauges and chokes attached to them that control the flow of oil. These are all housed on a structure called a template attached to which is a system of steel tubes, electrical and fiber optic cables that transport power and communication signals from the surface to the subsea equipment. Finally there is equipment to carry the oil to the surface. SPCS controls this entire system by sending and receiving data between the surface and the subsea equipment thus allowing the engineers at the surface to control and monitor the sub-sea equipment.

Problem Description. SPCS are subject to various industry and governmental regulations and undergo a process of certification by a third-party certification. In our case the SPCS was subject to a certification process against the IEC61508 standard for electrical, electronic, or programmable electronic systems that are used in safety-critical environments. The supplier of the system provides evidence that the system is compliant with the criteria set in the requisite standard. Hence, there should be a consistent interpretation of the standard being used by all parties involved. Without this explicit interpretation there can be problems between the certifier and the supplier due to the variance that exists. A systematic procedure is also needed for creating the necessary evidence, such that the supplier can properly interpret the standard in the context of its application domain and verify whether sufficient evidence exists to satisfy all the requirements of the standard [8].

Objective. *Certification Standards Modeling (A7).* The objective of using OCL is to assist system suppliers in establishing a relationship between a domain model of a safety-critical application and the evidence model of a certification standard.

Solution and Results. A conceptual model of the evidence requirements of a safety standard is created. This conceptual model is used as the basis for a UML profile of the standard. The UML profile is used for stereotyping the elements of a domain model of the system to be certified. When a stereotype from the profile is applied to a domain model element, it shows how that element fulfills the requirements from the standard. OCL constraints are added to the stereotypes to ensure certain properties of the stereotypes as well as to guide system developers in refining the domain model. When the OCL constraints associated with a stereotype are validated, they will start the guidance process for augmenting the domain model with other stereotypes. This may require the domain model to be updated so that the stereotype constraints are satisfied. Table 3 summarizes our results of applying OCL for certification in row A7.

3.3   Architecture Variability Modeling for Supporting Automated Product Configuration

Case Study Description. This case study is a product line of subsea control modules (SCMs) developed by FMC Technologies, Norway. SCMs control all the equipment and services located in the subsea, but communicates (via Network) with the topic control units. SCMs are deployed with software, which can be configured differently according to customers' requirements, some of which include environment factors (e.g., depth of the seabed), to control the subsea wells. An SCM contains subsea electronic modules, software applications deployed on them, and mechanical and electrical devices that are controlled and monitored by the software. The software application deployed to the control modules is configured mainly based on the number, type, and details of devices (e.g., sensors) connected to and controlled by the subsea electronic module on which the software application is deployed.

Problem Description. Integrated Control Systems (ICSs) are typically large-scale, highly configurable systems of systems such as SCMs. Such systems consist of large number of subsystems typically geographically distributed and connected through network. A family of ICSs share the same software code base, which is configured differently for each product to form a unique installation and, therefore, a large number of interdependent variability points are introduced by both hardware and software components. Due to the complexity of such systems and inadequate automation support, product configuration is typically error-prone and costly, and therefore an automated product configuration support is needed.

Objective. This application is about specifying the guidelines as OCL constraints for the purpose of automated product configuration in the context of ICSs (*A8*).

Solution and Results. We developed a UML-based product line modeling methodology (named as SimPL) that provides a foundation for supporting semi-automated product configuration in the specific context of ICSs [9]. The SimPL profile together with inherent features of UML (i.e., templates and packages) enables comprehensive modeling of variability points, tracing variability points to software and hardware model elements, and grouping and hierarchically organizing the variability points. As part of the SimPL methodology, we defined guidelines for modeling each view (e.g., software view, hardware view). To guide users through the process of applying SimPL, a modeling environment was constructed to automatically enforce six OCL constraints that correspond to these guidelines. Table 3 summarizes our results of applying OCL for specifying and evaluating constraints that correspond to modeling guidelines proposed as part of SimPL (Row A8).

3.4 Environment Model-Based Testing

Case Study Description. We apply the environment model-based testing to two industrial case studies. The first case study from WesternGeco is of a very large and complex control system for marine seismic acquisition. The system controls tens of thousands of sensors and actuators in its environment. The timing deadlines on the environment are in the order of tenths of seconds. The system was developed using Java. The second case study is an automated bottle-recycling machine developed by Tomra AS. The system under test (SUT) was an embedded device 'Sorter', which was responsible to sort the bottles into their appropriate destinations. The system communicated with a number of components to guide recycled items through the recycling machine to their appropriate destinations. It is possible to cascade multiple sorters with one another, which results in a complex recycling machine. The SUT was developed using C. Both the systems are Real-Time and Embedded Systems (RTESs) and were running in environments that enforce time deadlines in the order of tenths of seconds with acceptable jitters of a few milliseconds in response time.

Problem Description. RTESs typically work in environments comprising large numbers of interacting components. The interactions with the environment can be bound by time constraints. Violating such time constraints, or violating them too often for soft real-time systems, can lead to serious failures leading to threats to human life or the environment. For effective testing of industrial scale RTESs, systematic automated testing strategies that have high fault revealing power are essential. The system testing of RTESs requires interactions with the actual environment. Since the cost of testing in real conditions tends to be high, environment simulators are typically used for this purpose. For the industrial systems of WesternGeco and Tomra, we applied one such approach for black-box system level testing based on the environment models of the systems. These models were used to generate an environment simulator [10, 11], test cases, and obtain test oracles [3]. For test case generation, we applied various testing strategies, including search-based testing [12], adaptive random testing [13], and a hybrid approach combining these two strategies [12].

Objectives. *1) Test Data Generation (A1).* The objective of this application is to generate test data by solving OCL constraints in order to reach states in the environment that represent a failure of the SUT (the "error" states). *2) Test Oracle Generation*

(A2). The objective of this application is to evaluate OCL constraints to determine if the execution of a test case reached the "error" states or not.

Solution and Results. For the purpose of environment model-based testing, the environment of the SUT was modeled using our proposed UML & MARTE Real-time Embedded systems Modeling Profile (REMP) [14]. REMP provided extension to the standard UML class diagram and state machine notations, and used the MARTE profile for modeling timing details and non-deterministic events. The models developed were constrained by OCL for the purposes mentioned in the previous section. The structural details of an RTES environment were modeled as an environment domain model, which captures the information of various environment components, their properties, and their relationships. The behavioral details of the environment were modeled using the state machine notation annotated with REMP. Such state machines contain information of the nominal behavior of the components, their robustness behavior (e.g., breakdown of a sensor), and "error states" that should never be reached (e.g., hazardous situations). Table 3 summarizes the results of applying OCL in our context (rows A1 & A2).

4   Overall Discussion

In this section, we provide an overall discussion together with guidelines for practitioners based on our experience of applying OCL.

4.1   Selecting a Subset of OCL

From Table 4, we can see that in most of the applications, *select*, *collect*, and *forAll* were the most frequently used operations. Based on this observation, we can conclude that even though OCL provides a rich collection of constructs and operations, in practice the complete specification is not usually required. This means that for applying OCL in industrial applications one can select a well-defined subset of OCL that is sufficient to serve a required purpose. Note that this is similar to the use of a subset of UML and MARTE in practice as suggested in [1]. This also means that less training is required to teach the subset of OCL, which aids its adoption in industry.

4.2   Choosing a Meta Level

From the last column in Table 4, we can see that six out of eight applications are related to MBT, all of which required specifying constraints at M1 and enforcing these at M0. This observation is perfectly explainable because when dealing with test case generation we are very close to the system/software design and implementation (low level of abstraction). Recall that constraints specified at M1 correspond to the actual system variables of the design or implementation while at the M0 level these constraints are enforced based on the runtime values of the variables.

Table 4. Mapping of OCL applications to various purposes and meta level*

App.	Industry	Case Study	Domain	Modeling	Diagrams	Purpose	(Spec., Enf.)
A1	CCS, EES, REC	VCS, MSM, BRE	RTES	System Behavior, System Structure	CDs & SMs	CSolv	(M1, M0)
A2	CCS, EES, REC	VCS, MSM, BRE	RTES	System Behavior, System Structure	CDs & SMs	CE	(M1, M0)
A3	CCS	VCS, MSM, BRE	RTES	Environment Behavior	CDs, SMs, & ASMs	CE, CSolv	(M1, M0)
A4	CCS	VCS	RTES	System Behavior, System Structure, Environment Behavior	CDs & SMs	OQ	(M1, M0)
A5	CCS	VCS	RTES	System Behavior, System Structure, Environment Behavior, Architecture	CDs	CSolv, CE	(M1, M0)
A6	CCS	VCS	RTES	Class Diagram-based, State Based Variability	CDs & SMs	CSolv	(M1, M0)
A7	OGP	SPCS	ICS, RTES	Safety Standard	Profile, CDs	CE	(M2, M1)
A8	OGP	SCM	ICS, RTES	Architecture	CDs	CE	(M2, M1)

* CCS: Communication and Control System, EES: Energy Equipment and Services, REC: Recycling, OGP: Oil and Gas Production, VCS: Video Conferencing System, MSM: Marine Seismic Acquisition, BRE: Bottle Recycling, SPCS: Subsea Production Control System, RTES: Real-Time Embedded System, ICS: Integrated Control System, CD: Class Diagram, SM: State Machine, ASM: Aspect State Machine, Profile: UML Profile, SCM: Subsea Control Module, MM: Metamodel

For A7 and A8, as we were dealing with UML profiles, therefore we specified the constraints at the M2 level and these were enforced at the M1 level. Notice that in these two applications, our problems were at a higher meta level than implementation, i.e., architecture and design modeling of product lines for supporting configuration (A7) and standard modeling for supporting safety certification (A8). In these two cases, the resulting models to which the profiles were applied were UML class diagrams, which are at the M1 level.

Based on the above observations, we can conclude that constraint specification and enforcement at all applicable levels works in the same way (i.e., specified at one level and enforced in one level lower) and with pretty much the same set of OCL constructs. The only challenge, as far as we can see, is to select a right meta level for specifying constraints, which heavily depends on the problem to be solved. If the problem is related to the implementation, the most appropriate meta level is the pair (M1, M0) as is the case for (A1-A6). If we are dealing with UML profile, the obvious choice is to specify constraints at the M2 level and they will be automatically enforced at the profiled M1 level models. Moreover, the specification at the highest meta level (M3) is needed to enforce constraints at the M2 level, which is commonly used to define meta-models. This is suggested when there is a need in a particular industry to define a new MOF-based domain specific language to solve a particular problem in hand.

4.3   Choosing Diagram

In all our applications, class diagrams were used as the basis for modeling attributes that required specifying OCL constraints. In addition, for the applications where behavior was required to be modeled, we used state machines as our case studies exhibit state-based behavior. Of course, other behavioral diagrams (e.g., sequence diagrams) can also be used in other contexts. Based on this observation, we can then conclude that though choosing an appropriate diagram depends on application contexts; however at a minimum a UML class diagram representing various concepts required at various meta levels is needed to hold attributes required for specifying OCL constraints. Moreover, choosing a particular diagram does not impact what OCL constructs are applied and which meta level to use.

4.4   Selecting a Purpose of OCL

In our applications, the most common use of OCL was to perform evaluation (6 out of 8 applications) followed by solving (4 out of 8). In addition, recall that specification of constraints is required in solving, evaluating, parsing, and query as we discussed in Section 2. This observation can be explained from the fact that to support automation, e.g., test data generation, the specified constraints are required to be evaluated and/or solved. Of course, if an application is only for the purpose of bringing additional precision to models, specification of constraints is sufficient. Notice that as we discussed in Section 2.3., the most important step is OCL evaluation as it is also required for OCL solving and thus suggesting that OCL evaluation is at the core of any automated constraints manipulation activity. This is the reason that a wide variety of OCL evaluators exist, such as OCLE 2.0 [15], OSLO [16], IBM OCL parser [17], and EyeOCL Software (EOS) evaluator [18]. In all our applications except A7 and A8, we chose EOS as it is one of the most efficient evaluators for OCL. Notice that for A4 and A9, where we used OCL for querying, we again used EOS. For A7 and A8, we used the OCL evaluator built-in in IBM Rational Software Architect, because it has a good support for enforcing the constraints specified on UML profiles on M1 level models.

Several OCL solvers exist in the literature that translate OCL into other formalisms [19-24] such as Alloy and Satisfiability Problem (SAT) to solve them. In our industrial applications, we developed our own OCL Solver called EsOCL [4] based on search algorithms since the existing solvers either did not handle important features of OCL such as collections or their operations [19, 20], were not scalable, or lacked proper tool support [21].

5   Conclusion

This paper presents our experiences of applying the Object Constraint Language (OCL) on six industrial case studies. The case studies belong to diverse industrial domains including Communication and Control, Energy Equipment and Services, Recycling, and Oil and Gas Production. In these case studies, OCL is applied solving various industrial problems including model-based testing, safety certification, and automated product configuration. The results of the industrial case studies showed that a well-selected subset of OCL notations was sufficient for various problems for various purposes including constraint evaluation, solving, and querying. We found that OCL constraint specification and enforcement at various meta levels of MOF works in the same way, i.e., specified at M_x level and enforced at M_{x-1} where x={1, 2, 3}. OCL evaluation is a fundamental activity and is the core of all our industrial applications. Based on our findings, we presented guidelines for practitioners that can help them choose an appropriate purpose of OCL and meta level.

Acknowledgments. Muhammad Zohaib Iqbal was partly supported by ICT R&D Fund, Pakistan (ICTRDF/MBTToolset/2013) and by National Research Fund, Luxembourg (FNR/P10/03).

References

1. Iqbal, M.Z., Ali, S., Yue, T., Briand, L.: Experiences of Applying UML/MARTE on Three Industrial Projects. In: France, R.B., Kazmeier, J., Breu, R., Atkinson, C. (eds.) MODELS 2012. LNCS, vol. 7590, pp. 642–658. Springer, Heidelberg (2012)
2. Ali, S., Briand, L., Arcuri, A., Walawege, S.: An Industrial Application of Robustness Testing using Aspect-Oriented Modeling, UML/MARTE, and Search Algorithms. In: Whittle, J., Clark, T., Kühne, T. (eds.) MODELS 2011. LNCS, vol. 6981, pp. 108–122. Springer, Heidelberg (2011)
3. Arcuri, A., Iqbal, M., Briand, L.: Black-Box System Testing of Real-Time Embedded Systems Using Random and Search-Based Testing. In: Petrenko, A., Simão, A., Maldonado, J.C. (eds.) ICTSS 2010. LNCS, vol. 6435, pp. 95–110. Springer, Heidelberg (2010)
4. Ali, S., Iqbal, M.Z., Arcuri, A., Briand, L.: Generating Test Data from OCL Constraints with Search Techniques. IEEE Trans. Softw. Eng. 39(10), 1376–1402 (2013)
5. Ali, S., Briand, L.C., Hemmati, H.: Modeling Robustness Behavior Using Aspect-Oriented Modeling to Support Robustness Testing of Industrial Systems. Software and Systems Modeling 11(4), 633–670 (2012)
6. Ali, S., Yue, T., Briand, L.C.: Does Aspect-Oriented Modeling Help Improve the Readability of UML State Machines? Software & Systems Modeling 13(3), 1189–1221 (2014)
7. Laddad, R.: AspectJ in Action: Practical Aspect-Oriented Programming. Manning Publications (2003)
8. Panesar-Walawege, R.K., Sabetzadeh, M., Briand, L.: Supporting the verification of compliance to safety standards via model-driven engineering: Approach, tool-support and empirical validation. Information and Software Technology 55(5), 836–864 (2013)
9. Behjati, R., Yue, T., Briand, L., Selic, B.: SimPL: A Product-Line Modeling Methodology for Families of Integrated Control Systems. Information and Software Technology 55(3), 607–629 (2013)
10. Iqbal, M.Z., Arcuri, A., Briand, L.: Code Generation from UML/MARTE/OCL Environment Models to Support Automated System Testing of Real-Time Embedded Software. Simula Research Laboratory, Technical Report (2011-04) (2011)

11. Iqbal, M.Z., Arcuri, A., Briand, L.: Environment modeling and simulation for automated testing of soft real-time embedded software. Softw Syst. Model. 1–42 (2013)
12. Iqbal, M.Z., Arcuri, A., Briand, L.: Combining search-based and adaptive random testing strategies for environment model-based testing of real-time embedded systems. In: Fraser, G., Teixeira de Souza, J. (eds.) SSBSE 2012. LNCS, vol. 7515, pp. 136–151. Springer, Heidelberg (2012)
13. Iqbal, M.Z., Arcuri, A., Briand, L.: Automated System Testing of Real-Time Embedded Systems Based on Environment Models. Simula Research Laboratory, Technical Report (2011-19) (2011)
14. Iqbal, M.Z., Arcuri, A., Briand, L.: Environment Modeling with UML/MARTE to Support Black-Box System Testing for Real-Time Embedded Systems: Methodology and Industrial Case Studies. In: Petriu, D.C., Rouquette, N., Haugen, Ø. (eds.) MODELS 2010, Part I. LNCS, vol. 6394, pp. 286–300. Springer, Heidelberg (2010)
15. Chiorean, D., Bortes, M., Corutiu, D., Botiza, C., Cârcu, A.: OCLE. (September 2009), http://lci.cs.ubbcluj.ro/ocle/
16. Hein, C., Ritter, T., Wagner, M.: Open Source Library for OCL (2009)
17. Drusinsky, D.: Modeling and Verification using UML Statecharts: A Working Guide to Reactive System Design, Runtime Monitoring and Execution-based Model Checking. Newnes (2006)
18. Egea, M.: EyeOCL Software (September 2009), http://maude.sip.ucm.es/eos/
19. Aertryck, L.V., Jensen, T.: UML-Casting: Test synthesis from UML models using constraint resolution. Approches Formelles dans l'Assistance au Développement de Logiciels (AFADL 2003) (2003)
20. Benattou, M., Bruel, J., Hameurlain, N.: Generating test data from OCL specification. In: Proceedings of the Workshop:Workshop on Integration and Transformation of UML Models at ECOOP 2002 (WITUML) (2002)
21. Bao-Lin, L., Zhi-shu, L., Qing, L., Hong, C.Y.: Test case automate generation from UML-sequence diagram and OCLexpression. In: International Conference on Computational Intelligence and Security, pp. 1048–1052 (2007)
22. Clavel, M., Dios, M.A.G.D.: Checking unsatisfiability for OCL constraints. In: Proceedings of the Workshop: The Pragmatics of OCL and Other Textual Specification Languages at MoDELS 2009, Electronic Communications of the EASST, vol. 24 (2009)
23. Kyas, M., Fecher, H., Boer, F.S.D., Jacob, J., Hooman, J., Zwaag, M.V.D., Arons, T., Kugler, H.: Formalizing UML Models and OCL Constraints in PVS. Electron. Notes Theor. Comput. Sci. 115, 39–47 (2005)
24. Brucker, A.D., Krieger, M.P., Longuet, D., Wolff, B.: A specification-based test case generation method for UML/OCL. In: Dingel, J., Solberg, A. (eds.) MODELS 2010. LNCS, vol. 6627, pp. 334–348. Springer, Heidelberg (2011)

Model-Based Mining
of Source Code Repositories

Markus Scheidgen and Joachim Fischer

Humboldt-Universität zu Berlin,
Unter den Linden 6, 10099 Berlin, Germany
{scheidge,fischer}@informatik.hu-berlin.de

Abstract. The *Mining Software Repositories* (MSR) field analyzes the
rich data available in source code repositories (SCR) to uncover interesting and actionable information about software system evolution. Major
obstacles in MSR are the heterogeneity of software projects and the
amount of data that is processed. Model-driven software engineering
(MDSE) can deal with heterogeneity by abstraction as its core strength,
but only recent efforts in adopting NoSQL-databases for persisting and
processing very large models made MDSE a feasible approach for MSR.
This paper is a work in progress report on *srcrepo*: a model-based MSR
system. *Srcrepo* uses the NoSQL-based EMF-model persistence layer
EMF-Fragments and Eclipse's *MoDisco* reverse engineering framework
to create EMF-models of whole SCRs that comprise all code of all revisions at an abstract syntax tree (AST) level. An OCL-like language is
used as an accessible way to finally gather information such as software
metrics from these SCR models.

1 Introduction

Software repositories hold a wealth of information and provide a unique view of
the actual evolutionary path taken to realize a software system [17]. Software
engineering researchers have devised a wide spectrum of approaches to extract
this information; this research is commonly subsumed under the term *Mining
Software Repositories* (MSR). A specific branch of MSR uses statistical analysis
of code metrics gathered for each software revision to understand the evolution of software projects [16]. Recent advances in large-scale data processing
(i.e., NoSQL-databases and Map/Reduce-style processing) allowed to extend
this research to *large* or even *ultra-large* scale software repositories that comprise a large number of software projects [11]. Examples for large repositories
are the projects hosted under the umbrella of the *Apache Software Foundation* or
the *Eclipse Foundation*, and ultra-large repository examples are web-based software project hosting services like *GitHub* (250.000+ projects) or *SourceForge*
(350.000+ projects) [11]. But analyzing many heterogeneous software projects
has limits. While existing approaches [11,13,2,15] manage to abstract from different *code versioning systems* (e.g., CVS, SVN, Git), different programming languages with different syntax and semantics are still a major issue. The EU FP 7

D. Amyot et al. (Eds.): SAM 2014, LNCS 8769, pp. 239–254, 2014.

project FLOSS [13], for example, produced data sets for over 3000 libre software projects, but could only gather language independent text-based metrics, like *lines of code* (LOC). But many software evolution approaches [16,5,26,28] depend on object-oriented metrics (e.g., CK-metrics [8]) or more precise complexity-based size metrics (e.g., Halstead or McCabe) that can only be gathered by aggregating the occurrences of concrete language constructs and therefore require the analysis of *abstract syntax trees* (AST). Furthermore, other MSR techniques, like *implicit dependencies* [29] or mining for common API-usage patterns [21], also require a language dependent syntax-based analysis.

We hypothesize that MDSE methods and tools, like reverse engineering frameworks (e.g., *MoDisco* [7]) and the recent adoption of NoSQL-databases for persisting and processing very large models (e.g., [12,6,24]), allow us to implement an MSR-system that overcomes these issues and fulfills the following goals:

1. the potential to abstract from different programming languages and version control systems
2. syntax-based source code analysis, i.e., analysis of models for corresponding ASTs
3. high accessibility and low programming efforts through high-level languages
4. scalability through NoSQL-based model persistence that enables highly concurrent model processing

We started to implement a model-based MSR-system, coined *srcrepo*[1], in order to verify this hypothesis and research whether the stated goals are achievable.

Note that *srcrepo* only covers the analysis of *source code repositories* and does not deal with other aspects of software repositories, such as issue tracking systems, mailing-lists, Wiki-entries, etc., which are important additional data sources for many MSR techniques.

This paper is organized as follows. First, we describe the process of analyzing repositories with *srcrepo* and introduce all necessary components of our system. After that, we take a detailed look at some of these components: the used metamodel for versioned source code (Section 3), our model persistence layer *EMF-Fragments* [24] (Section 4), and an OCL-like DSL that can be used to calculate and aggregate software metrics (Section 5). The evaluation in Section 6 discusses our preliminary findings. We finally present related work and conclusions.

2   *srcrepo's* Analysis Process and Components

Figure 1 shows the basic process of a *srcrepo*-based analysis and all the entities that are involved.

The process starts with existing software projects as they are typically found in (ultra-)large scale software repositories like GitHub or SourceForge (top left). They usually entail a *source code repository* that is maintained by a *version control system* like CVS, Git, or SVN. The source code repository provides the

---

[1] http://github.com/markus1978/srcrepo

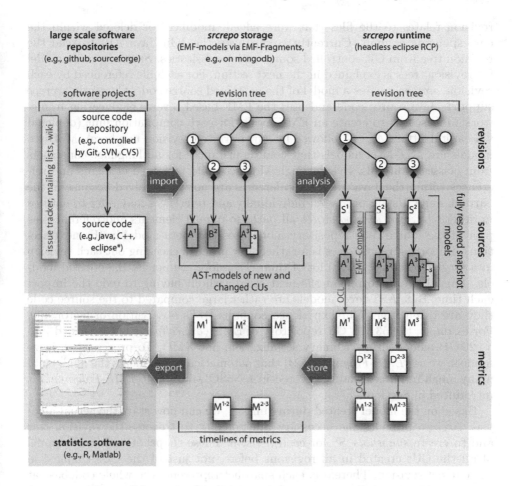

Fig. 1. Schematic visualization of the *srcrepo* analysis process

actual *source code* organized in files. These files represent the smallest compilable units of source code and are therefore referred to as *compilation units (CUs)*. Please note that CUs are only an organizational concept and not necessarily relate to a programming language construct, even though CUs sometimes contain a single class or module of the same name. Source code is written in a programming language, but the version control system only treats CUs as plain text files. Software projects also come with other repositories such as issue trackers, mailing lists, etc., which are not processed by *srcrepo*.

Now *srcrepo* provides the functionality to create an EMF-model from source code repositories as a single *import* step. First, *srcrepo* creates a model of the *revision tree*. The revision tree is a lattice of nodes each representing a single commit of changes to the source code repository. Each revision has a unique ID; for simplicity the figure shows revisions with numbers as IDs (*1 . . . 3*). Each revision relates to the files that were added, modified, or deleted within the corresponding commit. Currently *srcrepo* uses the JGit Java API to read the revision tree from Git controlled source code repositories. *Srcrepo*'s meta-model for revision trees is explained in the next section. For each file referenced by each revision, *srcrepo* creates a model of the contained source code. Currently *srcrepo* supports Java source code and uses the EMF-based reverse engineering framework MoDisco [7] to create an EMF-model for each compilation unit (depicted via capital letters $A \ldots C$ followed by superscripted revision numbers). MoDisco models are AST-level models that contain instances for all language constructs from classes to literals. Even though MoDisco collects named elements and references within the Java code, the references are not yet resolved because in the current step CUs are processed individually and references may refer to entities in other CUs. But *srcrepo* stores all paths to named elements and references as part of the source code repository model (see the meta-model in the next section). Importing repositories is a rather slow process: checking out each revision in a large repository takes a lot of time. Therefore, we persist the created models. This allows us to repeat the next steps without having to redo the import each time. But, AST-level models are rather large compared to the source code they are taken from. Our experience confirms [18]'s observation of factor 400. For example, the 53 MB Git repository of EMF (*org.eclipse.emf*) is turned into a 20 GB model (using a binary serialization, not XMI). To process such large models, we use *EMF-Fragments* [24] that automatically fragments the model into many small resources that are stored in a NoSQL-database. *EMF-Fragments* is introduced in Section 4.

Based on the model created during import, we can now start the actual analysis. *Srcrepo* provides the necessary functionality to traverse the revision tree and to create *snapshots* S^x for each revision. These snapshots contain a model of all the CUs created in all revisions before, not just of the CUs changed in the current revision. Therefore, each snapshot represents the whole codebase at the current revision. *Srcrepo* uses the stored data on named elements and references to resolve all references and create a fully linked model. Of course, we do not create all snapshots at once, but only a couple at a time. This allows us to perform this step within a single runtime (i.e., JVM) without running into memory issues. But this also means that snapshots have to be processed individually. Which is fine, since all software evolution and MSR methods are based on analyzing snapshots sequentially or on analyzing the differences between two successive snapshots.

Clients should have different very accessible options to analyze these snapshots. Currently, we are working on the option to use an OCL-like language to count and aggregate occurrences of language constructs (refer to Section 5). This is enough to calculate most existing code metrics (depicted by M^x). The language allows clients to write OCL-like expressions that are executed for the whole revision tree. Since snapshots can be analyzed individually, *srcrepo* can run these queries concurrently on different revisions. As future work, we plan to use *EMF Compare* to analyze the differences between snapshots. This is for example valuable to find *implicit dependencies* similar to [29], or to analyze typical change patterns/refactorings [27]. The results of *EMF Compare D^{x-y}* can also be processed via OCL. EMF-based model transformation languages are another option for analyzing snapshot models that we need to evaluate. Of course, there is always the possibility to use plain Java code, since all involved models are plain EMF-models.

The artifacts created during analysis (e.g., code metrics, metrics on differences) are also models (e.g., there is an OMG standard/meta-model for organizing software metrics[2]). These result models are also stored within the same storage that is used to persist the repository models. This allows us to maintain cross references between results and the entities that these results were created from (cross references not shown in Fig. 1). For example, we can use *srcrepo* to calculate McCabe's *cyclomatic complexity* for each method and link the resulting numbers to the corresponding methods. Thus, we calculate this metric once and can use it repeatedly in later analysis runs (e.g., use them as weights to calculate the CK-metric *Weighted Methods per Class* (WMC) [8].

As a final step, results are exported for the use in statistics software, such as R or Matlab. The statistics software can then be used to process and analyze the gathered "raw"-data into human readable charts and other forms of usable knowledge.

3   A Meta-Model for Source Code Repositories

Figure 2 shows the meta-model that we currently use for representing source code repositories.

The top part contains the elements used to model revision trees. A RepositoryModel contains revisions (Rev) that are connected via RevRelations (thus forming a lattice of revisions). Relations between revisions can be navigated both ways. The relation between two revisions contains all Diffs between those revisions. A Diff can reference a changed file. There can be a reference to a model of the file (AbstractFileRef).

In the middle part of the diagram, we have source code related constructs. A CompilationUnitRef is a concrete file reference targeting a model of a compilation unit. PendingElements and Targets are used to store references and named elements within code. We later use this data to resolve all references in snapshots models.

The lower part of the diagram shows (only) some elements from the MoDisco meta-model, which is used to represent the actual Java code. Each CompilationUnitRef refers to its own Model, i.e., we store a Java model for each CU separately. During analysis, *srcrepo* will merge the models of multiple CUs into snapshots and resolve all references stored within the individual models of the corresponding CUs.

---

[2] http://www.omg.org/spec/SMM/1.0/

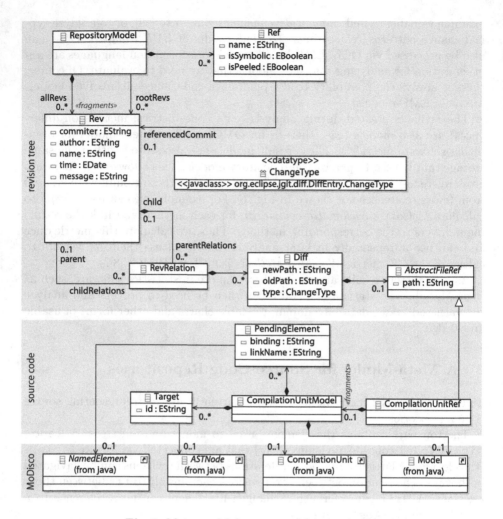

Fig. 2. Meta-model for source code repositories

4 Model Persistence in NoSQL-Databases

We build a model persistence framework for EMF [25] called *EMF-fragments* [22]. *EMF-Fragments* is different from frameworks based on object-relational mappings (ORM) like Connected Data Objects (CDO). While ORM mappings map single objects, attributes, and references to database entries, *EMF-Fragments* maps larger chunks of a model (*fragments*) to URIs that reference these fragments. Such fragmented models can then be saved to databases that allow us to store maps between keys (URIs) and values (serialized fragments). There is a wide range of such (distributed) data-stores including (distributed) file-systems and document-databases like Hadoop's *HBase* or *mongodb*.

EMF-Fragments uses and extends the regular EMF *resource* API [25]: each fragment is an EMF resource, a fragmented model is an EMF *resource set*. Resources have URIs (key) and can be serialized (value). *EMF-Fragments* uses EMF's *URI converters* to map URIs and serialized resources to database entries. EMF already supports on-demand loading (and later unloading) of resources, and *EMF-Fragments* simply triggers this functionality to automatically and transparently create, delete, save, and unload fragments/resources. *EMF-Fragments* only holds a few fragments in main memory at the same time and therefore can process arbitrary large models with limited main memory. *EMF-Fragments* automatically unloads fragments that are no longer used (*referenced* in Java terms) by clients. Note that at least the largest fragment has to fit into main memory, since fragments have to be loaded as a whole. To fragment a model, clients have to annotate their meta-models and designate references that shall fragment corresponding models. *EMF-Fragments* listens to changes on these references and creates and deletes fragments accordingly. Figure 3 exemplifies fragmentation on meta-model and model level.

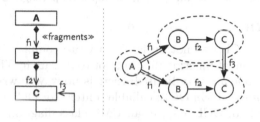

Fig. 3. Fragmentation of models

The *srcrepo* meta-model in Fig. 2 further exemplifies the use of *fragmenting* references, here annotated as UML stereotypes (i.e., with guillemets, set in italic). In consequence, each revision with all its `RevRelations` and `Diff` information is stored in an individual database entry. Each `CompilationUnitModel` is consequently stored in another database entry. The assumption is that single revisions and single compilation units will always fit into main memory. On the other hand, we usually analyze whole revisions and whole CUs, and therefore we would not benefit from further fragmentation. Should we, for example, discover that we often only look at parts of a CU (e.g., are only interested in class, field, and method declarations), we could further fragment the model (e.g., mark the reference between declaration and body as fragmenting) and therefore prevent the loading of irrelevant model parts. For a detailed discussion on how to design fragmentation refer to [24].

5   An OCL-Like Language for Ascertaining Software Metrics

5.1   Why OCL?

Even though OCL is called the *Object Constraint Language*, it can be used to write expressions with other return types than boolean. OCL was designed to easily navigate between model elements via their associations. To navigate multi-valued association ends comfortably, OCL provides a set of higher-order collection operations that allow to quickly collect, select, and otherwise process association ends. This makes OCL a good language to aggregate data about a model, while navigating that model. The following example OCL expression counts the classes contained in the top-level packages of a MoDisco model.

```
1 context Model:
2   self.ownedElements→collect(p | p.ownedElements)→size
```

Listing 1.1. OCL for collecting all types in all top-level packages of a MoDisco model

5.2   Why Not OCL?

Despite its merits, OCL was not designed to write complex "programs". OCL can be used to implement functionality but not to declare it. Therefore, concepts to structure OCL code are very limited: there is no way to write parameterized functions for example with-in OCL: callable context for OCL expressions has to be provided out-side of OCL, e.g., in an UML class diagram. Further, its side-effect free design makes it impossible to store results by means of creating and modifying new model elements, e.g., creating and filling a metrics-model.

Therefore, we wanted to extend OCL, or rather create a language that contains what we like about OCL. Similar to [14], where the authors mimic the syntax of model transformation languages in a very extensible internal Scala DSL, we transfered OCL's collection operations to Scala. Filip Krikava presents a way to transfer OCL's higher-order function syntax to Scala's lambda inspired function objects[3]. Besides its flexible syntax, Scala also provides type-inference. This allows us to omit most type information while retaining full static type safety and sensible code assist, which is essential when dealing with complex meta-models such as MoDisco's Java Model. The following shows the expression of the previous example in OCL-like Scala syntax.

```
1 def firstPackageLevelTypes(self: Model):Int =
2   self.getOwnedElements().collect(p⇒p.getOwnedElements()).size()
```

Listing 1.2. Collecting all types in all top-level packages with OCL-like collections in Scala

---

[3] http://www.slideshare.net/krikava/enriching-emf-models-with-scala

Instead of defining the context of the expression (line 1), we define a function with corresponding parameter and return type. The resemblance between the OCL expression body and the Scala body is apparent. We implemented these OCL-like collection operations (as declared in Listing 1.3) on top of Java `Iterables`; implicit conversions between `Iterables` and `OclCollections` provide these operations immediately to all Java and Scala collections including EMF's collections. Besides OCL's collect and select operations, we also added a few operations tailored for calculating metrics:

```scala
1  trait OclCollection[E] extends java.lang.Iterable[E] {
2    ...
3    def collect[R](exp:(E)⇒R):OclCollection[R]
4    def collectAll[R](exp:(E)⇒OclCollection[R]):OclCollection[R]
5    def collectNotNull[R](exp:(E)⇒R):OclCollection[R]
6    def collectClosure(exp:(E)⇒OclCollection[E]):OclCollection[E]
7
8    def select(expr:(E)⇒Bool):OclCollection[E]
9    def selectOfType[T]:OclCollection[T]
10
11   def aggregate[R,I](exp:(E)⇒I,start:()⇒R,aggr:(R, I)⇒R):R
12   def sum(exp:(E)⇒Double):Double
13   def product(exp:(E)⇒Double):Double
14   def max(exp:(E)⇒Double):Double
15   def min(exp:(E)⇒Double):Double
16   def avg(exp:(E)⇒Double):Stats[Double]
17
18   def run(runnable:(E)⇒Unit):Unit
19 }
```

Listing 1.3. Additional OCL-like collection functions defined in Scala

`collectAll` collects and flattens the result; `collectNotNull` behaves like collect, but omits `Null` values; `collectClosure` applies the expression recursively to the result until no more new elements are found. `selectOfType` selects elements of a certain type and returns a collection with casted values. `aggregate` allows to easily implement aggregation. `sum`, for example, is implemented as:

```scala
1  sum(exp:(E)⇒Double):Double =
2    aggregate[Double,Double](exp, ()⇒0, (a,b)⇒a+b)
```

5.3 Example Usage to Calculate CK-Metrics

The following demonstrates the OCL-like collections by implementing three of the CK-metrics [8]: *Weighted Methods per Class* (WMC)[4], *Coupling Between Object classes* (CBO), *Number Of Children* (NOC). To average these metrics

---

[4] Commonly weighted with unity or McCabe [16]. We use unity here.

```
1  def classes(model:Model):OclCollection[ClassDeclaration] = model
2    .getOwnedElements()
3    .collectClosure(pkg⇒ p.getOwnedPackages())
4    .collectAll(pkg⇒ pkg.getOwnedElements())
5    .collectClosure(typeDcl⇒ typeDcl
6      .getBodyDeclarations()
7      .selectOfType[ClassDeclaration]
8    )
9
10 def WMC(clazz:ClassDeclaration):Int = clazz
11   .getBodyDeclarations()
12   .selectOfType[MethodDeclaration]()
13   .size()
14
15 def CBO(clazz:ClassDeclration):Int = {
16   val types=new HashSet[AbstractTypeDeclaration]()
17   clazz.eContents()
18     .closure(e⇒ e.eContents())
19     .selectOfType[AbstractMethodInvocation]()
20     .collectNotNull(inv⇒ inv.getMethod())
21     .collectNotNull(meth⇒ meth.getReturnType())
22     .collectNotNull(typeAccess⇒ typeAccess.getType())
23     .select(typeDcl⇒ types.add(typeDcl)
24     .size()
25 }
26
27 def NOC(clazz:ClassDeclaration):Int = clazz
28   .getUsagesInTypeAccess()
29   .select(e⇒ e.eContainer()
30     .isInstanceOf[AbstractTypeDeclaration])
31   .size()
32
33 def averageWMC(model:Model):Double =
34   classes(model).avg(clazz⇒ WMC(clazz)).value
35 ...
```

Listing 1.4. Some CK-Metrics expressed in Scala with OCL-like collection operations

over all classes, we also demonstrate an operation that collects all classes in a model (line 1). Note that all required recursion (i.e., gathering all packages, in all packages, etc. and all the inner classes in all other potential inner classes, etc.) is covered through the use of collectClosure (lines 3 and 5). The meta-model excerpt of MoDisco in Fig. 4 explains the navigated classes and associations.

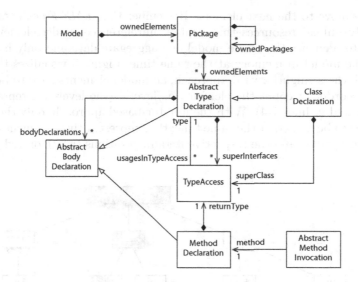

Fig. 4. Simplified excerpt of the MoDisco meta-model

5.4 Implementation

The straight forward method of implementing these OCL-like collection operations is to create a new collection for each operation call to hold the results. This approach, however, requires to keep all used collections in memory, even though one is just interested in an aggregation of these interim results. For instance, consider counting all classes in all revisions of a source code repository:

```
1  def countAllClasses(repo:RepositoryModel):Int = repo
2      .getAllRevs().
3      .collectAll(rev⇒ rev.getParentRelations())
4      .collectAll(parent⇒ parent.getDiffs())
5      .collect(diff⇒ diff.getFileRef())
6      .selectOfType[CompilationUnitRef]
7      .collectAll(classes(cu.getModel()))
8      .size()
```

Listing 1.5. Example aggregation of a large model

This would mean to create and keep in memory a list of all `ParentRelations`, all `Diffs`, ..., and all `ClassDeclarations`. If we wanted to count all calls of a certain method, for example, we would have to go even deeper and eventually hold most of the repository model in memory.

To retain scalability, we implemented the collection operations differently. Instead of creating collections that contain all the interim results, we create iterators that behave like collections containing the corresponding results. The iterators only hold references to the current element and loose these references when they move to the next element. Remember that *EMF-Fragments* can automatically unload resources that contain unreferenced model elements. This allows us to navigate the whole model and aggregate data and only have small parts of the model in memory at the same time. Figure 5 visualizes the difference. With the straightforward approach, all model elements have to be kept in memory in order to count the elements on level 4 (the levels 1-4 represent the results created in lines 1-4). With the iterator-based approach, only the red elements have to be loaded at the same time; they represent those elements that are currently collected from the respective iterator positions (white on red ground).

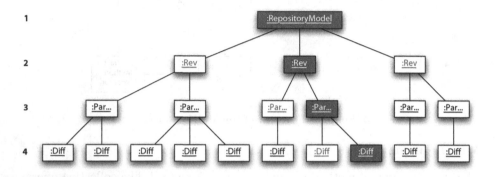

Fig. 5. Object diagram depicting the model elements involved in executing Listing 1.5

6   Current State, Problems, Limitations, and Future Work

Currently, the presented components of *srcrepo* work as described. With respect to the defined four goals (Section 1), we encountered the following problems in dealing with heterogeneous repositories (goal 1) and scalability (goal 4).

Our system *srcrepo* currently only supports Git-based source code repositories that contain Java code with Eclipse project meta-data. Most notably this metadata contains information about which files are actual sources and how the class-path looks like. We are convinced that our revision meta-model can work as an abstraction for other version control systems as well, and we are working on support for SVN as a proof of concept. Supporting other programming languages is a different class of problem. While the use of models, in principle, proliferates abstraction, it is not obvious that a *reasonable* abstraction (i.e., an abstraction that works for MSR) exists. MoDisco for example claims to be an extensible framework, but up to this moments it only supports Java and its meta-model is just an EMF-version of Eclipse's JDT datamodel. OMG's *Knowledge Discovery Metamodel* (KDM) (which, in addition to the given Java meta-model, is also supported by MoDisco) might be such a *reasonable* abstraction, but this has to be evaluated carefully. A different solution is to simply add meta-models for other languages. But this means that all parts of an analysis that are language specific, also have to be implemented for all other programming languages and their respective meta-models. An abstraction of the results (e.g., most software metrics can be defined for many languages) could still provide value: clients will need to deal with different languages during source code analysis, but not for studying the resulting metrics.

We also encountered performance issues that currently prevent a reasonable application of *srcrepo* on a large number of real life software repositories. These problems have three causes.

First, creating a snapshot model for each revision individually, involves a lot of repeated computation, since only a small part of the underlying *compilation units* (CU) actually changes from revision to revision. We are working on an incremental snapshot creation that merges differences into the snapshots of previous revisions and therefore reduces the workload drastically.

Secondly, CUs are atomic to *srcrepo*. When a CU changes, *srcrepo* will process that changed CU as a whole, even if only a small part has changed. This is fine for typically sized CUs, but in some seldom cases (especially when code generation is involved) CUs become very big. For example, the code repository of *EMF* itself contains a >3 MB CU. This massive Java file with >600.000 LOC has various aspects of EMF generated into it. Not only is it very large, but it also has a lot of dependencies to other parts of the source code. Thus, it also changes very often and therefore makes the problem even bigger. Obviously, we have to use a more granular unit as the smallest changeable part. Unfortunately, however, CUs are the smallest common nominator between the syntax-based view and the text-file-based view that version control systems offer. CUs and files can be directly mapped onto each other: each CU corresponds to a file. Finer units like class members on one side and distinct lines of text on the other side are much harder to map to each other. Therefore, we will always have to parse the whole CU, but we do not necessarily have to convert the whole AST into a model, and we certainly do not have to store the whole CU model. We can either map text-based difference information from the version control system onto the AST to determine which elements have actually changed, or employ some form of model comparison (e.g., *EMF Compare*) on ASTs/models.

Thirdly, at first glance, it should be easy to run most of an analysis in parallel, since all revisions can be analyzed individually. However, things become more complicated, if we introduce incremental snapshot creation as described as a possible solution to the first problem. We still have to implement concurrency that is sensitive to this issue.

As a general last limitation, *srcrepo* only analyzes source code repositories. For a lot of research (e.g., [21,16,5]) in MSR, this has to be integrated with other systems to analyze source code repositories in unity with other parts of software repositories, e.g., issues-tracking systems, mailing lists, Wiki's, etc.

7   Related Work

The field *Mining Software Repositories* is as old as software repositories; an overview of recent research can be found here [17]. A recent facet of this research is gathering large metrics-based data-sets from large and ultra-scale repositories. Our framework also aims at doing so.

The Floss project (EU Framework Programme 7) [13] gathered per revision data-sets of language independent text-based metrics from more than 3000 libre software projects. Their tool *Alitheia* [15] not only gathers metrics from source code (CVS, SNV, and Git), but also data from issue tracking and mailing lists. Thereby, the project goal was not to analyze this data, but to create a comprehensive common database for other researchers. *Sourcerer* [2] is a example for a language-dependent approach. In this project, over 4000 libre software Java projects have been mined for metrics based on class, field, and method declarations [9]. But, the project only gathered data from released revisions, not for whole repositories. Similar projects and tools are *BOA* [11] and Harmony[5].

Another source for related work is the recent adoption of NoSQL-databases [19,20,10] for the persistence of large models [3]. The use of document or graph databases promises better performance and scalability than traditional *object relational mapping* (ORM)-based technologies like CDO[6] or Teneo[7]. In [6,3], the authors implement EMF-persistence for graph databases. Morsa [12] stores individual objects as JSON-records in the document-database mongodb. Our own *EMF-Fragments*[8] stores individual EMF-resources in document-databases like HBase or mongodb. These approaches use different strategies to map objects and relations to their respective database-technology [23].

There are also attempts to create version control systems for models; [1] provides an overview of recent research. The approach in [4] is (to our knowledge) the first approach that uses a NoSQL-backend.

8   Conclusions

We presented *srcrepo*, a model-based system for the analysis of source code repositories and a proof of concept for a model-based approach to *Mining Source Code Repositories*. We presented 4 goals: (1) to abstract from heterogeneous repositories, (2) achieve syntax-based and not text-based analysis, (3) high accessibility, and (4) scalability. In respect to goal (1), we started to implement support for a single type of version control system and programming language. Consequently, we could not yet prove a possible abstraction from different programming languages and version control systems. But the model-based approach still offers this potential in principle. With respect to (2) and different from comparable systems, we were able to realize a language dependent, AST-level deep analysis. Furthermore, clients only have to write small OCL-like expressions to gather language dependent metrics from a vast amount of available software projects (goal 3). Although, all used technologies and components are prepared for concurrent execution, we encountered several issues for which we discussed possible solutions, and we are confident to realize goal (4) in the near future.

---

[5] http://code.google.com/p/harmony
[6] http://www.eclipse.org/cdo/
[7] http://www.eclipse.org/modeling/emft/?project=teneo
[8] http://github.com/markus1978/emf-fragments

References

1. Altmanninger, K., Seidl, M., Wimmer, M.: A survey on model versioning approaches. Intl. Journal of Web Information Systems (IJWIS) 5(3), 271–304 (2009)
2. Bajracharya, S., Ossher, J., Lepos, C.: Sourcerer: An internet-scale software repository. In: Proceedings of Search-Driven Development-Users, Infrastructure, Tools and Evaluation (SUITE 2009), an ICSE 2009 Workshop, pp. 1–4. IEEE Computer Society, Vancouver (2009)
3. Barmpis, K., Kolovos, D.S.: Comparative analysis of data persistence technologies for large-scale models. In: Proceedings of the 2012 Extreme Modeling Workshop, XM 2012, pp. 33–38. ACM, New York (2012)
4. Barmpis, K., Kolovos, D.: Hawk: Towards a scalable model indexing architecture. In: Proceedings of the Workshop on Scalability in Model Driven Engineering, BigMDE 2013, pp. 6:1–6:9. ACM, New York (2013)
5. Basili, V.R., Briand, L.C., Melo, W.L.: A validation of object-oriented design metrics as quality indicators. IEEE Trans. Softw. Eng. 22(10), 751–761 (1996)
6. Benelallam, A., Gómez, A., Sunyé, G., Tisi, M., Launay, D.: Neo4EMF, a scalable persistence layer for EMF models. In: Cabot, J., Rubin, J. (eds.) ECMFA 2014. LNCS, vol. 8569, pp. 230–241. Springer, Heidelberg (2014)
7. Bruneliere, H., Cabot, J., Jouault, F., Madiot, F.: Modisco: A generic and extensible framework for model driven reverse engineering. In: Proceedings of the IEEE/ACM International Conference on Automated Software Engineering, ASE 2010, pp. 173–174. ACM (2010)
8. Chidamber, S.R., Kemerer, C.F.: A metrics suite for object oriented design. IEEE Trans. Softw. Eng. 20(6), 476–493 (1994)
9. Cox, A., Clarke, C., Sim, S.: A model independent source code repository. In: Proceedings of the 1999 Conference of the Centre for Advanced Studies on Collaborative Research, CASCON 1999, p. 1. IBM Press (1999)
10. DeCandia, G., Hastorun, D., Jampani, M., Kakulapati, G., Lakshman, A., Pilchin, A., Sivasubramanian, S., Vosshall, P., Vogels, W.: Dynamo: Amazon's highly available key-value store. In: Proceedings of 21st ACM SIGOPS Symposium on Operating Systems Principles, SOSP 2007, pp. 205–220. ACM, New York (2007)
11. Dyer, R., Nguyen, H.A., Rajan, H., Nguyen, T.N.: Boa: A language and infrastructure for analyzing ultra-large-scale software repositories. In: Proceedings of the 2013 International Conference on Software Engineering, ICSE 2013, pp. 422–431. IEEE Press, Piscataway (2013)
12. Espinazo Pagán, J., Sánchez Cuadrado, J., García Molina, J.: Morsa: A scalable approach for persisting and accessing large models. In: Whittle, J., Clark, T., Kühne, T. (eds.) MODELS 2011. LNCS, vol. 6981, pp. 77–92. Springer, Heidelberg (2011)
13. FLOSSMetrics consortium: Flossmetrics final report: Free/libre/open source metrics and benchmarking. Tech. Rep. FP6-033982, FLOSSMetrics consortium (March 2010), http://www.flossmetrics.org/docs/fm3-final-report_en.pdf
14. George, L., Wider, A., Scheidgen, M.: Type-safe model transformation languages as internal dSLs in scala. In: Hu, Z., de Lara, J. (eds.) ICMT 2012. LNCS, vol. 7307, pp. 160–175. Springer, Heidelberg (2012)
15. Gousios, G., Spinellis, D.: A platform for software engineering research. In: Godfrey, M.W., Whitehead, J. (eds.) 6th IEEE International Working Conference on Mining Software Repositories, MSR 2009, pp. 31–40. IEEE (2009)

16. Gyimothy, T., Ferenc, R., Siket, I.: Empirical validation of object-oriented metrics on open source software for fault prediction. IEEE Trans. Softw. Eng. 31(10), 897–910 (2005)
17. Kagdi, H., Collard, M.L., Maletic, J.I.: A survey and taxonomy of approaches for mining software repositories in the context of software evolution. Journal of Software Maintenance and Evolution: Research and Practice 19(2), 77–131 (2007)
18. Kagdi, H.H., Collard, M.L., Maletic, J.I.: Towards a taxonomy of approaches for mining of source code repositories. ACM SIGSOFT Software Engineering Notes 30(4), 1–5 (2005)
19. Khetrapal, A., Ganesh, V.: HBase and Hypertable for large scale distributed storage systems a performance evaluation for open source Big-table implementations. Tech. rep., Purdue University (2008)
20. Lakshman, A., Malik, P.: Cassandra: Structured storage system on a P2P network. In: Proceedings of the 28th ACM Symposium on Principles of Distributed Computing, PODC 2009, p. 5. ACM, New York (2009)
21. Livshits, B., Zimmermann, T.: Dynamine: Finding common error patterns by mining software revision histories. In: Proceedings of the 10th European Software Engineering Conference Held Jointly with 13th ACM SIGSOFT International Symposium on Foundations of Software Engineering, ESEC/FSE-13, pp. 296–305. ACM, New York (2005)
22. Scheidgen, M.: EMFFrag – Meta-Model-based Model Fragmentation and Persistence Framework (2012), http://github.com/markus1978/emf-fragments
23. Scheidgen, M.: Reference representation techniques for large models. In: Proceedings of the Workshop on Scalability in Model Driven Engineering, BigMDE 2013, pp. 5:1–5:9. ACM (2013)
24. Scheidgen, M., Zubow, A., Fischer, J., Kolbe, T.H.: Automated and transparent model fragmentation for persisting large models. In: France, R.B., Kazmeier, J., Breu, R., Atkinson, C. (eds.) MODELS 2012. LNCS, vol. 7590, pp. 102–118. Springer, Heidelberg (2012)
25. Steinberg, D., Budinsky, F., Paternostro, M., Merks, E.: EMF: Eclipse Modeling Framework, 2nd edn. Addison-Wesley, Boston (2009)
26. Subramanyam, R., Krishnan, M.S.: Empirical analysis of CK metrics for object-oriented design complexity: Implications for software defects. IEEE Trans. Softw. Eng. 29(4), 297–310 (2003)
27. Williams, C.C., Hollingsworth, J.K.: Automatic mining of source code repositories to improve bug finding techniques. IEEE Trans. Software Eng. 31(6), 466–480 (2005)
28. Yu, P., Systä, T., Müller, H.A.: Predicting fault-proneness using OO metrics: An industrial case study. In: Proceedings of the 6th European Conference on Software Maintenance and Reengineering, CSMR 2002, pp. 99–107. IEEE Computer Society, Washington, DC (2002)
29. Zimmermann, T., Weißgerber, P., Diehl, S., Zeller, A.: Mining version histories to guide software changes. IEEE Trans. Software Eng. 31(6), 429–445 (2005)

Towards an Extensible Modeling
and Validation Framework for SDL-UML

Alexander Kraas

Poppenreuther Str. 45, D-90419 Nürnberg, Germany
alexander.kraas@gmx.de

Abstract. The Specification and Description Language (SDL) has been
a domain specific language that is well-established in the telecommunication sector for many years, but only a small set of SDL tools is available.
In contrast, a wide range of different kinds of tools can be used for various purposes, such as model transformation, for the Unified Modeling
Language (UML). The UML profile for SDL (SDL-UML) makes it possible to specify SDL compliant models in terms of a UML model. In this
paper, the extensible SDL-UML Modeling and Validation (SU-MoVal)
framework, which supports the specification and validation of models
that are compliant to Z.109, is presented. As an additional feature, the
SU-MoVal framework also provides an editor for the specification of a
textual notation that is mapped to corresponding SDL-UML elements.

Keywords: SDL-UML, Profile, Validation, Specification, Framework.

1 Introduction

Since many years a small set of tools for the Specification and Description Language (SDL) has been available, but without support for the latest edition of the
UML profile for SDL as specified in Z.109 [6]. In general, every UML compliant
editor should be capable to support the SDL-UML profile, so that stereotypes
can be applied to elements of a model. But this is not sufficient enough to be
compliant to Z.109, because all defined constraints of the SDL-UML profile have
to be validated by the used modeling tool. In addition, the latest edition of
Z.109 defines a set of metaclasses for the representation of SDL expressions that
a compliant tool shall also implement. However, it is also desirable for the con-
venience of the user to support a textual notation, which makes the specification
of statements and expressions possible.

Different research activities have addressed the definition of UML profiles as
well as metamodels for SDL [1,11,17]. Even if the mentioned works cover different
aspects, a few important issues are still open. In particular, the representation
and mapping of expressions to the abstract syntax of SDL are not addressed.
Furthermore, a concrete syntax, the handling of its short-hand notations, and
its mapping to particular model elements are also not taken into account. Apart
from research activities, a few commercial tools [3,10,16] that claim to support
Z.109 exist. As far as information is publicly available, it can be concluded that

D. Amyot et al. (Eds.): SAM 2014, LNCS 8769, pp. 255–270, 2014.

the common approach is to translate UML diagrams to corresponding constructs at the concrete syntax level of SDL. In contrast, the SDL-UML Modeling and Validation (SU-MoVal) framework [13] translates the textual notation for statements and expressions to corresponding elements of SDL-UML. The advantage of such an approach is that an entire SDL-UML model can be validated at model-level and a straightforward mapping to the abstract syntax of SDL is feasible.

The SU-MoVal framework rests upon the Eclipse IDE [14] and supports the graphical as well as textual specification of SDL-UML models. In addition, the standard compliance of models can be validated with SU-MoVal by a set of constraints defined in Z.109. Furthermore, the editor for the textual notation of SU-MoVal can be used to specify statements and expressions. In order to realize the framework, various QVT [9] model transformations are implemented. Even though other technologies could be used for the purposes of model validation and transformation, as far as possible, only open and standardized technologies were taken into account for SU-MoVal. That is because the main objective of SU-MoVal is to be extensible and maintainable by other parties, hence the usage of proprietary technologies should be avoided.

The rest of this paper is structured as follows. In Section 2, a brief overview of the UML profile for SDL is given, before the SU-MoVal framework is introduced in detail in Section 3. After that, the merits and shortcomings of SU-MoVal and the latest edition of Z.109 are discussed in Section 4 and in Section 5 a conclusion and an outlook to future work is given.

2   Overview of the Most Recent Version of SDL-UML

Before the SU-MoVal framework is discussed in detail, a brief overview of the UML profile for SDL (SDL-UML) as specified in the latest edition of Z.109 [6] is given in this chapter.

2.1   Notational Conventions

Due to the fact that in the following chapters grammar and semantics related issues of different standards are discussed, for the sake of clarity the subsequent notational conventions apply.

- A name written within guillemets («...») refers to an instance of a stereotype of the SDL-UML profile [6]. Otherwise, if a name written within guillemets is followed by the word 'stereotype', the name refers to the corresponding stereotype of the SDL-UML profile.
- An underlined Name starting with a capital letter refers to a metaclass of the UML Superstructure [8]. In addition, a property of such a metaclass is represented by an underlined name starting with a lower-case character.

2.2 The SDL-UML Profile and Its Stereotypes

Apart from a set of stereotypes, the most recent version of SDL-UML as defined in Z.109 [6] defines a package of additional metaclasses for the specification of expressions and another one with predefined data types. Subsequently, a brief introduction to the different parts of the SDL-UML profile is given.

Specification of Structural Aspects. In general, a set of stereotypes of SDL-UML is dedicated to the specification of structural aspects so that SDL agents and associated data types can be defined.

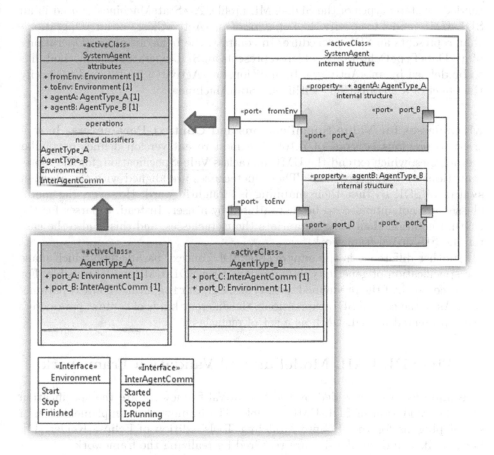

Fig. 1. Composite structure of an SDL-UML system model

As illustrated in Fig. 1, the central element of an SDL-UML model is an «ActiveClass» that represents an SDL system agent. Usually, this «ActiveClass» contains nested classifiers that define agent type definitions (represented by «ActiveClass»), interfaces (represented by «Interface»), data type definitions (represented by «DataTypeDefinition») and signals. In the given example, the nested classifiers of the `SystemAgent` «ActiveClass» are shown in terms of a class diagram. A further aspect that has to be specified is the internal structure of an «ActiveClass», which can be realized with a collaboration diagram as shown in Fig. 1. Usually, such a diagram only contains instances of the required «ActiveClass»es, its «Port»s and «Connector»s that are attached to them.

Specification of Behavior. For the behavior specification of an SDL-UML model, UML state machines and activities have to be used. Hence, appropriate metaclasses of the UML packages StateMachine, Activities, and Actions are extended by stereotypes of the SDL-UML profile. A «StateMachine» is used in an SDL-UML model to specify the behavior of an «ActiveClass» or an «Operation» that represents an SDL procedure. In contrast, the behavior of an «Operation» of a «DataTypeDefinition», which represents an SDL operator or a method, has to be defined by an «Activity». In addition, an «Activity» is also used to specify the effect of a «Transition» within a «StateMachine».

Metaclasses for Value Specifications and Context Parameters. In contrast to previous versions of Z.109, the most recent version defines particular metaclasses, which extend the UML metaclass ValueSpecification, for the representations of SDL expressions. These metaclasses are aligned with the abstract syntax of SDL so that their mapping is straightforward. However, the metaclasses are not intended to be instantiated by a user. Instead, a parser for the textual notation shall only instantiate the metaclasses, and this is also the case for the SU-MoVal framework.

Another difference is the support for SDL context parameters, which make the specification of generic type definitions for a SDL-UML model possible. For instance, some of the predefined data types, e.g., `String`, utilize context parameters. As in the case of SDL expressions, the different kinds of context parameters are represented in SDL-UML as a set of metaclasses.

3   The SDL-UML Modeling and Validation Framework

The main features provided by the SU-MoVal framework are the specification and the validation of SDL-UML models. The framework is implemented as a set of plug-ins for the 'Eclipse Modeling Tools' edition of Eclipse Kepler [14], because its standard plug-ins are required for realizing the framework.

Model Validation: One of the feature provided by SU-MoVal is the validation of SDL-UML models, which rests upon the OCL component of Eclipse. In order to validate models, constraints specified in the context of stereotypes and metaclasses of SDL-UML are evaluated. After validation, the result is displayed to the user in the 'Problems View' of Eclipse. Further details concerning the model validation are given in Section 3.1.

Modeling and Textual Notation: For the specification of structural and behavioral aspects of an SDL-UML model, a user is free to use the default UML
tree editor of Eclipse or the Papyrus UML modeling tool. Thanks to the extensibility mechanisms of EMF and UML, both tools can apply the SDL-UML profile
to a UML model without any customizations. However, only the UML tree editor
of Eclipse can directly display and instantiate the additional metaclasses defined
for SDL-UML. Also the validation component and the textual notation editor of
SU-MoVal can only be invoked from the UML tree editor at present. The textual
notation editor (see Section 3.2) of SU-MoVal can be accessed from the context
menu of the UML tree editor. The textual notation supports the specification
of SDL statements and expressions that are translated to corresponding SDL-
UML elements. At present, the textual notation editor only supports syntax
highlighting as well as type and syntax checks.

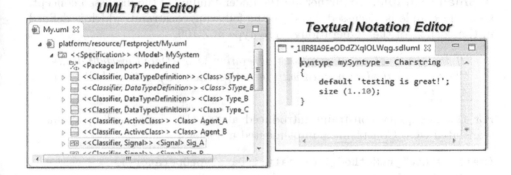

Fig. 2. The UML tree editor and the textual notation editor

Transformations: Before the textual notation editor can be invoked, required
type definitions of an SDL-UML model have to be extracted and transformed
into an internal format. For this purpose, a QVT transformation is executed
by the QVTo component of Eclipse. In addition, further QVT transformations
exist for mapping the textual notation to corresponding SDL-UML elements. All
implemented transformations of SU-MoVal are discussed in Section 3.3.

3.1 OCL-Based Model Validation

The model validation of SU-MoVal rests upon the build-in functionalities of
EMF. In order to define required constraints for the validation of an SDL-
UML model, the Object Constraint Language (OCL) [7] is utilized. The OCL
Constraints are specified in the context of stereotypes as well as metaclasses of
SDL-UML.

Challenges and Utilized Approach. For almost all stereotypes and meta-classes of SDL-UML as defined in Z.109 [6], constraints are specified in natural language. For an automatic validation by SU-MoVal, the constraints had to be manually translated to OCL Constraints, which are specified in terms of OCL Expressions. A challenge was that some of the constraints define complex conditions, which would entail large OCL Expressions. Furthermore, many constraints require the verification of similar conditions, which would also cause redundancies in corresponding OCL Expressions.

In order to cope with the challenge of too complex OCL Expressions and redundancies between them, a set of helper Operations owned by stereotypes and metaclasses of SDL-UML is specified. They implement common computations required and invoked by the Constraints. In general, the behavior of such an Operation is also implemented in terms of an OCL Expression.

A Small Example. To further aid the understanding of the discussed concept, a small example is discussed based on the following constraint, which is defined in the context of the «Operation» stereotype in Z.109:

> 'If the owner of an «Operation» Operation is a «DataTypeDefinition» Class, the method associated with the «Operation» Operation shall be an Activity.'

For the exemplary constraint introduced above, the corresponding manually translated OCL Constraint is implemented as follows:

```
(self.isDataTypeMethod() or self.isDataTypeOperator())
implies base_Operation.method
  ->forAll(isStereotypedBy('SDLUML::Activity'))
```

Only if the first or second condition specified in the first line of the constraint is fulfilled, the third condition after the **implies** keyword will also be verified. In all other cases, the constraint always evaluates to true. Both conditions specified in the first line are implemented in terms of calls to operations that encapsulate additional complex or large OCL Expressions. For instance, the OCL-based implementation of the first called Operation isDataTypeMethod() is defined as follows:

```
base_Operation.owner.oclAsType(uml::Classifier)
    .isImplicitlyStereotypedBy('SDLUML::DataTypeDefinition')
and self.isOperator = true
```

In the same way as for the discussed example, several common helper operations are also defined for other constraints, specified in Z.109 and requiring the computation of complex conditions.

Implemented Constraints and Operations. Even if most of the constraints specified in Z.109 could be translated to corresponding OCL <u>Expressions</u> and associated helper <u>Operations</u>, a small number of them could not be expressed in terms of OCL. That is because most of the affected constraints are formulated in a too general manner. Apart from OCL, Java was also used to implement helper operations, because the required functionality could not be implemented with OCL. A summary of the implemented constraints and operations is given in Table 1.

Table 1. Total number of constraints and operations

	Defined in Z.109	OCL implemented	Java implemented
Constraints	339	315	0
Operations	0	30	4

3.2   Editor for the Textual Notation

The textual notation editor (shown in Fig. 3) of SU-MoVal supports a subset of the concrete syntax of SDL so that the specification of statements and expressions is possible. Even if Appendix I of Z.109 [6] specifies an exemplary textual notation, this notation was not taken into account for the presented framework, because during its development the work for Appendix I had not been finished.

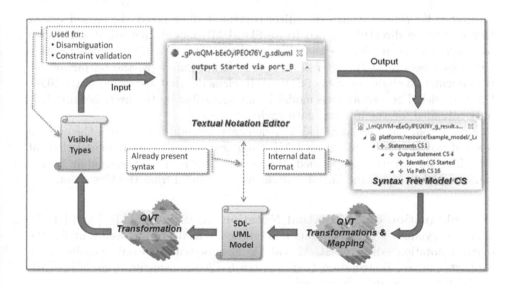

Fig. 3. Editor for the textual notation

The editor is generated by using the Spoofax Language Workbench [15], because its distinguished features fulfill most of the requirements already discussed in [2]. Apart from well-known features also provided by other editor construction kits, the Spoofax Language Workbench rests on a Scanner-less Generalized Left-Right (SGLR) parser that supports an efficient handling of syntax ambiguities by producing a parse forest instead of only a parse tree. If an ambiguity exists in the textual notation, a sub-tree for each syntactic alternative is produced so that the correct alternative can be selected after parsing.

Required Input and Output of the Editor. The textual notation editor has no direct access to an SDL-UML model so that required input and the output of the editor have to be transformed. The simplified workflow and the involved artifacts are illustrated in Fig. 3.

Extraction of Type Definitions. Type definitions specified in an SDL-UML model are utilized from the editor for disambiguating the syntax tree and for computing specified constraints of the textual notation (see Fig. 3). For this purpose, a particular QVT transformation is invoked, before the editor is opened. Starting from the element in an SDL-UML model for that a textual notation is specified, the transformation extracts all visible type definitions (see Section 3.3) and transforms them to an editor internal format. Later on, the extracted information can be accessed by the different components of the editor.

Output of the Editor. When the editor content shall be saved, the parsed syntax tree cannot be directly mapped to an SDL-UML model. Instead, it is mapped to a syntax tree model CS that is passed as input to a QVT transformation chain (see Section 3.3). After several transformation steps, the output of the transformation chain consists of SDL-UML elements that are stored in the SDL-UML model. The syntax tree model is not accessible by the user, because it is only intended for the internal data exchange.

Apart from the created SDL-UML elements, the editor also saves the entered textual notation in terms of an UML Comment owned by that model element for which the notation is specified. When the editor is opened once again for the same model element, the initial content will be loaded from the Comment.

Disambiguation of the Textual Notation. As discussed in [12] and [2], the concrete syntax of SDL contains ambiguities, which are also relevant for the textual notation editor of SU-MoVal. A disambiguation is only possible with context-sensitive information that is extracted from elements in an SDL-UML model before the editor is opened.

The relevant ambiguities of the textual notation are listed in Table 2. All ambiguities between the listed syntax alternatives are caused by the identifier parts (bold printed). When an ambiguity is identified, the disambiguation algorithm of the editor resolves the identifier within the list of visible type definitions.

Table 2. The different ambiguities

Alternative 1	Alternative 2
VariableAccess(**id**)	Literal(**id**)
TimerActiveExpression	ActiveAgentsExp(**id**)
CallStatement(ProcCallBody(**id**, ...))	CallStatement(RPCallBody(**id**, ...))
Destination_agentId(**id**)	Destination_pid(VariableAccess(**id**))

Constraints for the Textual Notation. Instead of utilizing an OCL-based approach as proposed in [2], the validation of constraints for the textual notation of SU-MoVal rests upon build-in capabilities of the Spoofax editor framework. The disadvantage of an OCL-based solution is a poor performance, because each time when the validation is invoked, the current parse tree has to be mapped to a new syntax tree model. In contrast, the constraint validation of Spoofax can directly operate on the internal parse tree. Hence, appropriate constraints are specified in terms of the Spoofax syntax. Subsequently, an example of such a constraint is given.

```
ResetClause(identifier, _)
  -> (identifier, $['[timerName]' must denote a timer!])
where
  timerName := <ID-to-fullQualifiedName> identifier;
  not(<is-timer-definition> identifier)
```

The purpose of the example constraint is to assure that the identifier of a reset clause refers to a visible timer definition. Therefore, a so-called matching rule (e.g., `ResetClause(identifier, _)`), which matches against a particular node in the syntax tree, has to be defined. If the matching condition is fulfilled, an error message will be created and displayed to the user. In addition, the corresponding location in the textual notation will be highlighted. As in the case of disambiguation, the component for constraint validation accesses the list of visible type definitions in order to determine correct type definitions.

3.3   QVT-Based Transformations

In order to implement required transformations at the level of SDL-UML and for the mapping of the textual notation to corresponding model elements, the Query/View/Transformation (QVT) [9] standard is utilized. In the following sections, an overview of the different kinds of transformations and their purposes within the SU-MoVal framework is given.

Challenges and Utilized Approach. Before going into details, general aspects of QVT, SDL-UML related challenges, and the utilized approach are discussed in this section.

General Aspects Concerning QVT. The QVT standard specifies two different kinds of transformation languages, namely the 'Relational Language' and the 'Operational Mappings'. The Relational Language makes it possible to specify bidirectional transformations between elements of different kinds of meta-models at a high level of abstraction, whereas the Operational Mappings are only unidirectional, but they are more powerful in their expressiveness. That is because Operational Mappings allow the specification of imperative expressions that can be utilized to define complex calculations. The following kinds of transformations are supported by Operational Mappings:

- **Model-to-Model Transformation:** For this kind of transformation, the source and target model are different. Typically, they are implemented as a complete rewrite system so that a particular mapping rule for each kind of element in the source and target model has to be present.
- **In-Place Transformation:** The same model is used as source and target for an in-place transformation. If only a few elements of a model shall be add or changed, the advantage of an in-place transformation is that there is no need to define a complete rewrite system. Instead, such transformations only consist of a small set of mapping rules.

SDL-UML Related Challenges. A case study concerning the general applicability of QVT for the transformation of SDL short-hand notations is already presented in [2]. However, this study covers only a small aspect concerning the applicability of QVT for mappings and transformations required in the context of SDL-UML. The main challenges that have to be taken into account for SU-MoVal are as follows:

1. **Transformation Models for Data Types:** A data type concept similar to that of the concrete syntax of SDL is defined for SDL-UML. Hence, relevant transformation models specified for SDL also apply for SDL-UML.
2. **Expansion of Short-Hand Notations:** So-called short-hand notations at the level of the textual notation have to be expanded to simpler constructs before further transformations or a mapping to SDL-UML elements are possible.
3. **Name Resolution:** Identifiers in the textual notation have to be resolved to fully qualified identifiers taking into account type definitions contained in an SDL-UML model.

Utilized Approach. The consequence of the challenges discussed above is that SDL-UML related transformations and mappings require complex computations. Therefore, only the Operational Mappings part of QVT is utilized for the SU-MoVal framework. That is because the Relational Language of QVT does not provide required syntactic constructs.

The QVT transformations of SU-MoVal are partitioned into two different transformation chains. One chain implements the transformation models associated with data types. The other chain realizes all transformations at the level of the textual notation and the mapping to SDL-UML elements. In addition, the

QVT transformations are implemented as in-place as well as model-to-model transformations.

Data Type Transformations. Since the data type concept of SDL-UML is similar to that of the concrete syntax of SDL, relevant transformation models specified for SDL data types also have to be applied to SDL-UML models. For the SU-MoVal framework, the required transformations are implemented as a transformation chain invoked before an SDL-UML model can be mapped to the abstract syntax of SDL or before the textual notation editor is used. The transformations $T_1 - T_3$ are implemented as in-place transformations applied to the same SDL-UML model, because only a few elements are added or changed by the transformations.

1. **Generic and implicit data type operations** are added by transformation T_1 that implements the relevant transformation models specified in Z.101 [4]. Transformation T_1 adds the two generic operations `equal` and `copy` to each «DataTypeDefinition». Furthermore, depending on the kind of a data type, also particular implicit operations have to be added. For instance, for `fieldA` of `Struct_A` shown in Fig. 4, a set of «Operation»s is introduced.
2. **Transformation of multi-valued properties** is realized by transformation T_2, because for SDL such a concept is not defined. Hence, the transformation model specified in Z.109 [6] is applied to elements that are stereotyped by «Property», «Parameter», or «Variable». For each multi-valued property, transformation T_2 creates a new «DataTypeDefinition» that subtypes an appropriated parameterized data type. In the given example, a new data type `Integer_Powerset` is created for `fieldA` of `Struct_A`. If the lowerValue is not 0 and/or the upperValue is not unbounded (specified by an *), an additional «Syntype» is introduced that restricts the bounds of the created «DataType-Definition» appropriately (e.g., `Integer_Powerset_1_10` in Fig. 4).
3. **Definition of inherited operations** is realized by transformation T_3 that implements the transformation model for inheritance specified in Z.102 [5]. Its purpose is to identify the set of inheritable «Operation»s and adding it to all subtypes of a «Classifier». In the given example, `method_A` of `SuperType` is inherited by `SubType`.

Mapping of the Textual Notation to SDL-UML Elements. In addition to the transformation chain for data types, a further chain (shown in Fig. 5) implements the mapping of the textual notation to corresponding elements of an SDL-UML model. Even if this chain is composed of several transformations invoked in sequential order, the chain can be divided into the following functional parts:

- Name resolution of identifiers (transformation T_4)
- Transformation of short-hand notations (transformations $T_5 - T_8$)
- Mapping of the textual notation to corresponding SDL-UML elements (transformation T_9)

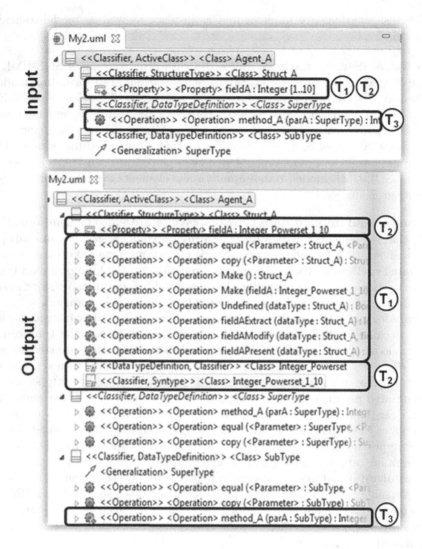

Fig. 4. Input and output of the data type transformation chain

Except for transformations T_4 and T_9, all other transformations shown in Fig. 5 are implemented as model-to-model (M2M) transformations. That is because for the transformation of short-hand notations at the level of the textual notation ($T_5 - T_8$), it is not only required to add or remove some elements in a concrete syntax model (CS). Instead, elements that correspond to a short-hand notation have to be transformed to other kinds of elements.

Name Resolution. Before short-hand notations can be expanded or the textual notation can be mapped to SDL-UML elements, all identifiers have to be resolved to qualified names, which is realized by in-place transformation T_5. Apart from

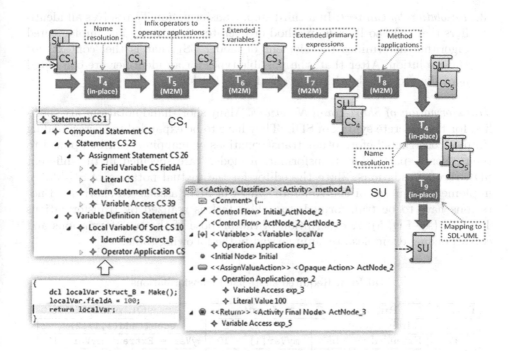

Fig. 5. Transformation chain for mapping the textual notation to SDL-UML

model CS_1, the SDL-UML model SU serves as further input required for the resolution of type definitions.

Transformation T_5 rests on the rules for name resolution specified in Z.101 [4]. However, for a proper adaption of the name resolution algorithm modifications were required. In particular, this is caused by the fact that in SDL-UML most of the type definitions are specified in terms of model elements, whereas in SDL this is realized at the concrete syntax level. Hence, the different parts of transformation T_5 are executed in the following order:

1. *Collection of Visible Type Definitions:* Starting from that SDL-UML element in model SU for which textual notation (represented by model CS_1) is specified, all visible model elements that represent type definitions (e.g., «DataTypeDefinition»s) are collected as a sequence of elements, taking into account the visibility rules of Z.101 [4].

2. *Resolution by Container:* This part resolves identifiers that are not referring to literals, operator or method signatures. At first, the 'container' for the resolution is identified. Usually, this is a particular element in the SDL-UML model M. However, the 'container' for local variable definitions can also be specified at the level of the textual notation (model CS_1). Hence, it is tried to resolve variable identifiers in model CS_1, before the algorithm proceeds in the SDL-UML model SU. For the resolution of all other kinds of identifiers, the sequence of visible type definitions (from step 1) is directly used.

3. *Resolution by Context*: In a third step, transformation T_5 resolves all identifiers that refer to literals, method or operator signatures. The implemented algorithm determines the element of model CS_1 that is the 'context' for the resolution. After that, the possible types for an identifier are computed according to the algorithm specified in Z. 101 [4].

Transformation of Short-Hand Notations. Many short-hand notations are specified for the concrete syntax of SDL. They have to be expanded to corresponding simpler constructs before other transformations or mappings can be applied to them. Hence, particular 'transformation models' are specified in the different SDL recommendations. Since the editor for the textual notation of SU-MoVal implements a subset of the concrete syntax of SDL, associated short-hand notations have to be transformed, too. This task is realized by transformations $T_5 - T_8$ (see Fig. 5). A description of the purpose of the transformations and corresponding examples are summarized in the following table.

Table 3. Required short-hand transformations

Transf.	Purpose	Input	Output
T_5	Infix operators	`(1 + 1) = 2`	`equal(add(1,1),2)`
T_6	Extended variables	`myVar[1] = 10`	`myVar = Extract(myVar, 10)`
T_7	Extended primary	`myVar[0]`	`Extract(myVar, 0)`
T_8	Method applications	`myVar.method_A()`	`method_A(myVar)`

Mapping of the Textual Notation to SDL-UML Elements. Before the mapping of model CS_5 to corresponding elements of the SDL-UML model SU, transformation T_4 has to be applied once again. That is because as a result of the transformation of short-hand notations, a lot of new operator application expressions are introduced and their identifiers need to be resolved, too. Afterward, each node of CS_5 is mapped to a corresponding SDL-UML element in model SU by in-place transformation T_9. All elements are added below that element in model SU for which the textual notation is specified. An example of the mapping of the textual notation to corresponding SDL-UML elements is given in Fig. 5.

Performance Issues. The execution of QVT transformations with the standard distribution of Eclipse QVTo rests on a two staged process. First of all, a transformation is compiled to an abstract syntax model of QVT and afterwards this model is interpreted. During the implementation of the SU-MoVal framework, it had been observed that the task of compilation takes approximately 75 percent of the entire execution time for a transformation. In order to increase the performance of SU-MoVal significantly, a patched version of QVTo is utilized, which makes it possible to directly execute a compiled transformation. In consequence, the compilation step of QVTo is never invoked and they are directly interpreted for all transformations discussed earlier.

4   Merits and Shortcomings

In this section, a brief summary of the merits and shortcomings concerning the SU-MoVal framework and Z.109 observed during the implementation is given. The identified shortcomings concerning Z.109 could be addressed by a revision of this recommendation in order to improve its applicability.

SU-MoVal Related Issues: The SU-MoVal framework has proved the general implementability of the latest edition of Z.109 [6]. An advantage of the framework is the possibility to validate an entire SDL-UML model based on the constraints specified in Z.109. In addition, the textual notation for statements and expressions decreases the time for specifying an SDL-UML model, because corresponding SDL-UML model elements do not have to be modeled in a graphical manner. Current drawbacks of SU-MoVal are the missing mapping to the abstract syntax of SDL and a subsequent code generation. In addition, a better integration into the Papyrus tool would be desirable in order to improve the usability.

Z.109 Related Issues: A notable feature of the latest edition of Z.109 is the representation of SDL expressions in terms of dedicated metaclasses so that an entire SDL-UML model can be validated and mapped to the abstract syntax of SDL in a straightforward manner. A drawback of the current edition of the recommendation is that some stereotypes, e.g., «ActiveClass» or «Pseudostate», represents different SDL constructs. In consequence, a contextual distinction within constraints and transformations is required for these stereotypes. A solution could be to introduce additional sub-stereotypes for each particular SDL construct (similar to the «DataTypeDefinition» stereotype). Furthermore, it could be considered to integrate the OCL constraint specifications of SU-MoVal in a new edition of Z.109.

5   Conclusion and Future Work

The presented SU-MoVal framework supports a textual notation for the specification of SDL statements and expressions as well as a mapping of them to corresponding SDL-UML elements. Apart from the textual specification of statements and expressions, the framework also provides a possibility to directly edit a model with the UML tree editor of Eclipse or the graphical UML modeling tool Papyrus. In addition, the validation of an entire SDL-UML model is supported, too.

For the future, it is planned to extend the presented framework with a mapping of SDL-UML elements to corresponding abstract syntax elements of SDL. In addition, the provided features of the editor for the textual notation shall be extended. Interested persons can obtain the latest version of the SU-MoVal source code from [13].

References

1. Grammes, R.: Formalisation of the UML Profile for SDL – A Case Study. Technical Report 352/06, Department of Computer Science, University of Kaiserslautern (2006)
2. Kraas, A.: A Model-Based Formalization of the Textual Notation for SDL-UML. In: Ober, I., Ober, I. (eds.) SDL 2011. LNCS, vol. 7083, pp. 218–232. Springer, Heidelberg (2011)
3. IBM: IBM Rational SDL and TTCN Suite 6.3, User Manual (April 2009)
4. International Telecommunication Union: Recommendation Z.101 (12/11), Specification and Description Language – Basic SDL-2010, http://www.itu.int/rec/T-REC-Z.101/en
5. International Telecommunication Union: Recommendation Z.102 (12/11), Specification and Description Language – Comprehensive SDL-2010, http://www.itu.int/rec/T-REC-Z.102/en
6. International Telecommunication Union: Recommendation Z.109 (10/13), Specification and Description Language – Unified modeling language profile for SDL-2010, http://www.itu.int/rec/T-REC-Z.109/en
7. Object Management Group: Object Constraint Language (OCL). Version 2.4. OMG Document Number: formal/2014-02-03, http://www.omg.org/spec/OCL/2.4/PDF
8. Object Management Group: OMG Unified Modeling Language (OMG UML), Superstructure. Version 2.4.1. OMG Document Number: formal/2011-08-06, http://www.omg.org/spec/UML/2.4.1/Superstructure/PDF
9. Object Management Group: Meta Object Facility (MOF) 2.0 Query/View/Transformation Specification. Version 1.1. OMG Document Number: formal/2011-01-01, http://www.omg.org/spec/QVT/1.1/PDF/
10. Pragmadev: Real Time Developer Studio User Manual, Real Time Developer Studio V4.3, www.pragmadev.com/downloads/UserManual.pdf
11. Prinz, A., Scheidgen, M., Tveit, M.: A Model-Based Standard for SDL. In: Gaudin, E., Najm, E., Reed, R. (eds.) SDL 2007. LNCS, vol. 4745, pp. 1–18. Springer, Heidelberg (2007)
12. Schmitt, M.: The Development of a Parser for SDL-2000. In: Proceedings of the Tenth GI/ITG Technical Meeting on Formal Description Techniques for Distributed Systems, pp. 131–142. Shaker Verlag (2009)
13. SDL-UML Modeling and Validation (SU-MoVal) framework, http://www.su-moval.org/
14. The Eclipse Foundation, Eclipse Kepler (4.3.2) – Eclipse Modeling Tools, http://www.eclipse.org/downloads/packages/eclipse-modeling-tools/keplersr2
15. The Spoofax Language Workbench, Spoofax 1.1, http://strategoxt.org/Spoofax/
16. UniqueSoft, UniqueSoft Modeling Tool Suite, http://www.uniquesoft.com/modeling-tool-suite.html
17. Werner, C., Kraatz, S., Hogrefe, D.: A UML Profile for Communicating Systems. In: Gotzhein, R., Reed, R. (eds.) SAM 2006. LNCS, vol. 4320, pp. 1–18. Springer, Heidelberg (2006)

SDL Implementations for Wireless Sensor Networks – Incorporation of PragmaDev's RTDS into the Deterministic Protocol Stack BiPS

Tobias Braun, Dennis Christmann, Reinhard Gotzhein, and Alexander Mäter

Networked Systems Group
University of Kaiserslautern, Germany
{tbraun,christma,gotzhein,a_mater09}@cs.uni-kl.de

Abstract. Predictable behavior of wireless sensor networks calls for deterministic protocols for network-wide synchronization and collision-free frame transmissions. Furthermore, the execution of these protocols requires tight scheduling under real-time constraints. In previous work, we have devised a framework called BiPS (Black-burst-Integrated Protocol Stack), which provides these functionalities. To achieve the required real-time behavior, BiPS has been implemented manually on bare hardware.

Higher-layer functionalities such as routing protocols or sensor applications are far less time-critical. Therefore, we strive for applying model-driven development, using SDL as abstract modeling language, and commercial tool environments to automatically generate implementations. In this paper, we present how we incorporate implementations generated with PragmaDev's Real-time Developer Studio (RTDS) into BiPS. Therefore, we have modified and extended the RTDS transition scheduler, and have placed it under the control of the BiPS scheduler. Furthermore, based on RTDS concepts, we have implemented an SDL environment that can access BiPS functionality, e.g., protocols of the MAC layer or hardware devices. In experiments on a wireless sensor node, we have demonstrated that our integration is fully operational and has advantages regarding efficiency and predictability.

1 Introduction

Though some time has passed since Wireless Sensor Networks (WSNs) have become a topic in research and industry, new application domains – e.g., in industrial and health care environments – increase their demands on the realization of such systems. In this regard, an ongoing trend is to develop WSNs for scenarios, in which communication among nodes must fulfill a predictable quality-of-service, which requires protocols and implementations to behave deterministically. Moreover, WSN nodes typically have strong hardware and energy limitations. Consequently, protocols and their implementations must also be efficient, thereby impeding the already challenging task.

To realize and evaluate deterministic protocols for WSNs, we have developed a protocol framework called *Black burst-Integrated Protocol Stack* (BiPS). BiPS

D. Amyot et al. (Eds.): SAM 2014, LNCS 8769, pp. 271–286, 2014.

provides several deterministic protocols, an application interface to access these protocols, and basic functionalities of an operating system (OS) to support distributed applications. Because several protocols provided by BiPS require time-critical execution, we have implemented BiPS manually and on bare hardware, i.e., without underlying operating system, to retain full control over hardware interrupts. For applications or higher-layer protocols, timing requirements are usually less strict, so hand-coding is often not required. Therefore, we have decided to adopt a model-driven approach, with SDL [16] as design language, which improves abstraction, reusability, and productivity. More specifically, we use PragmaDev's Real-time Developer Studio (RTDS, [20]), and interface BiPS with SDL implementations automatically generated with RTDS.

To incorporate SDL implementations into BiPS, we had, in the first instance, to realize the scheduling of the SDL systems in a way that does not compromise time-critical operations of BiPS. This was achieved by introducing a scheduling hierarchy, in which SDL runs with lower priority than more critical parts of BiPS. In a further step, an SDL environment implementation became necessary to integrate SDL systems into the data flow of BiPS's communication stack. Different to our previous work on SDL implementations [10], where the objective was conformance with SDL's formal ASM semantics and evaluation of language extensions, we now target timeliness, efficiency, and flexibility.

Our approach clearly states a trade-off between the pros and cons of hand-written and model-driven implementations. For several reasons, realizing BiPS in a fully model-driven way is no option: First, predictability and efficiency are no objectives of SDL, and are hardly achievable with automatically generated implementations. This is also a result of [2], where IEEE 802.15.4 [14] implementations are compared. Second, BiPS includes very platform-specific parts, making reusability as a major advantage of model-driven development obsolete.

The remainder of this paper is structured as follows: Section 2 presents an outline of BiPS and its interfaces. In Sect. 3, the integration of SDL implementations into BiPS is described in detail. Section 4 presents results of experimental evaluations with a small distributed system. After providing a survey of related work (Sect. 5), Sect. 6 concludes the paper and outlines future work.

2 Black Burst-Integrated Protocol Stack – Deterministic Protocols for Wireless Sensor Networks

The Black burst-Integrated Protocol Stack (BiPS) is a protocol framework for wireless sensor nodes [9]. By integrating Black Burst Synchronization (BBS) [12], BiPS achieves network-wide synchronization with bounded offset and bounded convergence delay, which paves the way for deterministic MAC protocols for multi-hop WSNs. BiPS additionally provides basic OS functionalities and an interface for applications in order to decouple time-critical protocol functionality from higher-layer protocols and applications. Up to now, BiPS includes four MAC protocols and has been implemented on the Imote 2 sensor platform [17], which is equipped with an IEEE 802.15.4-compliant [14] transceiver.

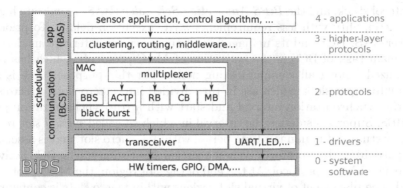

Fig. 1. BiPS architecture: interplay of applications, protocols, and schedulers

2.1 Overview

The architecture of BiPS is shown in Fig. 1. It is based on a layered structure and enables higher layers to abstract from the realization of lower layers. Execution is controlled by two schedulers (see Sect. 2.2). In layer 0, BiPS provides low level functionality to interact with the hardware. Among other things, this includes control of hardware timers and activation of DMA transfers. Layer 1 comprises hardware drivers for peripheral devices. This, particularly, includes a driver for the wireless transceiver, which is used by all MAC protocols of BiPS.

While layer 0 and 1 are hardware-specific by nature, layer 2, which incorporates all supported MAC protocols, abstracts from hardware details in most instances. However, full abstraction is not possible, because hardware limitations – e.g., the transceiver's transfer rate and switching delays – must be considered to calculate transmission delays and guard times. Currently, the MAC layer consists of a synchronization protocol (BBS), a contention-based protocol (CB), which is similar to Carrier Sense Multiple Access with Collision Avoidance (CSMA/CA), and three deterministic protocols: a reservation- and TDMA-based protocol (RB), the Arbitrating and Cooperative Transfer Protocol (ACTP) [6], and a protocol for mode-based communication (MB) [5]. Since both BBS and ACTP rely on a communication primitive called *black burst*, this functionality is encapsulated in a separate component.

Access to BiPS's MAC protocols is via a multiplexer (see Sect. 2.3), which realizes a homogeneous interface for higher-layer protocols (layer 3) and applications (layer 4). Time-criticality on these layers is usually less stringent, thereby enabling model-driven development of these layer – e.g., with SDL – and to focus on reusability and modularity.

2.2 Scheduling in BiPS

The execution of BiPS is controlled by two schedulers: The *BiPS Communication Scheduler* (BCS), which is responsible for running time-critical components of the protocol stack, and the *BiPS Application Scheduler* (BAS) to execute higher-layer functionality with less requirements w.r.t. execution delays. To prioritize BCS over BAS, BCS and its managed components run in interrupt mode.

The main task of BCS is the activation of MAC protocols, which has to be synchronized among all communicating nodes. For this purpose, time is subdivided into super slots, which are in turn divided into macro slots. Macro slots define the synchronization interval and start with a (re-)synchronization phase using BBS. Super slots define the interval in which so-called *virtual slot regions* recur. A virtual slot region is a time period within a macro slot that is associated with a particular MAC protocol. When a virtual slot region starts, BCS activates the associated MAC protocol. At the end of the slot region, the MAC protocol is stopped. The placement of virtual slot regions within macro slots is configurable and is based on the need of an application. If high data rates must be guaranteed, a possible super slot configuration would contain macro slots with many virtual regions, which are associated with the RB protocol. In parts of macro slots where no virtual slot region is placed, BCS switches the wireless transceiver off. Thereby, BiPS supports duty cycling with high flexibility. A further task of BCS is the deactivation of low-priority interrupts during time-critical sections. This affects, e.g., UART (Universal Asynchronous Receiver Transmitter) interrupts, which are suspended during synchronization phases.

BAS is an event-based non-preemptive scheduler for higher-layer functionalities. It is small-scale, since it does not manage processes or threads but handles function callbacks. To manage a component – i.e., an application or higher-layer protocol – by BAS, the component has to register one or several callbacks, which are identified in BAS by a unique id. To trigger the execution of this component, BAS provides an event system with a function called EVENT_emit, which must be called with the id of the corresponding callback. BAS, in turn, considers this execution request at the next scheduling decision. Since EVENT_emit can be invoked in interrupt mode, the function provides an interface to continue the processing of an event, which is announced in interrupt mode, after leaving the interrupt context. This is, for instance, used after the reception of a data frame, which is indicated by a MAC protocol running in interrupt mode, but should not entirely be handled in interrupt mode by higher-layer protocols due to its possibly costly processing.

2.3   BiPS Multiplexer – The MAC Data Interface for Applications

To temporally decouple applications from MAC protocols and to enable a loose coupling of MAC protocols in the framework, a multiplexer is introduced in BiPS. The multiplexer provides a homogeneous interface to all MAC protocols, though properties of a single transmission, which can be initiated by applications, may differ depending on the used MAC protocol.

The multiplexer comprises a set of TX queues – called TX transmission opportunities (TX TOs) – to store outgoing transmissions until the corresponding MAC protocol is activated. If an application or higher-layer protocol intends to transmit a frame, it does not invoke the MAC protocol directly, but enqueues

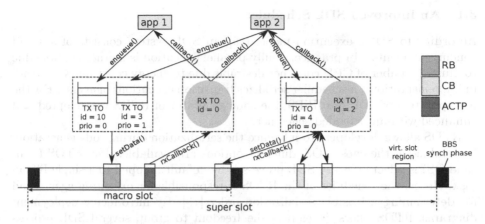

Fig. 2. Transmission opportunities in BiPS's multiplexer as application interface

the frame in a TX TO, which is addressed by an identifier and associated with a set of virtual slot regions. Several TX TOs can be assigned to the same virtual slot region, where each TX TO has a priority assigned. When a new virtual slot region begins, the first frame of the associated TX TO with highest priority is transferred to the MAC protocol that is responsible for this slot region. This protocol then tries to send the frame and informs the multiplexer about success or failure afterwards, which in turn informs the initiator, i.e., the application or higher-layer protocol, of the transmission. Similar to TX TOs, the multiplexer provides RX TOs, where applications can register a callback, which is invoked if data is received in an associated slot region.

The interplay of TX/RX TOs and applications, and the association of TOs to virtual slot regions is illustrated in Fig. 2. In this example, two applications access the multiplexer of BiPS, which comprises three TX TOs and two RX TOs. The super slot consists of two macro slots and six virtual slot regions. The example, particularly, highlights the following additional properties: First, one application can use several TX and RX TOs. Furthermore, TX/RX TOs can be associated with several slot regions. Thereby, BiPS enables a flexible mapping of transmissions to virtual slot regions and allows applications and higher-layer protocols to abstract from MAC protocol details like the placement of reserved transmission slots.

3   Interfacing PragmaDev's RTDS and BiPS

The integration of SDL systems into BiPS consists of two parts. First, code of the SDL system, which is automatically generated with PragmaDev's RTDS [20], has to be scheduled and executed without disturbing time-critical operations of underlying BiPS layers (Sect. 3.1). The second part covers the development of a flexible data interface between BiPS and the SDL system by providing a tailored but extensible SDL environment (Sect. 3.2).

3.1   An Improved SDL Scheduler

According to SDL's execution model [15], an SDL system consists of a set of concurrent agents[1]. In practice, a fully parallel execution is neither possible due to limited number of CPU cores nor desirable due to energy constraints. Instead, in implementations, a scheduler serializes transition executions of agents. For the incorporation of SDL into BiPS, the code generator of RTDS was adopted and enhanced with an extended scheduler.

RTDS allows developers to influence the serialization during code generation. Depending on the chosen OS, different options are available. If an RTOS (real-time OS) is selected, every SDL process is by default mapped to a single RTOS task. Hence, the scheduler of the RTOS is responsible for executing agents and for determining a feasible serialization order [19]. By introducing deployment diagrams, RTDS offers developers the freedom to group several SDL process instances into a single RTOS task. Since there is no parallelism within a task, an additional scheduler is required for intra-task scheduling. For executing SDL systems on bare systems, the single task solution has to be chosen due to its independence from external schedulers. Since this approach results in a mostly self-contained system, it is – together with RTDS's *rtosless* template – an ideal starting point for our BiPS integration. To interface the scheduler with BiPS, we have developed a new scheduler called BiPS SDL Scheduler (BSS), which is a modified and extended variant of PragmaDev's *CPPScheduler*.

Similar to *CPPScheduler*, BSS holds a global signal queue, which stores all pending SDL signals in FIFO order. The signals are processed in a non-preemptive way by executing corresponding target SDL processes. Since all processes are situated in the same address space, scheduling and execution of transitions does not require context switches. Timers are also stored in a global timer queue and ordered by their expiration. To prevent delay of time-critical operations of underlying BiPS layers, a scheduling hierarchy has been established, in which BAS executes BSS. Hence, BSS is, in terms of BiPS, just an interruptible application, whose execution is triggered via the event system of BAS.

The time basis of the SDL system and BSS, respectively, is not based on system ticks but derived from a hardware timer. Thereby, granularity of time is very fine (currently $1\,\mu s$) and coincides with time in other parts of BiPS. In this regard, it has also to be noted that different to the interpretation of SDL's SET construct in RTDS, which only accepts relative durations, we interpret the time value in SET as absolute time. Though our implementation supports the reconstitution of the original behavior by configuration[2], we feel confident that absolute times are more appropriate, since they are not prone to execution delays.

Figure 3 shows the realization of BSS in detail. After BAS starts the execution of BSS, the SDL time (represented by the keyword NOW in SDL) is updated with

---

[1] While SDL's semantics introduces several types of agents, most available SDL implementations support only SDL agents derived from SDL processes.

[2] Because in the implementation, RTDS uses the same data type for time and duration, the decision is an "either-or" one. Thus, we can not support absolute and relative times in SET.

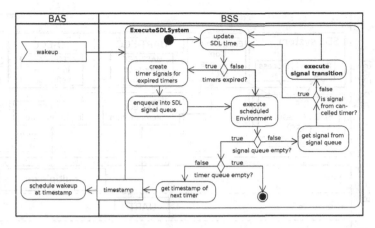

Fig. 3. UML activity diagram of the BSS

the hardware timer value. Then, for each expired timer, the respective SDL signal is created and stored in the SDL signal queue. Afterwards, if the environment has outstanding tasks, it is executed and its generated SDL signals are stored in the signal queue. Then, the first signal of the signal queue is processed by executing the respective SDL transition[3]. These steps are repeated until the signal queue is empty. In this case, BSS uses BAS to set its wake up time to the next timer expiration and returns the execution control back to BAS.

Besides timer events, other events – e.g., the reception of frames via the multiplexer – can wake up BSS to execute the SDL system (see also Sect. 3.2). If these events are announced by hardware interrupts, the event system of BAS is used to delay the events' processing until leaving interrupt mode.

3.2 Interfacing the SDL Environment

The SDL environment represents the interface between SDL system and underlying platform and is, for instance, used to access hardware peripherals. Communication between SDL system and SDL environment is asynchronous and via SDL signals that are sent over channels connected to the border of the SDL system. RTDS provides a basic template of the SDL environment, which is implemented as an independent SDL process. We have extended this template and have developed a modular and efficient SDL environment framework, which integrates so-called *Environment Control Components* (ECC). These are either hardware drivers or components to access further functionality of the underlying OS. Currently, this framework supports BiPS and basics of Linux. W.r.t. BiPS, ECCs are either hardware drivers, glue code to connect existing BiPS hardware

---

[3] SDL signals, which are saved in the process' current state, are also removed from the signal queue, buffered in a separate queue, and moved back to the signal queue after processing the last signal. Enabling conditions are not supported by RTDS.

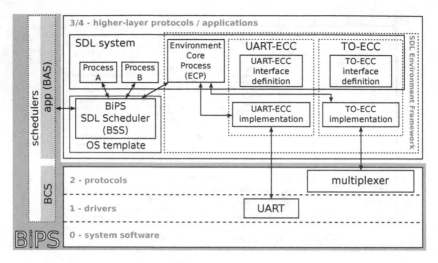

Fig. 4. Interface between SDL systems and BiPS

drivers, or interfaces to core functionalities of BiPS like access to TOs of the communication stack.

ECCs are self-contained and interact with the SDL system through the exchange of SDL signals. Hence, each ECC consists of two parts: interface definition and implementation. The interface definition is encapsulated in an SDL package and defines signal types and data structures to access an ECC's functionalities from within the SDL system. The implementation, on the other hand, is realized in C++. An ECC is executed by the SDL *Environment Core Process* (ECP) if an associated signal arrives in the environment or if the ECC requests an execution. This is, for instance, the case if a hardware interrupt has previously informed about an event, which has to be processed further.

Figure 4 shows an SDL system's structure with the new environment framework, and the interconnection with BiPS. The example includes two ECCs: The UART-ECC enables to access the hardware UART devices by utilizing the corresponding hardware driver of BiPS. The TO-ECC provides access to the multiplexer – and, thus, to the MAC protocols – of BiPS to send frames via the wireless channel and to forward received frames to the SDL system.

Similar to all other SDL processes, ECP is controlled by BSS, yet it does not consume SDL signals by itself but forwards them to the responsible ECC. During build time, compiler macros provided by the RTDS code generator are inspected to determine all required ECCs in order to compile and link them. Since extensibility has been one of the key requirements during design of the environment, we adopt a slightly modified variant of the well-known observer pattern [11] for a loose coupling between ECP and ECCs. The resulting class structure of the environment is shown by the UML diagram in Fig. 5. A new instantiated ECC first registers all accepted signal types it can process at the ECP by calling `registerSignal`. Hence, it acts as observer and the ECP

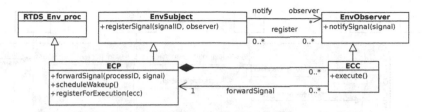

Fig. 5. UML class diagram of the environment framework

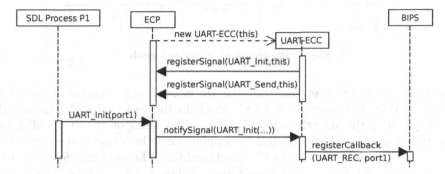

Fig. 6. Interplay of UART-ECC with BiPS, ECP, and an exemplary SDL process

forwards all signals received from the SDL system to the responsible ECC by calling `notifySignal` or discards them if there is no responsible ECC. The sequence diagram in Fig. 6 illustrates these steps for the UART-ECC.

To reduce overhead during runtime, RTDS determines target processes of SDL signals during code generation by using information about channels and signal paths in the SDL system. Therefore, generated code does not contain any equivalents to signal paths or channels, but target processes of signals are addressed by process identifiers. As consequence, such identifiers have also to be used to send SDL signals from ECP and ECCs to responsible SDL processes in the SDL system. To derive process identifiers from within the environment implementation, the names of SDL processes can be used, since RTDS provides a mapping between SDL process names and identifiers by C macros. This is often suggested as state-of-the-practice solution but dictates the designer to follow a – possibly undesired – naming convention. This also misleads to *dummy* processes in SDL specifications, which are only introduced to fulfill the naming convention and to forward signals to the actual target process.

In our opinion, a better and more generic solution is to use the observer pattern again. By enabling SDL processes to register themselves for signal types at ECCs during system startup, signals from the environment can be addressed to arbitrarily named processes. Thereby, neither ECCs nor the SDL system has to rely on naming conventions, and reusability of SDL system specifications is improved. To register signals at ECCs, SDL initialization signals are introduced, which are sent by SDL processes to the environment and contain the signal

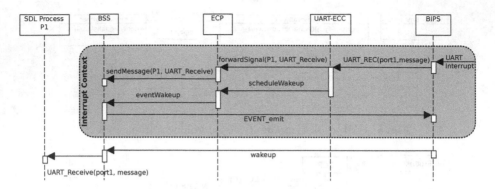

Fig. 7. Reception of incoming signals

type, for which the SDL process wants to subscribe. These signals are forwarded by the ECP to the responsible ECC, which in turn associates the requested signal type with the id of the sending process. Depending on the ECC, different subscribe signals or additional signal parameters may be introduced to enable a fine-granular distinction of an ECC's functionalities. This option is, for instance, used by the UART-ECC, which operates on all three UART ports of our Imote 2 platform but allows the subscription to single UART ports. Note that in this case, SDL signals of the same signal type, which have been generated due to data received on different UART ports, can be addressed to different SDL processes.

An example of the registration process is shown in Fig. 6. Here, SDL process P1 subscribes for the reception of incoming messages on UART port 1. The UART-ECC then registers its own callback at the UART driver provided by BiPS, which is invoked by the driver when data arrives on this port.

In the programming model of BiPS, events – like expirations of hardware timers or received frames – are indicated by a hardware interrupt, which suspends regular execution immediately to execute the associated interrupt handler. If the event is less time-critical, interrupt mode should, however, be left as fast as possible to preserve time-critical operations of BiPS's communication stack. Thus, only necessary operations should be performed and the event system of BAS should be used to continue event processing after leaving the interrupt mode. This strategy is adopted by ECCs to interact with BiPS in a compliant way. For this purpose, ECCs first register their own handler functions as callbacks in BiPS (see, e.g., UART-ECC in Fig. 6), which will be invoked in interrupt mode if a corresponding event occurs. If one of these handlers is executed, the ECC only performs short operations like storing data. As last step in the callback, they request the execution of BSS – and, thus, of the SDL system and of themselves – by calling the `scheduleWakeup` method provided by the ECP, which finally calls `EVENT_emit` of the event system of BAS. As soon as the interrupt mode is left, BAS executes the SDL system by starting BSS.

Figure 7 continues the scenario of Fig. 6 by presenting the handling of an incoming UART message. The message triggers a hardware interrupt and, therefore, causes the switching into interrupt mode. After the SDL signal has been created and inserted into the signal queue of BSS, ECC/ECP requests to wakeup BSS, which is then started by the BAS (depicted as part of BiPS in the figure) after the interrupt handler terminates.

4   Evaluation of SDL's Integration into BiPS

To evaluate SDL's integration into BiPS, we have conducted experiments with a distributed system providing TDMA-based medium access. The objectives of these experiments are twofold: First, functionalities of BSS, the interface between SDL time and hardware timer, and the SDL environment implementation are evaluated. Furthermore, we want to show that the presented hybrid integration approach with hand-written time-critical protocol functionalities and model-driven higher-layer functionalities has advantages over purely model-driven approaches regarding delays and predictability.

4.1   Evaluation Setup

Nodes in the experiments are Imote 2 sensor platforms [17]. They are based on Marvel's XScale processor PXA271 running with up to 416 MHz and are equipped with 256 kB SRAM, 32 MB SDRAM, and 32 MB Flash memory. Communication among nodes is performed with the integrated IEEE 802.15.4-compliant CC2420 transceiver. The evaluated scenario is illustrated in Fig. 8 and consists of three Imote 2. One of the nodes is depicted as master and synchronizes the network. Communication occurs in two pre-defined transmission slots and is originated by one of the slaves. In each slot, one frame is sent. To compare our hybrid solution to a purely model-driven approach with SDL, we have realized the scenario in two ways:

1. In the realization called SDL-MAC, synchronization and medium slotting are specified and implemented with SDL. This realization does not rely on functionalities of the BiPS MAC layer but uses drivers, system software, and the application scheduler of BiPS only. Synchronization is – similar to IEEE 802.15.4 [14] – based on beacon frames. For this purpose, an ECC is developed to interconnect BiPS's CC2420 driver with the SDL system. After detecting a frame's SFD (Start of Frame Delimiter), the CC2420 driver invokes a callback of this ECC, which in turn generates an SDL signal that

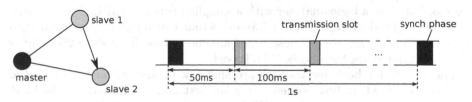

Fig. 8. Topology and medium slotting of the scenario

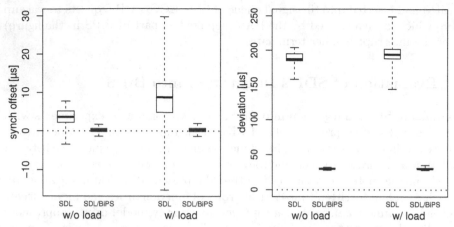

(a) Synchronization offset between slaves. (b) Deviation of data frames' transmission time from nominal transmission time.

Fig. 9. Evaluation results

is sent to the SDL system. Thereby, master, which sends beacon frames, and slaves can synchronize to the SFD, which is according to the data sheet signalized by the transceiver with an accuracy of about $3\,\mu s$.

2. The realization called `SDL/BiPS-MAC` utilizes the entire protocol stack of BiPS. Synchronization is performed by BBS. Data frames are still generated and consumed in an SDL system, which runs now on top of the BiPS MAC layer. Thus, different to `SDL-MAC`, data transfer is via TO-ECC, BiPS multiplexer, and the reservation-based MAC protocol.

SDL timers in the systems are set with absolute values (see Sect. 3.1). To evaluate the impact of load, we execute both realizations also with load, which is generated by additional SDL processes and very low (about 80 signals/sec).

4.2   Results

The systems are executed with and without load for a duration of 1000 seconds. Regarding results, we concentrate on two aspects: First, we investigate synchronization offset between slave 1 and slave 2 with `SDL-MAC` and `SDL/BiPS-MAC`. For this purpose, both slaves signalize synchronization via GPIO pins, which are monitored by a logic analyzer with a sampling rate of 50 MHz. Furthermore, we analyze the deviation of data frames' actual transmission time from their nominal transmission time. These times are determined from slave 2's point of view and printed via the node's UART port.

The results for both realizations are shown with and without load by box plots in Fig. 9, where box borders mark the first and third quartile. The black lines inside each box are medians. Whiskers mark min/max values.

The synchronization offset shown in Fig. 9(a) illustrates that even without load, the offset achieved by SDL-MAC (between $-3.4\,\mu s$ and $7.7\,\mu s$) is higher than with the hand-written BBS implementation of SDL/BiPS-MAC (between $-1.3\,\mu s$ and $1.7\,\mu s$). The gap even increases when the systems are executed with load. In this case, offset with SDL-MAC is between $-15.2\,\mu s$ and $29.8\,\mu s$, whereas offset with SDL/BiPS-MAC remains almost unchanged.

Similar outcomes can be observed regarding compliance with transmission slots, which are presented in Fig. 9(b). Here, the average deviation from the actual transmission time is with SDL-MAC more than 6 times higher than with the hand-written implementation of the reservation-based protocol in SDL/BiPS-MAC. In addition, variability is much higher with SDL-MAC: $46\,\mu s$ vs. $4\,\mu s$ without load and $105\,\mu s$ vs. $7\,\mu s$ with load. Thus, it can be concluded that SDL/BiPS-MAC is less prone to background load in the SDL system, whereas with SDL-MAC, the execution of the SDL transition, which initiates the frame transmission, is delayed due to load. Though the amount of load is very low in the presented scenario, the increase of variability is already clearly perceptible with SDL-MAC. It can furthermore be assumed that deviations will get worse if load is increased. The reason why the deviation also increases slightly for SDL/BiPS-MAC can be found in shared data structures of the SDL runtime and the BiPS multiplexer. In order to access them in a consistent way, interrupts have to be disabled temporarily, thereby deferring the processing of hardware interrupts and time-critical protocol parts of BiPS. For this reason, it is crucial to keep the times, in which interrupts are disabled, very small. However, since these times are almost constant, deviations with SDL/BiPS-MAC will hardly deteriorate with increasing load.

In summary, synchronization and compliance with transmission slots are much more accurate with the hybrid integration than with the pure SDL solution. Furthermore, the hybrid solution is almost imperceptible for load in the SDL system, thereby improving predictability of the overall system behavior.

5 Related Work

Before SDL systems can run on hardware, implementations must be derived from the specification. But although SDL's semantics has been described in an operational way [15], implementing and incorporating SDL into a hardware and software platform are challenging tasks due to many properties of SDL that do not hold in reality [21]. There are several text books [3,18] discussing general guidelines and alternatives regarding interfacing SDL systems with hardware platforms and OSs. In this regard, an important step is the realization of the SDL environment and the mapping of SDL processes to OS tasks.

Mitschele-Thiel [18] compares the three types of OS integrations introduced in IBM's SDL suite [13]: *Tight*, where each SDL process relates to an OS task, *light*, in which the entire SDL system runs in one task, and *bare*. With respect to the SDL environment, Mitschele-Thiel has no "master solution", since its realization depends on the system's application domain and properties of the underlying platform, but he compares alternatives like (a)synchronous inputs/outputs and interaction with hardware by interrupts and polling. A further role of the environment is discussed by Bræk and Haugen [3] and is regarding load control.

Interfacing SDL with software platforms is also considered by commercial SDL tools. RTDS of PragmaDev [20], for instance, maintains integrations for Windows, Linux, and various RTOS like VxWorks, FreeRTOS, and Nucleus; and also IBM's SDL Suite [13] supports inter alia Linux, Windows, VxWorks, and QNX. While these integrations cover scheduling and mapping of SDL's concurrent execution model to OS tasks, the realization of the environment – i.e., the transformation of SDL signals to/from platform-specific implementations – has to be provided manually, yet with driver support of the underlying OS. However, a common drawback is that signals generated by the environment and sent to the SDL system must be addressed by name, thereby dictating SDL process names or impeding generic environment implementations. By registering SDL processes at drivers during system startup, our integration does not suffer from this limitation and only required hardware devices have to be initialized.

There are also proposals describing the incorporation of SDL into light-weight (RT)OSs for embedded systems. Examples are Virtuoso [8], TinyOS [7], and Reflex [22]. For Virtuoso and Reflex, CAdvanced from IBM's SDL Suite [13] is used to generate code. The code generator for the TinyOS integration is not mentioned. All integrations follow a tight approach by mapping each SDL process to a task of the target OS, where the scheduler of TinyOS only supports a non-preemptive FIFO strategy. Virtuoso and Reflex also support preemptive and priority-based strategies. To interface the environment, the Virtuoso integration includes an intermediate layer, which provides interrupt routines and hardware drivers. Additionally, an environment task is introduced to map Virtuoso's signals to SDL signals. A similar solution was chosen for Reflex, where the SDL run-time environment is replaced by an OS integration layer. SDL processes and environment are realized by so-called Reflex activities, which are sub-divided into schedulable activities, which are SDL processes managed by the RTOS scheduler, and non-schedulable activities handling interrupts. Timers are stored in a global queue and checked for expiration at periodical system ticks. Thus, granularity of SDL timers is – different to our integration – limited to system tick intervals. A drawback of the Reflex integration is the addressing of signals, which is based on SDL process' names. For both other integrations, addressing of signals is not mentioned but is probably similar. This limitation also includes signals generated in the environment. A drawback of all RTOS integrations is the reduced coverage of SDL constructs like dynamic process instances.

Alvarez et al. in [1] present a different approach of accessing hardware by specifying each hardware component with two SDL processes. A *passive process* executing transitions as result of hardware interrupts, and an *active driver process*, which uses the passive process to access hardware and provides the interface to the SDL system. Together with their priority model, which is based on fixed transition priorities, this approach enables a flexible processing of external events, yet it generates an inefficient and less clear environment interface.

6   Conclusions

This paper proposes the incorporation of a commercial SDL tool into BiPS, a deterministic protocol stack for WSNs, which has been devised in previous works and implemented for Imote 2 nodes. The work, particularly, points out how scheduling of the SDL system is achieved without violating tight timing constraints of BiPS's protocols, and how the data interface between SDL and BiPS has been realized on the basis of the SDL environment. Referring to the environment, our solution supports a flexible addressing of signals from the environment to arbitrary named SDL processes, thereby not relying on dictated naming conventions. The incorporation follows a (very) light integration approach, in which SDL systems and their environments run on top of BiPS, using its services like event-based scheduling and hardware abstraction. By experiments with a small distributed system, the paper demonstrates that integrating SDL on top of a hand-written protocol stack is a good trade-off between manual and model-driven developments and their pros and cons w.r.t. efficiency, reusability, and maintainability.

This work shows our first steps with PragmaDev's commercial SDL tool RTDS. In future work, we are going to enhance scheduling within SDL systems, which is currently based on signal-based FIFO. This scheduling strategy is, however, not adequate in applications, which require prioritized transition executions to reduce reaction delays and to meet deadlines. One possible solution is the adoption of FreeRTOS[4], which is also supported by RTDS and has already been integrated into BiPS, where it is optionally used to complement the application scheduler. An additional open task is to investigate how SDL concepts like real-time signaling and real-time tasks, which have been proposed in previous works [4] and evaluated in prototype implementations, can be transferred to RTDS.

References

1. Álvarez, J.M., Díaz, M., Llopis, L., Pimentel, E., Troya, J.M.: Integrating Schedulability Analysis and Design Techniques in SDL. Real-Time Systems 24(3), 267–302 (2003)
2. Basmer, T., Schomann, H., Peter, S.: Implementation Analysis of the IEEE 802.15.4 MAC for Wireless Sensor Networks. In: 2011 International Conference on Selected Topics in Mobile and Wireless Networking (iCOST), pp. 7–12 (2011)
3. Bræk, R., Haugen, Ø.: Engineering Real Time Systems. Prentice Hall (1993)
4. Braun, T., Christmann, D., Gotzhein, R., Igel, A.: Model-driven engineering of networked ambient systems with SDL-MDD. Procedia Computer Science 10, 490 (2012), http://www.sciencedirect.com/science/article/pii/ S1877050912004206 ANT 2012 and MobiWIS 2012
5. Braun, T., Gotzhein, R., Kuhn, T.: Mode-based Scheduling with Fast Mode-Signaling – A Method for Efficient Usage of Network Time Slots. Journal of Advances in Computer Networks (JACN) 2, 48–57 (2014)

---

[4] http://www.freertos.org/

6. Christmann, D., Gotzhein, R., Rohr, S.: The Arbitrating Value Transfer Protocol (AVTP) - Deterministic Binary Countdown in Wireless Multi-Hop Networks. In: 2012 21st International Conference on Computer Communications and Networks (ICCCN), pp. 1–9 (August 2012)
7. Dietterle, D., Ryman, J., Dombrowski, K.F., Kraemer, R.: Mapping of High-Level SDL Models to Efficient Implementations for TinyOS. In: Euromicro Symposium on Digital System Design (DSD 2004), pp. 402–406. IEEE Computer Society (2004)
8. Drosos, C., Zayadine, M., Metafas, D.: Real-Time Communication Protocol Development - using SDL for an Embedded System On Chip Based on ARM Microcontroller. In: 13th Euromicro Conference on Real-Time Systems (ECRTS 2001), pp. 89–94. IEEE Computer Society (2001)
9. Engel, M.: Optimierung und Evaluation Black Burst-basierter Protkolle unter Verwendung der Imote 2-Plattform. Master's thesis, TU Kaiserslautern (2013)
10. Fliege, I., Grammes, R., Weber, C.: ConTraST - A Configurable SDL Transpiler and Runtime Environment. In: Gotzhein, R., Reed, R. (eds.) SAM 2006. LNCS, vol. 4320, pp. 216–228. Springer, Heidelberg (2006)
11. Gamma, E., Helm, R., Johnson, R., Vlissides, J.: Design Patterns – Elements of Reusable Object-Oriented Software, 37. print. edn. Addison-Wesley, Boston (2009)
12. Gotzhein, R., Kuhn, T.: Black Burst Synchronization (BBS) – A Protocol for Deterministic Tick and Time Synchronization in Wireless Networks. Computer Networks 55(13), 3015–3031 (2011)
13. IBM Corp.: Rational SDL Suite (2014), http://www-01.ibm.com/software/awdtools/sdlsuite/
14. Institute of Electrical and Electronics Engineers: IEEE Standard 802 Part 15.4: Low-Rate Wireless Personal Area Networks (LR-WPANs). IEEE Computer Society, New York, NY, USA (June 2011), http://standards.ieee.org/getieee802/download/802.15.4-2011.pdf
15. International Telecommunication Union (ITU): ITU-T Recommendation Z.100 Annex F: Formal Semantics Definition (2000), http://www.itu.int/rec/T-REC-Z.100-200011-I!AnnF1, http://www.itu.int/rec/T-REC-Z.100-200011-I!AnnF2, http://www.itu.int/rec/T-REC-Z.100-200011-I!AnnF3
16. International Telecommunication Union (ITU): ITU-T Recommendation Z.100 (12/11) - Specification and Description Language - Overview of SDL-2010 (2012), http://www.itu.int/rec/T-REC-Z.100/en
17. MEMSIC Inc.: Imote2 datasheet (2014), http://vs.cs.uni-kl.de/downloads/Imote2NET_ED_Datasheet.pdf
18. Mitschele-Thiel, A.: Engineering with SDL – Developing Performance-Critical Communication Systems. John Wiley & Sons (2000)
19. PragmaDev SARL: Real Time Developer Studio: User Manual (2013), http://www.pragmadev.com
20. PragmaDev SARL: Real Time Developer Studio (2014), http://www.pragmadev.com
21. Sanders, R.: Implementing from SDL. In: Telektronikk 4.2000, Languages for Telecommunication Applications. Telenor (2000)
22. Wagenknecht, G., Dietterle, D., Ebert, J.-P., Kraemer, R.: Transforming Protocol Specifications for Wireless Sensor Networks into Efficient Embedded System Implementations. In: Römer, K., Karl, H., Mattern, F. (eds.) EWSN 2006. LNCS, vol. 3868, pp. 228–243. Springer, Heidelberg (2006)

Formal Technical Process Specification and Verification for Automated Production Systems

Georg Hackenberg[1], Alarico Campetelli[1], Christoph Legat[2], Jakob Mund[1], Sabine Teufl[3], and Birgit Vogel-Heuser[2]

[1] Chair IV: Software & Systems Engineering, Technische Universität München, Boltzmannstr. 3, 85748 Garching
{hackenbe,campetel,mund}@in.tum.de

[2] Institute of Automation and Information Systems, Technische Universität München, Boltzmannstr. 5, 85748 Garching
{legat,vogel-heuser}@ais.mw.tum.de

[3] fortiss GmbH, An-Institut Technische Universität München, Guerickestr. 25, 80805 München
teufl@fortiss.org

Abstract. The complexity of automated production systems increases constantly due to growing functional requirements and engineering discipline integration. Early design steps include the cross-discipline specification of the system's technical process, while later steps have to ensure compatibility with the specification. Current specification techniques are able to describe and analyze certain properties on the specification level, however verification of the implementation with respect to the specification is a costly task. To overcome this situation we propose a formal modeling technique, which enables automatic verification of the implementation. We demonstrate the approach on a lab-sized automated production system and finally discuss its advantages and disadvantages.

Keywords: Automated production systems, technical process, formal method.

1 Introduction

Automated production systems are complex mechatronic systems whose engineering comprises various disciplines, e.g., mechanical, electrical, and software engineering. In the concurrent engineering process, efficient and effective collaboration between interdisciplinary engineering teams is important towards the projects' success [18,19]. Ensuring the correctness of a production system's design manually, i.e., ensuring the compliance with the technical process, is cumbersome and costly. For this reason, verification is performed only sparsely in practice increasing project risks drastically. Automating the verification would enable more frequent design examination for early detection and correction of design flaws. Therefore, ensuring the correctness of the design by automatic verification is one option to leverage a project's success.

D. Amyot et al. (Eds.): SAM 2014, LNCS 8769, pp. 287–303, 2014.

Various approaches for automatic verification exist, ranging from design-time to runtime techniques. For design-time verification, modeling tools provide specific extensions for formal analyses, e.g., Simulink Design Verifier[1] or SCADE Design Verifier[2], which allow to specify desired properties using temporal operators and assertions. In contrast, *Rhapsody in C++* [22] supports verification of UML models, while properties can be formulated using temporal patterns or a graphical notation called Life Sequence Charts [12]. Alternatively, Hugo/RT [2] offers UML communication diagrams for property definition. In contrast to design-time techniques, runtime techniques include runtime verification [4] and online/offline monitoring [21]. Both runtime verification and monitoring allow to express properties using for example temporal logics. While existing approaches already support the examination of a system's design with respect to desired properties both at design-time and at runtime, provided formalisms are not designed to be used within the automation domain (e.g., by process engineers). Rather, dedicated technical process modeling techniques are required, providing more suitable modeling vocabulary.

For technical process modeling various modeling notations exist. In particular, the application of notations originally developed in computer science are recently under investigation in the field of automated production systems. For example, Zor et al. [27] explore the adaption of the Business Process Model and Notation (BPMN) through domain-specific extensions such as parts flow connectors and material gateways. However, while intended for documentation purposes their approach lacks a formal foundation, making automatic verification infeasible. In contrast, Dijkman et al. [13] propose formal semantics for standard BPMN, but lack the necessary domain-specific extensions. Alternatively, the Formalized Process Description [24] provides a standard for technical process specification in the manufacturing domain. While in combination with a plant model the formalism is well suited for diagnosis [11], automatic design verification has not been targeted yet. Moreover, in the field of service-oriented manufacturing various process models exist for service orchestration [10,20,23]. While some of these models define execution semantics, the models typically are used during technical process implementation rather than specification and verification. Then, according to IEC 61131-3 [16] for developing field level control software, Sequential Function Charts provide a graphical programming language supporting the modeling of software processes. Also, state charts have been developed for the specification of control software [26]. Though providing formal semantics and verification capabilities, these approaches are not applied for technical process specification. In a nutshell, a variety of process specification languages have been defined for different purposes. However, the approaches are either not suited for technical process specification or do not provide necessary formal semantics.

Therefore, in Section 2 a dedicated formal approach to technical process specification and verification for automated production systems is presented. In particular, the approach allows developing both the process specification and the

---

[1] http://www.mathworks.de/products/simulink/

[2] http://www.esterel-technologies.com/products/scade-suite/

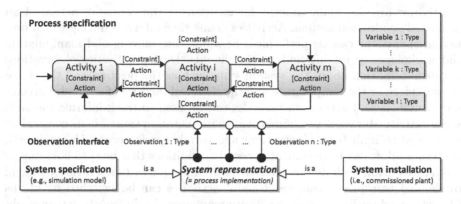

Fig. 1. Overview of the concepts and relations including process specfication and system representation connected through an observation interface

implementation independent of each other while achieving their semantic integration for automatic verification at design-time and runtime. The applicability of this approach is demonstrated based on a lab sized manufacturing system with an exemplified design process in Section 3. The demonstrator is reduced in size and complexity. Nevertheless, it is suitable for indicating the applicability for a basic class of manufacturing systems in a first step. It is shown that the verification can lead to an early detection of exemplary design flaws. The section concludes with a summary of experiences gained during executing the case study. Finally, the paper summarizes the findings and indicates necessary future work.

2   A Formal Approach

To explain our formal approach to technical process specification and verification, we first introduce a number of basic concepts and relations (Section 2.1), before going into details of their formalization (Section 2.2) and showing possibilities for automatic verification (Section 2.3).

2.1   Terminology

Figure 1 provides an overview of the core concepts and relations: We distinguish between (1) *process specification* and (2) *system representation*, which are connected and semantically integrated by an (3) *observation interface*.

Process Specification. As discussed in the previous section, the purpose of the process specification is to describe the expected behavior of automated production systems in a high-level and cross-discipline manner. To achieve this goal, we propose to describe technical processes in terms of (a) *activities*, (b) *observations*, (c) *variables*, (d) *transitions*, (e) *actions*, and (f) *constraints*. The terminology and the graphical notation are inspired by UML activity diagrams [3].

Activities are the main concept for structuring the course of action of an automated production system. Activities define time intervals during which production operations can be performed. Examples are moving and manipulating solid workpieces or mixing and stirring liquids. During activities observations provide information about the system state such as the position and the shape of a workpiece or the temperature and the chemical mixture of a liquid. Furthermore, variables and actions on variables can be used to track information such as the activity duration or cumulative energy consumption. Then, constraints can be used to limit both observations and variable assignments. Consequently, constraints allow one to document necessary conditions that need to hold during activity execution such as the activity duration, required temperature bands of liquids, and workpiece positions. Finally, activities can be switched by means of transitions describing possible activity sequences. Again, constraints over observations and variables are used to define the conditions that need to hold for switching activities. Examples are intermediate locations of workpieces or intermediate mixtures of liquids. At last, transition actions on variables can be used to track information across activities or to reset the tracking state.

The modeling technique is similar to input/output (i.e., I/O) automata [1]. However, the key differences are that the process specification does not include any outputs and the activities include the concept of constraints. Consequently, our notation reflects the needs of technical process engineers more closely.

Observation Interface. The purpose of the observation interface is to link process specification and system representation such that automatic process verification becomes feasible. Conceptually, the observation interface is modeled in terms of observation *ports* and *channels*, which is inspired by the FOCUS engineering method and underlying formalism [7]. The process specification defines the observation input ports, while the system representation provides the respective observation output ports. The port coupling is achieved by means of observation channels.

The interface concept allows one to decouple the process specification and the system representation, while achieving their semantic integration. Consequently, the system representation can be exchanged without the need for revising the process specification, e.g., when comparing automated production systems from different providers implementing the same technical process.

System Representation. The system representation finally constitutes the actual implementation of the process specification. Implementations typically include a number of mechanical, electrical and software elements. At this point we do not prescribe any particular representation format. Rather, we distinguish two general options both being suited for automated process verification: (a) *system specifications* and (b) *system installations*. System specifications describe the automated production system e.g., using MechatronicUML [5] or SysML4Mechatronics [17], while system installations represent the commissioned automated production systems themselves. However, note that for automated process verification the system representation needs to define an execution semantics and needs to implement the observation interface.

2.2 Formalization

To enable automatic verification, we first define the elements of a process specification in terms of mathematical sets and functions reflecting the concepts introduced in the previous section.

Definition 1 (Process specification). *A process specification P is an twelve-tuple $P = (A, M, N, O, V, T, a', v', f_1, f_2, g_1, g_2)$ with*

- *a finite set $A = \{a_1, \ldots, a_m\}$ of activities with $m \in \mathbb{N}$,*
- *a finite set $M = \{M_1, \ldots, M_n\}$ of observation domains with $n \in \mathbb{N}$,*
- *a finite set $N = \{N_1, \ldots, N_l\}$ of variable domains with $l \in \mathbb{N}$,*
- *a finite set $O = M_1 \times \cdots \times M_n$ of observations from observation domains,*
- *a finite set $V = N_1 \times \cdots \times N_l$ of variable assignments from variable domains,*
- *a finite set $T \subseteq A \times A$ of transitions,*
- *an element $a' \in A$ as initial activity,*
- *an element $v' \in V$ as initial variable assignments,*
- *an activity constraint function $f_1 : A \to \mathcal{P}(O \times V)$,*
- *an activity action function $f_2 : A \times O \times V \to V$,*
- *a transition constraint function $g_1 : T \to \mathcal{P}(O \times V)$, and*
- *a transition action function $g_2 : T \times O \times V \to V$*

such that the transition set T does not include self-transitions for any activity from the activity set A:

$$\forall (a_i, a_j) \in T : a_i \neq a_j \text{ with } 1 \leq i, j \leq m \text{ and } i, j \in \mathbb{N}$$

and only one transition in the transition set T is enabled by the transition constraint function g_1 at a time:

$$\forall a_i \in A : \bigcap_{(a_i, a_j) \in T} g_1((a_i, a_j)) = \emptyset \text{ with } 1 \leq i, j \leq m \text{ and } i, j \in \mathbb{N}$$

Note that a process specification P resembles a directed graph with vertices A and edges T. Furthermore, the constraint functions f_1 and g_1 specify possible combinations of observations $o \in O$ and variables $v \in V$, which are accepted while performing activities $a \in A$ or which are required in order to switch activities using transitions $(a_i, a_j) \in T$ with $1 \leq i, j \leq m$ and $i, j \in \mathbb{N}$. Finally, the action functions f_2 and g_2 define how to derive new variable assignments $v' \in V$ from observations $o \in O$ and previous variables assignment $v \in V$ during activities $a \in A$ and transitions $(a_i, a_j) \in T$ with $1 \leq i, j \leq m$ and $i, j \in \mathbb{N}$.

Based on process specification P, we define the concept of *observation traces* reflecting the input of the process specification and the output of the system representation respectively.

Definition 2 (Observation traces). *An observation trace τ_n for process specification $P = (A, M, N, O, V, T, a', v', f_1, f_2, g_1, g_2)$ is a finite or infinite sequence:*

$$\tau_n = (\omega_i)_{i=0}^{n}$$

with $\omega_i \in O$ representing observations and $n \in \mathbb{N} \cup \{\infty\}$ representing the length of the sequence.

Consequently, observation traces provide a record of system execution. Note that in theory observation traces can be of infinite length, which is important for exhaustive model checking as discussed in the following section.

Based on process specification P and the observation trace τ_n with $n \in \mathbb{N} \cup \{\infty\}$, we define the formal *process execution* semantics determining the order of action execution, constraint evaluation, and activity switching.

Definition 3 (Process execution). *A process execution π_n of process specification $P = (A, M, N, O, V, T, a', v', f_1, f_2, g_1, g_2)$ and observation trace $\tau_n = (\omega_k)_{k=0}^{n}$ with $n \in \mathbb{N} \cup \{\infty\}$ is a finite or infinite sequence:*

$$\pi_n = ((\alpha_k, \omega_k, \phi_k, \beta_k))_{k=0}^{n}$$

with $\alpha_k \in A$, $\omega_k \in O$, $\phi_k \in V$ and $\beta_k \in \mathbb{B}$ such that the sequence starts with the initial activity a' and the initial variable assignments v':

$$\alpha_0 = a', \phi_0 = v'$$

and given the domains of sequence indices D_1 and D_2 separating between the finite and the infinite case:

$$(n = \infty \Leftrightarrow D_1 = \mathbb{N}) \wedge (n \neq \infty \Leftrightarrow D_1 = \{k \in \mathbb{N} \mid k < n\})$$
$$(n = \infty \Leftrightarrow D_2 = \mathbb{N}) \wedge (n \neq \infty \Leftrightarrow D_2 = \{k \in \mathbb{N} \mid k \leq n\})$$

the transitions between the activities are included in the transition set T and supported by the transition constraint function g_1:

$$\forall k \in D_1 : \alpha_k \neq \alpha_{k+1} \Leftrightarrow (\alpha_k, \alpha_{k+1}) \in T \wedge (\omega_k, \phi_k) \in g_1((\alpha_k, \alpha_{k+1}))$$

and the variables are updated according to the activity action function f_2 and transition action functions g_2:

$$\forall k \in D_1 : \phi_{k+1} = \begin{cases} f_2(\alpha_{k+1}, \omega_{k+1}, \phi_k) & \text{if } \alpha_k = \alpha_{k+1} \\ f_2(\alpha_{k+1}, \omega_{k+1}, g_2((\alpha_k, \alpha_{k+1}), \omega_k, \phi_k)) & \text{if } \alpha_k \neq \alpha_{k+1} \end{cases}$$

and the boolean variables β_k contain the results of the activity constraint function f_1 respectively:

$$\forall k \in D_2 : \beta_k = true \Leftrightarrow (\omega_k, \phi_k) \in f_1(\alpha_k)$$

Essentially, a process execution π_n with $n \in \mathbb{N} \cup \{\infty\}$ extends the observation trace τ_n with activity, variable assignments, and activity constraint information. Note that transitions $(\alpha_k, \alpha_{k+1}) \in T$ with $k \in D_1$ occur between elements of the sequence π_n based on the observations $\omega_k \in O$ and variable assignments $\phi_k \in V$ of the former time point. Also, the effects of the transition actions $\phi'_{k+1} = g_2((\alpha_k, \alpha_{k+1}), \omega_k, \phi_k)$ with $k \in D_1$ on the variables $\phi_{k+1} \in V$ are hidden by the effects of the activity actions $f_2(\alpha_{k+1}, \omega_{k+1}, \phi'_{k+1})$. This design decision has been taken such that for every time point an activity as well as the activity constraints can be determined.

Finally, based on the process specification P, the observation trace τ_n, and the process execution π_n, the *process satisfaction* condition can be defined, determining whether an observation trace satisfies a process specification or not.

Definition 4 (Process satisfaction). *Given some process specification $P = (A, M, N, O, V, T, a', v', f_1, f_2, g_1, g_2)$, an observation trace $\tau_n = (\omega_k)_{k=0}^n$, and the respective process execution $\pi_n = (\alpha_k, \omega_k, \phi_k, \beta_k)_{k=0}^n$:*

$$\tau_n \text{ satisfies } P \Leftrightarrow \forall k \in D : \beta_k = true$$

with $n \in \mathbb{N} \cup \{\infty\}$ defining the sequence length and D representing the finite or infinite set of sequence indices:

$$(n = \infty \Leftrightarrow D - \mathbb{N}) \wedge (n \neq \infty \Leftrightarrow D = \{k \in \mathbb{N} : k \leq n\})$$

Consequently, the process specification P remains unsatisfied in case activity constraints $(\omega_k, \phi_k) \in f_1(\alpha_k)$ with $k \in D$ are violated, which are used to determine β_k. Note that a system specification satisfies a process specification P in case all possible observation traces τ_n with $n \in \mathbb{N} \cup \{\infty\}$ satisfy P.

2.3 Verification

Different verification techniques exist that allow one to check whether a process specification is fulfilled by incoming observation traces. Figure 2 shows the verification options and how the models and the properties for the verification tools can be derived.

In case an adequate system specification is given, model checking can be used for exhaustive verification of the process specification (i.e., with respect to all possible traces of the system). The formal model for the model checker is built from the system specification, the observation interface, and the process specification. Meanwhile, the formal property to be verified determines that the variable b_k remains always true. This way all finite and infinite observation traces are verified or a counterexample π_n is returned leading to an activity constraint violation in the last step. However, the application of model checking might not be feasible for some systems due to the complexity of the state space. One possibility to overcome this limitation is to apply bounded model checking instead. However, bounded model checking is limited to verification of finite traces with predefined length only, while the verification still is exhaustive (i.e., with respect to all possible traces of the system with predefined length).

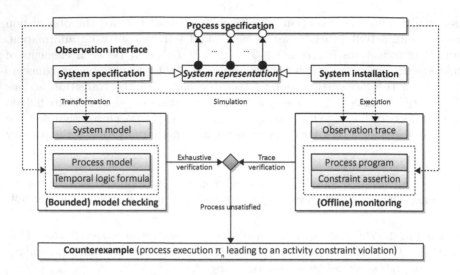

Fig. 2. Verification options including model checking of system specifications, offline monitoring of system specifications and installations, and counterexamples

Besides model checking other verification options exist which are applicable in case the formal system model cannot be built (i.e., no adequate system specification is available) or exhaustive verification is not feasible (i.e., the state space is too complex even for bounded model checking). In such cases we rely on observation traces only, e.g., obtained by simulation of the system specification or execution of the system installation. Checking whether an observation trace meets the process specification can be performed using online or offline monitoring [21]. As illustrated in Fig. 2, in our case the recorded executions are represented by the observation traces and the monitor is build from the process specification. The monitor verifies the same property as for model checking, i.e., the variable b_k must remain always true. Process monitoring in combination with simulation of the system specification or execution of the system installation requires less expertise, time, and memory as compared to model checking, but verifies the process specification for selected finite observation traces only. While this represents a drawback compared to model checking of system specifications, monitors are suited particularly well for verification of system installations.

3   An Academic Case Study

In the following, we apply the proposed approach to the pick and place unit (PPU) [15,25], a bench-scale lab demonstrator of a manufacturing system (cp. Fig. 3). The system consists of a *stack* for storing cylindrical workpieces (WPs), a *stamp* for stamping WPs, a *sorter* including a *conveyor*, two pneumatic *cylinders*, and three *ramps* for transporting, sorting, and storing WPs, as well as a *crane* for transporting WPs between the previous stations.

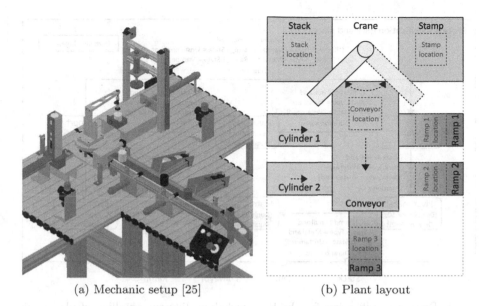

(a) Mechanic setup [25]   (b) Plant layout

Fig. 3. The pick and place unit (PPU) bench-scale lab demonstrator

For the study, the following requirements have been specified: The PPU must handle two types of WPs, *plastic* and *metallic*. During the process the latter should be *stamped*, while the former should be left *unstamped* (which is a common scenario for example in waste management). Moreover, both kinds of WPs should be transported from *stack* to *ramp 3* location within at most 25 seconds. Note that *ramp 1* and *ramp 2* locations remain unused, because in this study the PPU is not required to sort the WPs.

In the following, we describe the developed process specification before elaborating on the system specification. Further, we show how in the given case model checking helps to uncover a design flaw in the system specification and prove its subsequent correction.

3.1   Process Specification

The process specification for the PPU is depicted in Fig. 4. During design, it was decided to decompose the entire process into six activities and four observations. The activities are *wait, pivot plastic* WPs, *pivot metal* WPs, *stamp metal* WPs, *pivot metal* WPs again, and *transport* both types of WPs. In contrast, the observations describe WPs at *stack, stamp, conveyor*, and *ramp 3* location.

As shown in the process specification, the system is required to start with the wait activity. Then two transitions are defined, one for unstamped plastic and the other for unstamped metallic WPs at the stack location. When observing a plastic WP, the PPU switches to the pivot plastic activity for a maximum duration of 5 seconds. The activity ends as soon as an unstamped plastic WP is observed at the conveyor location. In contrast, for metallic WPs, a separate

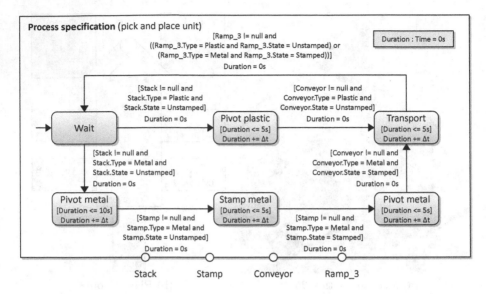

Fig. 4. Process specification for the PPU including different handling of plastic and metallic WPs

pivot metal activity is executed for a maximum duration of 10 seconds, and ends as soon as unstamped metallic WPs are observed at the stamp location. Then, the stamp metal activity is executed for a maximum duration of 5 seconds, which ends when stamped metallic WPs are observed at the stamp location. Subsequently, again a pivot metal activity is triggered for a maximum duration of 5 seconds, which ends exactly when stamped metallic WPs are observed at the conveyor location. Then, independent of the WP type and state, the transport activity is started for a maximum duration of 5 seconds, until a WP is observed at the ramp 3 location.

Overall the process ensures that both plastic and metallic WPs are processed in at least 25 seconds of time. In case a plastic WP is observed, the sequence of activities lasts at most 15 seconds. In case a metallic WP is observed, the sequence lasts at most 25 seconds instead. Also, in accordance to the requirements, only unstamped plastic or stamped metallic WPs can be observed at ramp 3 location.

3.2 System Specification

For this study, we decided to use AutoFOCUS[3] to model the system specification. AutoFOCUS is a reference implementation of the FOCUS formalism [7] and comes with NuSMV[4] integration [9] for model checking. FOCUS describes systems in terms of components, input/output ports, channels, and input/output

---

[3] http://af3.fortiss.org/
[4] http://nusmv.fbk.eu/

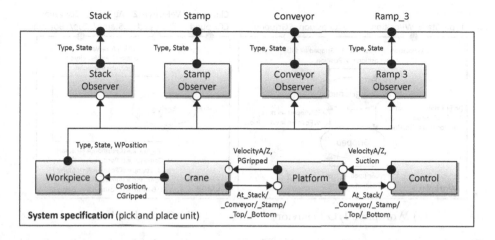

Fig. 5. Excerpt of a simplified system specification for the PPU including novel observer components

automata. The advantage of the tool chain is that the system specification can be verified with respect to the process specification. On the downside, the modeling technique is tailored to pure message exchange between components, which also has to be used to describe physical phenomena. However, it should be noted that extensions of FOCUS exist adding dense time [6] and continuous time [8] and spatial [14] phenomena. Though being more suitable for describing physical phenomena, these extensions are not used in the study as they are not yet supported by the reference implementation.

The system specification for the pick and place unit is shown in Fig. 5. Due to system complexity, we only focus on a part of the system specification including the *workpiece* (i.e., plastic or metallic WP), the *crane* to perform the *pivot* activities (see Section 3.1), a *platform*, a *control*, and several *observer* components. Note that the system specification assumes that only one WP is being processed by the PPU at a time, which is in accordance with the process specification.

Workpiece. The workpiece component is responsible for modeling the workpiece type (plastic or metallic), state (unstamped or stamped), and position (angular and lift). The component defines two input ports (*crane position* and *suction*) as well as three output ports (*type, state,* and *position*). The inputs are provided by the crane component, while the outputs are delivered to the observer components. Figure 6a shows the automaton specification of the input/output behavior of the workpiece component. The behavior is described in terms of two states: (1) *not gripped* and (2) *gripped*. In case the workpiece is gripped by the crane, the workpiece position (i.e., WPosition) is locked to the crane position (i.e., CPosition). Otherwise the workpiece position remains constant. The workpiece goes into the gripped state, if the workpiece position is equal to the crane

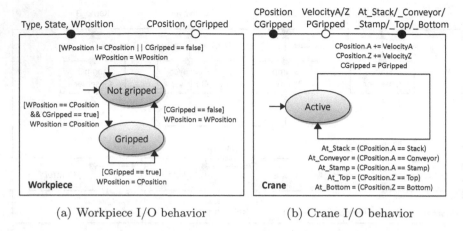

(a) Workpiece I/O behavior   (b) Crane I/O behavior

Fig. 6. Automaton specification of the input/output behavior for the workpiece and crane components

position and the gripped input is turned on. On the other hand, the workpiece goes back into the not gripped state as soon as the gripped input is turned off.

Note that the automaton does not include the type and state outputs of the workpiece, which are irrelevant for the interaction between workpiece and crane. Obviously, the type (i.e., plastic or metallic) remains constant, while the state depends on the interaction with the stamp, which is not the focus of this presentation.

Crane. The crane component is responsible for modeling the crane position (angular and lift) as well as the suction and position sensor outputs. The component defines three input ports (*angular velocity, lift velocity,* and *suction*) as well as seven output ports (*crane position, suction, at stack, at conveyor, at stamp, at top,* and *at bottom*). The inputs are provided by the platform component, while the first two outputs are forwarded to the workpiece component and the last five outputs are delivered back to the platform component. Figure 6b shows the automaton specification of the I/O behavior of the crane component. The behavior is described by means of a single state: *Active*. In this state angular and lift velocity are added to the crane position, while the suction input is forwarded to the workpiece unchanged and the position sensors fire selectively.

Platform. The platform component is responsible for modeling the physical connection between crane and control component. Consequently, the velocity and suction values are forwarded to the crane, while the position sensor values are delivered back to the control. An automaton specification of the I/O behavior is omitted here, however it should be noted that the platform introduces a message delay between crane and control. Technically, the delay is caused by

		Step	1	2	...	30	31	...	102	103
System model	Workpiece	WPosition	{A: 0, Z: 0}	{A: 0, Z: 0}	...	{A: 65, Z: 1}	{A: 70, Z: 1}	...	{A: 210, Z: 0}	{A: 210, Z: 0}
		...	...	...	...	...	...	...	...	...
	Crane	CPosition	{A: 0, Z: 0}	{A: 0, Z: 0}	...	{A: 65, Z: 1}	{A: 70, Z: 1}	...	{A: 210, Z: 0}	{A: 210, Z: 0}
		OSuction	false	false	...	true	true	...	false	false
		...	...	...	...	...	...	...	...	...
	...	...	...	...	...	...	...	...	...	...
Process model		Activity	Wait	Pivot metal	...	Pivot metal	Pivot metal	...	Pivot metal	Pivot metal
	Observations	Stack	{Type: Metal}	null	...	null	null	...	null	null
		...	...	...	...	...	...	...	...	...
	Variables	Duration	0.0s	0.1s	...	3.0s	3.1s	...	10.0s	10.1s
	Activity Constraint		true	true	...	true	true	...	true	false

Fig. 7. Counterexample returned by the model checker leading to an activity constraint violation in the last step

analog-digital converters, communication buses, and programmable logic controller execution semantics.

Control. The control component is responsible for adjusting crane velocity and suction based on the position sensor inputs. Again, due to space limitation the automaton specification of the I/O behavior is omitted. The automaton switches between different *pivot*, *lift*, and *wait* states controlling angular and lift velocities as well as suction, respectively. State switches occur based on the position sensor inputs from the crane as well as further information about the workpiece state (omitted in the presented system specification).

Observer. Finally, the observer components are responsible for defining the observation streams necessary to connect the system specification to the process specification (see Section 3.1). Based on the workpiece position, the observers decide whether to forward the input message including workpiece type and state to the respective observation output port.

3.3 Model Checking

Due to the selected tool chain (i.e., AutoFOCUS and NuSMV) we are able to perform exhaustive verification of the system specification with respect to the process specification using for example bounded model checking. Therefore, as described in [9] and Section 2.3, both the system specification and the process specification are translated into NuSMV modules.

For verification, the workpiece type is set to metallic, the workpiece state is set to unstamped, and the workpiece and crane positions are set to the stack location. Then, for bounded model checking, the analysis depth is set to 110

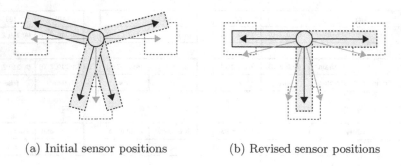

(a) Initial sensor positions   (b) Revised sensor positions

Fig. 8. Geometric explanation of the design flaw and its correction through manipulation of sensor positions

steps (covering the execution of the first pivot metal activity). Further, to indicate verification performance an analysis timeout of 50 seconds is used. Given these settings NuSMV fails to verify the absence of activity constraint violations within the timeout returning the counterexample shown in Fig. 7. In the counterexample, the process model correctly switches to the pivot activity after detecting unstamped metallic WPs at the stack location. Also, the WP transport seems to work correctly after suction is turned on. However, the WP is moved past the stamp location before the crane places the WP down and turns suction off. Consequently, the activity post condition (i.e., unstamped metallic WP at the stamp location) does not become true and the duration constraint is violated. After further examination of the counterexample, the cause of the problem is identified: as illustrated in Fig. 8a, the delay introduced by the platform component leads to a deviation between crane position sensor angles and final crane angles, which is why the WP moves past the stamp location.

To correct the design flaw, the angular position sensors are slightly displaced as shown in Fig. 8b. Also, a sensor is added to the conveyor location as the crane approaches the location from two sides. Finally, the control component is adjusted to accommodate for the novel input. Subsequently, given the same settings, NuSMV is able to verify the absence of activity constraint violations. However, note that only the first pivot metal activity is considered currently, while an exhaustive verification of the entire process has not been achieved yet.

4   Conclusion and Outlook

In this paper, we have introduced a dedicated formal approach to technical process specification and verification for automated production systems. In Section 2, we developed the underlying terminology (in compliance with existing approaches [3,27]) and provided the necessary mathematical definitions before describing verification options both at design-time and at runtime. Then, in Section 3, we showed how to apply the proposed approach to a bench-scale manufacturing system. The case study included the formal process specification as well as an excerpt of the system specification in AutoFOCUS. Moreover, model checking with NuSMV was used to uncover a design flaw caused by signal delays. Finally, one possibility to resolve the design flaw was discussed.

The case study showed the effectiveness of using an observation interface to decouple and semantically integrate process specification and system representation. In particular, high-level observations can be defined early during process specification, while a translation to these observations can be achieved easily later within the system's design to enable automatic verification. Furthermore, we have exploited the concept of variables and actions to model and constrain the duration of activities. Similarly, other performance characteristics such as energy consumption can be constrained. Finally, both model checking and simulation monitoring provide powerful tools for design-time verification, while monitoring also provides the link to system commissioning and operation. Overall, through the small set of concepts and different verification options we are able to provide a flexible basis for technical process specification and verification.

However, on the downside, both actions and constraints currently require lengthy textual notation, to which process engineers are not accustomed. To this end, we are working on graphical notations as well as the inclusion of language-level patterns. Moreover, we are working on extensions for process composition and synchronization to support parallel process execution. Also, we are investigating continuous-time rather than discrete-time process specifications. Then, we are exploring possibilities for process quality monitoring as compared to constraint monitoring. Finally, we are studying exhaustive verification performance as well as scenario-based testing as an alternative, scalable verification strategy.

References

1. Attie, P., Lynch, N.: Dynamic input/output automata: A formal model for dynamic systems. In: Larsen, K.G., Nielsen, M. (eds.) CONCUR 2001. LNCS, vol. 2154, pp. 137–151. Springer, Heidelberg (2001)
2. Balser, M., Bäumler, S., Knapp, A., Reif, W., Thums, A.: Interactive Verification of UML State Machines. In: Davies, J., Schulte, W., Barnett, M. (eds.) ICFEM 2004. LNCS, vol. 3308, pp. 434–448. Springer, Heidelberg (2004)
3. Bastos, R., Ruiz, D.: Extending uml activity diagram for workflow modeling in production systems. In: Proceedings of the 35th Annual Hawaii International Conference on System Sciences, HICSS, pp. 3786–3795 (January 2002)
4. Bauer, A., Leucker, M., Schallhart, C.: Runtime verification for ltl and tltl. ACM Trans. Softw. Eng. Methodol. 20(4), 14:1–14:64 (2011)
5. Becker, S., Brenner, C., Dziwok, S., Gewering, T., Heinzemann, C., Pohlmann, U., Priesterjahn, C., Schäfer, W., Suck, J., Sudmann, O., Tichy, M.: The mechatronicuml method - process, syntax, and semantics. Tech. Rep. tr-ri-12-318, Software Engineering Group, Heinz Nixdorf Institute University of Paderborn (2012)
6. Broy, M.: System behaviour models with discrete and dense time. In: Chakraborty, S., Eberspächer, J. (eds.) Advances in Real-Time Systems, pp. 3–25. Springer, Heidelberg (2012)
7. Broy, M., Stølen, K.: Specification and development of interactive systems: Focus on streams, interfaces and refinement. Springer (2001)

8. Campetelli, A.: Dynamic Sampling for FOCUS Hybrid Components. In: Ölveczky, P.C., Artho, C. (eds.) 3rd International Conference on Circuits, System and Simulation (ICCSS 2013), vol. 3(5), pp. 402–406 (2013); International Journal of Modeling and Optimization

9. Campetelli, A., Hölzl, F., Neubeck, P.: User-friendly Model Checking Integration in Model-based Development. In: 24th International Conference on Computer Applications in Industry and Engineering (CAINE 2011). The International Society for Computers and Their Applications (2011)

10. Cândido, G., Barata, J., Colombo, A.W., Jammes, F.: SOA in reconfigurable supply chains: A research roadmap. Engineering Applications of Artificial Intelligence 22(6), 939–949 (2009)

11. Christiansen, L., Fay, A., Opgenoorth, B., Neidig, J.: Improved diagnosis by combining structural and process knowledge. In: 2011 IEEE 16th Conference on Emerging Technologies Factory Automation (ETFA), pp. 1–8 (September 2011)

12. Damm, W., Harel, D.: LSCs: Breathing Life into Message Sequence Charts. Formal Methods in System Design 19(1), 45–80 (2001)

13. Dijkman, R.M., Dumas, M., Ouyang, C.: Semantics and analysis of business process models in bpmn. Inf. Softw. Technol. 50(12), 1281–1294 (2008)

14. Hummel, B.: Integrated Behavior Modeling of Space-Intensive Mechatronic Systems. Dissertation, Technische Universität München, München (2011)

15. Institute of Automation and Information Systems, Technische Universität München: The Pick and Place Unit Demonstrator for Evolution in Industrial Plant Automation (2014), http://www.ppu-demonstrator.org

16. International Electrotechnical Commission: IEC Standard 61131-3 (02/13): Programmable controllers – part 3: Programming languages (2013), http://webstore.iec.ch/webstore/webstore.nsf/Artnum_PK/47556

17. Kernschmidt, K., Vogel-Heuser, B.: An interdisciplinary SysML based modeling approach for analyzing change influences in production plants to support the engineering. In: IEEE International Conference on Automation Science and Engineering (CASE), Madison, WI, USA, pp. 1113–1118 (2013)

18. Kohn, A., Reif, J., Wolfenstetter, T., Kernschmidt, K., Goswami, S., Krcmar, H., Brodbeck, F., Vogel-Heuser, B., Lindemann, U.: Improving common model understanding within collaborative engineering design research projects. In: Chakrabarti, A., Prakash, R.V. (eds.) 4th International Conference on Research into Design. LNME, pp. 643–654. Springer India (2013)

19. Li, F., Bayrak, G., Kernschmidt, K., Vogel-Heuser, B.: Specification of the requirements to support information technology-cycles in the machine and plant manufacturing industry. In: 14th IFAC Symposium on Information Control Problems in Manufacturing, pp. 1077–1082 (2012)

20. Loskyll, M., Schlick, J., Hodek, S., Ollinger, L., Gerber, T., Pirvu, B.: Semantic service discovery and orchestration for manufacturing processes. In: 2011 IEEE 16th Conference on Emerging Technologies & Factory Automation (ETFA), pp. 1–8. IEEE (2011)

21. Maler, O., Nickovic, D.: Monitoring temporal properties of continuous signals. In: Lakhnech, Y., Yovine, S. (eds.) FORMATS 2004 and FTRTFT 2004. LNCS, vol. 3253, pp. 152–166. Springer, Heidelberg (2004)

22. Schinz, I., Toben, T., Mrugalla, C., Westphal, B.: The Rhapsody UML Verification Environment. In: 2nd International Conference on Software Engineering and Formal Methods, pp. 174–183. IEEE Computer Society (2004)

23. Shen, W., Hao, Q., Wang, S., Li, Y., Ghenniwa, H.: An agent-based service-oriented integration architecture for collaborative intelligent manufacturing. Robotics and Computer-Integrated Manufacturing 23(3), 315–325 (2007)
24. Verein Deutscher Ingenieure: VDI/VDE 3682 (09/05): Formalised process description (2005), https://www.vdi.de/nc/en/richtlinie/vdivde_3682-formalisierte_prozessbeschreibungen/
25. Vogel-Heuser, B., Legat, C., Folmer, J., Feldmann, S.: Researching evolution in industrial plant automation: Scenarios and documentation of the pick and place unit. Technical Report TUM-AIS-TR-01-14-02, Institute of Automation and Information Systems, Technische Universität München (2014), https://mediatum.ub.tum.de/node?id=1208973
26. Witsch, D., Vogel-Heuser, B.: PLC-statecharts: An approach to integrate UML-statecharts in open-loop control engineering – aspects on behavioral semantics and model-checking. In: 18th IFAC World Congress, pp. 7866–7872 (2011)
27. Zor, S., Leymann, F., Schumm, D.: A Proposal of BPMN Extensions for the Manufacturing Domain. In: Proceedings of the 44th CIRP Conference on Manufacturing Systems (ICMS 2011), Madison, WI, USA, pp. 1–6 (January 2011)

Prototyping SDL Extensions

Andreas Blunk and Joachim Fischer

Humboldt-Universität zu Berlin
Unter den Linden 6
D-10099 Berlin, Germany
{blunk,fischer}@informatik.hu-berlin.de

Abstract. Semaphores, process priorities, and real-time tasks are examples of SDL extensions which integrate concepts of real-time operating systems into SDL. Providing tool support for such extensions, requires time and effort to manually adapt existing modeling and analysis tools. We present an approach based on language extension which reduces the effort to obtain a text editor for modeling and a runtime efficient next-event simulator for model analysis. The approach allows to prototype extensions, i.e., evaluate their design and suitability by test and simulation. We discuss an application of our approach to a subset of SDL. In addition, we take the concept of semaphores from SDL-RT and bring it to the SDL subset by defining it as an extension. The approach is implemented only in parts yet, thus we present work in progress. We discuss working prototypes for the text editor and the simulator.

1 Introduction

The development of large and complex systems is best supported by domain-specific modeling languages (DSMLs) which allow to describe certain aspects of a system in a more concise and understandable way and which provide DSML-aware tool support for creating and analyzing system models.

The Specification and Description Language (SDL) [1] is a DSML which provides specific means for modeling structural and functional aspects of communicating reactive systems. The basic modeling concepts which SDL provides are on the one hand specific to the domain of reactive systems, and on the other hand general regarding the domain itself as they allow to model all kinds of reactive systems. When the application domain of SDL is even more specific, e.g., real-time systems, it may become necessary to extend the basic concepts of SDL. Such extensions keep being proposed. Examples are *semaphores* [2], process priorities [3], and real-time tasks [4].

These extensions can be seen as small DSMLs themselves. The problem with such small extensions is that they need to be supported by tools as well. During the development it may also become necessary to change an extension iteratively a number of times. Our research is targeted towards executable DSMLs where there is a need to analyze models by means of next-event simulation. A number of problems exist developing such DSMLs. 1) Adapting development tools manually

D. Amyot et al. (Eds.): SAM 2014, LNCS 8769, pp. 304–311, 2014.

costs a lot of time and effort. 2) Analyzing large models requires a runtime efficient simulator. When the base language is missing runtime efficient next-event specification primitives, the result can be inefficient long-running simulations. These problems hinder evaluating the suitability of an extension.

We propose an approach for defining an executable DSML by extending a discrete-event system modeling language. The approach has the advantage of providing DSML-aware tools for evaluating the design and suitability of a DSML by test and simulation at a low cost and with high runtime efficiency. We think that an editor, a debugger, and a simulator are important tools here. They allow models to be created, debugged, and analyzed during the initial design phase of a language. For model analysis, we use next-event simulation. Low language development cost is achieved by an immediate provisioning of DSML-aware tools. These tools are derived from a definition of a DSML specified as extension to the syntax, semantics, and debugging of the base language. By reusing concepts of a base language, the effort to define the DSML is reduced and runtime efficient simulations are enabled.

1.1   Contribution

In this paper, we apply our approach to a subset of SDL, named SDL_0. We show that an SDL text editor[1] as well as a runtime efficient simulator can be automatically derived from an extension-based definition of the language. At the moment, a full implementation of the approach does not exist. Therefore, this paper presents work in progress. We discuss working prototypes for the editor and the simulator.

In a first step, we define SDL_0 according to the SDL/PR syntax as an extension of our process-oriented discrete-event base language DBL [5]. The base language provides object-oriented description means, discrete-event specification primitives, and means for specifying active and passive objects. Event specification primitives are general. They can be used for modeling a wide variety of systems and they support implementing different higher level modeling approaches as DSMLs. In a second step, we define the SDL-RT [2] extension *semaphores* as a further extension of SDL_0.

The paper is structured as follows. In Section 2, we describe the implementation state of the approach. In Section 3, we present working prototypes for the application to SDL_0 and SDL-RT semaphores. In Section 4, we discuss the relevance of applying the approach to SDL. We conclude in Section 5.

2   Approach

The approach is partly implemented in a framework named DMX (Discrete-Event Simulation Modelling Framework with Extensibility) [7]. In the next paragraphs, the implemented and the not implemented parts of the framework are described.

---

[1] An SDL text editor allows SDL models to be created according to the SDL/PR textual syntax.

2.1 Implemented Parts

In [5], we describe our approach for defining the concrete and the abstract syntax of a DSML as extensions of the abstract syntax of DBL. The approach allows to define the concepts of a DSML as new forms of DBL concepts and to reuse DBL concepts inside DSML concepts. We also show how extensions are immediately supported by the DBL editor. As an example, the syntax of a simple state machine language is defined.

In [6], we describe an advancement of the approach for defining the execution semantics of extensions by a mapping to DBL concepts. We apply the advancement to the state machine language as well. We discuss a number of properties which we believe are essential for the efficient development of domain-specific simulation modeling languages and tools. We argue that runtime efficient executions are preserved by an efficient implementation of DBL event specification primitives.

In [8], we present a novel possibility for implementing context switches between concurrent processes in a highly runtime efficient way using C++. Context switches are one important part of a simulation core for process-oriented models. We name our core DBL Core. It will be the target of an executable mapping of DBL event specification primitives to C++. We prove the high runtime efficiency of DBL Core by a number of benchmarks in which we compare the core with other simulation cores implementing common C++ context switch techniques.

2.2 Not Implemented Parts

What is not implemented is an executable mapping of DBL to DBL Core. Also, other important parts of a simulation core are not implemented yet, most importantly a time-aware scheduler for events is still missing. There is also no support for debugging models at the level of DBL as well as at the level of a DSML. In addition, it is necessary to support a possibility of referring from one extension to parts of another extension. We intend to implement these parts in the future.

3   Application to SDL

3.1 Editor

SDL_0. The SDL_0 subset consists of the following SDL concepts: system definition, process definition, signal definition (without parameters), variable definition, timer definition, start state, simple state, final state, transition (with stimuli signal, timer, and none), task, output, set timer, and reset timer.

The syntax is defined according to SDL/PR in 76 lines written in a BNF-like grammar language. DBL concepts reused are variable, statement, and expression. In principle, the derived editor allows to create SDL_0 models. Problems encountered are connected to identifier resolution and parse conflicts imposed by the used LALR[2] parser algorithm.

---

[2] Look-Ahead, Left to right, Rightmost derivation parser.

Identifiers of SDL entities, e.g., processes and states, have to be globally unique as a resolution scheme cannot be defined. For DBL identifiers, e.g., variable definitions, the resolution scheme of DBL is reused if the identifier is defined in a regular DBL context. However, if the identifier is defined in the context of an extension, e.g., a variable defined in an SDL_0 process, then these identifiers are resolved in a global scope by default. For a language like SDL which defines namespaces, a description of identifier resolution is required. However, we are not concerned with such description during the prototyping phase of a language. There are approaches which allow to describe identifier resolution by using a suited DSML, e.g., the Name Binding Language NBL [9].

Parse conflicts are solved by adding additional keywords, e.g., the keywords signal and timer have to be used to distinguish them as stimuli which are part of an input definition. In SDL/PR, these additional keywords are not used.

SDL-RT Semaphores. The concept of SDL-RT semaphores is used for controlling access by multiple SDL processes to a shared resource. The concept consists of a semaphore definition and actions to *take* and *give* the semaphore.

The syntax of SDL_0 semaphores is defined according to SDL-RT semaphores in 32 lines of a BNF-like grammar. In principle, the SDL-RT syntax can be defined with our approach. However, we changed the syntax slightly to make using semaphores more concise. In SDL-RT, a *take* action has a return value for ERROR and OK. Here, one has to define a separate int variable and actions for evaluating its value after a *take* action. In SDL_0 instead, semaphores allow special timeout and failure actions to be specified in an ERROR and OK section as part of the same take action. Listing 1 shows the definition of an SDL_0 semaphore and Listing 2 shows taking and giving a semaphore.

```
semaphore SEM, kind=BINARY, policy=FIFO, initial=FULL;
```

Listing 1. Example of an SDL_0 semaphore definition.

```
take SEM with timeout=10,
  on ERROR {
    task { print time + ", " + active + ": take SEM ERROR"; } },
  on OK {
    task { give SEM; } };
```

Listing 2. Example of using the SDL_0 semaphore actions *take* and *give*.

3.2 Runtime Efficient Simulator

Execution Semantics Definition. The execution semantics of SDL_0 are defined as a mapping to DBL, similar to the semantics of the state machine language (SML) presented in [6]. The SDL system definition is mapped to a DBL class (as used in object-oriented programming) and a main function, which creates the system instance as an object of the DBL class. Each process definition is mapped to an *active* DBL class and each signal definition is mapped to a *passive* one. A corresponding instance for each process definition is created as well. Timer definitions map to an instance of a *fixed*[3] *Timer* class. Variables map to DBL variables and tasks map to DBL statements.

The semantics of process state machines are mapped as follows. An event pool variable is added to the DBL class of a process definition for saving signals and timers. The state graph is mapped to an event processing loop consisting of a DBL *wait-for-event* primitive at which execution is suspended until new signals are sent to the event pool. When another process sends a signal, it reactivates the process at the *wait* primitive with a *reactivate* primitive. The reactivated process resumes and processes the event, including the evaluation of conditions and the execution of transition actions.

In addition to standard SDL, event specification primitives of DBL can be reused. They allow to specify a *time event as a duration* for tasks and signals in order to simulate the time for processing and sending data in a real system. In addition, a process can be blocked and resumed by the event specification primitives *wait* and *reactivate*.

These primitives are used in the semantics description of the *take* and *give* actions. A semaphore definition is mapped to an instance of a *fixed Semaphore* class. In this case, the semantics of *take* and *give* can be defined independent of the concrete values provided for an instance of the semaphore extension. *Take* and *give* are simply mapped to corresponding calls to functions of a *Semaphore* object. The function *take* is implemented by using the *wait* primitive. At a *wait*, the execution of the current process is suspended until another process invokes a *reactivate*, which is used in the function *give* when a semaphore becomes available.

Wait and *reactivate* are DBL event specification primitives. Their execution results in context switches between processes. These context switches are implemented by a mapping to C++. Extensions can reuse this mapping as their semantics are defined as a mapping to DBL.

Context Switch in DBL Core. The simulation of a system, specified by an SDL_0 model, is realized by a sequential execution of processes according to a model time. This mechanism allows to simulate the concurrent execution of processes in a real system. Such simulation requires a high number of context switches between processes. A context switch consists of 1) a transfer of control and 2) a swap of function call stacks. In DBL Core, an efficient realization of these two parts is achieved by mapping 1) to an assigned goto and 2) to an emulation of function calls in pure C++.

The concept of assigned goto was introduced by the GNU Compiler Collection GCC under the name *Labels as Values*. In addition, it is also supported by a number of common C++ compilers[4]. An assigned goto allows to save the address

---

[3] A fixed class is independent of a concrete extension instance.

[4] Supporting compilers are GCC G++ v4.8, IBM XL C/C++ for Linux v9.0, Clang v5.02, and Intel C++ Compiler (ICC) v14.

of a label in a variable and to read its value when execution is to be resumed. Just as a regular goto, an assigned goto can only be used inside one and the same function. Therefore, the complete behavior of all process state machines has to be mapped to one large function.

A further difficulty when using an assigned goto is that regular function calls cannot be used anymore. This is because DBL functions can contain event specification primitives which result in context switches in functions. As a solution, function call stacks are emulated in pure C++. An area of memory is reserved for the stack of each process. For local variables and parameters, parts of this area are interpreted in the right way by pointer arithmetics and type casts. The complexity is hidden by the DBL to DBL Core mapping. A language developer works at the level of DBL and automatically gets a runtime efficient execution by this mapping.

In [8], we give a detailed description of the DBL Core and we provide results of a number of benchmarks. They show that runtime efficiency is very close to an Assembler-based core. In addition, it allows to make use of up-to-date C++ compiler optimizations.

Context Switch in PragmaDev RTDS. The only tool supporting SDL-RT is RTDS by PragmaDev [15]. RTDS allows to create SDL and SDL-RT models by means of a graphical editor. Standard SDL models can be analyzed by a next-event simulation according to timers specified in processes. In contrast, SDL-RT models can only be analyzed by executing them with the RTDS debugger according to a platform-dependent time. This means, time is provided by the operating system to RTDS. Thus, models can only be executed in real time, which is not appropriate for simulating a large system in a large time frame.

An SDL-RT model is executed by mapping it to a platform-specific C or C++ program first. After that, the program is compiled and executed. SDL concepts are mapped to real-time operating system concepts used by the RTDS runtime library. This platform specific mapping does not allow to simulate a model by using a time-aware next-event simulator. However, there is also a platform-independent mapping. Nevertheless, in this mapping one has to provide an implementation of time. There is no time-aware simulator provided by RTDS. One could define an implementation of time by changing the mapping to generate code which makes use of a C or C++-based discrete-event simulation library.

However, the mapping of semaphores in the platform-independent SDL-RT mapping, is already not that runtime efficient. This is because semaphores are mapped to SDL concepts. A *take* action in a process P_I is mapped to an invocation of a predefined semaphore *take* procedure. The procedure attempts to *take* a unit of a semaphore by sending a *take* signal to the corresponding process instance P_S which is initially created for each semaphore defined in an SDL-RT model. The *take* procedure blocks and waits for a success signal by P_S. All other signals, sent to P_I are saved in the meantime.

This mapping results in a context switch for semaphores which is less runtime efficient than the one implemented in DBL Core. If a language developer could reuse DBL event specification primitives, a runtime efficient execution could be achieved. Furthermore, runtime efficiency problems accumulate when take actions are used in SDL procedures. Here, a number of function calls are necessary in order to forward each signal. Therefore, the deeper the procedure call stack gets, the more inefficient this context switch approach will be.

4   Discussion of Relevance to SDL

We assume that models written in an extended language need to be analyzed by means of next-event simulation. In case of SDL, this assumption is only partly satisfied. For SDL models, two applications are important: (a) generating software components which are executed on a real system with specific hardware dependencies [10, 11] and (b) generating simulators which are used for performance evaluation [12–14]. This includes combinations in which target system programs and simulators are generated from the same SDL model. Therefore, the semantics of a concept added to SDL have to be considered with respect to target system execution as well as simulation.

In our approach, SDL models are solely used for simulation. Therefore, also the semantics of SDL are solely defined for simulation. The semantics are defined as a mapping to DBL event specification primitives. This poses a problem for certain concepts, which have a different meaning when executed on a target system. Such concepts require a direct mapping to target system primitives, e.g., remote procedure calls. When the semantics of such concepts are defined in terms of event specification primitives, then no separate target system mapping can be defined anymore. In a simulation, remote and local procedure calls may have the same meaning. But in a real system, they may not. They may map to primitives which are specific to each of many possible target platforms.

So what is the practical relevance of our approach to SDL? The aim of the approach is to prototype extensions and to evaluate their suitability by creating models and by running simulations. When a concept has reached a mature state, it can be added to SDL tools which support target system execution. Our approach supports the initial design phase of a concept by automatically providing modeling tools at a low cost. In addition, a highly runtime efficient simulator can be derived.

However, providing support for target system execution may still be possible by defining a special DBL to target system mapping. In this mapping, event specification primitives for *time* could be left out and primitives for *wait* and *reactivate* could be mapped to operations on threads or other process equivalent system primitives. However, the feasibility of such a mapping has to be investigated.

5   Conclusions

The definition of SDL-RT semaphores as an extension of the general discrete-event specification language DBL has the advantage of providing a next-event simulator for model analysis and a text editor for model creation at a low cost. The approach allows to prototype language extensions, i.e., to create and simulate example models during the initial design phase of an extension. We have shown several working prototypes which make us confident that the approach can be fully implemented in the future.

References

1. International Telecommunication Union: Recommendation Z.100 series, Specification and Description Language, http://www.itu.int/rec/T-REC-Z.100/en
2. SDL-RT Standard (2013), http://www.sdl-rt.org/standard/V2.3/pdf/SDL-RT.pdf
3. Christmann, D., Becker, P., Gotzhein, R.: Priority Scheduling in SDL. In: Ober, I., Ober, I. (eds.) SDL 2011. LNCS, vol. 7083, pp. 202–217. Springer, Heidelberg (2011)
4. Christmann, D., Braun, T., Gotzhein, R.: SDL Real-Time Tasks – Concept, Implementation, and Evaluation. In: Khendek, F., Toeroe, M., Gherbi, A., Reed, R. (eds.) SDL 2013. LNCS, vol. 7916, pp. 239–257. Springer, Heidelberg (2013)
5. Blunk, A., Fischer, J.: Prototyping Domain Specific Languages as Extensions of a General Purpose Language. In: Haugen, Ø., Reed, R., Gotzhein, R. (eds.) SAM 2012. LNCS, vol. 7744, pp. 72–87. Springer, Heidelberg (2013)
6. Blunk, A., Fischer, J.: Efficient Development of Domain-Specific Simulation Modelling Languages and Tools. In: Khendek, F., Toeroe, M., Gherbi, A., Reed, R. (eds.) SDL 2013. LNCS, vol. 7916, pp. 163–181. Springer, Heidelberg (2013)
7. Blunk, A.: Discrete-Event Simulation Modelling Framework with Extensibility (DMX), http://ablunk.github.com/dmx
8. Blunk, A., Fischer, J.: A Highly Efficient Simulation Core in C++. In: Symposium on Theory of Modeling and Simulation, Tampa, FL, USA (2014)
9. Konat, D.P.G., Vergu, V.A., Kats, L.C.L., Wachsmuth, G.H., Visser, E.: The Spoofax Name Binding Language. In: Proceedings of the 3rd Annual Conference on Systems, Programming, and Applications: Software for Humanity (SPLASH 2012), pp. 79–80. ACM, New York (2012)
10. Ahrens, K., Eveslage, I., Fischer, J., Kühnlenz, F., Weber, D.: The Challenges of Using SDL for the Development of Wireless Sensor Networks. In: Reed, R., Bilgic, A., Gotzhein, R. (eds.) SDL 2009. LNCS, vol. 5719, pp. 200–221. Springer, Heidelberg (2009)
11. Kavadias, C., Perrin, B., Kollias, V., Loupis, M.: Enhanced SDL Subset for the Design and Implementation of Java-Enabled Embedded Signalling Systems. In: Reed, R., Reed, J. (eds.) SDL 2003. LNCS, vol. 2708, pp. 137–149. Springer, Heidelberg (2003)
12. Brumbulli, M., Fischer, J.: SDL Code Generation for Network Simulators. In: Kraemer, F.A., Herrmann, P. (eds.) SAM 2010. LNCS, vol. 6598, pp. 144–155. Springer, Heidelberg (2011)
13. Kuhn, T., Geraldy, A., Gotzhein, R., Rothländer, F.: ns+SDL – The Network Simulator for SDL Systems. In: Prinz, A., Reed, R., Reed, J. (eds.) SDL 2005. LNCS, vol. 3530, pp. 103–116. Springer, Heidelberg (2005)
14. Fonseca i Casas, P.: Using Specification and Description Language to Define and Implement Discrete Simulation Models. In: Proceedings of the 2010 Summer Computer Simulation Conference (SCSC 2010), pp. 419–426. Society for Computer Simulation International, San Diego (2010)
15. PragmaDev - Real Time Development Tools, http://www.pragmadev.com

Author Index